The Public Press, 1900–1945

The Public Press, 1900–1945

The History of American Journalism

LEONARD RAY TEEL

The History of American Journalism, No. 5
James D. Startt and Wm. David Sloan, Series Editors

Westport, Connecticut
London

Library of Congress Cataloging-in-Publication Data

Teel, Leonard Ray.
 The public press, 1900–1945 : the history of American journalism / Leonard Ray Teel.
  p. cm. — (The history of American journalism, ISSN 1074–4193 ; no. 5)
 Includes bibliographical references and index.
 ISBN 0–275–98166–5
 1. Press—United States—History—20th century. 2. Journalism—United States—
History—20th century. I. Title. II. Series.
PN4867.T44   2006
071'.309041—dc22   2006003600

British Library Cataloguing in Publication Data is available.

Library of Congress Catalog Card Number: 2006003600
ISBN: 0–275–98166–5
ISSN: 1074–4193

First published in 2006

Praeger Publishers, 88 Post Road West, Westport, CT 06881
An imprint of Greenwood Publishing Group, Inc.
www.praeger.com

Printed in the United States of America

∞

#63390779

The paper used in this book complies with the
Permanent Paper Standard issued by the National
Information Standards Organization (Z39.48–1984).

10 9 8 7 6 5 4 3 2

For the historians and my able mentors Wm. David Sloan and James D. Startt
and
my wife, a historian in her own right, Katherine Winfield Teel

Contents

Series Foreword

Since the renowned historian Allan Nevins issued his call for an improved journalism history in 1959, the field has experienced remarkable growth in terms of both quantity and quality. It can now be said with confidence that journalism history is a vital and vitalizing field full of scholarly activity and promise.

The new scholarship has widened the field's horizons and extended its depth. Today, especially with new bibliographic technologies at their disposal, journalism historians are able to explore literature pertinent to their studies to a greater extent than was previously possible. This expansion of literary sources has occurred in conjunction with other advances in the use of source materials. Today's historians incorporate primary and original records into their work more than was common when Nevins issued his call, and they also utilize sources produced by the electronic media. As the source foundation for journalism history has grown, so its content has undergone a substantive expansion. Previously neglected or minimized subjects in the field now receive fairer and more-concerted treatment. Contemporary journalism history, moreover, reflects more consciousness of culture than that written a generation ago.

Growth, however, has created problems. Abundance of sources, proliferation and diversity of writing, and the stimulation of new discoveries and interpretations combine to make scholarship in the field a formidable task. A broad study covering journalism history from its beginnings to the present, one combining the rich primary materials now available and the older and newer literature in the field, is needed. The History of American Journalism series is designed to address this need. Each volume is written by an author or authors who are recognized scholars in the field. Each is intended to provide a coherent perspective on a major period, to facilitate further research in the field, and to engage general readers interested in the subject. A strong narrative and interpretive element is found in each volume, and each contains a bibliographical essay pointing readers to the most pertinent research sources and secondary literature.

The present volume, the fifth in the series, examines journalism in the first half of the twentieth century. It was a time when the press grew as a business and as a profession as it faced major challenges through domestic and international crises. As the other volumes in the series do, this volume focuses on the nature of journalism during the years surveyed, chronicles noteworthy figures, examines the relationship of journalism to society, and provides explanations for the main directions that journalism was taking.

Preface

In the forty-five years from 1900 to the end of World War II, the modern character of American newspapers was forged in the context of dynamic changes in the world and the nation. This tumultuous period spans the Progressive Era, a world war in Europe, a decade of prosperity, the Great Depression, and a second, global world war. Journalists charted, more or less successfully, the stream of political, economic, and social changes. In the economic realm, newspaper publishers faced serious competition from revitalized magazines, the immediacy of radio, and a glamorous movie industry; some fought new media, some embraced it, some sold out. In the end there were fewer owners, some of whom came to be called moguls.

So pronounced was the role of public opinion in this period that the media were frequently targeted in efforts to restrict their freedom of expression. Criticism and challenges came from presidents, Congress, and the Supreme Court. Some of the harshest commentaries came from a new breed of press critics whose aim was not merely condemnation but institutional reform.

The Public Press: 1900–1945 focuses on the mainstream press, both magazines and newspapers. Yet it also gives attention to minority newspapers and radio as they influenced the direction of the media establishment. The book traces the movement of mainstream commercial journalism toward a vision of professionalism and public responsibility, articulated in 1904 by Joseph Pulitzer. As he distanced himself from the so-called yellow press, Pulitzer bequeathed part of his fortune to build a school of journalism and provide the prizes that would annually remind journalists of what was considered excellence. Pulitzer, standing almost alone, contended that specialized scholastic training could raise journalism to the level of a profession with noble standards. While many of Pulitzer's peers disagreed on the value of college courses, within a decade journalism education was being adopted into college curricula. As other critics of the press joined the discourse, the movement toward responsibility to a public gained momentum, resulting in both the expansion of college programs and an agreement on a codes of ethics such as that adopted in 1923 by the American Society of Newspaper Editors.

While this initiative toward a professional and public press took root, the movement often went astray, prompting prodding from unsparing press critics, among them Will Irwin, Walter Lippmann, and George Seldes. In a serious critique of American news coverage of the Russian Revolution, Lippmann and Charles Merz concluded that journalists' reports amounted to "a disaster.... a case of seeing not what was, but what men wished to see."

The body of press criticism throughout the period testifies to the struggle between old ways and new. By 1900, the successful evolution of the commercial press, blessed with money and editorial independence, had presented owners and journalists alike with opportunity to articulate, discover, and practice something spirited and soulful, a commitment to a vision of public service. Through war and peace, men and women in journalism came to recognize and often realize the intellectual and spiritual character of the American press.

As with other authors in this series, I have relied as much as possible upon primary and contemporary sources. Newspapers, magazines, newsreels, government studies, interviews, correspondence, autobiographies, articles, essays, and speeches from the period constitute the basic documentation. Histories and biographies that were dependent upon primary sources were useful for their contributions to the historiographical conversation about events and trends in this dynamic period. By relying on primary sources, I have tried to illuminate the realities of the period.

Leonard Ray Teel
Atlanta, 16 March 2006

Acknowledgments

The research for this book was conducted over a period of sixteen years in libraries and archives. The number of archives is literally countless because of the extensive efforts of Margie Patterson's Interlibrary Loan staff in the Georgia State University Library, who secured a multitude of publications and books from numerous collections around the country. I am appreciative of the assistance of other librarians and staff who assisted me in collecting original articles and documents from the Library of Congress, the British Public Record Office, Emory University, the University of North Carolina, the Peabody Awards radio archives at the University of Georgia, the National Archives, the National Museum of American History, and the U.S. Bureau of the Census.

I am indebted also to the efforts of numerous students who helped me locate hundreds of magazine and newspaper articles in a systematic search across the span of forty-five years. My thanks go to Qing Tian, Zhiqiang Yan, Ling Lu, Frances Masamba, Megan Beall, Sarah Halim, Adrienne Proeller, Francesca Cesa Bianchi, Na Ni, Rasha Ramzy, Miglena Sandmeier, Rachel Ramos, Vidushi Sinha, Eva Ulmer, Miila Derzett, Boriana Milanova, Zehra Barlas, and Ghalib Shatnawi. I appreciate also the students who read sections of the manuscript and helped compile the index: James Bratton, Stacy Schmitt, Shanna Gildersleeve, Jin Zhao, and Katie Hawkins.

I owe a special debt to colleagues who assisted in locating archives or who encouraged me in numerous other ways throughout the research and writing of this work, especially Wm. David Sloan of the University of Alabama, James D. Startt of Valparaiso University, Shirley Biagi of the University of California–Sacramento, Patrick Washburn of Ohio University, Stephen Ponder of the University of Oregon, and Kathleen Endres of the University of Akron. Toward the end, no one was more help than Phyllis Mueller, whose professional eyes right away spotted my inconsistencies and duplications.

1

Emergence of a Public Press

An able, disinterested, public-spirited press, with trained intelligence to know the right and courage to do it, can preserve that public virtue without which popular government is a sham and a mockery.
—Joseph Pulitzer, "The College of Journalism," 1904

Very early in the twentieth century, various forces contested publicly concerning the roles and responsibilities of the free press in the United States. The ensuing discourse in newspapers, magazines, and trade publications, signaled recognition of the importance of the press not only for its owners and employees but also for an imagined American *public*. Advocates of change linked the practice of journalism to the health of the democracy, citing its need to both effectively advocate for the public and frame political issues. In a remarkable wave of self-examination, critics and publishers alike joined in the discourse, altogether urging numerous and monumental efforts. Some sought to reform practices thought to be tarnishing the image of journalism; some sought to rein in the influence of advertisers upon content; some advocated a stronger watchdog approach to government; some recommended better training at the university level. In general the movement during the first decade and ensuing years sought through reform and education to elevate journalism to the status of a profession serving the public and respected by it.[1]

Certainly one of the less-respectable trends was the "yellow" press. But by 1900, even the trend's chief architects, William Randolph Hearst and Joseph Pulitzer, seemed to be changing their colors, clothing themselves less garishly, in public responsibility. When in September 1900 a hurricane-driven tidal wave laid waste to Galveston, Texas, both Hearst and Pulitzer responded by sending aid. About 10 days after the storm killed almost 6,000 people, Clara Barton, founder of the American Red Cross, arrived in Galveston aboard a train carrying carbolic acid and other desperately needed disinfectants sent by Pulitzer and the *New York World*. Outdoing Pulitzer, Hearst sent, "at the editor's expense," three express relief trains from New York, Chicago, and San Francisco, each carrying physicians, nurses, and medical supplies. Hearst also donated $50,000 for Galveston orphans. For Hearst's papers, Winifred Black wrote about the "terrible, sickening odor" of bodies. When she wrote that the hurricane uncovered a cemetery, Hearst's *New York Journal*, in a capitulation to sensationalism, headlined that story, "Even the Graves Give up Their Dead."[2]

Concurrent with this discourse over the role of the press, economic developments were changing the nature of urban journalism. In city after city, the diversity of press ownership and the numbers of independent voices contracted dramatically as buyouts, closings, and mergers accelerated. Begun by a few visionary entrepreneurs, the economic trend absorbed undercapitalized newspapers, reducing the variety of voices in cities where, previously, as many as a dozen or more papers had competed. Inspired by record-setting profits, investors developed national chains, or groups, headed by individuals, families, or corporations and encompassing numerous newspapers, news agencies, and, eventually, radio stations. Although contemporary critics, among them Oswald Garrison Villard, lamented the disappearance of choices as fatal to press freedom, advocates of "combinations" asserted that profitability strengthened independence. Writing in an American magazine, the prosperous British publisher Alfred Harmsworth predicted that through combinations the "press would be raised to such a commanding position that its freedom would be greater than ever."[3]

Concern over these and other issues gathered momentum due to the increased impact of journalism upon American society. By 1900 there was little doubt remaining that the newspaper press had become increasingly influential and essential as a force in national affairs. The nation had grown from coast to coast, now almost 3,000 miles wide with 75.9 million people in 45 states. Newspapers and magazines had been both stimulators and beneficiaries of the dramatic extension of communication and transportation that, by 1900, crisscrossed and united the nation through telegraph lines, railroads, and, more recently, telephone networks. Transoceanic links with Europe had expanded as well with the laying of cables under the Atlantic.[4]

Periodic advances in technology had ushered in a new era for American printing and publishing. "The modern newspaper is one of the greatest powers in the world," one observer noted in 1902. "In no other field have the mechanical advancements been so many, so wonderful, and so pronounced." With machines setting type and producing curved plates for multi-cylindered presses, big-city newspapers were produced in various daily editions at rates exceeding 25,000 an hour.[5] Technology was keeping pace with demand as more and more newspapers reached the circulation plateau of 100,000. At the same time, accuracy and speed of reporting advanced with the increasing diffusion of typewriters and telephones.

Beyond its news services, the press engaged in stimulating public opinion on a national scale, notably focused in 1900 on the political wisdom of new global military ventures by a traditionally isolationist America. The widening reach of American journalism into foreign reporting mirrored the country's steadily increasing interest in world events. Since victory in the Spanish-American War, areas of American involvement now stretched into Asia as far as the Philippine Islands. There, U.S. troops were entangled in a guerrilla war with Filipinos revolting for independence. On New Year's Day, 1900, a report from Manila about Philippine "insurgents" sparked a national debate at the start of the presidential campaign. Bombs, guns, and ammunition apparently belonging to Filipino nationalists had been discovered in a Manila house. According to a story in the *Washington Post*, "Filipino insurgents were planning an uprising against American forces. Reliable reports from native spies show that ... 2000 insurgents massed at Mt. Ararat ... command steep and narrow trails and are prepared to roll boulders down on advancing troops."[6] Such news dispatches disturbed the body politic more frequently as newspapers hired journalists to follow the flag.

War and domestic issues had increased not only readership but also the number of newspapers and magazines in circulation. Amid this proliferation, editors and publishers sought ways to distinguish their newspapers and magazines. One emerging trend was a movement toward achieving standards that could increase credibility. The movement was inspired in part by a gradual departure from the excesses of sensationalism that had been branded yellow journalism. While the yellows had flourished mainly in New York, criticism of sensationalism had tainted the reliability of newspapers generally. In the first years of the century, first Adolph Ochs at the *New York Times*, followed by Joseph Pulitzer at the *New York World*, sought to profit from credibility as a bedrock principle for long-term success.

On the business side, the impetus toward credibility inspired a parallel movement in accountancy. Now that advertisers provided publications with most of their income, publishers increasingly recognized that they needed a system to audit and authenticate circulation statistics, which formed the basis of advertising rates. Although circulation claims continued to be unsubstantiated, a movement for industry reform was clearly underway.

Testifying to the changing nature of American journalism, elder newspapermen reminisced with nostalgia about journalism in the preceding era. In books and articles they recalled the age's great editors and documented modes of operation. Some newsmen retired with a bang, writing memoirs that read like exposés. Fremont Older, after 23 years as editor of the *San Francisco Bulletin,* acknowledged in his "confessional" that the *Bulletin* "was for years on the pay-roll of the Southern Pacific Railroad and of other public corporations at a time when it was pretending to fight for civic righteousness," and that its owner "did not scruple to solicit money from candidates and political parties in return for the paper's support." Other journalists criticized Older's confessions because "revelations of the secrets of his profession are regarded as 'bad form.'" One *Bulletin* writer, Bailey Millard, cited "a code of ethics which bars any self-respecting employee, after leaving a job, from going over to a competing firm and revealing the secret of his former employers." In explaining himself, Older underscored a relatively new *public* ethic that elevated the *public* interest. He wrote:

A newspaper is not a private undertaking, and an employee of a newspaper has other obligations than to help the owner make money. The public interest enters in quite as fully as it does into the operations of street cars.... What newspapers say forms public opinion and public opinion forms almost everything else.[7]

Such a public ethic seemed no longer attainable to Older's contemporaries, who argued that increasing concern for profit drove owners to publish whatever might increase circulation. Amid such "timorous inanity of the respectable commercialized press and the insanity of the yellow journalism," one critic worried, "Where is the chance for light and leading for this newspaper-reading country?" As profitable investment properties, the press "might well have already become a 'trust,' and been completely lost to public benefit and behoof."[8]

During the first years of the twentieth century, publishers of leading newspapers and of a new style of national magazines asserted themselves as guardians of the public interest. Despite arguments that they were economically biased, the publishers presented themselves as independent agents, as public servants acting apart from the interests of political officeholders or advertisers. This concern for the public interest generated an effort to elevate goals of truth and objectivity—a movement toward standards of professional practices. Significantly, the concept of journalism as a "public trust" arose in speeches and discussions. Robert Underwood Johnson, whose career on the editorial staff of the *Century* magazine spanned 40 years, told the new Columbia School of Journalism that the magazine editor "regards his office as a public trust."[9]

The insistence that newspapers had "other obligations than to help the owner make money" recognized that urban dailies, notably the newer evening editions, had become rich investment opportunities. By 1900 one trend was well established for buying and modernizing undercapitalized dailies. Another model, adopted by Edward Willis Scripps, his family, and partners, was to establish cheap new dailies for underserved audiences, especially urban workingmen. Amid a proliferation of small labor papers, Scripps had shrewdly moved into the cities, where he offered a pro-labor, anti-monopolistic newspaper for a penny. By 1900, Scripps's venture, inspired by his half-brother's experimental *Detroit Evening News*, had succeeded in Cleveland, Cincinnati, and other cities in the Midwest and West. Scripps's "league" of newspapers, the first to be identified as a "chain," managed to make millions while espousing a philosophy of concern for the economic well-being of his target audience—the mass of the laboring class—and expressly opposing the rich.[10]

In the debate over the public interest, critics most often attacked the publishers whose newspapers emphasized sensationalism at the expense of accurate news and information, the so-called yellow press. One British critic observed that perhaps the yellow press's "greatest offense is its policy of perverting the truth in the interest of a mere tawdry sensationalism, of encouraging the American people to look for a thrill in every paragraph of news, of feeding them on a diet of scrappy balderdash."[11] Among the harshest critics were rival American newspapermen. "How to disable this machine of perpetual motion is the greatest problem that confronts our social philosophers," wrote one veteran journalist, Horace White.[12] The successful dime-magazine publisher Frank Munsey discredited yellow journalism from a business standpoint, arguing that the yellow newspapers' techniques were ultimately suicidal: sensationalism ruined credibility. Even fact-based yellow journalism, he stated, "presents the truth so hysterically that it looks like a lie." Munsey made that assessment in 1900, when, with his mind set on acquiring a New York daily, he assigned one of his magazine writers, Hartley Davis, to survey the city's newspapers. Davis concluded that the "distinguishing mark of the so-called 'yellow journalism'" was the "presentation or 'playing-up' of news," including "huge headlines of a startling nature, big and striking illustrations, and heavily leaded type."[13]

There was more to that genre than self-promotion and the screaming headlines some called "scare-heads." Multicolumn banner headlines were part of a bold new graphic approach to displaying news with colorful layouts that featured illustrations, maps, and photographs, sometimes greatly enlarged.[14] In the West, the *Denver Post* became famous for its red headlines. Big headlines helped sell evening papers on the streets. But even newsboys complained about "Extra" editions with huge headlines but insignificant stories. In 1900, one boy was troubled that "newspapers make us pay six cents for ten extras because some jay in New Jersey has painted his barn red."[15]

While these graphic elements appealed to mass audiences, including the "quarter-educated" immigrant population, the yellow press damaged its credibility with a wider public by use of anonymous sources and questionable interviews and stories.[16] Before he became president, Theodore Roosevelt publicly accused William Randolph Hearst's *New York Journal* of completely fabricating an interview with him—"an invention from beginning to end."[17] In considering journalistic ethics in 1902, press critic Charles Connolly denigrated the yellow press, in which

news is featured not according to its objective truth or public interest but with a view of bringing out some novel, unique, or hitherto undeveloped phase ... which appeals more to the eye and prejudices of the reader than to his intellect; which introduces, colors, and suppresses facts in conformity with its own editorial policy, the orders of its business office, and the dictates of its proprietor; and which never misses an opportunity to chronicle its own achievements for the benefit of humanity, and to boast of its extensive circulation as compared with its competitors.[18]

Hearst defended yellow journalism as serving the public better than the old-style journalism. Countering detractors, he asserted in 1902 that yellow journals were disliked by some "because they speak the truth, and that is the reason also that they are liked by the majority of the reading public in America." His most prominent editor, Arthur Brisbane, proudly accepted the label of yellow journalist. Declaring that the genre was "Real Journalism"—"the journalism of action, and responsibility"—Brisbane asserted that barking critics belonged to "the journalism of the past."[19]

This new brand of journalism, in Brisbane's view, promoted "deeds of active energy," including public charity. He reminded readers of Hearst's response to the hurricane that had devastated Galveston.[20] Pulitzer as well engaged in public charity. At Christmas in 1900, his *Evening World* distributed hot chicken dinners to about 6,000 people, an act duly noted by the trade paper the *Fourth Estate*, which said it was "the first time in the history of the New York press when a great newspaper has, solely at its own expense, undertaken to do so much for the poor of the city." At Christmas 1902, Hearst, newly elected to Congress, and competitive even in charity, had 75 of his trucks deliver 100,000 packages of toys to poor children in his New York City district.[21]

Some critics acknowledged that the yellow press often served the public interest, notably by conducting crusades. These crusades often represented the interests of the voiceless working class against big business monopolies and government corruption. Brisbane cited Hearst's efforts to fight government corruption by renting halls and organizing mass meetings to protest "franchise steals" in New York. Both Pulitzer and Hearst "have not only saved millions of dollars to the public, but have fought a stimulating fight for democracy against plutocracy and privilege," wrote the British critic Sydney Brooks. "The Yellow Press, in short, has proved a fearless and efficient instrument for the exposure of public wrongdoing." When little Marion Clarke was kidnapped, Brisbane noted, it was Hearst who put up a $5,000 reward and "plastered the country" with thousands of posters that led to the girl's return.[22]

While the practice of crusading against abuses and promoting public benefits was not a new feature of American journalism, the yellow press emphasized it, whether for economic motives or a sense of public responsibility or both. Hearst certainly learned from the financial successes of Pulitzer in St. Louis and New York and of Scripps in Cleveland and the rest of the Midwest. Both men had created dailies that advocated reform and appealed to the masses of the working class. That approach had led to fortune. As circulation soared, so did advertising revenues.[23]

The yellow-press phenomenon, though it spread to other major city dailies, showed signs of peaking shortly after 1900. Munsey expressed the view in 1900 that "the evil carries with it its own antidote." He reasoned that the yellow papers had "made new readers" and the new readers eventually would want better journalism. "It is absolutely true that when men begin to read at all, their taste is swiftly developed, and soon they demand better things."[24] The decade's leading critic of journalistic practices, Will Irwin, discounted the impact of yellow journalism. He concluded that the great majority of editors in the early 1900s "still served news and editorial in fashion much more intellectual than the public wanted, still appealed to the mind rather than the heart."

Hearst, whose competition for circulation with Pulitzer during the Spanish-American War generated the greatest frenzy of yellow journalism, became the exception rather than the rule, remaining committed to sensationalism for its own sake after others had distanced themselves from it, Irwin noted. Hearst, said Irwin, "came to reject all news stories which did not contain that thrill of sensation loved by the man on the street and the woman in the kitchen." One Hearst editor, Arthur McEwen, told Irwin, "What we're after is the 'gee-whiz' emotion. We run our paper so that when the reader opens it he says: 'Gee-whiz!'"[25]

For a few more years Hearst exemplified the yellow press, although he retreated somewhat from extreme sensationalism, probably for political more than economic reasons. Politically, yellow journalism became a liability for a man who had determined to run for president in 1904. During and after the 1900 presidential campaign, Hearst's newspapers supported Democrat William Jennings Bryan and engaged in a personal assault on Republican President William McKinley as a tool of big business. When McKinley was assassinated in September 1901, Republican critics blamed the Hearst press, which had repeatedly attacked McKinley, recalling that after McKinley's second inauguration, editorial writer Arthur Brisbane stated, "If bad institutions and bad men can be got rid of only by killing, then the killing must be done."[26] Such "reckless utterances" in the "public press," contended the new president, Theodore Roosevelt, "appeal to the dark and evil spirits of malice and greed, envy and sullen hatred." Such authors "cannot escape their responsibility for the whirlwind that is reaped." After the assassination, Hearst, as if to put the *New York Journal's* yellowness behind him and affirm his patriotism, changed the paper's name to the *New York American.*[27]

In 1902, when Hearst campaigned and won the first of his two terms in Congress, he reined in the attacks on corruption in government. Economically, having established a massive circulation, Hearst now could afford to cater to a class of readers and advertisers attracted to newspapers that did not attack what they believed to be their interests. His former brand of yellow journalism was now widely discredited. Critics conceded that the yellows had created new readers, notably among immigrants, especially in New York City, and among women entering a new era of gender consciousness. "All the time," Will Irwin later asserted, "these people were reading up"—out of yellow journalism. For many of them, by the end of the decade "shallow melodrama interested them no more."[28]

Sensationalism, however, did not die, as evidenced by the coverage of crimes whose mere facts were eye catching. While publishers claimed that they were supplying a "public demand," critics assailed such "demand" as "prefabricated," contending that content pandered to the public merely for profit. One critic, while crediting most newspapers for public service, assailed "a minor part of the press"—the mass-circulation dailies—as "catalogues of crime" that seek "consciously, and with almost insane activity, to outrage private right and shock public decency, lest over stimulated and jaded readers should find in a rival sheet a mess of social slime and human misery more to their vitiated taste."[29]

The magnetism of a murder case engaged most newspapers, especially when the crime entangled celebrities. On June 25, 1906, all 15 New York newspapers and others in the United States and Europe detailed the "crime of the century" when millionaire Harry Thaw shot and killed famous New York architect Stanford White during a rooftop theatrical performance. The morning *New York Times'* multiple-deck headlines encapsulated the crime: "Thaw Murders Stanford White; Shoots Him on the Madison Square Garden Roof," followed by reference to Thaw's motive involving his young wife, the lovely showgirl Evelyn Nesbit: "'He Ruined My Wife,' Witness Says He Said." The third deck described pandemonium: "Audience in a Panic: Chairs and Tables Are Overturned in a Wild Scramble for the Exits."[30] Trial testimony gave readers a glimpse into the private clubs of the city's wealthy class among whom White socialized. Nesbit testified that when she was sixteen White had drugged and raped her in his secluded apartment in the tower atop Madison Square Garden where he hosted private parties. Hearst's *Evening Journal* reported that "the flash of that pistol lighted up an abyss of moral turpitude, revealing powerful, reckless, openly flaunted wealth."[31] After one jury could not reach a verdict, a second jury found Thaw not guilty on grounds of insanity, and he served seven years in a prison for the criminally insane.

The movement toward a more publicly responsible press gained with each convert from the yellow press. In the East the most remarkable convert was the publisher who in the 1890s had rivaled Hearst to serve the yellow diet consisting of exaggerations, crime, scandal, caricatures, and gossip. Beginning in 1903, Joseph Pulitzer, owner of the *New York World,* sprang surprisingly into the leadership of the movement for a more responsible press, advocating university curriculum in journalism. "Suddenly the *World* dropped the whole game, changed almost in a week from yellow to merely sensational," Will Irwin wrote, concluding that "Pulitzer perceived the end of this madness.... He must have known it could not last."[32]

Seeking profit along the path of respectability, Pulitzer positioned his *World* to appeal to a better-educated class of reader. Socially, fellow wealthy socialites in 1891 had denied him the respectability that came from being listed in the *Social Register,* probably in part because of his newspaper's policy—"without fear or favor"—which portrayed some of them as robber barons.[33]

If social respectability was not Pulitzer's primary objective, professional respectability was, of the sort being stressed by Adolph Ochs at the rival *Times.* In the world of New York journalism, it did not escape Pulitzer that Ochs had achieved financial success, surpassing 100,000 in circulation, by 1900. Ochs had made his mark with a vision. Biographer Gerald Johnson claimed that while "the merely greedy never looked beyond money, the really big men of that period always grasped at something beyond money and the biggest accepted blithely the responsibility that goes with power."[34]

In 1903 Pulitzer publicly challenged leaders and critics of the press to dedicate themselves to the intellectual requirements of journalism. That year, worried enough by chronic ill health to consider his will, he publicly promised $2 million to establish a professional school of journalism at Columbia University.[35] His urgency in establishing the school arose no doubt from his sense of mortality and his self-serving desire to leave a positive lasting impression upon history, in contrast to the besmirched legacy of yellow journalism. He had first mentioned the idea publicly in 1884 shortly after buying the *World.*[36] Now he devoted himself to pushing the idea through with Columbia's new president, Nicholas Murray Butler.

Universities had been slow to introduce journalism courses. Although journalism had flowered into a big business with some aspirations to public service, both academics and newspapermen considered the teaching of newspaper skills as a matter for on-the-job training. Both groups generally resisted the notion that specific journalistic skills were suitable for a university curriculum. However, there was some agreement that college graduates could be better prepared for journalism if they had a broad study of the liberal arts with a concentration in writing. In 1900, the few journalism courses offered were usually embedded in English programs with literature and composition curricula.[37]

For his school, Pulitzer insisted on appointing an advisory board comprised of eminent academics and journalists. His naming of educators at rival universities—Harvard University President Charles W. Eliot and Andrew D. White, president of Cornell University—led to frustrating delay. Columbia's Butler "has shown a spirit of jealous objection to the most eminent men on the Advisory Board; and a desire to fill their places with small incompetent men disqualified under our agreement," Pulitzer complained to former Columbia president Seth Low, to whom, he reminded, he had submitted the idea in 1892. "I beg that you will use your influence with President Butler to make him realize that success depends upon him; and that he will be morally responsible if there is a failure."[38] Afterward, opposition to his nominations dissipated.

Pulitzer's choices for the board were among the leading figures of journalism in the East and Midwest. The list included *New York Tribune* publisher Whitelaw Reid; *Brooklyn Eagle* editor St. Clair McKelway; Samuel Bowles, owner of the *Springfield Republican*, whose newspaper had been called a "school of journalism"; and the *Boston Globe*'s General Charles H. Taylor, who had "placed that paper upon a pinnacle of prosperity." Other newspapers were represented: the *New York Times* by editor Charles Ransom Miller; the *New York Sun* by editor-in-chief Edward Page Mitchell, who had succeeded the great Charles A. Dana; the *Chicago Daily News* by publisher Victor Fremont Lawson, a leading figure in the modernized Associated Press; and the *Philadelphia Press* by the lesser-known Samuel Calvin Wells. Pulitzer also included the noted Associated Press general manager Melville Elijah Stone.[39]

Critics of Pulitzer's concept argued that a special curriculum for journalists was at best pointless, at worst a hindrance. Months before Pulitzer announced the bequest, the editor of the *New York Evening Post*, Horace White, told him "that I could see no need of a School of Journalism" and afterward maintained in a lengthy essay that "the university has nothing to teach journalists in the special sense that it has to teach lawyers, physicians and engineers." Without expressing disrespect for Pulitzer's journalistic career, White lamented the flourishing of profitable yellow journalism. He wondered what use the school would be if "no self-respecting youth will prepare himself for future connection with a yellow journal."[40] Expecting such comments, Pulitzer had alerted New York editors of his bequest and that "the comments of the news paper press ... are to be permanently preserved in the University."[41]

White spoke also for those doubtful about routing young men through a school of journalism that might divert them from essential studies. What a journalist needed, White insisted, were good teachers of fundamental subjects—English composition, law, economics, history, and some of the "whole troop of sciences" that had emerged since his own college years. In his journalistic experience, dating from 1854, "a nose for news cannot be cultivated at college.... [That] is something which can be trained only in a newspaper office." Columbia should "leave him to learn journalism afterwards by practice."[42] Likewise, an editor of the *Independent* contended that "what the tyro needs is ... a wide knowledge of human history and achievement, with some emphasis on the art of self-expression."[43]

Given the identification of the *World* with the yellows, some critics challenged both gift and giver. The *Independent* editorial demeaned Pulitzer's bequest as "specious." Such a school would provide, one editorialist wrote, "a shallow concentration on the passing concerns of the day, and these again can better be learned in the world than in the school." Journalism's (and Pulitzer's) reputation for yellow journalism was another compelling reason for keeping journalism out of the colleges. The same editorialist concluded that "the thing most of all demanded in the education of the future writer is that his education shall be entirely severed from the methods of the press, that his mind shall be drawn away from the 'fresh-coined lie.'"[44]

Some shared Pulitzer's belief that training could professionalize journalism. Acknowledging "much difference of opinion as to the value of such a school," *Popular Science Monthly* editorialized, "Schools of journalism will probably soon be regarded as equally essential" as those "for the church or for teaching." Columbia's school of education had become a model, and the "school of journalism will doubtless repeat this history." The school could serve as "selective agencies," eliminating "those quite unfit" before graduation. Graduates "are likely to be better men than those who do not [receive a journalistic education]—employers run less risk in choosing them." Moreover, graduates "will probably deserve advancement better and secure it more easily than those who spend the same years in a newspaper office."[45]

Editors at the *Outlook* wrote enthusiastically about the two-year curriculum, saying it was time to move on from "lectures in journalism" to "systematic training for newspaper work in a fully equipped institution established solely for that purpose." Graduates "would have a great superiority over one of equal ability who depended solely on his native cleverness and adaptability." They seconded Pulitzer's choice of an advisory board of experienced newspaper editors, educators, and distinguished public figures, which "must give the public confidence that the school will be carried on in a dignified and confident manner."[46]

At last Pulitzer joined the discourse, defending his vision with an air of experience and sarcasm.[47] In a 39-page manifesto, he pounced on "criticisms and misgivings, many honest, some shallow, some based on misunderstanding, but the most representing only prejudice and ignorance." Caustically addressing the "born, not made" critics, he replied that the "only position that occurs to me which a man in our Republic can successfully fill by the simple fact of birth is that of an idiot." Granting that some were born with "news instinct," he argued that "if news instinct as born were turned loose in any newspaper office in New York without the control of sound judgment bred by considerable experience and training, the results would be much more pleasing to the lawyers than to the editor." To those who demeaned college studies in favor of newsroom experience, he said the only training recruits received was their own "blunders costly to the aspirant" and to the newspaper. The system "works by natural selection and the survival of the fittest, and its failures are strewn along the wayside." Only in rare cases, Pulitzer asserted, as when Horace Greeley tutored Henry Raymond, did a journalist receive worthwhile instruction from an editor.

What is the actual practice of the office? It is not intentional, but only incidental training—it is not apprenticeship—it is work, in which every participant is supposed to know his business. Nobody in a newspaper office has the time or the inclination to teach a raw reporter the things he ought to know before taking up even the humblest work of the journalist.[48]

Other professions had grown away from the "shop" idea that once prevailed. In law and medicine, "it is recognized that better results are obtained by starting with a systematic equipment in a professional school." Replying to those, like Horace White, who contended that colleges' general courses sufficed for journalists, Pulitzer underscored the modern trend toward specialization. "The spirit of specialization is everywhere," he argued, and journalists must adapt.

The object of the College of Journalism will be to dig through this General scheme intended to cover every possible career or work in life, every profession, to select and concentrate only upon the things which the journalist wants, and not to waste time on things he does not want.[49]

To those who claimed that tries at journalism studies had failed, he said those attempts had been "Lilliputian," limited to "pretentious 'correspondence schools'" or series of lectures "in which gentlemen of more or less experience in journalism have expressed some general ideas about the requirements of the profession." The effect, if any, was in "convincing the student that he would do better to choose some other profession." All part-time, piecemeal journalism instruction underestimated the importance of the profession to democracy and the need for specialized preparation. Pulitzer's concluding argument certainly suggested his own hope of escaping the tattoo of "base" yellowness. He also intimated that he had glimpsed the dark hazards to the republic of a press exclusively preoccupied with profit-taking seeking more heat than light. Almost like one who has pulled back from an abyss, Pulitzer now championed a crucial role in the republic for succeeding generations of journalists, well prepared, serious, and intelligent, who could vitalize a public-spirited press.

Our Republic and its press will rise or fall together. An able, disinterested, public-spirited press, with trained intelligence to know the right and courage to do it, can preserve that public virtue without which popular government is a sham and a mockery. A cynical, mercenary, demagogic press will produce in time a people as base as itself. The power to mould the future of the Republic will be in the hands of the journalists of future generations. This is why I urge my colleagues to aid the important experiment which I have ventured to endow.[50]

Even as Pulitzer published his manifesto, a new generation of editors was contributing to his vision of a public press. In the transition from heat-seeking yellows to a more publicly responsible journalism, magazine editors of general-interest magazines provided leadership. These new publications, among them *McClure's, Munsey's,* and *Cosmopolitan,* all attuned to timely topics and well illustrated, showcased serious and entertaining writing and gave new emphasis to investigations and other nonfiction. Their marketing strategy reached a mass audience by undercutting the standard price of 25 to 35 cents a copy, offering their magazines for 15 cents or a dime. Their subsequent surges in circulation—reaching from 350,000 to 650,000 by 1900—attracted abundant advertising and lavishly compensated for the reduced prices. Confronted with competition, some older leisurely literary magazines continued to publish fiction and poetry but paid increasing attention to this new appetite for public affairs and political commentary. Nonetheless, *Century,* the *Atlantic Monthly, Harper's,* and *Scribner's* continued to lose audiences, and by 1900 circulations had fallen to between 150,000 to 165,000. Some editors of older magazines left to join the prosperous newcomers, or to start new ventures in which they could share in the profits. This was the career path for Walter Hines Page, a former ambassador to Great Britain. After editing *Forum,* Page infused new life into the *Atlantic Monthly,* after which he joined Frank N. Doubleday in establishing Doubleday, Page and Company and in

September 1900 launched a popular magazine, *World's Work*, which Page could call "mine." The magazine's public crusades championed conservation of national resources and exposed pension frauds.[51]

Financed by the price revolution, the new magazines catered to the tastes and needs of a wider range of readers. Their content gave a truer representation of the nation as a whole, from the upper crust to the lower classes; urban and rural; East, West, and South. More so than before, magazines had become the first truly national medium, outdistancing city newspapers and reaching from coast to coast. Magazines bridged sectionalism, offering stories of national interest and import while showcasing ample advertisements that stimulated demand for national brands of soaps and soups.

Amid the emergence of mass-circulation magazines, other periodicals gained special audiences. Some analyzed current events, among them *Arena* and *Forum, Review of Reviews,* and the *Literary Digest,* the last of which trumpeted its review of "Topics of the Day."[52] Others featured well-researched nonfiction on diverse political, economic, and social issues. The serious, in-depth journalism in *McClure's* and *Collier's* found a receptive audience, which, in turn, encouraged more such stories.[53] There seemed to be so much more to write about and more writers emerging to do the work. As never before, readers began to clip and save stories. One serious reader, responding to the proliferation of information, published an article in *World's Work* explaining his system for binding and cataloguing stories under wide-ranging headings: Historical Incidents, Biographical Sketches, the Stage, and the just-concluded South African War, the contents of which alone numbered 314 pages.[54]

Some of the new mass-audience magazines generated healthy profits through regional and national advertising. Magazines offered two distinct advantages over newspapers: geographic reach and elite audiences. With circulations reaching beyond their cities of publication, ads for national brands such as Bon Ami household cleanser and Cream of Wheat reached distant customers who were more demographically predictable, at least in education and income, than readers of newspapers. As with newspapers, most of the income came from advertising rather than purchase prices, and ad rates varied according to circulation. Rising to become circulation and advertising leaders were Cyrus H. K. Curtis's two magazines, the monthly *Ladies' Home Journal,* edited by Edward Bok, and the *Saturday Evening Post,* which published stories by leading journalists and authors and was edited by George Lorimer. For a time *Munsey's* claimed the largest circulation of any magazine in the world. Largely from the simple expedient of reducing his magazine's price to a dime, by 1900 Frank Andrew Munsey, at the age of 46, had become prosperous.

The national advertising benefited publishers and editors in another significant way. Independence from local advertising granted more freedom from censorship and suppression of content. By contrast, newspapers, which depended mostly upon local advertising, especially from department stores and local governments, were vulnerable to the advertisers' direct influence upon content. Some newspapers survived almost solely upon government ad contracts. The practice of awarding government advertising for publicity or for suppression of news had been documented; less traceable was manipulation or suppression of news for the benefit of commercial advertisers or moneyed interests. In 1909, when George Seldes was a beginning reporter in Pittsburgh, he learned that "well-disciplined" local newspapers seldom carried news unfavorable to the city's philanthropic banker Andrew Mellon, as when Nora Mellon sued for divorce. Department stores also got special consideration for the volume of advertising money they spent. One day, Seldes wrote that the son of a major department-store owner was accused of sexually assaulting one of the store's salesgirls. His newspaper did not publish his story. Seldes said his city editor explained that his story was given "to the business office; they will blackmail that store for the next 20 years; you'll see larger ads from now on." When Seldes later became a leading critic of the press, he cited the case to show how local newspaper owners thought they profited more by catering to advertisers than by providing news to the public.[55]

Publishers' concerns for advertisers and competitors often constrained impulses toward reform at the local level. However, local advertisers had far less influence on magazines published for a national audience. With the increase in national brands—advertised coast to coast—a national publication could risk insulting a locality and keep afloat financially. This was a contributing reason why magazines and not newspapers took the lead in publishing what Pulitzer called "public-spirited" journalism.

During the first decade of the 1900s, national magazines exercised an influence in politics and society that often exceeded the impact of newspapers. Some publishers accepted the challenge to expose social, political, and economic ills. By 1903, 11 years after its founding by Samuel S. McClure, a Scotch-Irish immigrant, *McClure's* had a healthy circulation of about 400,000 and was notable for well-written, fact-based investigations attacking monopolistic business practices and political corruption. The articles "elicited an immediate response from the press, and undoubtedly had a strong influence upon the public mind," McClure wrote in his autobiography.[56] The sell-out success of the January 1903 issue encouraged other publishers to identify and document misdeeds and systemic corruption. In time, rival magazines—*Collier's*, the *American, Cosmopolitan* (purchased by Hearst), *Everybody's, Pearson's*, and the *Ladies' Home Journal*—amplified the impact of *McClure's*.

In the first years of the century, commonly termed the Progressive Era in American politics, investigative journalists set the agenda for the press as a whole. There was a direct relationship between the public press and reform of public policy, historian Richard Hofstadter has argued. "To an extraordinary degree the work of the Progressive movement rested upon its journalism," Hofstadter concluded. "The fundamental critical achievement of American Progressivism was the business of exposure, and journalism was the chief occupational source of its creative writers."[57] With a greatly expanded interest in the "commonwealth," socially responsible reporter-reformers were now addressing themselves to the "public." Their targets were usually government and big business and alleged profiteering at the expense of the public. In promoting a Progressive view of reality, the press, especially in magazines, emphasized that "evil-doing" among the most respectable people was found in many walks of life and should be considered "as a widespread breaking of the law."[58]

In agenda setting, magazine journalists led the way. The extraordinary January 1903 issue of *McClure's* carried three investigative articles documenting evasions of law and ethics. The second of Lincoln Steffens's investigations of municipal corruption exposed "The Shame of Minneapolis," a city run, in McClure's words, "by crooks and incompetents."[59] The issue carried the third installment of Ida M. Tarbell's 19-part series (1902–1904) exposing the "force and fraud" John D. Rockefeller used to build the Standard Oil Company. And Ray Stannard Baker's "The Right to Work" documented the torments of nonstrikers during the 1902 coal-mine strike in Pennsylvania. Taken together, those three articles showed American contempt for law, *McClure's* editorial contended. "We are doing our worst and making the public pay."[60]

McClure, like Pulitzer, had emigrated from Europe in the mid-1860s with an idealistic view of America. McClure "believed that the government of the United States was the flower of all the ages—that nothing could possibly corrupt it." Years later he concluded that while the Civil War had opened "easy avenues of corruption," the "American people went on believing that they were still what they had once been, but they were not." Upon learning of the collaboration of politicians and criminals in Minneapolis, he thought it "unbelievable," "appalling," and "incomprehensible" and concluded that "the dishonest administration of public affairs in our cities has come about largely through carelessness."[61]

McClure made a lasting contribution to professional standards, notably in the way journalists specialized in certain public issues about which they wrote knowledgeably. "I had to invent a new method in magazine journalism," he wrote. He had identified a "fundamental weakness" in American journalism—a "carelessness" he attributed in part to a paucity of expertise. Economics, government, and other "highly specialized activities of modern civilization were very generally reported by men uninformed in the subjects upon which they wrote." As a remedy, he adapted a technique from the *Times* of London, which hired experts for reporting on "all subjects requiring special knowledge." Second, he gave his writers more time, altering the pattern of payment that rewarded quantity rather than quality. He decided "to pay my writers for their study rather than for the amount of copy they turned out—to put the writer on such a salary as would relieve him of all financial worry and let him master a subject to such a degree that he could write upon it, if not with the authority of the specialist, at least with such accuracy as could inform the public and meet with the corroboration of experts."[62] At the end of his career, he calculated the average cost of his pioneering effort in specialization and expertise. Steffens had averaged four articles a year at $2,000 each. Tarbell had been more expensive, providing three Standard Oil articles per year at a cost of $4,000 each.[63]

As McClure established himself as a leader of journalistic reform in the Progressive Era, the era's most prominent political reformer, Theodore Roosevelt, early on established a working relationship with the press. From his experience in state and federal government, President Roosevelt carried to the presidency an appreciation of the mutual usefulness of the press-public relationship. While maintaining President McKinley's system for keeping the press informed of White House developments through frequent and timely press releases, Roosevelt also met person-ally with reporters. Immediately after taking the oath in September 1901, he began meeting with journalists, who before long were producing a stream of stories about Roosevelt's initiatives. Frequently, Roosevelt chatted privately with journalists who kept his confidence.[64] In these private exchanges, Roosevelt probed the journalists, tested his own ideas and slogans, and listened to their views. Lincoln Steffens claimed credit for suggesting Roosevelt's "Square Deal" slogan, and Ray Stannard Baker claimed Roosevelt borrowed his phrase "fetish of competition."[65]

Journalists' revelations of corporate manipulation and greed helped advance Roosevelt's reform agenda. In 1903, the *McClure's* portrayal of Rockefeller and his Standard Oil Company as the ultimate corporate-trust villains helped create a climate favorable to passage of Roosevelt's preferred antitrust legislation. Before the vote, the press helped politically by embarrassing six U.S. senators identified as taking orders from Standard Oil to defeat the antitrust bill.[66] This revelation fueled growing criticism of the questionable loyalties of U.S. senators, who at the time were not elected by popular vote but were appointed by state legislatures, commonly to support party and corporate interests.

Investigative reporters traced some problems to the lack of government regulation of big business. In 1905, *McClure's* began publishing Ray Stannard Baker's five-part series exposing the railroads' power to manipulate rates to control business, especially in the West and South. Once again the Rockefellers and the fellow rich were vilified. Baker said the Revolutionary War issue of taxation without representation was squarely before us again. The cry arises from every part of the country that the railroad "baron" does not tax fairly and equally. He is charged with making the taxes low and easy for his rich favorites—the Rockefellers, the Armours, and their like, and is charged with making the taxes high and hard for the farmer, the small struggling manufacturers and shippers, and all the vast unorganized mass of produces and consumers.... with using his great power to practice extortion.... with secretly paying back part of the taxes to his rich favorites by a device called the "rebate."[67]

Baker detailed how the railroads' fat purses satisfied their "private interest which wishes to defeat the public will, to break the law, to enjoy the fruits of unrestrained power."

Baker's series was credited with focusing public outrage against the railroads and encouraging Roosevelt to support legislation to strengthen the Interstate Commerce Commission. On February 8, 1906, Roosevelt summoned Baker to the White House on the day after the House of Representatives passed the Hepburn Bill to regulate railroad rates. In his notebook, Baker conceded that while the House vote of 324 to 7 was "phenomenal ... a great victory for the President," the "great struggle is to come" among the appointed senators. As though visiting royalty, Baker noted that the "President received me at one o'clock." As he often did, Roosevelt talked while being shaved. It seemed to Baker that the barber's chair was "too fragile for his great weight." While being lathered, Roosevelt "launched into a discussion of the railroad legislation." As he told Baker, "the railroad senators" wanted to limit the rate-regulation authority of the Interstate Commerce Commission, "throwing the rate controversy into the courts," where railroad lawyers could leverage victory or delay. When Baker had a chance to talk, as the barber worked on Roosevelt's chin, he suggested the stronger remedy then favored by many: "governmental ownership of the railroads." Roosevelt "objected forcibly," saying "that he knew better than anyone else could how inefficient and undependable government employees were & what a disaster it would be to have them control great business enterprises like the railroads."[68]

By 1906, a crusading brand of investigative journalism had become regular fare in magazines, much to the embarrassment of numerous politicians and businessmen. While the sparks of the crusading journalism can be traced back to Pulitzer's concern for the public welfare and beyond, the fire this time was more intense. These new articles were better researched and, appearing in magazines—sometimes presented in a series continuing for months in several issues—were much longer and had more duration in the public discourse. The authors were often inspired by new ideologies and philosophies imported from Europe, in part by the scathing Socialist critiques of laissez-faire capitalism initiated in the mid-1800s by Karl Marx and Friedrich Engels. Then, too, humanitarian philosophies bred during the Industrial Revolution in England heralded the "greatest good for the greatest number."

At the turn of the century, writers searching for the soul of America looked at the country through these new lenses and found much to criticize. While the nation had become a world power with a great navy and mounting wealth, the journalists sought to prove that much of the wealth was gained through cheap labor that kept the laboring class subservient, poor, and unhealthy. Millionaires, among them the Vanderbilts, owned railroads and set shipping rates that influenced the price of goods. Tycoons of energy—coal and oil—epitomized by John D. Rockefeller, a man wealthy beyond imagination, practically owned their laborers. After an era of relatively unrestrained laissez-faire capitalism, these and other tycoons—Andrew Carnegie in steel, Andrew Mellon and J. Pierpont Morgan in finance—had developed a powerful economy enjoyed by the few. What rights should workers have? What education should be afforded child laborers? What quality and safety were afforded the working class in their homes, their food? Through the lens of these news ideologies, early twentieth-century journalists reexamined the relationships among politicians, business tycoons, and laborers. In some cities, Socialist newspapers emerged, voicing opposition, as in Boston, to the "Republican and Democratic wings of the capitalist party" that have never "done anything for the workmen in these places."[69]

The assault on political corruption eventually impugned the United States Senate. In 1906, David Graham Phillips, a novelist trying his hand at investigative reporting, attacked an encrusted klatch of senators in his astounding series "The Treason of the Senate." It was published in *Cosmopolitan* magazine, which Hearst had purchased in May 1905.[70] As a congressman, Hearst was making his first venture into popular 10-cent magazines, aiming to profit from the trend of exposing corruption by those in power and to reach a new audience more affluent than the immigrants and laborers who bought his newspapers. He strengthened the magazine's staff by drawing from his newspapers' most prominent writers. The staff and well-paid contributors included Ambrose Bierce from California, novelists Jack London and Upton Sinclair, and some with Socialist leanings, among them the politician Charles Edward Russell and the novelist Phillips.[71] Hearst also examined proofs, noted his editor, George D'Utassy. "Each month the Chief took a copy, and in his loose running handwriting made comments on the margins of the pages" that "showed us where and how we could improve the next issue."[72]

Phillips's nine "Treason" installments, beginning in March 1906 and appearing monthly through November, demonstrated Hearst's effort to transcend merely sensational yellows to fact-based exposé journalism. Hearst's insistence on verifying facts delayed publication of the first installment until Phillips supplied more proof. "Violence is not force. Windy vituperation is not convincing," Hearst told editor George D'Utassy. "I had intended an exposé. We have merely an attack.... We want more definite facts throughout. Supply them where you can. Then run the article if you want, and we will try to get the others later."[73] Hearst's editors placed responsibility for accuracy on the author, with the first installment's front page carrying the phrase "according to Mr. Phillips."[74] One month later, the second installment carried a correction at the end. An "Editor's Note" conceded that one statement in March had been "untrue" and requested that "any other publication which may have reprinted such statement will publish this correction."[75]

Phillips's political journalism ranks among the most comprehensive and far-reaching of the decade. While the exposés of Ida Tarbell, Ray Stannard Baker, and others revealed systemic injustices by *private* corporations, Phillips attacked perceived systemic violations of *public* trust. While Lincoln Steffens had exposed political corruption in cities, Phillips increased the stakes, carrying the battle to a high realm of national public life, the U.S. Senate. His series alleged that a cabal of senators, by deceitfully serving not the people but the corporate "interests" and their private fortunes, had committed treason against the Constitution.[76]

The series detailed how special interests worked through the state legislatures, which very often chose senators favorable to "the interests." He demonstrated how key Senate Republicans and Democrats conspired in a "merger" to promote corporate greed and defeat the public interest. His work gave a boost to two movements resulting in significant reforms. One reformed the cozy government-business alliance, ushering in federal regulation of various businesses operating in interstate commerce. The second movement led to a Constitutional reform to permit popular direct election of senators, replacing election by legislatures. By 1913 direct election was passed as the Seventeenth Amendment to the Constitution. Phillips can also be credited with providing impetus for a Constitutional federal income tax, also approved in 1913 by the Sixteenth Amendment.

Phillips was perhaps the most literary of the investigative writers. Having already written novels on the subject of industrial and political corruption,[77] he brought to journalism some of the techniques of fiction—a grand theme, characters, plot, intrigue, and style. With the theme of treason, he explored the personal histories of the cast of Senate leaders and their cohorts, rooting his narrative in history, biography, and contemporary fact. He explained how they plotted with one another, usually in secret but with the results in plain view. His style was that of a storyteller confident of virtue and contemptuous of villainy, hypocrisy, and thievery. In his first paragraph, he wasted no time in portraying his disdain for the U.S. Senate:

One morning, during this session of the Congress, the Senate blundered into a discussion of two of its minor disreputables, Burton and Mitchell, who had been caught with their fingers sliding about in the change of the people. The discussion on these change-pocket thieves was a fine exhibition of "senatorial dignity and courtesy," which means, nowadays, regard for the honor and dignity of the American people smugly sacrificed to the Senate's craftily convenient workshop of the Mumbo-Jumbo mask and mantle of its own respectability.[78]

Phillips challenged that respectability generally and specifically, naming the offending senators. He portrayed their "treachery" as a perversion of democracy and a commonwealth in favor of oligarchy, rule by a wealthy class. He detailed how powerful senators used their votes to channel billions of dollars to the rich from the "incredible prosperity" made possible by the industrial working class. Phillips attributed the success of the treason to a pattern of public lies and popular neglect of politics:

Politics does not determine prosperity. But in this day of concentrations, politics does determine *the distribution of prosperity.* Because the people have neglected politics, have not educated themselves out of credulity to flimsily plausible political lies and liars, because they will not realize that *it is not enough to work, it is also necessary to think,* they remain poor, or deprived of their fair share of the products, though they have produced an incredible prosperity.[79]

While Phillips was attacking the integrity of the Senate, another investigative writer, Upton Sinclair, published his disturbing novel, *The Jungle,* in which he portrayed the nation's unregulated meat packers as oppressive exploiters of labor and, more importantly for consumers, a threat to the nation's health because of grossly unsanitary conditions. Public questions about the safety of packed meat had been raised at least since the Spanish-American War, when soldiers complained that meat rations were "embalmed." In 1904, Sinclair, in his mid-20s and inspired by the Socialist agenda for reform, developed the research technique of immersion. For seven weeks, on assignment for a Socialist weekly newspaper, the *Appeal to Reason,* he immersed himself in the culture of the laborers in "Packingtown," the huge slaughterhouse operations in Chicago. The resulting novel portrayed the human drama of the "wage slaves of the Beef Trust" and the unsanitary conditions in which meat was processed and packed for shipment to consumers. In 1905 much of his novel was serialized in the *Appeal to Reason,* which urged readers to buy the forthcoming book for its "unsparing realism and tense excitement."[80]

After confirming facts and cutting some of Sinclair's Socialist digressions, Doubleday, Page and Company published the novel. The timing was critical for lawmaking, since the Senate was debating Roosevelt's recommendation for a law to regulate interstate commerce in "misbranded and adulterated foods, drinks, and drugs." While Sinclair's chief concerns were the plight of the workers and the Socialist goal of equalization of wealth, consumers reacted with concern for their stomachs. Drawing upon his wealth of observed detail, Sinclair showed the butchering of wounded, diseased, and pregnant animals as well as working conditions that left men injured and disabled. Contemporaries credited *The Jungle*'s shocking scenes as responsible for "rousing public opinion to the point where it demanded general legislation."[81] No work of fiction had ever so quickly prompted legislation.

At the White House, Sinclair's exposé moved Roosevelt to act. A copy of *The Jungle* sent to him by a sympathetic senator "both fascinated and repulsed" the president. Sinclair wrote to Roosevelt, asking for an investigation. Then Doubleday, Page and Company sent the proofs of its *nonfiction* article, based on its independent investigation supporting Sinclair's allegations, and scheduled to be published in May. Roosevelt responded by asking for his own "absolutely secret" investigation.[82]

Simultaneously, public concern about the purity of drugs and the honesty of drug manufacturers was heightened in Congress largely because of another investigative series. "The Great American Fraud," a 10-part series, began appearing *Collier's* in October 1905. The writer, Samuel Hopkins Adams, who formerly wrote for *McClure's*, attacked the hazard of fraudulent "patent medicines" that claimed to alleviate or cure illness or disease. Guarding against counterattacks, Adams employed a new investigative technique: laboratory testing. He arranged for chemical and pharmaceutical analyses that supported his charge of fraud. "Gullible America," Adams began, spent about $75 million a year on patent medicines that contained "huge quantities of alcohol, an appalling amount of opiates and narcotics … drugs ranging from powerful and dangerous heart depressants to insidious liver stimulants." He also attacked medical journals for not taking a stand, as well as newspapers and magazines for helping to perpetrate the fraud by accepting some $40 million in advertising, which, if refused, would enrich the nation "not only in lives and money, but in drunkards and drug-fiends saved." Among the more-popular brands advertised widely was Mrs. Winslow's Soothing Syrup, containing unmentioned narcotics, but recommended "for children teething." One ad pictured the medicine on a nightstand next to a mother in bed with two small, happy children.[83]

The journalistic assault on politicians and businessmen provoked a counterattack articulated by the president in 1906. Roosevelt appeared to be especially nettled by Hearst's attack on the "treason" of the Senate. Evidently he wanted also to avoid the appearance that he used his cozy press relationships to manipulate the Senate, as claimed by at least one senator, Benjamin R. Tillman of South Carolina.[84] Then, too, zealous press crusaders seemed to be claiming ownership of the reform movement, giving Roosevelt little or no credit for past or proposed reforms. Worse, Phillips's series for Hearst described Roosevelt as both a dupe of the Senate clique and a compromiser who settled for weakened legislation out of "the desire to feel that he had 'done something,' the desire to get credit with the people for accomplishment."[85]

In his attack, Roosevelt distanced himself politically from scandalmongers and Socialists, who focused unrelentingly and grimly on what they perceived as the system's evils. On March 17, in comments at the off-the-record Gridiron Club dinner hosted by House Speaker Joseph Cannon, Roosevelt referred to a recent magazine article he had read "with great indignation," presumably Phillips's allegations of treason, and suggested that the writer had a depraved interest in scandal.[86] Roosevelt equated such journalists with the fixated character in John Bunyan's allegory *The Pilgrim's Progress*—Bunyan's "man that could look no way but downwards with a muck-rake in his hand."[87]

As the *Cosmopolitan* series on the Senate continued, Roosevelt emphasized the muckrake theme in his most remembered speech, which would later be considered a "landmark of American public address."[88] On April 14, at the laying of the cornerstone of the House Office Building, the president asserted that "men with the muckrake are often indispensable to the well-being of society, but only if they know when to stop raking the muck." Although the president presumably aimed the epithet at Hearst, *Cosmopolitan*, and Phillips, "muckrake" soon applied to all those of like mind who were fixated on exposing America's ills: the "muckrakers."[89]

Coming from a president with a history of supporting reform efforts, the surprising accusation that muckrakers were destructive bruised the egos of Phillips, Ray Stannard Baker, Lincoln Steffens, and Ida Tarbell, among others. Before the April 14 speech, Baker had urged Roosevelt not to repeat the Gridiron Club remarks, but the president told Baker he wanted to clarify his "muckraking" remarks by having them "reported in full."[90] As such the speech served to divide the press into camps, isolating the muckrakers. In response, Phillips, in his May "Treason" installment, attacked the anti-muckraking, sycophant press—the "conspicuous newspaper servants of the 'interests' since the present series on the 'Treason of the Senate' was announced." In the June installment, Phillips continued his assault on "the press of the interests," expanding it to "all those newspapers that do not look beneath surfaces or remember history."[91] And in his August installment, Phillips dismissed the "muckraking" epithet as irrelevant to the central debate on betrayal of the public interest:

Admit that it is "muck-raking" to write and publish the records of Senate, the biographies of the senators as made by themselves. Still, how does the epithet "muck-raker" change the fact of senatorial treason to the people, incessant, flagrant, deliberate?[92]

As Congress ended its 1906 session, journalists justifiably could take credit for some remarkable legislative reforms. On June 29, Roosevelt signed the Hepburn Act, in which the Senate had finally conceded railroad rate regulation to the Interstate Commerce Commission that

Ray Stannard Baker had championed. On June 30, he signed the Meat Inspection Act, vindicating Sinclair's work.[93] On the same day, he signed the Pure Food and Drug Act, advancing the cause for which Samuel Hopkins Adams had crusaded. The muckrakers had contributed to ameliorate some of the gross abuses of unregulated capitalism, while at the White House Roosevelt had extended federal authority over political, economic, social, and public-health matters previously dealt with, if at all, by private enterprise or the states.

On the other hand, conservatives could also claim victories. As some muckrakers noted, powerful interests represented in the Senate had forced numerous compromises. Although mandatory inspection of meat was required, the provision for dating the inspection labels was deleted to placate the chair of the Senate Agriculture Committee, who was a stockbreeder, thus permitting packers to sell old cans of meat.[94] Although the pure-drug law eliminated most dangerous ingredients, it set no standards of purity and did not outlaw patent medicines.[95] Ironically, patent-medicine producers benefited at least temporarily, because federal regulation thinned competition while boosting sales among consumers, who thought the new law ensured the safety and effectiveness of self-medication.[96]

The railroad legislation had also been compromised. In his final November installment, Phillips lamented that senators had "nullified" the impact of several bills by inserting "vague" language. He noted that although the Interstate Commerce Commission could set "just and reasonable" railroad rates, the Senate "for the obvious reason of treachery to the people refused to define what 'just and reasonable' means." He envisioned that the "interests" would continue to control Congress through the "terror" of withholding campaign contributions. Phillips stressed the grip that money had upon legislation: "The greatest single hold of 'the interests' is the fact that they are the 'campaign contributors'" who "make sure of getting their money back, with interest, compound upon compound." It was no coincidence that the "chief servant of the money power in the Senate," Senator Nelson W. Aldrich of Rhode Island, was the father-in-law of John D. Rockefeller Jr.[97] "A corrupt system," Phillips concluded, "will continue to be until the people think, instead of shout, about politics."[98]

Despite corrective steps, Phillips and other muckrakers could agree that capitalists and conservatives successfully maintained the status quo. Roosevelt's complaint that the muckrakers offered few alternatives was subsequently expanded to apply to most political movements during the Progressive Era. As the muckrakers themselves noted, an ill-informed and unempowered public could not match the influence of "the interests." They could have agreed with historians, who claimed that, despite liberal and Socialist attacks, conservatism triumphed as moneyed capitalists worked through the political system to advance industrialism.[99] On the other hand, apart from material and legislative gains, the muckrakers have been credited with elevating the status of journalism while energizing the public psyche.[100] By asserting moral values, the muckraking movement did achieve some intangible results. Occasionally the courts acted where Congress and the president did not, as in the breakup of the Standard Oil Company advocated by Ida Tarbell's series in *McClure's*.[101]

While journalists crusaded for reforms in numerous political, economic, and social institutions, newspapers nevertheless resisted significant reforms within their own newsrooms. One of the most dramatic reform movements of the era—the advocacy of women's rights—met with little cooperation from publishers and editors. Although newspapers employed women, editors normally cloistered women to report on "fashions, household matters, art, book reviews," and "beauty matters," as one female educator noted in 1900. Hopefully, she asserted that, despite male "jealousy" and "the sacrifice of many social advantages," women with a liberal college education "may accomplish much good. All kinds of reform pertaining to humanity at large may find voice through the medium of her pen." Among newspapermen "in every way she must prove herself his 'better half.'"[102]

In 1901, the *Ladies' Home Journal* surveyed newspaper women and male newspaper editors about career prospects for a "girl" in journalism. Responding to *Journal* editor Edward Bok's question whether they would approve of a having a "young daughter" working in a daily-newspaper office, 39 of the 42 women and all 30 men rejected the idea.[103] The women surveyed generally reflected upon the hard edge of the profession. One noted the "absolutely uncertain" career aspect and the "harmful effect upon a girl's health." Another testified to "a dreadful sense of freedom which unconsciously deteriorates into all sorts of license of language and behavior." The newspaper office itself, said another, "establishes her on a footing with men that is not wise.... It makes her overcome every day obstacles that tend to harden her: to lessen her illusions about gentleness and the personal self-respect needed." Another cited the "absolute danger for any girl in the intimate, free and easy life of a newspaper office—a life from which social restraints are in a very great measure removed." One said a young woman "gets too close to the Tree of Knowledge" and comes "in contact with those votaries of sin." Among three positive responses, one said a woman could "find a splendid field of work in journalism" if she had these requirements: "brains, health, great strength of character, and clearness of head," expects no "drawing room" courtesies, and shows the "perfectly cool, professional manner a business woman should wear." A second claimed, "My best education and happiest experiences have come to me through my newspaper work."[104]

Male editors thought the business too rough for the feminine nature. An editor with 20 women staffers said he "would rather see his daughter starve" than have her hear or see "what the women on my staff have been compelled to hear and see." Some agreed that newspaper work disturbed young women's personalities. Despite being "extremely careful" in making story assignments, a veteran editor concluded, "I have noticed a steady decline in that innate sense of refinement, gentleness and womanliness." Another cited such a decline in "a woman who, five years ago, was the daintiest, the prettiest and the most womanly creature that every started out on the hard path of the reporter." A western editor claimed he was so unimpressed that he "cut down my women editors and reporters from twelve to two."[105]

While the press resisted internal changes, some reformers wished for a more-ethical press or even a "Christian" press guided by Christian values. By 1900, as noted in *Outlook,* daily newspapers compromised with religious pressure by devoting more space to church news.[106] This token recognition by dailies did not satisfy ardent Christians. In Kansas in March 1900, Charles M. Sheldon undertook a one-week experiment with the staff of the *Topeka Daily Capital* to demonstrate what a newspaper would look like if each journalist did "everything as he believed Jesus would do it." Some Christian clerics criticized that as "blasphemous," "sacrilegious," and "irreverent," objecting "to the thought of Jesus' taking any part in such a prosaic and material thing as a daily paper." The publicity drew about 40 journalists to Topeka to report on the experiment.[107] Sheldon's first issue, in which he converted a "brief notice" into a newspaper campaign raising food and funds for famine relief, featured the famine in India. When the son of a Kansas senator committed suicide, Sheldon's paper "turned down a long account of the tragedy" and expressed sympathy. In another departure from tradition, his business manager "turned down thousands of dollars" worth of questionable advertisements. Nevertheless, the paper made $30,000 profit that week, largely because advance reports about the experiment had attracted subscribers around the world. At the end of his week, Sheldon concluded that journalists' criticism that his paper was "dull and uninteresting" was mostly because he published no "scandal and sensational divorce cases." He shortened crime reports, emphasizing, he noted, "the cause, and if possible the remedy." Rejecting yellow journalism, Sheldon asserted: "It is childish and useless to report human frailty simply for the sake of creating a morbid mental sensation in the reader; yet this is the regular and stupid fashion of reporting human sin adopted by those dailies which print elaborate stories of human lapses."[108]

Other efforts at publishing a Christian newspaper were underway. In Boston, Mary Baker Eddy, founder of the Church of Christ, Scientist, and author of the best-selling *Science and Health,* had begun in 1898 by publishing a weekly paper, the *Christian Science Sentinel,* to, as she said, "hold guard over Truth, Life and Love." Eight years later, on November 25, 1908, she launched the daily *Christian Science Monitor*. Eddy, then 87, rejected the tenor of daily journalism that gave the impression that "it is too dangerous to live." Instead, she wanted her *Monitor* "to injure no man, but to bless all mankind." In the first issue, a Pennsylvania editor praised the *Monitor* as exemplary for the newspaper industry. He predicted that Eddy would prove "there is such a thing as newspaper success along non-sensational lines" and that "there will follow a widespread readjustment of news policies." The first issue's front page featured a story from Washington about the unveiling of a statue of Civil War General Phil Sheridan, a local court injunction asking that striking shoe workers not interfere with 500 to 800 men hired to replace them, and rapid progress on a "Great Dam Across the Charles River Basin."[109]

Apart from exceptional cases, newspaper content continued to be influenced largely by competitive forces. Business and profit margins, more often than ethics, seemed to guide editors in the composition of front pages. In the larger cities, the economic trend of capitalist competition, bankrolled by increasingly sophisticated finance, tended toward monopoly, resulting in the rise of media chains and empires through buyouts, mergers, closings, and cross-media ownership. By 1900, publishers had identified this trend "for good or ill," wrote the British publisher of the *London Daily Mail*, Alfred Harmsworth. On the modern publishing landscape, he foresaw controllers of "unlimited capital" with "the power to undersell" buying out rival newspapers and establishing national chains, or combinations, patterned after the organizational efficiency of centralized business trusts. "The whole tendency of the times, both in American and Great Britain," Harmsworth concluded, "is toward the concentration of business affairs in the hands of a few." He viewed the trend as a positive development that improved the quality of news and distribution with its "practical monopoly of all the best writers and news-services of the whole world." Concentration of ownership on a grand scale could lead to greater influence for the public press, exemplified by the journalism of Pulitzer and Hearst, Harmsworth noted. "Would not such a journal effectually revive the waning influence of the newspaper upon the life and thought of the nation?"

Imagine, then, the influence which would be exerted if an overwhelming majority of the newspapers in the United States spoke with the same voice, supported the same principles, and enunciated the same policy! Such a state of things would be a terror to evil-doers and to the supporters of anything inimical to the commonwealth.[110]

Harmsworth said he was "quite alive to the darker side" of monopolistic business trusts. He anticipated concerns about the influence of megapublishers and their impact upon freedom of the press. He conceded the possibility that "a great newspaper monopoly might, in bad hands, become nothing less than a national disaster.... In the hands of a weak man—still more so in the hands of an unprincipled one—such an influence might work great mischief. But I am a firm believer in the sound sense and practical power of the people." Discounting the argument that concentration would be a "fatal blow at freedom of the Press," he envisioned that the press "would be raised to so commanding a position that its freedom would be greater than ever."[111]

Some of the new generation of American newspaper owners had accumulated capital in very different businesses and had little or no background in newspapering. In the East, Frank Munsey built his wealth from a chain of groceries, office buildings, a hotel, banking, and stock speculation before plunging into the magazine trade. Intent on maximizing profit, he had slashed the price of *Munsey's* magazine from a quarter to a dime, increased circulation, and raised advertising revenue. Before venturing capital in newspapers, he had his writer Hartley Davis survey New York papers' content, machinery, techniques, and personnel—from publishers to pressmen to paperboys. As Davis noted, Munsey believed a publisher succeeded if he understood "what people want sufficiently far ahead to present it to them in advance of the actual demand." Davis's extensive investigation of "the great newspapers" served as industrial snooping for Munsey's private agenda—to share in the profits of New York's Park Row. The newspapers clustered there in lower Manhattan included the *Sun, Tribune, Times, Press,* Hearst's *Journal,* and Pulitzer's *World.* Only the *Herald* was uptown, at 35th Street. Park Row, Davis wrote, "is to the newspaper world what Wall Street is to finance."[112]

Reflecting his publisher's own business views, Davis stressed efficiency. Amid intense competition, newspapers had become expert at "beating time," exhibiting "the mechanical genius of the age"—telegraph, typewriters, typesetters, giant presses, and motorized delivery trucks. "Reporters click off their stories on typewriters—they save time." Desirable to any profit-seeking publisher, Davis noted, was the labor situation, both reliable and cheap, from editors down to the streets, where hundreds of "bright and active" newsboys hawked the numerous editions. Added to that, he reported, the "devotion, loyalty and energy which its employees give the newspaper... cannot be underestimated.... They take the most desperate chances to get their copy into the office on time, without hope of reward in money or glory. It is simply part of the business."[113]

By 1901, New York City newspapers rivaled other big businesses. The mass-production presses cost as much as $100,000. Hearst's *Journal* had 14 presses, each of which in one hour could produce 96,000 eight-page papers with five colors on front and back, or 24,000 32-page editions. The presses devoured paper—in one day as many as 1,400 half-ton rolls of newsprint. Twine and wrapping paper to bundle newspapers cost as

23. Mott, *American Journalism*, 573; Thomas C. Leonard, *The Power of the Press: The Birth of American Political Reporting* (New York: Oxford University Press, 1987).

24. Davis, "Journalism of New York," 233.

25. Will Irwin, "The American Newspaper: A Study of Journalism in Its Relation to the Public—the *Fourth Current*," *Collier's*, February 18, 1911, 15.

26. *New York Journal*, April 10, 1901. Earlier, the Hearst columnist in Washington, Ambrose Bierce, commenting on the assassination of Kentucky Governor-Elect William Goebel in February 1900, wrote that the assassin's bullet was now "speeding here / To stretch McKinley on his bier." Ambrose Bierce, "A Thumbnail Sketch," in *Collected Works* (1912; repr., Staten Island, NY: Gordian Press, 1960).

27. W. A. Swanberg, *Citizen Hearst: A Biography of William Randolph Hearst* (New York: Galahad Books, 1961), 195.

28. Will Irwin, "The American Newspaper: A Study of Journalism in Its Relation to the Public—the Spread and Decline of Yellow Journalism," *Collier's*, March 4, 1911, 19–20.

29. "Lawlessness and the Press: Topics of the Time," *Century*, May 1911, 146, 148.

30. "Thaw Murders Stanford White," *New York Times*, June 26, 1906, 1.

31. *Evening Journal*, June 26, 1906, 1.

32. Irwin, "The *Fourth Current*," 17, 24.

33. Denis Brian, *Pulitzer: A Life* (New York: John Wiley & Sons, 2001), 163–64. Brian noted that one of Pulitzer's secretaries said that "most wealthy socialites seem to look upon any sort of connection with J. P. as a very malignant [form] of leprosy and yet they have nothing definite to say against him." In a Republican era, Pulitzer was a steadfast Democrat, while many of his fellow millionaires were Republicans.

34. Gerald Johnson, *An Honorable Titan: A Biographical Study of Adolph S. Ochs* (New York: Harper & Brothers, 1946), 216–17.

35. Pulitzer eventually pledged $1 million up front and "conditionally promised a second million" in his will if he approved of the progress being made. "The School of Journalism of Columbia University," *Popular Science Monthly*, October 1903, 570. See Brian, *Pulitzer: A Life*, 286.

36. In 1884, Pulitzer wrote on the editorial page that "We are thinking of opening a Lyceum or school for the development of reporters, but our plans are not yet perfected." *New York World*, December 7, 1884, 4, cited in George Jeurgens, *Joseph Pulitzer and the New York World* (Princeton, NJ: Princeton University Press, 1966), 26.

37. C. F. Bacon, "College Literature and Journalism," *Critic* 37 (July 1900): 21–30.

38. Joseph Pulitzer to Seth Low, September 18, 1903, container 3, Pulitzer Papers, Manuscript Division, Library of Congress (hereafter LOC). Pulitzer said that in 1892 he "submitted the idea to President Low of Columbia, when it was declined." When the bequest was announced, Pulitzer worried that Low might have forgotten that he had received Pulitzer's original offer. From Europe, Pulitzer telegrammed his staff to "REMIND SETH LOW SAME PROPOSITION MADE HIM NINETYTWO." Joseph Pulitzer to Bradford Merrill, August 13, 1903, container 3, Pulitzer Papers. Butler proposed "suitable" additional advisors in a letter. Nicholas

much as $3,000 a week. The payrolls of New York dailies, according to the *Fourth Estate*'s trade survey, ranged from $30,000 to $60,000 a week, despite generally low wages. At the *Journal*, which "pays the highest wages known" in the newspaper industry, the direct payroll included 2,000 persons, not counting its correspondents and about 6,000 agents and newsboys. To cut costs, the *Journal* "has the largest factory for colored and black inks in the country. It makes its own rollers and almost everything it uses." In this transition era, the *Journal* still used horses for delivery of papers and "makes its own wagons and harnesses."[114]

The large Sunday papers with "an enormous quantity of advertising" had become profit leaders. Davis recognized the organizational genius of Morrill Goddard, "the father of the modern Sunday newspaper," first at Pulitzer's *World* and then at Hearst's *Journal*. With his own staff of reporters and editors, together with a magazine concept, "stirring articles," big headlines, larger illustrations, color, and comics, Goddard had increased the *Sunday World* circulation from 200,000 to 600,000 and then the *Sunday Journal* from 100,000 to 600,000. No doubt Munsey was fascinated that Sunday editions were setting circulation records, making about three-fourths of the total profits of a big newspaper and influencing content in the afternoon and morning papers. Davis concluded that the Sundays were "from the countingroom standard, the most important edition of the newspaper." These papers, produced apart from the newsroom's obsession with "beating time," were "the most important feature of the new journalism." The time and effort devoted to the Sundays confirmed Munsey's theory that "the countingroom" ruled journalism.[115]

Within a generation, Munsey spent millions buying numerous newspapers. In his effort to increase efficiency and profit, he experimented with changing prices, size, and features, ultimately killing some of the weaker papers, merging them with stronger papers, or selling them. Among his purchases were the *New York Daily News*, the *Boston Journal*, the *Washington Times*, and the *Baltimore News*. He founded the *Philadelphia Times*.[116] Munsey amassed a fortune of $40 million and a reputation as a "killer" of newspapers and a "gravedigger," but he set a pattern for the twentieth-century press.[117] Munsey was emulated and copied as businessmen bought and sold newspapers as commodities, merging or killing the weaker ones.

Among those who followed this pattern in the Midwest was Ira Clifton Copley. In the Midwest, the profitability of newspapers attracted the former congressman, who had made a fortune supplying Illinois customers with natural gas and electricity. Starting in Illinois in 1905 with the purchase of the *Aurora Beacon*, he bought and merged the competitive *Aurora Daily News*. Eventually he acquired 24 newspapers in the Midwest and West, killing the unprofitable ones among them.[118] Building upon his experience with public utilities, Copley brought to newspapering "the principle that the safest investment is a monopoly serving so many customers so well that it discourages competition."[119] Eventually he followed the trail blazed by Scripps and invested in newspapering in San Diego.[120]

Looked upon as an industry, big-city dailies were proving to be profitable, spurred on by improved technology, a cheap labor force, and increasingly literate mass urban populations—a fertile field for advertisers seeking a medium. Looked upon as a national resource shielded by the Constitution, the newspaper field now attracted more talented newspapermen eager to exercise opportunities to reach the masses and policy makers, challenge the status quo, and induce change. Simultaneously, for diverse reasons, media barons and their journalists worked in tandem to establish an economically viable and editorially influential public press.

NOTES

1. Concern for professional issues was evidenced by the emergence of two new trade publications, the *Fourth Estate* and *Editor and Publisher*, which joined the *Journalist*, published since 1884, and *Newspaperdom*, started in 1892.

2. Arthur Brisbane, "Yellow Journalism," no. 4 in "The American Newspaper," *Bookman*, June 19, 1904, 400–2; Sharon Murphy, "Winifred Black," in *Biographical Dictionary of American Journalism*, ed. Joseph McKerns (New York: Greenwood Press, 1989), 48–49; Erik Larson, *Isaac's Storm: A Man, a Time, and the Deadliest Hurricane in History* (New York: Vantage Books), 244.

3. Oswald Garrison Villard, "Frank A. Munsey: Dealer in Dailies." *Nation*, 20 June 1923, 713; Oswald Garrison Villard, *The Disappearing Daily: Chapters in American Newspaper Evolution* (New York: Alfred A. Knopf, 1944); Alfred Harmsworth, "The Simultaneous Newspapers of the Twentieth Century," *North American Review* 172 (January 1901): 90.

4. Michael Howard and Wm. Roger Louis, eds., *The Oxford History of the Twentieth Century* (Oxford: Oxford University Press, 1998), 129–31; Judy Crichton, *America 1900: The Turning Point* (New York: Henry Holt, 1998), 4; Richard W. Bulliet, ed., *The Columbia History of the 20th Century* (New York: Columbia University Press, 1998), 383–84.

5. Charles B. Connolly, "The Ethics of Modern Journalism," *Catholic World* 75 (July 1902): 453.

6. "Plot in Manila," *Washington Post*, January 1, 1900, 1; J. M. Roberts, *Twentieth Century: The History of the World, 1901 to 2000* (New York: Viking, 1999), 104.

7. "Fremont Older's Exposé of Newspaper Ethics: A Startling Recital of Secret and Unwritten History of San Francisco and California," *Current Opinion* 66 (January 1919): 39–40.

8. "The Newspaper Industry," *Atlantic Monthly*, June 1902, 745, 751.

9. Robert Underwood Johnson, "The Responsibilities of the Magazine," address to the School of Journalism at Columbia University, *Independent*, December 26, 1912, 1489.

10. By 1900, working-class newspapers proliferated in cities, constituting a "golden age for working-class newspapers"—a mix of radical, Socialist, Wobbly,

and anarchist publications, many in German and other languages. See Karla Kelling, "The Labor and Radical Press 1820–the Present: An Overview and Bibliography," Labor Press project, http://faculty.washington.edu/gregoryj/laborpress/Kelling. While championing the workingman, Scripps lived a life of relative luxury. After he discovered San Diego in 1890, he ran his newspaper empire from his 400-acre villa at nearby Miramar, or from offshore aboard his yacht. The other San Diego newspaper, the *Union*, frequently lampooned and caricatured Scripps as antilabor and lawless. In 1919, it headlined a lawsuit by a workman on Scripps's ranch. Calling Scripps a "Feudal Baron" the article's headline read: "Injured Man Declared Forced to Labor until He Becomes Human Junk." In 1923, during Prohibition, the *Union* reported the seizure of 166 bottles of wine from Scripps's yacht *Ohio*. When asked how his own newspaper should handle the story, Scripps replied, "Hell, it's news, isn't it?" Walter S. J. Swanson, *The Thin Gold Watch: A Personal History of the Newspaper Copleys* (New York: Macmillan, 1964), 128.

11. Sydney Brooks, "The American Yellow Press," *Living Age*, January 13, 1912, 71.

12. Horace White, "The School of Journalism," *North American Review* 176 (January 1904): 21.

13. Hartley Davis, "The Journalism of New York," *Munsey's*, November 1900, 233.

14. W. Joseph Campbell, *Yellow Journalism: Puncturing the Myths, Defining the Legacies* (Westport, CT: Praeger, 2001), 7–8; Frank Luther Mott, *American Journalism: A History, 1690–1960*, 3d ed. (New York: Macmillan, 1962), 539.

15. Davis, "Journalism of New York," 233.

16. Mott, *American Journalism*, 539.

17. Roosevelt's distaste for Hearst's journalism dated at least from March 1898. As assistant secretary of the navy, Roosevelt denied the *Journal's* claim that its reporter had interviewed him. "The alleged interview with me in to-day's *New York Journal* is an invention from beginning to end. It is difficult to understand the kind of infamy that resorts to such methods." He denied the article's claim that he praised the Washington dispatches as "most commendable and accurate" and claimed he "never in public or private commended the *New York Journal*." *New York Evening Post*, March 21, 1898; see also Willard G. Bleyer, *Main Currents in the History of American Journalism* (Boston: Houghton Mifflin, 1927), 375–76; and Edmund Morris, *Theodore Rex* (New York, Random House, 2001), 437, 439.

18. Connolly, "Ethics of Modern Journalism," 453–54.

19. Hearst's defense, given in an interview with a reporter for the *London Express*, was reprinted in the trade press. William Randolph Hearst, "Hearst Defends So-Called Yellow Journalism; Says They Are Disliked by Some Because They Persist in Telling the Truth," *Fourth Estate*, September 13, 1902, 4; Brisbane, "Yellow Journalism," 400.

20. Brisbane, "Yellow Journalism," 402.

21. "Dinners for the Poor; Evening World to Make 6,000 Persons Happy on Christmas," *Fourth Estate*, December 22, 1900, 13; "Hearst Makes It a Joyous Christmas for the Poor," *Fourth Estate*, December 27, 1902, 9.

22. Brisbane, "Yellow Journalism," 402; Brooks, "The American Yellow Press," 75.

Murray Butler to Joseph Pulitzer, August 17, 1903, container 3, Pulitzer Papers. Formerly dean of philosophy, Butler succeeded Low in 1901 at the age of 39; his books included *The Meaning of Education* (1898) and *True and False Democracy* (1908).

39. Don Carlos Seitz, *Joseph Pulitzer: His Life & Letters* (New York: Simon & Schuster, 1924), 140, 459–61.

40. White, "School of Journalism," 25, 26, 28, 31. White also served as a first vice president of the Associated Press. His own scholarship was evident in his textbook, *Money and Banking* (1895). Though he died in 1916, his text in 10 editions was used in classrooms through the 1930s. Marvin N. Olasky, "Horace White," in *Biographical Dictionary of American Journalism*, 738–39.

41. Bradford Merrill to New York editors, August 18, 1903, container 3, Pulitzer Papers.

42. White, "School of Journalism," 26, 28.

43. "Editorials: A School of Journalism," *Independent*, August 27, 1903, 2061.

44. "Editorials: A School of Journalism," 2061–62.

45. "The School of Journalism," *Popular Science Monthly*, 569–70.

46. "A School of Journalism," *Outlook*, August 22, 1903, 968–69.

47. Joseph Pulitzer, "The College of Journalism," *North American Review* 178 (May 1904): 641–80. The 39-page essay was condensed into two pages in *Review of Reviews*, June 1904, 735–37. Pulitzer's secretary instructed the business manager, Don Carlos Seitz, to send copies of the *North American Review* treatise to 10 persons. Alfred Butes to Don Carlos Seitz, May 4, 1904, container 4, Pulitzer Papers. A month after publication, Butes told editorial executive Bradford Merrill that Pulitzer "very carefully revised and corrected the North American article—in which by the way were two or three bad printer's blunders. This revised copy has just been sent to Dr. Butler who wishes to reprint the article in pamphlet form. He has been told to send the proof to you, and when you receive it Mr. P. begs that you will read it at least three times, seeing that his corrections and alterations are all properly made and that in this process, no new mistake creep in!" Butes to Bradford Merrill, June 15, 1904, container 4, Pulitzer Papers.

48. Ibid., 647.

49. Ibid., 649.

50. Pulitzer, "The College of Journalism," 680.

51. Mott, *American Journalism*, 590; Page established *World's Work* precisely because he wanted a proprietary interest in the magazine world so that he "shall not work to build up a good piece of machinery and then be turned out to graze as an old horse is," as he wrote to the historian Roscoe Thayer. Walter Hines Page to Roscoe Thayer, December 5, 1900, in Burton J. Hendrick, *The Life and Letters of Walter H. Page* (Garden City, NY: Doubleday, Page, 1923), http://www.lib.byu.edu/~rdh/wwi/memoir/Page/Page02.html. At the *Atlantic*, Page published an early treatise by Woodrow Wilson and later would be named U.S. ambassador to England and Germany by President Wilson.

52. The "Topics of the Day" was sometimes featured on the magazine cover by its publisher, Funk & Wagnalls. "Topics of the Day," *Literary Digest*, June 20, 1908, 1.

53. John Tebbel and Mary Ellen Zuckerman, *The Magazine in America* (New York: Oxford University Press, 1991), 66.

54. M. B. Corse, "The Best Plan to Save Magazine Literature," *World's Work*, September 1901, 1222–24.

55. George Seldes, *Freedom of the Press* (Garden City, NY: Garden City Publishing, 1937), 22–23, 27; James Parton, "Falsehood in the Daily Press," *Harper's New Monthly,* July 1874, 271.

56. S. S. McClure, *My Autobiography* (New York: Frederick A. Stokes, 1914), 243.

57. Richard Hofstadter, *The Age of Reform: From Bryan to F.D.R.* (New York: Alfred A. Knopf, 1955), 185.

58. Ibid., 210.

59. McClure, *Autobiography,* 242.

60. Judith Serrin and William Serrin, *Muckraking! The Journalism That Changed America* (New York: New Press, 2002), 146, 150–51.

61. McClure, *Autobiography,* 241, 266.

62. Ibid., 266.

63. Donald A. Ritchie, *American Journalists: Getting the Story* (New York: Oxford University Press, 1997), 174; McClure, *Autobiography,* 243–45.

64. Stephen Ponder, *Managing the Press: Origins of the Media Presidency, 1897–1933* (New York: St. Martin's Press, 1998), 18.

65. Morris, *Theodore Rex,* 712.

66. Morris, *Theodore Rex,* 206–7.

67. Ray Stannard Baker, "Railroad Rebates," *McClure's,* December 1905.

68. Ray Stannard Baker, notebook no. 2, Manuscript Division, LOC, 1–5.

69. "They Combine to Beat Us; But We Shall Make a Good Showing in Twenty Towns Tomorrow," *Boston Daily Socialist,* December 7, 1903, 1. The short-lived eight-page newspaper was published by the Socialists' candidate for mayor of Boston and succumbed after the election, according to Jon Bekken, Suffolk University, Boston.

70. Hearst had ignored his editors' advice against magazine ventures and started a successful automotive magazine, *Motor,* in 1904. In 1905 he ignored financial advice from *Motor* editor George D'Utassy that he could buy *Cosmopolitan* for less than $400,000 if he waited. "Perhaps you are right," Hearst replied, "but price is only one consideration. If I don't buy now, [John Brisben] Walker may find another purchaser, or Walker may make money in his automobile business and not want to sell. Or the magazine may continue to deteriorate and not be worth anything. You say we can make money with it. I assume you mean 'real money!' … If you do, buy now instead of waiting, and start to make money." In less than three years *Cosmopolitan* increased circulation more than tenfold, from fewer than 100,000 to more than a million, and had more advertising that the two closest competitors. Cora Baggerly Older, *William Randolph. Hearst, American* (New York: Appleton-Century, 1936), 256–57.

71. David Nasaw, *The Chief: The Life of William Randolph Hearst* (Boston: Houghton Mifflin, 2000), 190–92.

72. Quoted in Older, *Hearst,* 257.

73. Quoted in Ibid., 257–258.

74. David Graham Phillips, "Treason," March 1906, 487.

75. David Graham Phillips, "Treason," April 1906, 638. The correction related to a candidate for federal district attorney who, because he "had been caught stealing trust funds," was rejected by Roosevelt. "Mr. Phillips has since ascertained that this statement was untrue, and that the reason for the failure of his candidacy

much as $3,000 a week. The payrolls of New York dailies, according to the *Fourth Estate*'s trade survey, ranged from $30,000 to $60,000 a week, despite generally low wages. At the *Journal*, which "pays the highest wages known" in the newspaper industry, the direct payroll included 2,000 persons, not counting its correspondents and about 6,000 agents and newsboys. To cut costs, the *Journal* "has the largest factory for colored and black inks in the country. It makes its own rollers and almost everything it uses." In this transition era, the *Journal* still used horses for delivery of papers and "makes its own wagons and harnesses."[114]

The large Sunday papers with "an enormous quantity of advertising" had become profit leaders. Davis recognized the organizational genius of Morrill Goddard, "the father of the modern Sunday newspaper," first at Pulitzer's *World* and then at Hearst's *Journal*. With his own staff of reporters and editors, together with a magazine concept, "stirring articles," big headlines, larger illustrations, color, and comics, Goddard had increased the *Sunday World* circulation from 200,000 to 600,000 and then the *Sunday Journal* from 100,000 to 600,000. No doubt Munsey was fascinated that Sunday editions were setting circulation records, making about three-fourths of the total profits of a big newspaper and influencing content in the afternoon and morning papers. Davis concluded that the Sundays were "from the countingroom standard, the most important edition of the newspaper." These papers, produced apart from the newsroom's obsession with "beating time," were "the most important feature of the new journalism." The time and effort devoted to the Sundays confirmed Munsey's theory that "the countingroom" ruled journalism.[115]

Within a generation, Munsey spent millions buying numerous newspapers. In his effort to increase efficiency and profit, he experimented with changing prices, size, and features, ultimately killing some of the weaker papers, merging them with stronger papers, or selling them. Among his purchases were the *New York Daily News*, the *Boston Journal*, the *Washington Times*, and the *Baltimore News*. He founded the *Philadelphia Times*.[116] Munsey amassed a fortune of $40 million and a reputation as a "killer" of newspapers and a "gravedigger," but he set a pattern for the twentieth-century press.[117] Munsey was emulated and copied as businessmen bought and sold newspapers as commodities, merging or killing the weaker ones.

Among those who followed this pattern in the Midwest was Ira Clifton Copley. In the Midwest, the profitability of newspapers attracted the former congressman, who had made a fortune supplying Illinois customers with natural gas and electricity. Starting in Illinois in 1905 with the purchase of the *Aurora Beacon*, he bought and merged the competitive *Aurora Daily News*. Eventually he acquired 24 newspapers in the Midwest and West, killing the unprofitable ones among them.[118] Building upon his experience with public utilities, Copley brought to newspapering "the principle that the safest investment is a monopoly serving so many customers so well that it discourages competition."[119] Eventually he followed the trail blazed by Scripps and invested in news-papering in San Diego.[120]

Looked upon as an industry, big-city dailies were proving to be profitable, spurred on by improved technology, a cheap labor force, and increasingly literate mass urban populations—a fertile field for advertisers seeking a medium. Looked upon as a national resource shielded by the Constitution, the newspaper field now attracted more talented newspapermen eager to exercise opportunities to reach the masses and policy makers, challenge the status quo, and induce change. Simultaneously, for diverse reasons, media barons and their journalists worked in tandem to establish an eco-nomically viable and editorially influential public press.

NOTES

1. Concern for professional issues was evidenced by the emergence of two new trade publications, the *Fourth Estate* and *Editor and Publisher,* which joined the *Journalist,* published since 1884, and *Newspaperdom,* started in 1892.

2. Arthur Brisbane, "Yellow Journalism," no. 4 in "The American Newspaper," *Bookman,* June 19, 1904, 400–2; Sharon Murphy, "Winifred Black," in *Biographical Dictionary of American Journalism,* ed. Joseph McKerns (New York: Greenwood Press, 1989), 48–49; Erik Larson, *Isaac's Storm: A Man, a Time, and the Deadliest Hurricane in History* (New York: Vantage Books), 244.

3. Oswald Garrison Villard, "Frank A. Munsey: Dealer in Dailies." *Nation,* 20 June 1923, 713; Oswald Garrison Villard, *The Disappearing Daily: Chapters in American Newspaper Evolution* (New York: Alfred A. Knopf, 1944); Alfred Harmsworth, "The Simultaneous Newspapers of the Twentieth Century," *North American Review* 172 (January 1901): 90.

4. Michael Howard and Wm. Roger Louis, eds., *The Oxford History of the Twentieth Century* (Oxford: Oxford University Press, 1998), 129–31; Judy Crichton, *America 1900: The Turning Point* (New York: Henry Holt, 1998), 4; Richard W. Bulliet, ed., *The Columbia History of the 20th Century* (New York: Columbia University Press, 1998), 383–84.

5. Charles B. Connolly, "The Ethics of Modern Journalism," *Catholic World* 75 (July 1902): 453.

6. "Plot in Manila," *Washington Post,* January 1, 1900, 1; J. M. Roberts, *Twentieth Century: The History of the World, 1901 to 2000* (New York: Viking, 1999), 104.

7. "Fremont Older's Exposé of Newspaper Ethics: A Startling Recital of Secret and Unwritten History of San Francisco and California," *Current Opinion* 66 (January 1919): 39–40.

8. "The Newspaper Industry," *Atlantic Monthly,* June 1902, 745, 751.

9. Robert Underwood Johnson, "The Responsibilities of the Magazine," address to the School of Journalism at Columbia University, *Independent,* December 26, 1912, 1489.

10. By 1900, working-class newspapers proliferated in cities, constituting a "golden age for working-class newspapers"—a mix of radical, Socialist, Wobbly,

and anarchist publications, many in German and other languages. See Karla Kelling, "The Labor and Radical Press 1820–the Present: An Overview and Bibliography," Labor Press project, http://faculty.washington.edu/gregoryj/laborpress/Kelling. While championing the workingman, Scripps lived a life of relative luxury. After he discovered San Diego in 1890, he ran his newspaper empire from his 400-acre villa at nearby Miramar, or from offshore aboard his yacht. The other San Diego newspaper, the *Union,* frequently lampooned and caricatured Scripps as antilabor and lawless. In 1919, it headlined a lawsuit by a workman on Scripps's ranch. Calling Scripps a "Feudal Baron" the article's headline read: "Injured Man Declared Forced to Labor until He Becomes Human Junk." In 1923, during Prohibition, the *Union* reported the seizure of 166 bottles of wine from Scripps's yacht *Ohio.* When asked how his own newspaper should handle the story, Scripps replied, "Hell, it's news, isn't it?" Walter S. J. Swanson, *The Thin Gold Watch: A Personal History of the Newspaper Copleys* (New York: Macmillan, 1964), 128.

11. Sydney Brooks, "The American Yellow Press," *Living Age,* January 13, 1912, 71.

12. Horace White, "The School of Journalism," *North American Review* 176 (January 1904): 21.

13. Hartley Davis, "The Journalism of New York," *Munsey's,* November 1900, 233.

14. W. Joseph Campbell, *Yellow Journalism: Puncturing the Myths, Defining the Legacies* (Westport, CT: Praeger, 2001), 7–8; Frank Luther Mott, *American Journalism: A History, 1690–1960,* 3d ed. (New York: Macmillan, 1962), 539.

15. Davis, "Journalism of New York," 233.

16. Mott, *American Journalism,* 539.

17. Roosevelt's distaste for Hearst's journalism dated at least from March 1898. As assistant secretary of the navy, Roosevelt denied the *Journal's* claim that its reporter had interviewed him. "The alleged interview with me in to-day's *New York Journal* is an invention from beginning to end. It is difficult to understand the kind of infamy that resorts to such methods." He denied the article's claim that he praised the Washington dispatches as "most commendable and accurate" and claimed he "never in public or private commended the *New York Journal.*" *New York Evening Post,* March 21, 1898; see also Willard G. Bleyer, *Main Currents in the History of American Journalism* (Boston: Houghton Mifflin, 1927), 375–76; and Edmund Morris, *Theodore Rex* (New York, Random House, 2001), 437, 439.

18. Connolly, "Ethics of Modern Journalism," 453–54.

19. Hearst's defense, given in an interview with a reporter for the *London Express,* was reprinted in the trade press. William Randolph Hearst, "Hearst Defends So-Called Yellow Journalism; Says They Are Disliked by Some Because They Persist in Telling the Truth," *Fourth Estate,* September 13, 1902, 4; Brisbane, "Yellow Journalism," 400.

20. Brisbane, "Yellow Journalism," 402.

21. "Dinners for the Poor; Evening World to Make 6,000 Persons Happy on Christmas," *Fourth Estate,* December 22, 1900, 13; "Hearst Makes It a Joyous Christmas for the Poor," *Fourth Estate,* December 27, 1902, 9.

22. Brisbane, "Yellow Journalism," 402; Brooks, "The American Yellow Press," 75.

23. Mott, *American Journalism*, 573; Thomas C. Leonard, *The Power of the Press: The Birth of American Political Reporting* (New York: Oxford University Press, 1987).

24. Davis, "Journalism of New York," 233.

25. Will Irwin, "The American Newspaper: A Study of Journalism in Its Relation to the Public—the *Fourth Current*," *Collier's*, February 18, 1911, 15.

26. *New York Journal*, April 10, 1901. Earlier, the Hearst columnist in Washington, Ambrose Bierce, commenting on the assassination of Kentucky Governor-Elect William Goebel in February 1900, wrote that the assassin's bullet was now "speeding here / To stretch McKinley on his bier." Ambrose Bierce, "A Thumbnail Sketch," in *Collected Works* (1912; repr., Staten Island, NY: Gordian Press, 1960).

27. W. A. Swanberg, *Citizen Hearst: A Biography of William Randolph Hearst* (New York: Galahad Books, 1961), 195.

28. Will Irwin, "The American Newspaper: A Study of Journalism in Its Relation to the Public—the Spread and Decline of Yellow Journalism," *Collier's*, March 4, 1911, 19–20.

29. "Lawlessness and the Press: Topics of the Time," *Century*, May 1911, 146, 148.

30. "Thaw Murders Stanford White," *New York Times*, June 26, 1906, 1.

31. *Evening Journal*, June 26, 1906, 1.

32. Irwin, "The *Fourth Current*," 17, 24.

33. Denis Brian, *Pulitzer: A Life* (New York: John Wiley & Sons, 2001), 163–64. Brian noted that one of Pulitzer's secretaries said that "most wealthy socialites seem to look upon any sort of connection with J. P. as a very malignant [form] of leprosy and yet they have nothing definite to say against him." In a Republican era, Pulitzer was a steadfast Democrat, while many of his fellow millionaires were Republicans.

34. Gerald Johnson, *An Honorable Titan: A Biographical Study of Adolph S. Ochs* (New York: Harper & Brothers, 1946), 216–17.

35. Pulitzer eventually pledged $1 million up front and "conditionally promised a second million" in his will if he approved of the progress being made. "The School of Journalism of Columbia University," *Popular Science Monthly*, October 1903, 570. See Brian, *Pulitzer: A Life*, 286.

36. In 1884, Pulitzer wrote on the editorial page that "We are thinking of opening a Lyceum or school for the development of reporters, but our plans are not yet perfected." *New York World*, December 7, 1884, 4, cited in George Jeurgens, *Joseph Pulitzer and the New York World* (Princeton, NJ: Princeton University Press, 1966), 26.

37. C. F. Bacon, "College Literature and Journalism," *Critic* 37 (July 1900): 21–30.

38. Joseph Pulitzer to Seth Low, September 18, 1903, container 3, Pulitzer Papers, Manuscript Division, Library of Congress (hereafter LOC). Pulitzer said that in 1892 he "submitted the idea to President Low of Columbia, when it was declined." When the bequest was announced, Pulitzer worried that Low might have forgotten that he had received Pulitzer's original offer. From Europe, Pulitzer telegrammed his staff to "REMIND SETH LOW SAME PROPOSITION MADE HIM NINETYTWO." Joseph Pulitzer to Bradford Merrill, August 13, 1903, container 3, Pulitzer Papers. Butler proposed "suitable" additional advisors in a letter. Nicholas

Murray Butler to Joseph Pulitzer, August 17, 1903, container 3, Pulitzer Papers. Formerly dean of philosophy, Butler succeeded Low in 1901 at the age of 39; his books included *The Meaning of Education* (1898) and *True and False Democracy* (1908).

39. Don Carlos Seitz, *Joseph Pulitzer: His Life & Letters* (New York: Simon & Schuster, 1924), 140, 459–61.

40. White, "School of Journalism," 25, 26, 28, 31. White also served as a first vice president of the Associated Press. His own scholarship was evident in his textbook, *Money and Banking* (1895). Though he died in 1916, his text in 10 editions was used in classrooms through the 1930s. Marvin N. Olasky, "Horace White," in *Biographical Dictionary of American Journalism*, 738–39.

41. Bradford Merrill to New York editors, August 18, 1903, container 3, Pulitzer Papers.

42. White, "School of Journalism," 26, 28.

43. "Editorials: A School of Journalism," *Independent*, August 27, 1903, 2061.

44. "Editorials: A School of Journalism," 2061–62.

45. "The School of Journalism," *Popular Science Monthly*, 569–70.

46. "A School of Journalism," *Outlook*, August 22, 1903, 968–69.

47. Joseph Pulitzer, "The College of Journalism," *North American Review* 178 (May 1904): 641–80. The 39-page essay was condensed into two pages in *Review of Reviews*, June 1904, 735–37. Pulitzer's secretary instructed the business manager, Don Carlos Seitz, to send copies of the *North American Review* treatise to 10 persons. Alfred Butes to Don Carlos Seitz, May 4, 1904, container 4, Pulitzer Papers. A month after publication, Butes told editorial executive Bradford Merrill that Pulitzer "very carefully revised and corrected the North American article—in which by the way were two or three bad printer's blunders. This revised copy has just been sent to Dr. Butler who wishes to reprint the article in pamphlet form. He has been told to send the proof to you, and when you receive it Mr. P. begs that you will read it at least three times, seeing that his corrections and alterations are all properly made and that in this process, no new mistake creep in!" Butes to Bradford Merrill, June 15, 1904, container 4, Pulitzer Papers.

48. Ibid., 647.

49. Ibid., 649.

50. Pulitzer, "The College of Journalism," 680.

51. Mott, *American Journalism*, 590; Page established *World's Work* precisely because he wanted a proprietary interest in the magazine world so that he "shall not work to build up a good piece of machinery and then be turned out to graze as an old horse is," as he wrote to the historian Roscoe Thayer. Walter Hines Page to Roscoe Thayer, December 5, 1900, in Burton J. Hendrick, *The Life and Letters of Walter H. Page* (Garden City, NY: Doubleday, Page, 1923), http://www.lib.byu.edu/~rdh/wwi/memoir/Page/Page02.html. At the *Atlantic*, Page published an early treatise by Woodrow Wilson and later would be named U.S. ambassador to England and Germany by President Wilson.

52. The "Topics of the Day" was sometimes featured on the magazine cover by its publisher, Funk & Wagnalls. "Topics of the Day," *Literary Digest*, June 20, 1908, 1.

53. John Tebbel and Mary Ellen Zuckerman, *The Magazine in America* (New York: Oxford University Press, 1991), 66.

54. M. B. Corse, "The Best Plan to Save Magazine Literature," *World's Work*, September 1901, 1222–24.

55. George Seldes, *Freedom of the Press* (Garden City, NY: Garden City Publishing, 1937), 22–23, 27; James Parton, "Falsehood in the Daily Press," *Harper's New Monthly*, July 1874, 271.

56. S. S. McClure, *My Autobiography* (New York: Frederick A. Stokes, 1914), 243.

57. Richard Hofstadter, *The Age of Reform: From Bryan to F.D.R.* (New York: Alfred A. Knopf, 1955), 185.

58. Ibid., 210.

59. McClure, *Autobiography*, 242.

60. Judith Serrin and William Serrin, *Muckraking! The Journalism That Changed America* (New York: New Press, 2002), 146, 150–51.

61. McClure, *Autobiography*, 241, 266.

62. Ibid., 266.

63. Donald A. Ritchie, *American Journalists: Getting the Story* (New York: Oxford University Press, 1997), 174; McClure, *Autobiography*, 243–45.

64. Stephen Ponder, *Managing the Press: Origins of the Media Presidency, 1897–1933* (New York: St. Martin's Press, 1998), 18.

65. Morris, *Theodore Rex*, 712.

66. Morris, *Theodore Rex*, 206–7.

67. Ray Stannard Baker, "Railroad Rebates," *McClure's*, December 1905.

68. Ray Stannard Baker, notebook no. 2, Manuscript Division, LOC, 1–5.

69. "They Combine to Beat Us; But We Shall Make a Good Showing in Twenty Towns Tomorrow," *Boston Daily Socialist*, December 7, 1903, 1. The short-lived eight-page newspaper was published by the Socialists' candidate for mayor of Boston and succumbed after the election, according to Jon Bekken, Suffolk University, Boston.

70. Hearst had ignored his editors' advice against magazine ventures and started a successful automotive magazine, *Motor*, in 1904. In 1905 he ignored financial advice from *Motor* editor George D'Utassy that he could buy *Cosmopolitan* for less than $400,000 if he waited. "Perhaps you are right," Hearst replied, "but price is only one consideration. If I don't buy now, [John Brisben] Walker may find another purchaser, or Walker may make money in his automobile business and not want to sell. Or the magazine may continue to deteriorate and not be worth anything. You say we can make money with it. I assume you mean 'real money!' … If you do, buy now instead of waiting, and start to make money." In less than three years *Cosmopolitan* increased circulation more than tenfold, from fewer than 100,000 to more than a million, and had more advertising that the two closest competitors. Cora Baggerly Older, *William Randolph. Hearst, American* (New York: Appleton-Century, 1936), 256–57.

71. David Nasaw, *The Chief: The Life of William Randolph Hearst* (Boston: Houghton Mifflin, 2000), 190–92.

72. Quoted in Older, *Hearst*, 257.

73. Quoted in Ibid., 257–258.

74. David Graham Phillips, "Treason," March 1906, 487.

75. David Graham Phillips, "Treason," April 1906, 638. The correction related to a candidate for federal district attorney who, because he "had been caught stealing trust funds," was rejected by Roosevelt. "Mr. Phillips has since ascertained that this statement was untrue, and that the reason for the failure of his candidacy

was not his character, which is above reproach, but was his zealous espousal of the [Senator Thomas] Platt side of the New York factional warfare."

76. The allegation of treason was based on the Constitution, Article III, Section 3: "Treason against the United States shall consist only in levying war against them, or in *adhering to their enemies, giving them aid and comfort*" (Phillips's italics). Phillips' premise was that the corporate "interests" were "enemies" in a greedy conspiracy enacted through the senators' "treachery." Phillips, "Treason," March 1906, 487.

77. Phillips' novels *The Master Rogue* (1903), *The Cost* (1904), and *The Deluge* (1905) portrayed industrial corruption, and *The Plum Tree* (1905) showed politicians as taking orders from big business. They suggested "the need for reform and government regulation." Robert Miraldi, "David Graham Phillips," *Biographical Dictionary of American Journalism,* 556.

78. Phillips, "Treason," March 1906, 487–88.

79. Ibid. Italics in original.

80. "The Jungle: A Tale of the Beef Trust," advertisement, *Appeal to Reason,* December 9, 1905, 4. The *Appeal to Reason* was a new Socialist weekly newspaper based in Girard, Kansas, whose editors focused on social justice and the rights of labor. The newspaper had a national circulation of more than 500,000 in 1904 when it sent Sinclair to Chicago to examine conditions in the stockyards in the wake of an unsuccessful strike.

81. Oscar Edward Anderson Jr., *The Health of a Nation: Harvey W. Wiley and the Fight for Pure Food* (Chicago: University of Chicago Press, 1958), 194–95.

82. Anderson, *The Health of a Nation,* 189. According to Anderson, Roosevelt wanted an investigation "independent of the Department of Agriculture," so he asked Charles P. Neill, U.S. labor commissioner, and James B. Reynolds, a New York reformer, to "make a study that would not be open to attack as a 'whitewash.'" Edmund Morris says Roosevelt asked Secretary of Agriculture James Wilson for a "first-class man to be appointed to meet Sinclair ... get the names of witnesses ... and then go to work in the industry." Morris, *Theodore Rex,* 439.

83. Samuel Hopkins Adams, "The Great American Fraud," *Collier's,* October 7, 1905, 14, 15, 29. Chemical testing protected the magazine against a lawsuit. In 1904, *Ladies' Home Journal* editor Edward Bok published an editorial condemning "the 'patent-medicine' curse." The company that produced Doctor Pierce's Favorite Prescription sued for libel and a jury fined the magazine $16,000. See "The 'Patent-Medicine' Curse," *Ladies' Home Journal,* May 1904, 21; July 1904, 18; see also J. Harvey Young, *The Toadstool Millionaires* (Princeton, NJ: Princeton University Press, 1961), 213, 216–23, 247.

84. Morris, *Theodore Rex,* 446.

85. Phillips, "Treason," August 1906, 375–76; "Treason," November 1906, 81–82. Phillips contended that Roosevelt retained President McKinley's attorney general, Philander Knox, as an unlikely watchdog against "the interests" because Roosevelt was "charmed by his engaging personality and manifest abilities," even though Knox had been handpicked by financier J. Pierpont Morgan, "the big man of the steel corporation."

86. Morris, *Theodore Rex,* 439.

87. John Bunyan, *The Pilgrim's Progress* (New York: Pocket Library, 1957), 2:194.

88. Lucas, "Muck-Rake," 452. While the muckrake metaphor made the speech memorable, Lucas contended that the speech was at least equally important for Roosevelt's endorsement of increased federal control over interstate commerce—then being debated in the Senate—and support for a federal inheritance tax and income tax, which he supported in subsequent messages to Congress. Taken as a whole, Lucas argued that the April 14 speech "reflected TR's increasing disenchantment with political and economic conservatism, and marked a significant step in the breaking of his alliances with Wall Street, the Old Guard, and other representatives of economic and political standpatism." Lucas, "Muck-Rake," 452, 459.

89. Quoted in Morris, *Theodore Rex*, 439–40; Serrin and Serrin, *Muckraking!* 154.

90. Theodore Roosevelt to Ray Stannard Baker, April 9, 1906, Roosevelt Papers, cited in Lucas, "Muck-Rake," 455.

91. Phillips, "Treason," May 1906, 11; "Treason," June 1906, 131.

92. Phillips, "Treason," August 1906, 377.

93. Roosevelt's secret investigation of the meatpackers "vindicated everything Upton Sinclair had written in *The Jungle,* but supplied extra details so disgusting that Roosevelt could not bring himself to release them." Morris, *Theodore Rex*, 447.

94. Morris, *Theodore Rex,* 447.

95. Young, "Toadstool Millionaires," 248.

96. Ibid., 248.

97. Phillips, "Treason," April 1906, 631, 633, 635.

98. Phillips, "Treason," November 1906, 84.

99. Gabriel Kalko, *The Triumph of Conservatism: A Reinterpretation of American History, 1900–1916* (London: Free Press of Glencoe, 1963), 304–5.

100. Hofstadter, *The Age of Reform,* 210.

101. On May 1, 1911, the Supreme Court, under the Sherman Antitrust Act, ordered the dissolution of the Standard Oil Company and the American Tobacco Company. In the Standard Oil case, the court enunciated the *rule-of-reason doctrine,* indicating its belief that the government should not attempt to outlaw "every" combination in restraint of trade but should confine action to those contracts that result in an "unreasonable" restraint of trade. The enunciation of this doctrine marked a turning point in the court's attitude toward the so-called trusts. William L. Langer, ed., *An Encyclopedia of World History* (Boston: Houghton Mifflin, 1948), 830.

102. Marian Ainsworth-White, "The Higher Education of Women: Women in Journalism," *Arena,* June 1900, 669–72.

103. Edward Bok, "Is the Newspaper Office the Place for a Girl?" *Ladies' Home Journal,* February 1901, 18.

104. Ibid.

105. Ibid.

106. "Religious Journalism," *Outlook,* August 2, 1902, 821.

107. Charles M. Sheldon, "The Experiment of a Christian Daily," *Atlantic Monthly,* November 1924, 624–33.

108. Ibid.

109. Mary Baker G. Eddy, "Something in a Name," *Christian Science Monitor,* November 25, 1908, editorial page; Frank Bell, managing editor of the *Harrisburg Telegraph,* sent his praise in a November 2 letter reprinted on the editorial page. The front-page headlines read: "Unveil Statue of Gen. Sheridan at Washington,"

"Ask Injunction against Chelsea Shoe Workers," and "Construction Work Rapidly Progresses on Great Dam across the Charles River Basin," *Christian Science Monitor*, November 25, 1908, 1. See also Norman Beasley, *The Cross and the Crown: The History of Christian Science* (Boston: Little, Brown, 1952).

110. Alfred Harmsworth, "The Simultaneous Newspapers of the Twentieth Century," *North American Review* 172 (January 1901): 72, 79, 80–83, 85, 89–90.

111. Ibid.

112. Davis, "Journalism of New York," 217–18, 233.

113. Ibid.; "Electric Typewriter," *Fourth Estate*, September 28, 1901, 4; "Delivery by Automobiles," *Fourth Estate*, March 24, 1900, 5; "A New Time Saver; How the Graphophone Aids the Typewriter," *Fourth Estate*, December 21, 1899, 7.

114. "The Cost of a Big Daily; Interesting Inside Facts concerning William R. Hearst's *New York Journal*," *Fourth Estate*, November 30, 1901, 12.

115. Davis, "Journalism of New York," 217–33.

116. Munsey later killed the *New York Daily News* and the *Philadelphia Times* and sold the *Boston Journal*, the *Washington Times*, and the *Baltimore News*. Jack H. Colldeweih, "Frank Andrew Munsey," in *Biographical Dictionary of American Journalism*, 499–500.

117. George Britt, *Forty Years—Forty Millions: The Career of Frank A. Munsey* (New York: Farrar & Reinhart, 1935), 295–301.

118. Swanson, *The Thin Gold Watch*, 55.

119. Julia Crain Zaharopoulos, "Ira Clifton Copley," in *Biographical Dictionary of American Journalism*, 133.

120. Swanson, *The Thin Gold Watch*, 1, 114, 120–21.

2

Journalism in Transition

Our newspapers are sharper, quicker, more moderate, nearer to the truth and to sound principles of sociology, than the newspaper of twenty or thirty years ago.

—Will Irwin, "The American Newspaper," 1911

By 1906 the nation was bound together by the sinews of railroads, steamships, wagon trails, the postal system, the telegraph, and, more than ever, by the press. The continuing population trends of immigration from overseas and migration from rural to urban areas supported the publication of more newspapers than ever before. From coast to coast, newspapers and magazines contributed to a national consciousness. Competing news-gathering agencies knit thousands of local newspapers into the fabric of the nation. Larger metropolitan papers routinely considered the relevancy of distant news. Magazines, increasing in both number and scope, employed writers who crafted nonfiction and social, political, and economic criticism.[1]

The nation's press demonstrated its maturation and reach in the reporting of disasters that struck the extremities of the country. As with the Galveston hurricane in 1900, the press in 1906 treated as a national concern the earthquake and fire that destroyed the city of San Francisco. The shock occurred at 5:15 A.M. on Wednesday, April 17. The earthquake crumpled the city's infrastructure, bursting water mains. Lacking water to battle flames that engulfed block after block, firefighters dynamited buildings in the fire's path. By daybreak a tower of smoke could be seen 100 miles away. Across the country, newspapers featured eyewitness accounts from victims, including celebrities drawn to the city by its cultural life—notably the operatic tenor Enrico Caruso and actor John Barrymore. In the New York newsroom of the *Sun*, Will Irwin penciled a memorial about the sea-fogged San Francisco streets he knew so well. Under editor Franklin P. Matthews's headline, "The City That Was," Irwin wrote:

The old San Francisco is dead. The gayest, lightest hearted, most pleasure loving city of the western continent, and in many ways the most interesting and romantic, is a horde of huddled refugees living among ruins. It may rebuild; it probably will; but those who have known that peculiar city by the Golden Gate and have caught its flavor of the Arabian Nights feel that it can never be the same. It is as though a pretty, frivolous woman had passed through a great tragedy. She survives, but she is sobered and different. If it rises out of the ashes it must be a modern city, much like other cities and without its old atmosphere.[2]

Across a continent, four days apart by the swiftest train, the two publics, West and East, were joined through the immediacy of transcontinental journalism.[3]

Magazines, less immediate but more complete, gave deep dimension to the disaster. *Collier's Weekly* trumped the competition by publishing a 2,500-word eyewitness account by Jack London, famous for his novel set in Alaska, *The Call of the Wild*. That day, London left his perch across the bay and sought out the heart of the terror in the midst of the city, where rich and poor citizens were carting or dragging trunks of possessions ahead of walls of flames. Firefighters could not halt the "onrush of the flames...Near to the flames, the wind was often half a gale, so mighty was the suck." London portrayed the desperation of the survivors.

All night these tens of thousands fled before the flames.... They held longest to their trunks, and over these trunks many a strong man broke his heart that night. The hills of San Francisco are steep, and up these hills, mile after mile, were the trunks dragged.... Before the march of the flames were flung picket lines of soldiers.... One of their tasks was to keep the trunk-pullers moving.... Often, after surmounting a heart-breaking hill, they would find another wall of flame advancing upon them at right angles.... In the end, completely played out, after toiling for a dozen hours like giants, thousands of them were compelled to abandon their trunks. Here shopkeepers and soft members of the middle class were at a disadvantage. But the working-men dug holes in vacant lots and backyards and buried their trunks.[4]

The homeless hungered for help and guidance. The disaster had silenced the city's major newspapers. Jack London had witnessed "the tottering walls of the *Examiner* building, the burned-out *Call* building." Fantastic rumors circulated among the survivors "huddled in parks and squares, their houses gone, death or famine or thirst a rumor and a possibility." The only newspaper published on April 18 was the *Daily News*, whose staff had produced the issue by hand just before its building was destroyed. Its "Extra" edition, issued from 1308 Mission Street, headlined "HUNDREDS DEAD!" and listed victims, telegraph-style:

Max Fenner, policeman, killed in collapse Essex Hotel. Seven firemen killed in collapse of brick power house, Valencia and 7th. Frank Corali, buried, beneath basement floor of burning lodging house 6th and Mission. Heard crying "For God's sake, help me."[5]

Editors and some reporters of the three major San Francisco newspapers boated across the bay to the office of the *Oakland Tribune*. There they published a joint *Call-Chronicle-Examiner*. The public's frantic craving for that first edition proved to Will Irwin how they needed news as much or more than bread or blankets. "News," he concluded, was "the main thing, the vital consideration to the American newspaper." The modern usefulness of news had surpassed the historic influence of opinion.

When at dawn the paper was printed, an editor and a reporter loaded the edition into an automobile and drove it through the parks of the disordered city, giving copies away. They were fairly mobbed; they had to drive at top speed, casting out the sheets as they went, to make any progress at all. No bread wagon, no supply of blankets, caused half so much stir as did the arrival of the news.[6]

Irwin's fascination with the public's uses of and gratifications from news led him toward serious research on the production of news as a national commodity. In 1908, when he was freelancing for *Collier's* and other magazines, his writing caught the attention of Columbia University President Nicholas Butler. With Joseph Pulitzer's health failing, the university needed to move ahead on planning curriculum for the School of Journalism to be funded from his bequest. Butler, who that year published his inquiry, *True and False Democracy*, found in Irwin a journalist with scholarly aptitude and professional integrity. He asked him to travel and research journalistic standards and practices with the goal of recommending how they could be improved through training. Irwin was to interview newspaper editors and publishers in the United Sates and Europe.[7]

In 1909 Irwin began work on a series of articles on the public press to be published in *Collier's*. He benefited from a growing body of articles and books critical of the press and advocating reforms. In response, publisher Rob Collier wanted his magazine to take the muckraker's approach to analyzing the defects of American newspapers. Irwin, however, elevated the assignment beyond standard muckraking into what his biographer called "an analytical, historical, definitive study" of the state of journalism in the Progressive Era. He studied American journalism, past and present. He probed one of the most persistent criticisms—that publishers' commercial and political considerations had corrupted journalism by dictating news and editorial decisions. But he also identified positive contributions and trends. The series was a milestone for Irwin, establishing him as the leading expert on the journalism of his day.[8]

His "study of American journalism in its relation to the public" took more than a year. The 15-part series appeared in *Collier's* from January through July 1911. In the first installment, he reviewed the state of press criticism—allegations mainly by professors, "who preach to an imperfect world," and plaudits principally from newspaper men "eager to defend their own profession."

The condemners say that the metropolitan newspaper has grown venal: that advertisers and great financial interests control it; that its sensationalism has vitiated the public taste; that it has lost all power of leadership in good causes. The defenders answer that it is more free and independent than ever before; that it gives its readers better mental pabulum than they want; that it leads our civilization; that it has more influence than ever the written word exercised before .... Truth and justice lie somewhere between their extreme views.[9]

Irwin confirmed that the production of news had become a basic public necessity, a bonding feature of modern American life coast to coast. In arguing that political endorsements and opinion pages had become less influential than the news, Irwin was confirming the view of the previous generation's leading press critic, E. L. Godkin, editor of the *Nation*. Godkin's comparison of newspaper endorsements and election outcomes led him to conclude that "the influence of the press has undergone great diminution in all parts of the country."[10]

As Irwin compiled a catalog of great reporters' stories, he concluded that journalists were generally capable of reporting factually and truthfully. Yet he understood certain handicaps, limitations, and pressures: They worked without a guiding code of ethics; they were at times driven by circumstances to violations of decency and privacy or to exaggerate or sensationalize; they depended too often on biased information from the increasing numbers of press bureaus.[11]

Corruption of the production of news, he concluded, occurred mainly through interference from editors, who took cues directly from publishers. Following this trail, he documented how publishers' personal agendas interfered with the public interest. Publishers also responded to the special interests of major advertisers and businessmen who wielded financial power, which the *Collier's* artist portrayed as a cudgel. In short, with some exceptions, special interests and commercialism contaminated the contents of the press. This corruption resulted in distortions or organized lying and suppression, endangering the public interest.[12]

While Irwin attested to the misguided power and questionable health of the public press, he underscored its strengths and potential. "This is a transition period," he wrote, in which despite "evils and excesses ... the curve of progress appears to run upward." While documenting the sins of yellow journalism, he found that the "yellow influence" had ebbed as journalists and the public became more educated, and publishers, even Pulitzer and Hearst, found more-profitable styles. "Our newspapers are sharper, quicker, more moderate, nearer to the truth and to sound principles of sociology, than the newspaper of twenty or thirty years ago."[13]

Irwin prophesized that the future of the press depended upon the new generation of "trained and specialized talent." In analyzing trends in the history of American journalism, he concluded that great advances had come when the older editors gave way to the new, as when the generation of the great Horace Greeley was succeeded after the Civil War by the editors of Godkin's era. In his parting words, he urged the transfer of the "supreme power [that] resides in men of that older generation. Could the working journalists of our own age tell us as frankly as they wished what they think and see and feel about the times, we should have only minor points to criticize in American journalism."[14] He worried, however, that contemporary publishers who wielded "supreme power" were driving journalism with a strictly commercial outlook. Frank Munsey was busy acquiring and killing newspapers. Hearst was expanding his empire of newspapers and magazines to New York, Chicago, Boston, Atlanta, San Francisco, and Los Angeles, putting his stamp on every publication.

While yellow journalism had faded, another luminous creation now competed with the news for the attention of readers. Since the introduction of Sunday comics, the lure of entertainment had proved profitable. Newspaper comics and cartoons expanded from occasional appearances to daily comic strips after November 15, 1907, when the first successful strip was published by the *San Francisco Chronicle*. Drawn by sports cartoonist Harry Conway "Bud" Fisher, the comic strip featured a "checked-suited, felt-hatted, chinless, mustachioed" horse-race bettor named Augustus Mutt. *Mr. Mutt* was soon purchased by Hearst's *Examiner* and became *Mutt and Jeff* when Fisher introduced Mutt's comic partner—a "pint-sized, silk-hatted illogician." Within a few years, Fisher's income soared, and comic strips had become an American staple featuring married couples, kids, adventures, girls, animals, and slapstick.[15]

In Chicago, Hearst was battling for circulation against one of the new generation of publishers, Robert M. McCormick, who was chosen as president of the *Chicago Tribune* in 1911. McCormick soon outdid Hearst at his own game of seeking the pennies of the common man. Rivalries among seven newspapers—including Hearst's *Chicago Evening*

American and morning *Chicago Examiner*—escalated into a true circulation war with weapons as diverse as money and guns. In the front offices, executives offered cash to hire rival papers' best employees. On Chicago's streets, "the wagon bosses who delivered papers to the stands and the newsboys became remarkably persuasive…. The rotary press found great cooperation in the Colt automatic, the dirk, the blackjack, and other shelf hardware."[16]

In the thick of the circulation war, newspapers found an ally in the newly popular medium of motion pictures. McCormick increased the *Tribune*'s readership overnight by merging the entertaining narratives of the movies with the pages of the daily paper. McCormick saw how picture-show stories could be at least as popular as comic strips. Motion pictures offered lengthy stories that newspapers could serialize and synchronize to appear simultaneously on page and screen. Secretly, McCormick bid for picture-story rights. On December 29, 1913, *The Adventures of Kathlyn* opened in theaters and simultaneously "flared out upon the world through the columns of the *Chicago Tribune* and newspapers to which the *Tribune* syndicated the story." Circulation jumped by 10 percent. McCormick had added to the orthodox *Tribune*'s elite readership 35,000 regulars from a different audience, the "emotion-hungry" nickelodeon filmgoers. Hearst's attempt to duplicate the feat in Chicago failed, largely because his "comic-stripped" papers had already tapped into that class of readers.[17]

While such entertaining features attracted additional audiences, accurate and timely reporting of news arguably best served the public. As Will Irwin and other critics argued, expanded and serious news coverage distinguished newspapers as great. Nothing evidenced the impact of news coverage better than press response to economic and social problems. Between November 1909 and February 1910, the press covered the first massive strike of female workers in the United States—popularized as the "women's movement strike" and "the uprising of the thirty thousand." The strike targeted New York City and Philadelphia sweatshop factories, where thousands of women and girls worked six days a week in unsafe conditions, sewing fashionable waist-length shirts called shirtwaists. That so many women had joined America's working class was in itself news, a significant departure from the stereotype of wife, mother, and homemaker. The factory working class included mostly girls over 15 and unmarried women, many of them European immigrants. Led by the Women's Trade Union League and the International Ladies Garment Workers Union, the strike was the first major effort to organize working-class women in the profitable garment industry. Little of the industry's income trickled down to the workers, who earned barely more than a subsistence wage, ranging from $2.50 to $4 a week for girls to $9 a week for experienced young women.[18]

During the strike, the press noted that upper-class women joined picketing strikers, most of whom were teenage girls. The society ladies also provided bail money for strikers jailed on charges of disturbing the peace, loitering, prostitution, or assault. This support from prominent women added significance and public sympathy and induced factory owners to make some settlement.[19] In their partial settlement, women at the Triangle Shirt Waist factory in New York did not gain their demand for adequate fire escapes from the factory's eighth, ninth, and tenth floors. Nor did the women win their demand for unlocked doors. They had protested the foreman's practice of locking the doors while the women worked for fear they might take breaks or steal needles and thread.[20]

When the Triangle factory went up in flames, the press's extensive coverage underscored the tragic consequences of not granting the women's demands for safer working conditions.[21] One Saturday afternoon, March 25, 1911, a sudden, intense fire swept through the lint-filled air of the factory, trapping employees behind a locked door and above the collapsed fire escape. Within 30 minutes, workers suffocated or "were burned to death or killed by jumping to the pavement below." The death toll was 147, mostly women and girls. The *New York World* gave the first five pages of its Sunday paper to the tragedy. So did the conservative *New York Times*, whose managing editor, the brilliant and astute Carr Van Anda, had been directing evermore extensive news coverage since taking control in 1904. In the 21 years of the Van Anda era, the *Times* set a model for twentieth-century news gathering by confirming that "stark fact, simply told, was more powerful than any purple writing."[22]

Front-page stories and photographs now attested that factories were horrible death traps. Flames, the *Times* noted, "spread with deadly rapidity through flimsy material used in the factory." When firemen arrived, ladders reached no higher than the sixth floor. Witnesses watched panicked women and girls at windows and ledges, some of them waiting or clinging to the building briefly, then jumping. "The crowd yelled, 'Don't Jump!' but it was jump or be burned," reported the *New York Times*. The *World's* eyewitness wrote, "They jumped with their clothing ablaze. The hair of some of the girls streamed up of flame as they leaped. Thud after thud sounded on the pavement."[23]

Because nearly all the dead were women and girls, the press now focused more intently on the plight of women laborers working in dangerous factory conditions. Fifty bodies were found bunched behind an iron door that had been locked.[24] Stories revealed that elevators did not work and that the owners knew of an exit through which they had escaped unharmed across rooftops. Hearst's *New York Evening Journal* accused the owners of murder.[25] The press also blamed city inspectors. The Triangle's owners, Max Blanck and Isaac Harris, were tried for manslaughter and acquitted by a jury that was "smuggled" out by a rear door to avoid the crowd outside. For code violations, the owners paid small fines. Blanck opened another business elsewhere under much the same conditions.[26]

The Triangle fire and its aftermath raised questions in other cities. Newspapers and magazines increased public awareness of the plight of girls and women in the workforce. In 1910 they numbered more than 8 million aged 15 and older.[27] In Chicago, the *Tribune* questioned whether its city's employers were "gambling with death to save a little money." An editorial asked whether Chicago's inspectors were inadequate, incompetent, overworked, or "winking at law evasion."[28] National magazines cited "lessons" learned from the Triangle and other factory fires in New York and Newark, focusing on safety standards, inspections, fire drills, fire prevention, and firefighting. A. E. McFarlane muckraked for *McClure's* on the plight of workers in New York's "tower factories" and for *Collier's* described the Triangle story as "a rotten risk."[29]

The Triangle fire and the perception of injustice helped generate some legal reforms. A campaign by the Women's Trade Union League resulted in the creation of a New York Factory Investigation Commission, which recommended improved working conditions. Women had been working 59 hours a week; the state reduced the work week to 54 hours. Nonetheless, labor organizers considered the progress minimal and stressed that the best protection was "a union strong enough on the shop level to enforce the law and to agitate around safety issues."[30]

While mainstream newspapers and magazines gave only occasional attention to such disasters, reformers created or located alternative media by which to spread their nontraditional messages and advocate legislation to improve human and civil rights. The women's suffrage movement and ethnic, racial, and labor organizations voiced issues of discrimination and championed civil and economic rights in publications such as *Women's Journal,* and the *Crisis* (1909), and the social, labor, and farm press. The reform spirit inspired and enlivened journals of opinion, whose readers were interested in the *meaning* of events and in new ideas and new books. Some intellectuals took cues from England, where liberal thinkers had founded several journals that, according to social historian Jacques Barzun, "countered the press lords' organs and their giant circulations." In the United States, the political philosopher Herbert Croly in 1909 published his seminal *The Promise of American Life,* advocating an agenda for establishing political and economic balance through social and governmental activism. The book stimulated sponsors to engage Croly in launching in November 1914 a progressive-liberal journal, the *New Republic,* which joined the *Nation* as a leading forum of opinion.[31]

In some states, women had been winning the right to vote and using it. In Denver, Caroline Nichols Churchill continued publishing her pro-suffrage newspaper, the *Queen Bee,* a generation after Colorado granted women the right to vote in 1893, announcing proudly that the

West was "The Land for Women!" In 1911, when California became the sixth and largest state to approve women's suffrage, Charlotta Spears Bass, co-owner with her husband of the African American newspaper in Los Angeles, the *California Eagle,* followed up by supporting a voter-registration campaign and advocating national women's suffrage. In this battle they had to overcome the resistance from Congress as well as anti-suffragettes, among them Annie Nathan Meyer, founder of Barnard College in New York, who disagreed that women's votes would cure the ills of American political life.[32]

Early in the century, the growth of concentrated African American urban populations with increasing literacy encouraged the birth and growth of several weekly newspapers. The papers specialized in reporting community social news generally ignored by the white press, while editorials articulated issues ranging from slum clearance to voting rights. The *Afro-American,* founded in Baltimore by John Henry Murphy in 1892, was joined during a fertile five-year period by numerous papers, most notably by Robert Sengstacke Abbott's *Chicago Defender* (1905), James H. Anderson's *Amsterdam News* in Harlem (1909), and Robert Vann's *Pittsburgh Courier* (1910), and Plummer Bernard Young's Norfolk, Virginia, *Journal and Guide* (1910). African American newspapers in turn often supported the National Association for the Advancement of Colored People (NAACP), founded in 1909 with its own publication, the *Crisis,* edited by William Edward Burghardt Du Bois.[33]

By 1900, hundreds of publications catered to America's industrial laborers, often propagating socialist, radical, or anarchist views that were denied access to mainstream publications. Many were printed in German and other immigrant languages. The most successful socialist publication nationally was the *Appeal to Reason,* which had serialized Upton Sinclair's exposé of the capitalist exploitation of labor in the meat-packing plants of Chicago. In Seattle, a center of union activity in the West, the *Union Record* became the city's best-known labor newspaper. Launched as a weekly in 1900, it went daily in 1918 with six to eight pages "in response the insistent demand of labor for a fair and adequate presentation of its case to the public. It has no grudges to satisfy and no axe to grind." It was joined between 1900 and 1910 by the *Socialist: The Workingman's Paper,* which abrasively proclaimed its weekly Socialist Party mission "to organize the slaves of capital to vote their own emancipation."[34]

Outside the cities, America's farmers sought their own publications. Between 1900 and 1910, when farm population grew from 44 million to 50 million, there were 458 listed publications claiming 15 million in circulation. Although many farmers traditionally rejected "book farming," others read the farm press regularly for information about agricultural practices and farm politics, banking, and credit, as reflected by the publication titles: *Successful Farming,* the *Progressive Farmer,* the

National Stockman and Farmer, Wallaces' Farmer, Western Farm Life, and the *Banker-Farmer.* Recent research has demonstrated that agricultural journalists (who usually were not farmers) were ambitious about agenda setting. So impressive was the extent of the farm press that by 1905, Iowa State University had established a course in agricultural journalism.[35]

Among urban newspapers, the *New York Times* was fast distinguishing itself as a model for American journalism, both in quality and profitability. By 1911, after 15 years of Adolph Ochs's practice of reinvesting profits in developing the news organization, the *Times* exercised a persuasive influence on press standards in New York and to some extent nationally. Devotion to Ochs's credo—"All the News That's Fit to Print"—was paying off financially, and this commercial success was not lost on other publishers. Since 1900, daily circulation of the *Times* more than doubled from 82,000 to 187,000, while the circulation of the Sunday edition more than tripled from 39,000 to 128,000. Advertising lineage doubled from 4 million to 8 million. Then in one year, 1912, circulation escalated 17 percent on the daily and 23 percent on the Sunday editions, in part because of Van Anda's unmatched direction of news coverage of the sinking of the ocean liner *Titanic.*[36]

That drama began at the *Times* with an Associated Press bulletin. The few words, received at 1:20 A.M. on Monday morning, April 15, reported that the White Star Line steamship on its maiden voyage had sent a distress message to the Marconi wireless station in Cape Race, Newfoundland. The message at 10:25 P.M. said the *Titanic* had "struck an iceberg" and required "immediate assistance." Within minutes, Van Anda mobilized the newsroom and got information over the phone from *Times* correspondents in Halifax and Montreal. Convinced that the "unsinkable" ship was sinkable, he stopped the presses and inserted the AP bulletin with the headline, "Titanic Sinking in Mid-Ocean; Hit Great Iceberg." The headline for the next edition was even more descriptive: "New Liner Titanic Hits an Iceberg; Sinking by the Bow at Midnight; Women Put off in Lifeboats; Last Wireless at 12:27 A.M. Blurred." The final edition declared what the liner's company would not confirm, that the *Titanic* had sunk. While other newspapers merely published the AP bulletin or published "rumors" or wrong information, the *Times'* "reporting triumph ... did much to kindle early public interest in the disaster."[37]

Van Anda and his editors organized follow-up coverage with military efficiency. Renting a floor in a hotel near where the rescue ship, the *Carpathia,* would dock with survivors, they appointed field reporters and newsroom rewrite men, arranged for press passes to the pier, and hired taxicabs. The *Times* wanted interviews with the heroic captain of the *Carpathia,* Arthur H. Rostron, and with the *Titanic's* crew and passengers, notably the White Star Line director J. Bruce Ismay. Van Anda tracked down his friend Guglielmo Marconi, the wireless inventor, and led him to the pier. Marconi managed to take a *Times* reporter with him on board, past the police barrier. With this full-scale campaign, the *Times* devoted 15 of its 24 pages to the disaster: the 1,517 dead, the 706 survivors, and heroes on both ships. The front-page headline on April 19 relayed the human tragedy as seen from the lifeboats: "745 Saw Titanic Sink with 1,595, Her Band Playing." It told how: "Hit Iceberg at 21 Knots and Tore Her Bottom Out." It quoted Captain Edward J. Smith's last words: "I'll Follow the Ship." And it underscored sacrifice: "Many Women Stayed to Perish with Their Husbands."[38]

Although news coverage of the aftermath continued for months with stories about the accident inquiry and about relief efforts for the survivors, the April 19 issue established a new norm for comprehensive news reporting. "Trade journals warmly praised it, here and abroad," wrote *Times* historian Meyer Berger. "Long afterward, when Carr Van Anda, visiting in London, called at Lord Northcliffe's *Daily Mail*, Northcliffe's editor opened a desk drawer at his right hand. In it lay the *New York Times* of April 19, 1912. He said: 'We keep this as an example of the greatest accomplishment in news reporting.'"[39]

The *Times* also excelled that year in covering the nation's most peculiar four-way presidential race, which one historian regarded as "a defining moment in American history ... a conflict between progressive idealism ... and conservative values." Challenging Republican President William Howard Taft's reelection was his old political ally, former president Roosevelt, running as a progressive candidate with his own independent Progressive Party, thus splitting the Republican vote. The main beneficiary of the Republican split was the progressive Democratic candidate, Woodrow Wilson, governor of New Jersey and past president of Princeton University. Added to the mix was the reform-minded Socialist Party candidate, Eugene V. Debs, destined to poll more votes than in his first two runs for the presidency. All four seemed committed to limiting what the muckrakers had revealed as the "excesses of big business, symbolized by the great trusts, which had accompanied the rise of industrial capitalism." But Roosevelt and Wilson appeared to be the true progressives, and the campaign became a forum for reform on issues that muckrakers, social workers, and clergy had publicized: child labor, factory hours and conditions, the conservation of natural resources, and women's suffrage.[40]

In the final months before the election, Roosevelt's party predicted Taft would run a poor third, behind Debs, and Republicans accused Roosevelt of seeking to elect Wilson. Wilson, viewing Roosevelt as his main opponent, told American workers that Roosevelt would "make the people nothing more than mere wards and puppets" of a national board headed by capitalists. In November, Taft won only Vermont and Utah, Roosevelt won California and five other states totaling 88 electoral votes, Debs won a remarkable 6 percent of the vote but no states, and Wilson, with only

42 percent of the popular vote, won an overwhelming majority in the Electoral College. Roosevelt viewed Wilson's victory as a win for progressives and wired his congratulations. The Democratic *New York World,* in the first election since Pulitzer's death in 1911, hailed Wilson's victory as "a mandate of the people to restore confidence."[41]

Although the press devoted extensive space to domestic reforms during Wilson's first term, troubles in Europe gradually stole attention from domestic affairs. Teased at first by U.S. adventures in Cuba and the Philippines, more Americans now considered developments in Europe as impinging on their own lives. In response, U.S. newspapers, magazines, and news agencies took a lead in breaking with the national tradition of isolationism. Coverage of foreign news shifted during these years from the occasional to the systematic, from the spectacular stories to coverage of foreign politics, economics, and society.

Surveys of editors indicated the commercial value of overseas news gathering. Americans seemed to want news from Europe, especially if it was light and not ponderous. In a 1913 survey of member newspapers, the AP news chief in New York, Charles Kloeber, learned that editors rated the other services' news from Paris as "more snappy and interesting." Kloeber advised Paris bureau chief Elmer Roberts that, without "trying to conduct a correspondence school of journalism," he would appreciate "a judicious mingling of the bright and serious." Over time, more advisories asked Roberts to adjust style, focus, length, speed, and comprehension. Other cables thanked him, once for a story about "blind masseurs" and another about sea turtles. In 1914, with the outbreak of war, he shifted into high gear and wrote several "excellent" biographical sketches of French wartime commanders about whom information had been "practically unavailable."[42]

NOTES

1. Three more states were admitted before World War I: Oklahoma (1907), New Mexico, and Arizona (both 1912). In 1900, 60 percent of the people lived in rural areas, and 40 percent lived in urban areas; in 1990, only 25 percent lived in rural areas, and 75 percent in urban areas; between 1901 and 1910, 2 million immigrants came from Italy alone. U.S. Census Bureau Public Information Office, 2001. The number of publications peaked in 1914 at 2,250 dailies, 12,500 weeklies, and 600 semiweeklies. Mott, *American Journalism,* 549.

2. Robert V. Hudson, *The Writing Game: A Biography of Will Irwin* (Ames: Iowa State University Press, 1982), 53–54.

3. Will Irwin, "The Power of the Press," pt. 1 in "The American Newspaper: A Study of Journalism in Its Relation to the Public," *Collier's,* January 21, 1911, 15–18.

4. Jack London, "The Story of an Eye-Witness: The San Francisco Earthquake," *Collier's Weekly,* May 5, 1906, in *The Mammoth Book of Journalism,* ed. Jon E. Lewis (New York: Carroll & Graf Publishers, 2003), 107–13.

5. "Hundreds Dead! Fire Follows Earthquake, Laying Downtown Section in Ruins—City Seems Doomed for Lack of Water," *San Francisco Daily News,* April 18, 1906. Copyright 1906 by Charles A. McDonald, reprinted in *An American Time Capsule: Three Centuries of Broadsides and Other Printed Ephemera* (Washington, DC: Library of Congress, 2000–ongoing). http://memory.loc.gov/. See also Dan Kurzman, *Disaster! The Great San Francisco Earthquake and Fire of 1906* (New York: William Morrow, 2001), 220.

6. Will Irwin, "What Is News?" pt. 5, *Collier's,* March 18, 1911, 16.

7. Will Irwin, *The American Newspaper,* ed. Clifford F. Weigle and David G. Clark (Ames: Iowa State University Press, 1969), xi.

8. Hudson, *The Writing Game,* 68.

9. Irwin, "The Power of the Press," pt. 1, 15. Typical of the critical articles of the day was "Is Sane and Honest Journalism Possible?" *Review of Reviews,* January 1910, 93–94.

10. E. L. Godkin, "The Influence of the Press," *Nation,* November 25, 1897, 410.

11. Irwin, "The Reporter and the News," pt. 7, "The American Newspaper," *Collier's,* April 22, 1911, 19–20, 35–36.

12. Irwin, "The Editor and the News," pt. 6, *Collier's,* April 1, 1911, 18–19, 28; Irwin, "The Advertising Influence," pt. 9, *Collier's,* May 27, 1911, 15–16, 23–25; Irwin, "The Unhealthy Alliance," pt. 10, *Collier's,* June 3, 1911, 17–19, 28; Irwin, "Our Kind of People," pt. 11, *Collier's,* June 17, 1911, 17–18; Irwin, "The Foe from Within," pt. 12, *Collier's,* July 1, 1911, 17–18, 30.

13. Irwin, "The Voice of a Generation," pt. 15, "The American Newspaper," *Collier's,* July 29, 1911, 15.

14. Ibid., 15, 25.

15. Stephen Becker, *Comic Art in America: A Social History of the Funnies, the Political Cartoons, Magazine Humor, Sporting Cartoons and Animated Cartoons* (New York: Simon & Schuster, 1959), 33–36. *Mutt and Jeff* made Fisher a rich man. In 1913, he left Hearst and syndicated his strip through the Wheeler Syndicate for $1,000 a week plus 80 percent of the gross syndicate sales; his syndicate earnings within a few years reached $4,600 a week, not counting vaudeville appearances, books, and toys. Hearst resorted to an old ploy, publishing an imitation of the strip until Fisher won a court order against him.

16. Terry Ramsaye, *A Million and One Nights: A History of the Motion Picture Through 1925* (New York: Simon & Schuster, 1926), 657.

17. Ibid., 660–62.

18. S. Comstock, "Uprising of the Girls," *Collier's,* December 25, 1909, 14–16; W. Mailly, "Working Girls' Strike: The Shirtwaist Makers of New York," *Independent,* December 23, 1909, 1416–20; M. B. Sumner, "Spirit of the Strikers," *Survey,* January 22, 1910, 550–55; Lois W. Banner, *Women in Modern America: A Brief History* (New York: Harcourt, Brace, Jovanovich, 1974), 66; Meredith Tax, *The Rising of the Women* (New York: Monthly Review Press, 1980), 205–6, 210–11; Woods Hutchinson, "The Hygienic Aspects of the Shirtwaist Strike," *Survey,* January 22, 1910, 545; Elizabeth V. Burt, "Women in the Workplace: Newspaper Coverage of the Triangle Shirt Waist Factory Fire, 25 March 1911," paper presented at the American Journalism Historians Association Conference, Billings, Montana, October 3, 2003.

19. "True and False Sympathy in Strikes," *Century,* March 1910, 791–92.

20. M. F. Scott, "What the Women Strikers Won," *Outlook,* July 2, 1910, 480–81; "Philadelphia Shirtwaist Strike Settled," *Survey,* February 19, 1910, 757–58; S. A. Clark and E. Wyatt, "Shirtwaist Makers and Their Strike," *McClure's,* November 10, 1910, 70–86; Banner, *Women in Modern America,* 66–67; Tax, *The Rising of the Women,* 203, 234.

21. Burt, "Women in the Workplace." Burt cites the anti-labor and anti-immigrant mentality noted in Foster Rea Dulles and Melvin Dubofsky, *Labor in America: A History,* 5th ed. (Arlington Heights, IL: Harlan Davidson, 1953), 1–20; Daniel J. Tichenor, *Dividing Lines: The Politics of Immigration Control in America* (Princeton, NJ: Princeton University Press, 2002); Alan M. Kraut, *Silent Travelers: Germs, Genes, and the "Immigrant Menace"* (New York: Basic Books, 1994); John Higham, "Another Look at Nativism," *Catholic Historical Review* 44 (1958): 147–58.

22. "141 Men and Girls Die in Waist Factory Fire; Trapped High up in Washington Place Building; Street Strewn with Bodies; Piles of Dead Inside," *New York Times,* March 26, 1911, 1; Burt, "Women in the Workplace"; Meyer Berger, *The Story of the "New York Times," 1851–1951* (New York: Simon & Schuster, 1951), 201.

23. "154 Killed in Skyscraper Factory Fire; Scores Burn, Others Leap to Death," *New York World,* March 26, 1911, 1, in Burt, "Women in the Workplace." The fire stories and editorials circulated nationally through the press agencies; Banner, *Women in Modern America,* 67–68.

24. Leon Stein, *The Triangle Fire* (New York: J. B. Lippincott, 1952), 168; Meredith Tax, *The Rising of the Women,* 234.

25. "The Murdering of Those Unhappy Girls on Saturday," *New York Evening Journal,* March 28, 1911, editorial page, in Burt, "Women in the Workplace."

26. "Triangle Owners Acquitted by Jury; Harris and Blanck Leave Court with a Strong Police Guard to Protect Them; The Jurors Smuggled Out; Throng in the Street Hisses and Reviles the Defendants—To Be Tried on Another Indictment," *New York Times,* December 28, 1911, 1; Tax, *The Rising of the Women,* 236. Protesting against weak law enforcement, the publication of the Industrial Workers of the World alleged that Blanck and Harris—"these butchers for profit"—had "rented a condemned building and proceeded to again defy the law." *Solidarity,* April 15, 1911, in Tax, *The Rising of the Women,* 264. Blanck allegedly chained the door of his newly rented factory while 150 workers were inside,, for which he was fined $20. Burt, "Women in the Workplace."

27. Banner, *Women in Modern America,* 60–61; Tax, *Rising of the Women,* 30.

28. "Again," *Chicago Tribune,* March 27, 1911, 8.

29. A. E. McFarlane, "Fire and the Skyscraper: Problem of Protecting the Workers in New York's Tower Factories," *McClure's,* September 1911, 466–82. Twenty months later, McFarlane dug deeper into the story in "Triangle Fire: The Story of a Rotten Risk," *McClure's,* May 17, 1913. *McClure's* also published M. A. Hopkins's study of the "Newark Factory Fire," *McClure's,* April 11, 1911, 663–72. *Survey* in one issue linked two fires: "New York and the Asch Fire," *Survey,* July 15, 1911, 578–80; and "New Jersey and the Newark Fire," *Survey,* July 15, 1911, 575–78. See also "The Lessons of the Equitable Building Fire," *Scientific American,* January 20, 1912, 62.

30. "New York Plans to Lessen Fire Risks," *Survey,* April 29, 1911, 180–82; Burt, "Women in the Workplace"; Tax, *Rising of the Women,* 236.

31. Jacques Barzun, *From Dawn to Decadence: 1500 to the Present: 500 Years of Western Cultural Life* (New York: HarperCollins, 2000), 684; Herbert Croly, *The Promise of American Life* (1909; repr., New York: Capricorn Books, 1964). See Charles Forcey, *The Crossroads of Liberalism: Croly, Weyl, Lippmann, and the Progressive Era 1900–1925* (New York: Oxford University Press, 1961); and Byron Dexter, "Herbert Croly and the Promise of American Life," *Political Science Quarterly* 70 (1955): 197. Walter Lippmann, who joined the *New Republic,* characterized Croly as "the first important political philosopher" of the twentieth century. David Levy, *Herbert Croly of the New Republic: The Life and Thought of an American Progressive* (Princeton, NJ: Princeton University Press, 1985), xi.

32. "Western Women Wild with Joy over the Victory in Colorado," *Queen Bee,* November 1893, 1, in "This Shall be the Land for Women," Women of the West Museum, Boulder, Colorado, http://www.autry-museum.org/explore/exhibits/suffrage/suffrage; Annie Nathan Meyer, "Women's Assumption of Sex Superiority," *North American Review* 178 (1904): 103–9; cited in Robert A. McCaughey, "Annie Nathan Meyer," http://www.columbia.edu/~rr91/3567/sample_biographies.

33. Leonard Ray Teel, "The African-American Press and the Campaign for a Federal Anti-lynching Law, 1933–34: Putting Civil Rights on the National Agenda," *American Journalism* 8, no. 2–3 (1991): 84–107.

34. "The Workingman's Ticket: Debs and Harriman at the Head," *Socialist,* August 17, 1900, 1; Dirk Hoerder, *The Immigrant Labor Press in North America, 1840s–1970s* (New York: Greenwood Press, 1987), vols. 1–3; John Graham, ed. *"Yours for the Revolution": The Appeal to Reason, 1895–1922* (Lincoln: University of Nebraska Press, 1990); Karla Kelling, "The Labor and Radical Press 1820–the Present: An Overview and Bibliography," Labor Press Project, http://faculty.washington.edu/gregoryj/laborpress/Kelling; Jon Bekken, "'No Weapon so Powerful': Working-Class Press at the Turn of the Century," *Journal of Communication Inquiry* 12 (Summer 1988): 104–19; Elliott Shore, *Talkin' Socialism: J. A. Wayland and the Role of the Press in American Radicalism, 1890–1912* (Lawrence: University of Kansas Press, 1988); *The American Labor Press: An Annotated Directory* (Washington, DC: American Council on Public Affairs, 1940).

35. W. S. Crowe, *Batten's Agricultural Directory* (New York: George Batten, 1908), 15, cited in Stuart E. Shulman, "The Origin of the Federal Farm Loan Act: Agenda-Setting in the Progressive Era Print Press" (PhD diss., University of Oregon, 1999), chapter 5. See also Stuart E. Shulman, "The Progressive Era Farm Press: A Primer on a Neglected Source of Journalism History," *Journalism History* 25 (Spring 1999): 25–32.

36. Berger, *Story of the "New York Times,"* 569.

37. Berger, *Story of the "New York Times,"* 194–96; John P. Eaton and Charles A. Haas, *Titanic: Triumph and Tragedy* (New York: W. W. Norton, 1986), 181, 209. Headlines in Hearst's New York *Evening Sun* on April 15 were misleading or erroneous. The Wall Street night edition declared that "Titanic's Passengers Are Transshipped" and the final edition headlined: "All Saved from Titanic after Collision." Armed with new facts a day later, the *Evening Sun* headlined, "Hope for More Titanic Survivors Faint."

38. Berger, *Story of the "New York Times,"* 197–201; Eaton and Hass, *Titanic,* 192–98.

39. Eaton and Hass, *Titanic*, 192–198; Berger, *Story of the "New York Times,"* 201.

40. James Chace, 1912: *Wilson, Roosevelt, Taft & Debs—the Election That Changed the Country* (New York: Simon & Schuster, 2004), 6–8.

41. "Taft a Poor Third, Says Gov. Johnson; Bull Moose Mate Predicts Debs Will Poll More Votes than President in Illinois," *New York Times*, September 23, 1912, 2; "Colonel's Aim to Beat Taft; Angry at Steel Exposures, Says Hilles, and Now Seeks to Elect Wilson," *New York Times*, September 24, 1912, 7; "Ignore Party Labels, Wilson Tells Labor; Says Roosevelt Would Make the People Puppets of a National Board Headed by Capitalists," *New York Times*, September 3, 1912, 3; "Roosevelt Meets Defeat Buoyantly; Progressives Must Win in the End, He Says, after Wiring Congratulations to Wilson," *New York Times*, November 6, 1912, 6; "Local Press Writes Wilson's Duty Large; Victory a Mandate of the People to Restore Confidence, Says the *World*," *New York Times*, November 6, 1912, 6.

42. Charles E. Kloeber to Elmer Roberts, January 13, 1913; January 18, 1913; January 22, 1913; March 20, 1913; November 21, 1913; and July 2, 1915; box 1, Elmer Earle Roberts Papers, Manuscript Department, Southern Historical Collection, University of North Carolina, Chapel Hill.

3

The War over There

A new kind of warfare—a warfare of engines and machines and anonymous units—now was being carried forward on a scale never before dreamed of by mortal minds.

—Irvin S. Cobb, in Belgium, 1914

The German invasion of Belgium in August 1914 and the outbreak of a general war in Europe on August 4 suddenly challenged the U.S. press to expand coverage. Few U.S. newspapers and magazines had adequate staffs in Europe, and communications facilities were inadequate. The transatlantic cables speeded news dissemination, but after the British cut the cables between Germany and America, news from the Continent filtered in mostly from England. Wireless communication brought bursts of short, carefully worded bulletins censored by the warring countries, not enough to satisfy immigrants and others anxiously awaiting news. Some American publishers responded by agreeing to cooperate in news gathering. In New York, the *Times,* the *World,* and the *Tribune* pooled some of their war news, and some newspapers and news agencies pooled resources to offset the cable costs.[1]

Editors immediately recognized the immensity of the conflict, the "spectacle of Mars stalking across Europe," as the *Outlook* described it. Newspapers that already had focused on the ultimatums and declarations began devoting even more space to the invasion of Belgium. The time-zone differences benefited the U.S evening newspapers. Since events in Belgium, Britain, France, Germany, and Moscow occurred several hours earlier than in New York, the evening papers could publish European news the same day, sometimes crowding out local and national news.[2]

Apart from the news, editorial opinion reflected profound discouragement. In a national survey of press opinion one week after the outbreak of war, the *Outlook* reported a sense that civilization had descended into a great abyss. The *San Francisco Chronicle* predicted that this would be "the most devastating war in European history." The *Philadelphia North American* asked, "What does this mean but that our boasted civilization has broken down?" The *New York Herald* asked, "Is Christian civilization a failure?" The *New York Sun* concluded that a "feeling of depression, of sadness, almost of bitterness, must possess every thinking person as Europe flames into war" and asked if humankind's fate was to basely devour or be devoured. The *Atlanta Constitution* noted that despite progress in science, medicine, and commerce, and "conquest of the air and water," there has been no "conquest of the murderous human instinct."[3]

Most editorialists blamed the German government and special interests and cited the need to replace absolutist rulers with democracies. The *Springfield Republican* called the German "audacity" in violating the neutrality of neutral Belgium and Luxemburg "more villainous than anything that has occurred in international relations since the time of Frederick the Great." In the German-American heartland, the *St. Louis Republic* blamed the German government, not the German masses: "No two things could be further apart than the spirit of the German War Office and the spirit of Germany.... The cure for war is democracy—'the consent of the governed.'" The *Buffalo Commercial* condemned Europe's entangling security alliances, which, by committing allies to join in war, "are now seen as they are, a peril and a curse." Louisville's *Courier-Journal* blamed "big business," as did the *Philadelphia Public Ledger,* which said, "the ultimate issue, stripped of all the subordinate but vital hopes involved, is commerce." The *Ledger,* among other newspapers, forecast Germany's doom because of a "scarcity of provisions." The *Boston Transcript,* the *Hartford Courant,* and the *Wall Street Journal* agreed that the British fleet would be the deciding factor. "This," declared the *Chicago Tribune,* "is the twilight of the kings. Western Europe of the people may be caught in this debacle, but never again."[4]

The impact of the conflict commanded so much attention that within the first week of the war, freelance journalists, staff reporters, and artists were steaming to Europe. At least nine American journalists shipped out in the first four days, hoping to be accommodated as representatives from a neutral country. Just after midnight on August 5, hours after the British declaration of war against Germany, five American reporters sailed from New York on the British liner *Lusitania,* including two correspondents fresh from the U.S. war in Mexico, Frederick Palmer with *Everybody's* magazine and the flamboyant Richard Harding Davis, who had been roused from a respite at his farm. Davis, staying with his wife in a $1,000-a-day suite, would be freelancing for the *New York Tribune* and several papers in the Wheeler Syndicate for $600 a day plus expenses. At the age of 50, he was the most experienced, respected, and highest-paid war correspondent, noted for his style and daring during a generation of covering wars. Armed with a revolver, seeking action and adventure in combat, he had established a heroic "glamour-boy" school of war reporting that appealed to readers and editors.[5] Only three years earlier, however, he had written an "obituary" for war correspondents, noting that the increasing speed of news dissemination in the Spanish-American War and the Russo-Japanese War had delivered a "death sentence." Now that war news could be cabled and printed within a day and relayed to the enemy, correspondents were as unwelcome as spies, he maintained.[6]

Two days later, the immensely popular magazine journalist Irvin S. Cobb sailed with another three reporters on the *St. Paul* after receiving a brief telegram from *Saturday Evening Post* editor George Horace Lorimer: "Seems like this here war has done busted right in our face. Your ship sails Thursday." Lorimer provided a letter of introduction from Secretary of State William Jennings Bryan, traveler's checks, a letter of credit, $6,000 in gold coins, and a revolver.[7]

The fact that the United States in 1914 remained "neutral" in the conflict seemed to benefit these American journalists who rushed to cover the war from all sides. But the concept of neutrality was, for various economic, political, social, and historical reasons, misleading or confusing, and allegiance to official neutrality was strained. Economically and politically, the Wilson administration, while urging Americans to remain partial, still insisted on maintaining American trading rights with the warring nations, conceivably benefiting Germany and drawing criticism from Britain. On the other hand, American citizens had more in common socially and historically with the Anglo-Saxon world than with the Germanic. By the third month of the war, editors' drift away from neutrality seemed to be confirmed by a magazine poll. Of 367 editors who replied, most (242, or 65.9%) considered themselves officially neutral, although some indicated they were inclined to be "pro-Ally" or anti-German. Other editors, mostly in the East and South, acknowledged they were pro-Ally (105, or 28.6%). The editors favoring the Germans (20, or 5.4%) were mostly in the Midwest. At the *New York Times*, where the editorial policy was pro-Ally, editorial writer Elmer Davis later wrote that "the Germans saw from the first that the balance of opinion was against them, and they made desperate efforts in their tactful way to turn the scales."[8]

In the first days of the war, that distinction of neutrality immediately gave the Americans arriving in Belgium a clear advantage over British journalists. Back in London, the British military, suddenly dealing with a wartime press, delayed granting permits to British news reporters throughout August.[9] British editors for some time would benefit from reports in the

U.S. press. On August 18, Richard Harding Davis and Cobb had dinner at the luxurious Palace Hotel, an unofficial base for correspondents, where they caught up on what they had missed and tried to locate the battlefront. One eyewitness, American correspondent Granville Fortescue, who was then sending reports to London's *Daily Telegraph*, told of the Belgian resistance and the massive German shelling of Belgian forts at Liège. The forts had been blasted away by what Cobb described weeks later as a barrage of German "devil devices"—one-ton, four-foot-long shells, each with the impact of a hurricane, an earthquake, a volcano, and a "flaming meteor."[10]

To get to the battle front, correspondents took any available vehicle. They rented cars or taxis or carriages or rode on public trains and troop trains. Some used dogcarts. Otherwise, they walked.[11] On August 19, Cobb's foursome took a taxi north as far as the driver would go, until they heard guns and saw smoke from the German siege and conquest of Louvain (Leuven). On foot, Cobb's group met the massive German army now marching toward Brussels. As he wrote in his *Post* article published months later after he returned to New York, "We watched the gray-clad columns pass until the mind grew numb at the prospect of computing their number."[12]

Davis had a similar reaction to the massive German army but managed to get the story published within a day. On August 20, he witnessed the first of the gray-clad Germans marching into Brussels, thousands upon thousands, but he could not leave Brussels. To get the story out, Davis asked an Englishman to carry it to London. Drawing upon his sense for significant detail and metaphor, Davis's 14 paragraphs for British and American readers conveyed awe and menace in the machinelike movement of the tramping iron boots and horses' hoofs, rolling pack wagons, and siege guns.

Brussels, Friday, August 21, 2 P.M.—The entrance of the German army into Brussels has lost the human quality. It was lost as soon as the three soldiers who led the army bicycled into the Boulevard du Regent and asked the way to the Gare du Nord. When they passed the human note passed with them.

What came after them, and twenty-four hours later is still coming, is not men marching, but a force of nature like a tidal wave, an avalanche or a river flooding its banks. At this minute it is rolling through Brussels as the swollen waters of the Conemaugh Valley swept through Johnstown.

At the sight of the first few regiments of the enemy we were thrilled with interest. For three hours they had passed in one unbroken steel-gray column we were bored. But when hour after hour passed and there was no halt, no breathing time, no open spaces in the ranks, the thing became uncanny, inhuman. You returned to watch it, fascinated. It held the mystery and menace of fog rolling toward you across the sea.... Like a river of steel it flowed, gray and ghostlike.[13]

One week later, Davis, traveling by troop train, reported the destruction of Louvain and the Germans' execution of noncombatants. Davis reported that the military governor of Brussels had ordered the noncombatants killed as retaliation for the killing and wounding of 50 Germans by what the governor termed "a blinded and maddened" population. He said he pieced together that story despite being locked up for a time. "The Germans were burning it, and to hide their work kept us locked in railroad carriages. But the story was written across the sky, was told to us by German soldiers incoherent with excesses; and we could read it in the faces of women and children being led to concentration camps and of citizens on their way to be shot."[14]

Official neutrality did not guarantee safety, and American journalists constantly risked their personal security. While neutral-nation status gave them confidence and some access, they were handicapped by traveling without official accreditation from the warring countries. Some managed to get a *laissez-passe* (pass permit) issued by military authorities, but these often restricted them to Brussels. Reporters were frequently stopped and questioned by Belgian or German troops. Some were accused of spying or held on suspicion. Davis's passport photo showed him wearing a decorated British military jacket, leading one German officer to accuse him of being an English officer out of uniform. Davis was told he would be shot. Eventually he persuaded another officer that he was an American journalist, and the Germans released him.[15]

Irvin Cobb and four other Americans, emboldened by their neutral status, set off to find the fighting. While Cobb was mainly writing for a magazine, the others were intent on daily news stories—Roger Lewis for the Associated Press, Harry Hansen for the *Chicago Daily News,* and James O'Donnell Bennett and artist John T. McCutcheon for the *Chicago Tribune.* They followed the path of the war's destruction toward the French border. Wandering by dogcart and bicycle, they followed a trail of freshly abandoned battlefields, ruined towns, bodies, and refugees. Years later, Cobb recalled:

We decided then—and I'm sure we were right about it—that an enormous psychic force was being focused upon the immediate spots where we chanced to be; that all over the civilized globe millions on millions of human beings had their thoughts concentrated where, behind the smoke screens of gunfire and the veils of manufactured secrecy, a new kind of warfare—a warfare of engines and machines and anonymous units—now was being carried forward on a scale never before dreamed of by mortal minds.[16]

They found the German army at Beaumont, but it would be a long time before they could report the story. In his *Saturday Evening Post* series two months later, Cobb stated that a German colonel who spoke good English addressed them politely, "I do not understand how you came here, you gentlemen. We have no correspondents with our army."[17] Suspecting them to be British spies, the commanders detained them then put them under guard on a train headed to Germany with boxcars of captured and wounded French soldiers and three other captured journalists—an American, a Frenchman, and a Belgian. After a two-day journey, on August 30, the five were held in a town just across the German border. Together the correspondents wrote an appeal directly to Emperor Wilhelm II, translated into German, contending that the release of the neutral American reporters would help the German press image in America.[18]

Surprisingly, their appeal was answered by a document, signed by the emperor, permitting them to travel behind German lines in exchange for some good publicity in the United States. By now the Germans realized their captive journalists could help discredit anti-German publicity in the U.S. press. A flood of allegations of German atrocities against noncombatants in Belgium streamed from refugees. Richard Harding Davis's dispatches about the destruction of Louvain and military executions were perhaps the most factual reporting of German treatment of civilians. The atrocity stories gained some currency because of a lack of sympathy for the erratic Emperor Wilhelm. *World's Work* quoted Wilhelm as saying in 1910 that he was "the instrument of the Lord, without heeding the views and opinions of the day, I go my way." With his "mailed fist" policy, "the Emperor finds himself isolated, fighting half the world with little sympathy from the other half."[19] The *New York Tribune* contended that "German conduct in Belgium has set progress toward civilized warfare back a hundred years." They cited "the burning of Louvain on August 26, and the killing of noncombatants in Antwerp by bombs dropt [sic] from Zeppelins flying over the city…. Furthermore, in spreading floating mines in the North Sea, Germany has been guilty of an infraction of the Hague agreement." In contrast, the *Literary Digest* challenged stories of barbarism because the "case against Germany" was "based principally upon dispatches from sources hostile to her…. Many of our editors are skeptical."[20]

At the request of their German captors, Cobb and the other U.S. journalists signed a statement that rebutted stories of atrocities as "groundless." Their telegram, which the *New York Times* published on September 7, portrayed German soldiers as respectful.

In spirit we unite in rendering the German atrocities groundless, as far as we are able to. After spending two weeks with and accompanying the troops upward of 100 miles we are unable to report a single instance unprovoked.

We are also unable to confirm rumors of mistreatment of prisoners or of noncombatants….

Everywhere we have seen Germans paying [for] purchases and respecting property rights as well as according civilians every consideration….

Refugees with stories of atrocities were unable to supply direct evidence.[21]

Although the Germans were satisfied with the statement and granted the group easy access to the German battlefront, this first message from the missing men was received with suspicion by some, who discounted it as a product of torture. Later, the journalists attested that their statement was sincere. In time, the exposure of atrocity propaganda during the German invasion would be one of the most responsible wartime contributions of American journalists.[22]

Cobb spent weeks observing the war along the German battlefront. As opposing forces were stalemated in trenches, Cobb interviewed a German officer who referred to the contested area as "a stretch four miles long and a half-mile wide that is literally carpeted with bodies of dead men. They weren't all dead at first. For two days and nights our men in the earthworks heard the cries of those who still lived and the sound of them almost drove them mad." Cobb wrote: "I stood there and I smelled that smell.... Beneath its bogus glamour I saw war for what it is—the next morning of drunken glory."[23]

Cobb enjoyed one more benefit of neutrality status. En route home he stopped over in England where he was granted the only journalistic interview of the war with the British secretary of war, Lord Horatio Kitchener. While Kitchener could have learned about the German army from Cobb, Cobb gained enough for a *Saturday Evening Post* article, which was eagerly excerpted in a British press starved for war news. Notably, Kitchener discounted hopes that the war would last only three months, confiding his belief that it would continue for three years and cost millions of lives. When the story appeared, Kitchener said Cobb fabricated the entire interview.[24]

Away from the front, it was hard to sort fact from fiction, but that became one of the responsible contributions of the neutral American press. In London, Edward Price Bell, the respected chief of the *Chicago Daily News* foreign service, refused to believe most atrocity allegations circulating in the British press, cabling to America only cases witnessed by reputable persons. During the last week of August, Bell noted, "Many of the stories published here have been sheer invention"—either "pure fakes" or stories based on "gossips of refugees or soldiers broken from their ranks." He instructed *Daily News* reporters to "report only what they see or what they can obtain from credible sources."[25]

After the first month of the war, strict British and French military regulations sought to keep journalists away from the battlefront in France and instead supplied carefully worded bulletins. This was partly to prevent battle news from informing the enemy and partly to keep news about the dead and wounded from affecting recruitment of volunteers. Five weeks into the war, news reports were so censored and uninformative that Associated Press general manager Melville Stone asked his Paris bureau chief, Elmer Roberts, to reduce cable tolls, which were running as much as $1,500 a day. Stone advised "cutting out all matter that is not actual news." In the United States, he reasoned that "the first flush of news interest in everything relating to it [the war] will have subsided to a certain degree." Further pieces about refugees, individual experiences, and human interest stories "will be repetitions of those that have already been told."[26] Chafing under the censorship in 1916, Roberts tried to persuade the French to grant interviews that "would build up a mental impression in the minds of millions of Americans of the absolute solidity and strength of France and her certainty of victory."[27]

Given the demand for real news, and some news leaks, the British War Office in September assigned Major Ernest D. Swinton as an official "eyewitness" to go with the army and supply the press with detailed reports. Meanwhile, most reporters clumped together in Paris, where, it was said, they had everything they could want, except news. During the fall of 1914 and early in 1915, Cobb, Davis, and other newspapermen gave up or went home to write uncensored stories. Finishing his book for Scribner's, Cobb wrote late in 1914: "Those who are carrying on this war behind a curtain, who have enforced this conspiracy of silence, tell you that in good time the truth will be known. It will not.... This is a world war, and my contention is that the world has a right to know, not what is going to happen next, but at least what has happened."[28]

Whatever the limits on U.S. journalists, censorship of the press in England was tighter, largely because major publishers were officially enlisted to support the national effort. From the top down, British publishers maintained strict allegiance to the Defence of Realm Act, by which the government, in direct cooperation with a council of newspaper publishers, effectively suppressed negative war news that "might create public criticism of the conduct of the war or depress the nation."[29] In October and November 1914, while a mighty German offensive threatened to break through British positions around the Belgian city of Ypres to reach the sea, the English public "did not know—actually were in total ignorance of the fact—that there ever had been such as thing as the battle of Ypres" until months later, wrote United Press war correspondent William Shepherd. "Lord Northcliff, the king of British publishers, with almost unlimited influence in British affairs, knew of the battle, as did all the other publishers of England, but, for some mysterious reason working in British affairs, they did not publish the story." Although the "iron hand of the censor is on the news," Shepherd added, the censorship "has broken down or has been evaded by American correspondents."[30]

British press restrictions almost guaranteed that American papers frequently scooped the London press. George F. Allison, a British citizen working in London for the Hearst papers, recalled, "There as a wild scramble for photographs of anything appertaining to the war." In the fall of 1914, rumors that a German torpedo had sunk the British battleship

H.M.S. Audacious were denied by the British. But Allison, while drinking at the bar of the London Press Club, learned that a Belfast editor had photographs of the sinking, taken by a tourist aboard a nearby ocean liner off the coast of Ireland. The editor, reluctant to publish the pictures, dealt them to Allison, who sent them to New York where the Hearst papers scored a sensational scoop.[31]

Seeking to defeat the censorship, some American reporters got closer glimpses of the war by joining the Red Cross as ambulance attendants and hospital orderlies. After being arrested for sneaking to see the fighting at Ypres, Will Irwin worked as a stretcher bearer for three days near Ypres.[32] Irwin's persistence found a humanistic opening in the censorship when the British commander at Ypres, Field Marshal Sir John French, sought a way to publicize his soldiers' valor, and his own, in fighting back assaults by successive German regiments. Using documents and accounts sent through intermediaries, Irwin visualized the series of battles and wrote a flowing descriptive narrative, "The Splendid Story of the Battle of Ypres." Under contract, he sold his story to the *New York Tribune*, and Lord Northcliffe bought British rights for simultaneous publication in his London *Daily Mail*. In what the *Daily Mail* termed a "noble epic," Irwin colored the vocabulary of battle with historic, romantic, and heroic allusion:

In all this torn, bleeding province of fire and death the action rose to separate battles which would have been famous in old wars…. The English had really held—technically—really, they had won the climactic action in that long battle which must determine the future course of this war…. The American Civil War has been called the most terrible in modern history. In this one long battle Europe lost as many men as the North lost in the whole Civil War.[33]

Although British journalists, who were denied such information, stressed that Irwin had not actually seen the battle, the American became an instant celebrity in London. The surprised United Press war correspondent William Shepherd noted that "within a week Irwin became the most famous journalist in England. His picture was published in the British newspapers…. The story was published in pamphlet form and sold on the news-stands through the British Isles." London's *British Weekly* declared that "no message from any correspondent during the war has surpassed [Irwin's] in merit and interest…. Few of us at home had the faintest idea of the peril in which our Army, our nation, and our Empire were placed in this battle." By contrast, Shepherd thought that "the American public took the story as a commonplace, quite in line with their habit of receiving the best war news first."[34]

With the war stalemated in trench fighting, the Germans in April 1915 introduced a new weapon, a horrific toxic gas. Shielded by a haze of smoke and wearing masks to filter out the debilitating gas, German troops broke past the Allied trenches at Ypres. Because of censorship, British reports at first revealed little of the shock and horror of "asphyxiating gases." By contrast, Irwin, writing to New York from France, published a more-detailed story a day after a shorter, less-graphic version was printed in Britain. Datelined "North of France, April 24," his story referred to the gas in the second paragraph:

Then on Thursday the Germans suddenly threw in that attack its asphyxiating bombs, which will doubtless become famous in this war. It succeeded in breaking the line of French near Bixschoote, although not to such an extent as the Germans claim in today's communiqué.[35]

One day later, the *Times* of London carried one paragraph, but Irwin cabled five, portraying the ghastly, crippling effect on soldiers and emphasizing a premeditated violation of the Hague Convention of 1899. A "greenish-gray and iridescent" vapor had "settled to the ground like a swamp mist and drifted toward the French trenches on a brisk wind," he wrote. "Its effect on the French was a violent nausea and faintness, followed by an utter collapse.... The German troops, who followed up this advantage with a direct attack, held inspirators in their mouths.... Everything indicates long and thorough preparation for this attack."[36] Irwin had sorted through German propaganda claims that the British had earlier started the use of poison gas—using "shells and bombs emitting asphyxiating gases."[37] Field Marshal French had denied the German claim as "doubtless made to justify use of these gases."[38] By April 23, the Germans discounted the danger of "gases which do develop on the explosion of German shells." By April 29, a leading German newspaper defended the use of "poisonous gases" in self-defense. Frederick Palmer, then biding his time in Britain, noted how the British publicized the gas attacks "to make the most of this latest horror of German frightfulness... to stir belligerent spirit and neutral indignation."[39]

Amid such reports, the neutrality of the American press was seriously questioned. A crucial challenge to neutrality came one month later as German submarine warfare suddenly struck American interests. On May 7, off the coast of Ireland, a German U-Boat torpedoed the famous British Cunard cargo and passenger steamship *Lusitania*, killing 1,195 men, women, and children, among them 128 Americans. The news created a period of anti-German hostility. "Washington Believes that a Grave Crisis Is at Hand" stated a *New York Times* headline on May 8. For days newspapers published stories of survivors' ordeals, unidentified bodies, and mass burials. President Wilson responded by sending a warning to Germany. Secretary of State William Jennings Bryan, regarding Wilson as tilting toward a pro-Allied stance, resigned in protest on June 9. Although tensions abated, the memory that Germans had killed innocent U.S. noncombatants remained. In the sweep toward pro-British sentiment, the Hearst newspapers were notable exceptions, as were the *Washington Post* and papers in the Midwest and West—the *Cincinnati Inquirer, Cleveland Plain Dealer, Milwaukee Sentinel, Los Angeles Times*, and *San Francisco Chronicle*.[40]

On the European front in June 1915, the press finally gained access to the armies, largely because the British and French militaries realized that certain stories could be useful. Months earlier, the British had accredited eight trusted reporters, whose dispatches could be censored and sanitized, but had delayed granting them access during the shocking German advance. Now, the military authorized five of the eight to represent the five groups of British newspapers. Two others could report for the British Commonwealth nations and the Allies. The eighth would report for all the U.S. press. Officials with the three major press associations—Roy Martin of the Associated Press, Roy Howard of the United Press, and W. Orton Tewson of the International News Service—agreed reluctantly to accept censorship in exchange for access. For their one reporter they chose Frederick Palmer. "I wanted the appointment," Palmer later wrote. "It was my one chance for a close view of the gigantic conflict which had been the subject of world imagination and alarm.... I should see the ultimate in the drama of war, no matter how little or how much of it I could tell at the time." By contrast, the uncompliant Will Irwin, now blacklisted by the British and French and subject to arrest, was kept at a distance from the war.[41]

In Britain, the censorship and other restrictions on civil liberties were rationalized by both military leaders and newspaper publishers. "War kills liberalism," Winston Churchill, as first lord of the Admiralty, observed in 1914. Most British publishers soon joined in strict allegiance to the Defence of the Realm Act. With direct cooperation from a council of newspaper publishers, the government effectively suppressed negative war news that "might create public criticism of the conduct of the war or depress the nation."[42]

Some embarrassing secrets did slip through the British censorship and into the U.S. press, subsequently reverberating in European newspapers. In the summer of 1916 a letter sent to the United States by a member of Parliament revealed that a German flyer had bombed the British ammunition sheds in France, causing "the biggest explosion that the world has ever had." The air strike had damaged support for British soldiers during that summer's massive offensive in the Battle of the Somme.[43] The story in the *New York Times* reported that "the commands had been warned against such a huge collection of ammunition."[44] Further, publication of the story in a neutral nation's reputable press confirmed German prowess in the air war, legitimizing a wartime claim for Germany. The German press then circulated its own story.

Other U.S. correspondents covered the war from Germany. In the summer of 1916, Herbert Bayard Swope of the *New York World* returned to Germany, where he had spent the first four months of the war in 1914. In 19 long articles, he contrasted "the picture of the wild exaltation of 1914 with the serious, somber, Germany of to-day." He observed "seventy million people with their backs against the wall ... and not a quitter among them. And that is why, if peace is dependent upon a forthright German defeat, peace is still remote; for a nation unified by such a spirit is far from being humbled."[45]

More than any other U.S. journalist, Swope had access to key leaders in German politics, economics, and society. He interviewed German ministers, traveled in German-occupied Belgium and northern France, and toured the combat area near the Somme River, where an incoming artillery burst landed only yards from him. He interviewed the ace German pilot Oswald von Boelcke and two young British pilots taken prisoner and scheduled for execution for using incendiary ammunition. Their lives were spared because Swope told U.S. Ambassador James Gerard, who interceded.[46]

Just two months before the Germans declared unrestricted submarine warfare, Swope reported that "advocates of greater ruthlessness in the war" would risk "wide open" warfare despite "its certainty to involve America."[47] On the voyage home with the ambassador, Swope wired to the *World* a story discounting any German interest in having President Wilson help seek peace. The story, headlined "Gerard Is Coming Solely to Tell of U-Boat Menace," appeared when the two landed in New York. The subsequent series, which was reprinted in seven other newspapers, began with a front-page piece headlined "9,000,000 Here Are Ready to Do Her Bidding to Make Kulture Rule World, Germany Believes." Swope quoted Gerard's response to speculation that, if the United States declared war on Germany, there were 500,000 Germans in the United States who would rise up in arms. "There may be, but there are five-hundred thousand lamp posts in America to string them up on if they ever tried it." While the series was commended by the New York press and some national magazines, it offended the pro-German and German-language press, which labeled Swope's work anti-German propaganda, erroneous, or slander.[48]

Swope's series in the *World* and shortly afterward in the book *Inside the German Empire* set a new standard for international correspondence. It was a level of excellence Joseph Pulitzer had hoped to honor when he bequeathed some of his wealth to create the Pulitzer Prizes. In 1917, when Columbia University awarded the first two prizes, one went to Swope for international reporting, and one to the *New York Tribune* for an anti-German editorial essay.[49]

The prizes called attention to the fact that the Columbia School of Journalism was playing an active role in establishing criteria for excellence in journalism. The school had welcomed its first class in 1912, the year after Pulitzer died. The first director, the veteran journalist Talcott Williams, regarded journalism as a "calling" and pledged that "the student must feel the arduous, unremitting daily pressure of the newspaper office or he will not be ready for it, when it comes, and grow soft, instead of being annealed and tempered by his study for his calling."[50]

The faculty, curriculum, and facilities stressed the connection between academic rigor and excellence in the field. The new building at 116th and Broadway had a floor devoted to research materials for history, politics, and economics. In drafting the blueprint for research, Columbia's distinguished economic and political historian Charles A. Beard intended "to inspire our students to care about the government of their country and its relation with other countries, to show them how to get accurate information on the living issues about us, and to train them in the ideal of efficiency ... what we may call applied Politics."[51] Because the building was not completed until the second year, the first-year senior news laboratory was nestled snugly in Hamilton Hall, evidenced by a photograph of Professor Robert E. MacAlarney's class at work on typewriters.[52]

An exemplary first-year student was Carl W. Ackerman. Graduating with a degree in literature in 1913, he went to work for the United Press and in the fall of 1914 was assigned to cover the Washington embassies of the warring nations. At the German embassy he recalled hearing "fantastic ideas about how to win the war." Associating with ambassadors and press officers, he built a reputation as an astute writer on Germany such that in 1915 the United Press sent him to Berlin. In January 1917, the acerbic Henry Louis Mencken of the Baltimore *Sun* arrived in Berlin and was there just long enough to confirm his love of things German, denigrate the American correspondents for their "continuous boozing in the bar of the Adlon Hotel," and discount them as "men who would hardly qualify as competent police reporters at home." The best, he thought, was the *Chicago Tribune*'s James O'Donnell Bennett. Mencken was unimpressed with Ackerman, whom he called "a mediocre reporter of extremely unpleasant personality." Mencken's time in Berlin was less than a month, cut short when Wilson broke off diplomatic relations with Germany on February 1, 1917. Ackerman left Berlin when the United States entered the war.[53]

NOTES

1. Meyer Berger, *The Story of the "New York Times,"* 209. Cable rates were expensive and varied. By 1917 reporters paid a "double urgent" rate of 75 cents a word if they wanted to publish battlefield stories the day they occurred. James D. Startt and Debra Reddin van Tuyll, "The Media and National Crises, 1917–1945,"

in *The Media in America: A History,* ed. Wm. David Sloan, 5th ed. (Northport, AL: Vision Press, 2002), 323.

2. "American Opinion on the War: A Poll of the Press," *Outlook,* August 15, 1914, 907–8; Mott, *American Journalism,* 632.

3. "American Opinion on the War," 907–8.

4. Ibid. Some saw religious foundations for war. In Lewiston, Maine, the *Journal* viewed the war as "the fruit of a false national ambition and of imperialism and special privilege fighting against Christian internationalism."

5. Davis's ship also carried Gerald Morgan of the *Metropolitan Tribune* and Frederick Palmer of *Collier's* magazine, who was soon to be the only U.S. correspondent accredited by the British to report for the Associated Press, the United Press, and the International News Service; both Morgan and Palmer had been with Davis in 1904–1905 covering the Russo-Japanese War and a few months earlier reporting on the Mexican conflict. Emmet Crozier, *American Reporters on the Western Front, 1914–1918* (New York: Oxford University Press, 1959),16–17; Anita Lawson, *Irvin S. Cobb* (Bowling Green, Ohio: Bowling Green State University Popular Press, 1984), 113; Phillip Knightley, *The First Casualty: The War Correspondent as Hero and Myth-Maker from the Crimea to Kosovo* (Baltimore: Johns Hopkins University Press, 2000), 123.

6. Richard Harding Davis, "The War Correspondent: In Nine Years His Condition Has Changed from That of a Welcome Free Lance with Complete Independence to That of a Prisoner and a Suspected Spy," *Collier's,* October 7, 1911, 21–22.

7. Lawson, *Cobb,* 113. Also sailing on Cobb's ship were Will Irwin, the muckraker of journalism, for *Collier's Weekly* magazine, Arnot Dosch of *World's Work,* and for the *Chicago Tribune* John McCutcheon, who was also an illustrator of Cobb's books; Davis's ship also carried Gerald Morgan of the *Metropolitan Tribune.*

8. Jürg Martin Gabriel, *The American Conception of Neutrality after 1941,* rev. ed. (Hampshire, UK: Palgrave Macmillan, 2002), 24–28; James D. Startt, "The Media and Political Culture," in *The Significance of the Media in American History,* ed. James D. Startt and Wm. David Sloan (Northport, AL: Vision Press, 1994), 191–98; "American Sympathies in the War," *Literary Digest,* 14 November 1914, 939–41, 974–78; Elmer Davis, *History of the "New York Times," 1851–1921* (New York: New York Times, 1921), 342.

9. Crozier, *American Reporters,* 35.

10. Fred Gus Neuman, *Irvin S. Cobb: His Life and Achievements* (New York: Beekman Publishers, 1974), 176.

11. Irvin S. Cobb, "Sherman Said It—Looking for War in a Taxicab—and Finding It," *Saturday Evening Post,* October 17, 1914, 6–9, 65–68.

12. Lawson, *Cobb,* 116.

13. Richard Harding Davis, "German Army Flows Like a River of Steel," *News Chronicle* (London), August 23, 1914, in Wm. David Sloan, Julie K. Hedgepeth, Patricia C. Place, and Kevin Stoker, *The Great Reporters: An Anthology of News Writing at Its Best* (Northport, AL: Vision Press, 1992), 72–75. The English courier was E. A. Dalton, who traveled at night in cars and wagons, hiding alongside the road and crawling for about a mile until he reached the coast and boarded a refugee boat. First published in London's *News Chronicle,* Davis's story appeared

the following day in the *New York Tribune*. Considered the finest of Davis's war reporting, the story continues to be anthologized in the twenty-first century: "Saw German Army Roll on Like Fog," in *The Mammoth Book of Journalism: 101 Masterpieces from the Finest Writers and Reporters,* ed. Jon E. Lewis (New York: Carroll & Graf Publishers, 2003), 122–24; see also Gerald Langford, *The Richard Harding Davis Years: The Biography of a Mother and Son* (New York: Holt, Rinehart and Winston 1961); "Richard Harding Davis," in *Dictionary of American Biography* (New York: Scribner, 1946–1958), 5, 144–45; Thomas Connery, "Richard Harding Davis," in *Biographical Dictionary of American Journalism,* 168–70.

14. Richard Harding Davis, *New York Tribune,* August 31, 1914, in *Voices of the Past: Key Documents in The History of American Journalism,* ed. Calder M. Pickett (New York: Macmillan, 1977), 230. For the German position, see the proclamation of General Baron von Bissing, German military governor of Belgium, August 29, 1914, in *Source Records of the Great War,* ed. Charles F. Horne and Walter F. Austin (Indianapolis, Indiana: American Legion, 1923), 57–59.

15. Crozier, *American Reporters,* 44–46, 50–52.

16. Irvin S. Cobb, *Exit Laughing* (Garden City, NY: Garden City Publishing, 1942), 178.

17. Irvin S. Cobb, "Being a Guest of the German Kaiser," *Saturday Evening Post,* October 24, 1914, 14.

18. Cobb, "Guest of the German Kaiser," 15, 48–50; Lawson, *Cobb,* 118–21.

19. "Darkest Side of the Great War," *Literary Digest,* September 12, 1914, 442; "The Kaiser and the Mailed Fist," *World's Work,* September 1914, 71.

20. "Darkest Side," *Literary Digest,* 441.

21. Crozier, *American Reporters,* 41–42, 54; Quoted in Lawson, *Cobb,* 121–22.

22. Crozier, *American Reporters,* 42; "Discrediting the Stories of German Atrocities," *Current Opinion,* November 1914, 302; James D. Startt, "The Media and Political Culture," in *The Significance of the Media in American History,* ed. James D. Startt and Wm. David Sloan (Northport, AL: Vision Press, 1994), 188.

23. Irvin S. Cobb, *Paths of Glory* (New York: G. H. Doran, 1915), 292–93, in Lawson, *Cobb,* 122, 127.

24. Lawson, *Cobb,* 126.

25. *Chicago Daily News,* August 31, 1914, 3, in James D. Startt, *Journalism's Unofficial Ambassador: A Biography of Edward Price Bell, 1869–1943* (Athens: Ohio University Press, 1979), 52, 53.

26. Melville E. Stone to Elmer Roberts, August 31, 1914, box 1, Roberts Papers.

27. Elmer Roberts, February 16, 1916, box 1, Roberts Papers.

28. Crozier, *American Reporters,* 7; Richard Harding Davis, *With the Allies* (New York: Scribner's Sons, 1914), 240.

29. Phillip Knightley, *First Casualty,,* 100. British models for censorship and propaganda were emulated in other countries. The system of co-opting newspaper publishers in voluntary censorship councils was adopted in wartime by the United States in 1917 and again in 1942. The British propaganda organization, Knightley noted, "became the model on which [Joseph] Goebbels based that of the Germans some twenty years later."

30. William G. Shepherd, "Confessions of a War Correspondent," *Everybody's,* February 1917, 181.

31. George F. Allison, *Allison Calling: A Galaxy of Football and Other Memories* (London: Staples Press, 1948), cited in Louis Pizzitola, *Hearst Over Hollywood: Power, Passion, and Propaganda in the Movies* (New York: Columbia University Press, 2002), 135–36.

32. Crozier, *American Reporters*, 89, 91.

33. "An American War Correspondent," *Literary Digest*, April 24, 1915, 954–55.

34. Due to limited sources, Irwin gave no credit to the French army and too much to Sir John French. Crozier, *American Reporters*, 91–93; "American War Correspondent," 954; Shepherd, "Confessions," 181.

35. Will Irwin, "The German Army Dispersed Chlorine Gas over Allied Lines at Ypres on 22 April 1915," *New York Tribune*, April 25, 1915, 1.

36. Will Irwin, "Poison Gas Enters Modern Warfare," *New York Tribune*, April 27, 1915, in Pickett, *Voices of the Past*, 232–33. The story was datelined Boulogne, April 25. The *Times'* story, sent on April 25, appeared on April 26. Early in April the British had learned from prisoners of a German plan to use gas "contained under pressure in steel cylinders, and, being of a heavy nature, will spread along the ground without being dissipated quickly." "A New German Weapon; Poisonous Gas for Our Troops; The Control of Modern Battles," from eyewitness Major Ernest D. Swinton, *Times* (London), April 9, 1915. Swinton's report, dated April 6, referred to gas in the third paragraph. Germany had signed the Hague Convention of 1899, which prohibited gas warfare. At the Hague Peace Conference of 1899, 26 states were represented. One convention defined laws of war; it prohibited gas warfare and dumdum bullets, prohibited for five years the use of projectiles thrown from balloons, and provided for better treatment of war prisoners and wounded.

37. "A British Attack," *Times* (London), April 19, 1915, 8. The German claim, reportedly issued from Berlin, came from Great Army Headquarters in Amsterdam.

38. "The British Advance; Hand-to-Hand Fighting; Heavy Losses," from Sir John French, April 19, *Times* (London), April 21, 1915, 8.

39. "Asphixiating Gases in Warfare," from German wireless news, *Times* (London), April 24, 1915, 8; "Through German Eyes. Poisonous Gases. A Quick and Painless Death," *Times* (London), April 29, 1915, 6; Frederick Palmer, *With My Own Eyes: A Personal Story of the Battle Years* (Indianapolis, Indiana: Bobbs-Merrill, 1933), 313.

40. One body never recovered was that of multimillionaire Alfred Vanderbilt, who would have been on the *Titanic* but for a change of plans. "Lusitania Sunk by a Submarine, Probably 1,260 Dead; Twice Torpedoed off Irish Coast; Sinks in 15 Minutes; Capt. Turner Saved, Frohman and Vanderbilt Missing; Washington Believes that a Grave Crisis Is at Hand," *New York Times*, May 8, 1915, 1; T. A Bailey, *The Lusitania Disaster* (New York: Free Press, 1975); J. M. Taylor, "Fateful Voyage of the Lusitania," *MHQ: Quarterly Journal of Military History* 11 (3): 18–27; Mott, *American Journalism*, 616.

41. Palmer, *With My Own Eyes*, 301–16; Crozier, *American Reporters*, 93, 104.

42. Knightley, *First Casualty*, 86, 100.

43. Joseph King to George Raffalovich, August 22, 1916, 2, transcript of shorthand notes, British Intelligence KV 2/823, Public Record Office, England (hereafter referred to as PRO).

44. King to Raffalovich, 2, as reported in *New York Times,* September 3, 1916.

45. Herbert Bayard Swope, *Inside the German Empire: In the Third Year of the War* (New York: Century, 1917), x–xi, 39. The first installment appeared November 4, 1916, just days ahead of the 1916 presidential election; the book based on the series, *Inside the German Empire,* appeared in January 1917, one month before President Wilson broke relations with Germany.

46. Ely J. Kahn, *The World of Swope* (New York: Simon & Schuster, 1965), 174–83.

47. Swope, *German Empire,* 64;

48. Kahn, *Swope,* 174–83. The German-language newspapers included the *German Herald* and *Germania.*

49. Boylen, *Pulitzer's School,* 52. By 1931, the school had established academic standards and could judge whether an journalist esteemed in the newsroom could convert successfully to the ivory tower. When in 1931 Swope was recommended by *World* publisher Ralph Pulitzer to be the school's first dean, he was rejected by Columbia President Nicholas Murray Butler. Butler conceded that Swope was a "brilliant and attractive gentleman" but "could not, I feel sure, ever be turned into an academic person, even if all the universities in the country were to unite their efforts upon him." Butler to Ralph Pulitzer, February 11, 1931, Ralph Pulitzer Center, Columbia University Archives, in James Boylan, *Pulitzer's School: Columbia University's School of Journalism, 1903–2003* (New York: Columbia University Press, 2003), 64.

50. Boylan, *Pulitzer's School,* 25–30.

51. While teaching history and politics at Columbia (1904–1917), Beard joined James Harvey Robinson in promoting the teaching of history that would encompass all aspects of civilization, including economics, politics, intellectual life, and culture. Together they wrote *The Development of Modern Europe* (1907) and compiled an accompanying book of readings. Beard was especially concerned with the relationship of economic interests and politics. His study of the conservative economic interests of the men at the Federal Constitutional Convention, *An Economic Interpretation of the Constitution* (1913), caused much stir; he also wrote *Economic Origins of Jeffersonian Democracy* (1915) and *The Economic Basis of Politics* (1922). His interest in city government led to *American City Government* (1912) as well as the long-standard *American Government and Politics* (1910). After resigning from Columbia during World War I, he helped to found the New School for Social Research and was director (1917–1922) of the Training School for Public Service in New York City.

52. Boylan, *Pulitzer's School,* 25, 27, 28, 30. Another student in the class photograph (following p. 182) is Hollington K. Tong, who during World War II established the school's branch in Chungking, China.

53. Carl W. Ackerman to the Library of Congress, March 18, 1963, Introductory Letter for the World War I Scrapbook, box 158, Ackerman Papers. After his journalism career, Ackerman directed public relations for General Motors. In March 1931 he was chosen as the school's dean and for a generation was influential in the awarding of the Pulitzer Prizes; H. L. Mencken, *A Memoir: Thirty-five Years of Newspaper Work,* ed. Fred Hobson, Vincent Fitzpatrick, and Bradford Jacobs (Baltimore: Johns Hopkins University Press, 1994), 60–65.

4

Mobilizing Public Opinion

Improperly trained men have seriously misled a whole nation.
—Walter Lippmann and Charles Merz, "A Test of the News," 1920

President Wilson won reelection in November 1916 largely because, as his campaign slogan emphasized, he kept the country out of the European war. That theme seemed to resonate most strongly with Americans farthest from the East Coast and Europe; California's electoral votes in the final hours tipped the victory away from the confident Republican challenger, Charles Evans Hughes.[1]

Three months later Wilson broke off diplomatic relations with Germany, and five months after the election, on April 2, 1917, he asked for a declaration of war against Germany, which Congress approved on April 6. In allying with Britain and France, the president blamed Germany's "military masters" for defeating his policy of keeping America neutral. In a Flag Day address in June, he asserted, "It is plain enough how we were forced into the war." He described "extraordinary insults and aggressions." He said Germany had planted "spies and conspirators," some at the highest level in the Germany embassy in Washington, who "spread sedition amongst us." He referred to Germany's secret strategy outlined in the decoded Zimmerman Telegram: "They tried to incite Mexico to take up arms against us and to draw Japan into a hostile alliance with her."[2]

Most importantly, Wilson conceded, his political stance since 1914 that America's neutrality should protect its freedom of the seas to carry on international trade had failed. He placed full blame on Germany. "The military masters of Germany denied us the right to be neutral," Wilson stated. "They sought by violence to destroy our industries and arrest our commerce.... They impudently denied us the use of the high seas and repeatedly executed their threat that they would send to their death any of our people who ventured to approach the coasts of Europe.... The flag under which we serve would have been dishonoured had we withheld our hand." Now at war, Wilson did not mention advisors' earlier warnings that his neutrality policy was failing, in part, because he displayed "un-neutral" leniency toward the British blockade and sea mines while protesting vehemently against Germany's declaration of unrestricted submarine warfare.[3]

The U.S. declaration of war led almost immediately to the most comprehensive restrictions on freedom of the press ever issued by the federal government. Though there was an ostensible effort to balance freedom with national security, the momentum shifted quickly toward establishing centralized control of news flowing to the public from the government and the military. Wilson and leading Cabinet members completed a plan to centralize government information about national defense and war mobilization. On April 13, the secretaries of state, war and the navy formally asked the president to create a Committee on Public Information, which would include them and a civilian executive director. Indicating a necessary curtailment of First Amendment rights, they stressed concerns about national security and "premature or ill-advised" news reports:

Even though the cooperation of the press has been generous and patriotic, there is a steadily developing need for some authoritative agency to assure the publication of all the vital facts of national defense. Premature or ill-advised announcements of policies, plans, and specific activities, whether innocent or otherwise, would constitute a source of danger.[4]

The secretaries also recommended efforts to rally public support. "America's great present needs are confidence, enthusiasm and service, and these needs will not be met completely unless every citizen is given the feeling of partnership that comes with full, frank statements concerning the conduct of the public business." They asserted that the agency's "two functions—censorship and publicity—can be joined in honesty and with profit. While there is much that is properly secret in connection with the departments of the Government, the total is small compared to the vast amount of information that it is right and proper for the people to have."[5]

One day later, Wilson's 39-word executive order established the Committee on Public Information, composed of the three secretaries and a civilian executive director.[6] Although technically a committee, the CPI's scope and authority made it seem more like a ministry of information. To head the CPI, the secretaries recommended a civilian chairman.

They preferred "some writer of proved courage, ability, and vision, able to gain the understanding cooperation of the press and at the same time rally the authors of the country to a work of service."[7] The director would be expected to win over millions of undecided Americans—many west of the Mississippi who just a few months earlier had reelected Wilson because "He Kept Us out of War." A more difficult task would be limiting the impact of publications by antiwar radicals and socialists and German sympathizers.

In appointing the director, Wilson bypassed his Cabinet members, instead choosing a journalist, George Creel.[8] In selecting a working journalist, Wilson also bypassed the British method of co-opting its newspaper proprietors. The British had quickly involved leading publishers in official capacities as masters of the press, controllers of war news, and consultants on propaganda. These included the respected and feared publisher of the *Times* of London, Alfred Harmsworth (Viscount Northcliffe). In 1918, another member of the House of Lords, the new principal owner of the *Daily Express*, Max Aitken (Baron Beaverbrook), was named wartime minister of information. By contrast, Wilson, rather than seeking overt control and suppression, sought a process to persuade publishers to exercise self-censorship. As Harold Lasswell noted, Wilson's concept required a civilian journalist of "tremendous energy, but little reputation"—advantageous if "the humbler journalist" were freer from professional "animosities" accruing to a publisher, which might "impair his usefulness." Creel possessed what Lasswell termed an essential talent: "intimate knowledge of the group to which they are supposed to appeal."[9]

Creel had professional and political credentials and possessed energy enough for the massive task of mobilizing press *and* public cooperation. As a journalist and author he was an ardent Progressive, campaigning for local and national reforms and ultimately supporting Wilson's candidacy. In Kansas City from 1899 to 1909 he edited the weekly *Independent,* promoting municipal ownership of utilities, women's rights, and laws restricting child labor, and later publishing an exposé of child labor, *Children of Bondage.* In 1910, he demonstrated political toughness, resigning as an editorial writer on the *Denver Post* rather than endorsing party-machine candidates. Subsequently he wrote for Denver's *Rocky Mountain News,* served a year as Denver's appointed police commissioner, worked in various national reform efforts, and freelanced for New York magazines.[10]

Creel also had credibility among Socialist and radical journalists. In 1914 he sided with striking coal miners at the Ludlow, Colorado, mine disaster. After armed guards attacked the strikers' tent camp, killing women and children, Creel worked with Socialist muckraker Upton Sinclair and radical writer John Reed to rally public support for the miners and against mine owner John D. Rockefeller Jr.[11] Another of the causes he supported was women's suffrage.[12] Yet nothing in Creel's career gained him as much notoriety as when, at the age of 40, he became the nation's chief publicist and censor.

Whatever the publicity requirements of the CPI, Wilson may have thought of the committee primarily as a way to control wartime information flowing from his administration to the public, an extension of controls he had attempted during peacetime. From the beginning of his administration, Wilson suffered information leaks to the press, in part because of the proliferation of publicists working in the various executive-branch departments. He had considered establishing a "publicity bureau," what one scholar has likened to a ministry of information. That peacetime initiative led naturally, in wartime, to creation of the CPI.[13]

Creel and Wilson collaborated on statements relating to censorship. Considering the potential for confusion, they shared a mutual interest in speaking with one voice. To that end, Creel submitted public pronouncements to the president, who read them with care. Wilson wrote notations that he had inserted "a few verbal alternatives," but at least once the president made a significant deletion: He struck two penciled lines through Creel's forecast that the Allies would require "the payment of indemnities."[14]

Recognizing the urgency of censorship for national security, they articulated plans for an idealistic if unrealistic censorship that would protect the right of dissent. Wilson sought to avoid the image of centralized state censorship associated with enemy authoritarian governments. In a "Preliminary Statement to the Press" on May 17, the president stressed his aversion to a "system of censorship" that was so excessive that it suppressed reasonable criticism.

I can imagine no greater disservice to the country than to establish a system of censorship that would deny to the people of a free republic like our own their indisputable right to criticize their own public officials. While exercising the great powers of the office I hold, I would regret in a crisis like the one through which we are now passing to lose the benefit of patriotic and intelligent criticism.[15]

With war declared, Congress was considering what the *Nation* warned were two "menacing" censorship bills. They were unnecessary, the journal's editors reasoned, because every "reputable newspaper is ready and willing to censor itself." The bills, it argued, were aimed "to prevent infringements by the conscienceless or careless few. But that ought not to be made the excuse for giving undue powers to the President.... Much evil has occurred in Europe since August 1, 1914, because the censorship has not been confined to military news, and has too often garbled the truth."[16]

Creel prevailed in promoting a middle ground on censorship. The CPI policy stressed that newspapers should practice *voluntary* censorship, regularizing to an institutional level the occasional, common practice of self-censorship. To standardize voluntary censorship, Creel sought agreement with news organizations and newspaper owners to cooperate with guidelines for screening news to protect the U.S. military effort and to publish news that supported the national war effort. For public credibility, Creel announced that the press was "at liberty to give full publicity" to the system of censorship. "It is well to let the people know just what it is that the Committee proposes and desires, so that there may be the least possible impairment of public confidence in the printed information presented to it."[17]

Beyond the censorship, the CPI sought publicity—propaganda advocating wartime goals. The CPI needed the cooperation of the mass media to publicize and promote solidarity among Americans now engaged in industrial America's first total war. To make the world "safe for democracy," Wilson pledged in the war message to Congress, "We can dedicate our lives and our fortunes, everything that we are and everything that we have." The war in Europe taught that "every country brought the whole nation into arms and the utilization of the non-combatant population and its resources had become as important as the training of troops, the production of matériel, and the direction of armies in the field."[18]

Very soon CPI mobilized most of the press to voluntary censorship and, with Wilson's support, survived occasional attacks from the press. Three months into the war, the *New York Times* accused the CPI of circulating "misinformation" about an alleged attack by a German submarine on an American transport ship and called for Creel's dismissal. "As for Mr. Creel, it is evident that in his present position he is out of place, that his abilities, whatever they may be, are misapplied, misdirected. His long training in another field of publicity, where emotion and imagination count for much and accuracy is of minor importance, has evidently disqualified him for the service he has been called upon to perform."[19]

To rally public support for home front goals, the CPI targeted diverse publications reaching women, farmers, blacks, and ethnic populations. America's mass media would be called upon to assist in promoting, with urgency, military conscription, mobilization of four million troops, increased agricultural production, manufacture of weapons and munitions, efficiency initiatives, war-bond drives, and alertness to thwart German spies and espionage.

This total mobilization had been planned months before the war by Wilson's Council on National Defense and its Advisory Commission. The commission developed publicity initiatives to promote war goals and counter opponents of the war, specifically Socialist opposition. By March 12, 1917, the advisors had "produced a general programme of co-operation and fought consistently to counteract propaganda of the non-war Socialists." As soon as the CPI was established on April 14, the commission "used the resources of publicity to insure unanimity of patriotic conviction." The CPI was to be instrumental in "a genuine attempt at a complete transition from the doctrine of individualism and free competition to one of centralized national cooperation which was properly symbolized in the pregnant phrase—'work or fight.'"[20]

The voluntary censorship code had to be fine tuned in July, partly because newspapers continued to publish information deemed helpful to the enemy. On July 30, Creel cited "repeated and serious violations of the voluntary censorship" because of alleged "misunderstandings or lack of positive information." That day the CPI issued a list of 21 regulations to make "necessary secrecies so complete and explicit as to leave no room for honest ignorance or dishonorable evasion." In addition to a "general request that there be no published mention of the arrival of American troops at European ports," the CPI stated that it wished to conceal information about troop train or boat movements, number and identity of troops, officers and ship captains, and locations of bases, ports, friendly or enemy ships, munitions, minefields, aircraft, war material, and wartime experiments. Within hours, the rules were received in the Associated Press bureau in Paris, where bureau chief Elmer Roberts added them to censorship concerns of the French.[21]

As the reality of total war became manifest, distinctions blurred between journalism and propaganda and between patriotic constructive opinion and dangerous criticism. While most journalists cooperated with the mobilization, many grew "self-conscious about the manipulability of information" amid wartime propaganda and the increasing practice of what would become known as public relations.[22] The CPI's wartime propaganda reached farther in 1918 when Creel extended his work to Britain, Russia, and other European countries "to stiffen moral[e] and determination" and "counteract German propaganda."[23]

The sense of total war was projected from the pages of the daily press and magazines. Overseas news in the evening papers included reports of the morning's conflicts on the French front, especially any news of Americans soldiers, and occasionally reports of efforts to reach a peace accord, complicated by the Russian Revolution and Russia's separate peace with Germany, which freed thousands of German troops to shift from the Russian front to fight in France. In 1918, in addition to a new Allied military expedition into Russia, political news focused on "political readjustments in Europe that might be expected to follow the end of the war, and ... presentation of the claims and possibilities of the various nationalist revolutionary movements." Late in 1918, stories lauded the success of allied war propaganda, and days before the Armistice, George Creel praised U.S. efforts to spread democracy.[24]

Domestically, the press reported on the nation at war. There was widespread interest in decisions by local Selective Service boards that in 1917 and 1918 registered about 24 million men aged 18 to 45, deferred some, and drafted others, sending them to be trained and shipped to Europe. Some stories questioned the war and the sacrifice of sons and daughters. Another focus was the mobilization of home-front labor in the war effort and exhortations to economies, home gardening, savings, and purchase of Liberty Bonds to help finance the war. The Washington press covered war costs and loans and Congressional legislation deemed urgent to support the troops overseas, mobilize citizens on the home front, and deal with dissent.[25]

Some journalists seeking a new role in the war joined the administration in Washington. Will Irwin, whose right eardrum was damaged by a shell blast on the Italian front, took a six-month break to chair Creel's new foreign division for American propaganda. Walter Lippmann, whose thoughtful essays on government and politics in the *New Republic* had won the attention of President Wilson and the friendship of Secretary of War Newton D. Baker, served in four posts in 1917 and 1918. As Baker's assistant on various committees, Lippmann met with American Federation of Labor President Samuel Gompers and Assistant Secretary of the Navy Franklin D. Roosevelt. Late in 1917 Lippmann directed the Inquiry, a secret group developing data for Wilson's Fourteen Points peace proposal. Next he was commissioned as a captain and worked with the British Propaganda Division, directing American propaganda to the Germans. His last assignment was on the staff of Wilson's key advisor, Colonel Edward House.[26]

In Washington, too, Wilsonian idealism was soon sacrificed to the exigencies of the crisis, resulting in further curtailment of civil liberties. The president's articulated tolerance for "patriotic and reasonable criticism" and the public's "indisputable right to criticize their own public officials" did not extend to critics deemed to be a threat to national security. Three months into the war, Congress and the Wilson administration acted to muzzle dissident voices considered seditious by the Espionage Act of 1917. Antiwar dissenters whose publications had been more or less tolerated during American neutrality would soon be muzzled on the grounds they harmed the nation's military effort and endangered soldiers and sailors overseas. Congress's right to enact such laws when there was "a clear and present danger" was subsequently upheld in 1919 by the U.S. Supreme Court in *Schenck v. United States.*

Emergency postal legislation, which had taken effect on June 15, 1917, empowered the postmaster general to exclude from the mail publications containing material considered to be treasonable. By November, Postmaster General Albert S. Burleson ruled that 44 publications were either nonmailable or had their second-class mail permits revoked for content. Most of the banned publications were socialist, radical, or German ethnic publications, including the official Socialist Party newspaper, *American Socialist*; the *Milwaukee Leader*; the *New York Call*; and the *Masses*, a monthly magazine. The government banned the *Masses* in August 1917 in part because of its antiwar cartoons.[27] Some publications voiced the Socialist viewpoint that the war benefited capitalists; others advocated resistance to conscription. One issue of the prestigious the *Nation* was banned because an article criticized labor leader Samuel Gompers for cooperating with the administration's labor policies.[28] By October, another law required German-language papers to supply English translations of articles about the war and the U.S. government.

In 1918, Hearst and his newspapers were accused of a pattern of disloyal editorials. In New Jersey and New York, politicians and citizens groups acted to prevent circulation of his New York papers—the *New York American* and the *Evening Journal*. The most prominent critic, former president Roosevelt, cited a half-dozen editorials written before and after the United States went to war that were favorable to Germany. Roosevelt said Postmaster General Burleson had failed "to deal with Mr. Hearst's papers as it has dealt with certain other papers." Rival New York editors joined against Hearst, who was then a potential candidate for governor. The *Evening Post* said Roosevelt's argument "has great force." The *World* said Roosevelt was "substantially correct" that Hearst was patriotic in some editorials but in others attacked England and Japan "in the most offensive way." The *Tribune*, which had earlier questioned Hearst's loyalty, wondered about Hearst's "singular and sinister immunity" from federal action. Hearst's vocal defenders included three U.S. senators, one of whom asserted that, despite Hearst's earlier editorials, he had now "given most loyal support to all war-measures."[29] Hearst responded that Roosevelt suffered from the "mental and moral deterioration" and "childish mental processes" of "his old age."[30]

Mainstream newspapers with overseas correspondents led a major effort to cover the role of the American Expeditionary Forces. Leading war correspondents earned name recognition seldom achieved in peacetime. Coming with previous experience during the U.S. military intervention in Mexico in 1916–1917 were Floyd Gibbons for the *Chicago Tribune* and Damon Runyon with Hearst's *New York American*. In Mexico both had established good relationships with General John J. Pershing, who now commanded the American forces in France. Gibbons got his first exclusive story en route to Europe when the British SS *Laconia*, on which he was traveling, was torpedoed in February 1917.

At this moment the ship gave a sudden lurch sideways and forward. There was a muffled noise like the slamming of some large door at a good distance away....

Every man in the room was on his feet in an instant.... Then came five blasts on the whistle....

The ship sank rapidly at the stern until at last its nose stood straight up in the air. Then it slid silently down and out of sight like a piece of disappearing scenery in a panorama spectacle.

In June 1918 after the American assault in the Belleau Wood, Gibbons was wounded by machine-gun fire; he lost an eye and afterward wore an eye patch like a badge of distinction.[31]

Runyon's distinctive stories about American soldiers in France boosted his popularity throughout the Hearst press and led after the war to Hearst's syndication of his columns and articles. In his slangy style, which became known as "Runyonese," he had referred to the war as "a rough-house" and "a squabble" and declared, "I am brought up to believe that the U.S. can tie its hands behind it, and put its feet in a hole, and still lick anybody in the world."[32]

A cluster of writers worked in Paris for *Stars and Stripes*, a newspaper created in Pershing's headquarters. The roster included editor Harold Ross, who had written for several U.S. newspapers and covered the 1913 murder trial of Leo Frank for Hearst's *Atlanta Georgian*; in 1917 he enlisted, went AWOL, and avoided punishment by persuading the military that he was of better use as an editor. Alexander Woollcott, a drama critic at the *New York Times*, took leave during the war to serve in a hospital unit in France then was transferred to the newspaper. Grantland Rice, the sportswriter whose article at the *Atlanta Journal* had catapulted Georgian Ty Cobb into major league baseball, took leave from the *New York Tribune* to serve in the field artillery and write for Ross's paper. Also there on leave from the *New York Tribune* was humor columnist Franklin Pierce Adams, who had joined the intelligence service. Ross's writing was often serious, advising that the American soldier on leave in France should behave, "indulge in no excesses that will impair his efficiency," and remember to "hold all women as sacred." Adams's good humor shone through in his ode to the fizzy American ice cream soda, a finer drink than *vin* or *bière*. Woollcott was remembered for his tale of an American marine and a faithful trench dog named Belle for whom he fashioned a gas mask and whose puppies were nurtured through battle.[33]

Others went into battle for the first time. Heywood Broun and his bride, Ruth Hale, shipped to Europe for their honeymoon, he to report for the *New York Tribune* and she to write for the Paris edition of the *Chicago Tribune*. U.S. correspondents were required to wear military uniforms and submit to strict censorship, two rules that Broun resisted. In France he bypassed the censorship; when he returned to the United States and criticized the war effort, the military revoked his war credentials.[34]

While most female reporters worked on society news and on small-town papers, a few gained military accreditation to cover the war. The exemplar of small-town journalism was Sadie L. Mossler, "the hen editor," who acknowledged in 1918 the "great cry for women's advancement" but insisted women should "not seek out the crowded, hostile cities, but remain in the smaller places where their work can stand out distinctly." By contrast, Peggy Hall and Rheta Childe Dorr found distinction in hostile situations, writing for widespread audiences. Hall was the first woman to receive War Department press credentials. She reported from France and later from Russia with the American military expedition. Hall's stories circulated through the Newspaper Enterprise Association. Dorr, a champion of women's rights, was already in her 40s and well known through her work on New York's *Evening Post* and for national magazines, and as editor of the *Suffragist.* Her European dispatches to the *New York Evening Mail* were syndicated to 21 newspapers, and after the war she continued to write from Prague.[35]

This sharing of news reports became common practice for newspapers without their own war correspondents. Most U.S. newspapers relied on syndicates, on the Associated Press and competing wire services, on other newspapers, and of course on the Committee on Public Information and other government and military announcements.

George Seldes covered the American front for a syndicate that provided stories to several papers, including the *Atlanta Constitution,* the *Los Angeles Times,* and the *St. Louis Globe-Democrat.* He had gone to London in 1916 and met up with Gibbons, Runyon, and Broun after he went to France in 1917. Although he agreed to wear the military uniform, he violated other restrictions as he bolted from the pack of reporters to get his own stories. In September 1918, Seldes scooped the pack when the Germans retreated after four years in St. Mihiel, a town described as "a dagger in the heart of France." Dashing by car and on foot, Seldes was the first American to arrive. Townsfolk hoisting the French flag shouted, *"Vive l'Amerique!"* and hailed him as a liberator hours before the arrival of General Pershing and French General Henri-Philippe Pétain. Other correspondents, Seldes noted, "were chagrinned they had not been able to witness the entry."[36]

Two months later, immediately after the Armistice, Seldes and three other reporters disregarded a prohibition against crossing the Armistice line. They left behind the lavish and giddy victory celebrations and headed to be the first Americans in Berlin. Instead, in Frankfurt, amid the demobilization and the Socialists' bid for power, they managed to interview German General Paul von Hindenberg. "Who won the war?" they wanted to know, partly because the American soldiers had received little credit. Seldes reported that Hindenberg, admittedly ready to retire from the army, was "faintly amused at our diplomacy" and gave a long critique in German, which was translated by the group's spokesperson.

I will reply with the same frankness. The American infantry in the Argonne won
the war.
To begin with I must confess that Germany could not have won the war—that is,
after 1917. We might have won on land. We might have taken Paris. But after the
failure of the world food crops of 1916 the British food blockade reached its greatest effectiveness in 1917. So I must really say that the British food blockade of 1917
and the American blow in the Argonne of 1918 decided the war for the Allies.

Hindenberg continued to assess why the Germans lost the war and how
they could have won the peace. Then he "bowed his head and tears
flooded his pale, watery eyes. His huge bulk was shaken. He wept for
his 'poor fatherland.'" Unfortunately for Seldes, the army suppressed
his story of Hindenberg's concession to American soldiers—technically
because Seldes had violated the Armistice travel ban, but politically
because the American papers in France and the Allied press were giving
credit to the French, British, Italian, and Belgian victories.[37]
    War coverage established the reputation of other journalists. In 1917
Carl Ackerman left the United Press in Berlin, traveled in Europe and
Mexico, contributed to the *New York Tribune* and the *Saturday Evening
Post,* and published his first book on Germany and his second on Mexico.
After the Bolshevik Revolution, *New York Times* managing editor Carr Van
Anda hired him in 1918 to report from Siberia on the fate of forces fight-
ing the Bolshevik army and on the reported execution of Czar Nicholas
II. Traveling 5,000 miles on the Trans-Siberian Railway, he reached the
village of Ekaterinburg, where he interviewed a servant of the czar
and a nun who took eggs and milk to the czar's family and confirmed
they had been executed four months earlier on July 16. The failure of
the counterrevolutionaries, Ackerman concluded, could be blamed on
lack of timely support from the Wilson administration and the Allies.
But he also acknowledged the power of the revolutionaries. In 1919, he
wrote to Colonel House at the Paris peace conference, warning about the
Bolsheviks' mission: "Bolshevism is a revolutionary movement not at all
confined to Russia and Europe, but evident even in the United States,
which has as its object the razing of the world in order to reconstruct it."[38]
The postwar threat of a Bolshevik conspiracy in the United States soon
became a mantra of politicians, echoed in the press and rising to a pitch
of hysteria.
    The actions of organized labor fueled fears that Bolsheviks were plot-
ting to destabilize American society and overthrow the government.
Seeking higher wages and job security, several groups of workers went
on strike, including steelworkers, coal miners, and the Boston police. A
series of unexplained bombings heightened what became known as the
Red Scare. At the *Emporia Gazette,* William Allen White acknowledged
"the silly terror of Bolshevism in the hearts of the American people."

He criticized the "cruel raids" and deportations of nearly a thousand suspect aliens that were carried out by U.S. Attorney General Mitchell Palmer. Palmer's actions put him in consideration for the Democratic presidential nomination in 1920. After a bomb damaged his house on June 2, 1918, Palmer had vowed, "These attacks will only increase the activities of our crime-detecting forces." In the East, Walter Lippmann characterized Americans as "scared out of their wits." Just three years later he contended in *Public Opinion* that democracy depended upon people who often acted upon fiction and stereotypes. Referring to Palmer, he noted that "counterfeit reality" occurs in high places, as when "an Attorney-General, who has been frightened by a bomb exploded on his doorstep, convinces himself by the reading of revolutionary literature that a revolution is to happen on the first of May 1920."[39]

Newspapers' political cartoons suggested the mood of 1919, depicting strikers, anarchists, and Bolsheviks trying to create the sort of chaos that led to the Communist revolution in Russia. Sympathy won by workers in wartime ended abruptly with the massive strikes. In his cartoon "Where Public Sympathy Gets Off," Ding Darling in the *New York Tribune* depicted the driver of a car who sympathized with so many hitchhiking strikers that he was crowded out of his own car. A cartoon in the *New York Evening Telegram* showed the feet of labor headed down steps marked "strikes—walkouts" "disorder—riots," "Bolshevism—murders" and "Chaos." "The Gauntlet Flung Down" by Nelson Harding in the *Brooklyn Eagle* depicted an anarchist's bomb at the doorstep of free government. A *Baltimore American* cartoon suggested that the anarchist's bomb would "Bomb-erang" back at him. In Oregon, the *Portland Telegram* depicted a member of the newly formed American Legion holding the butt of his infantry rifle like a baseball bat poised to swing about the "Sock It Hard" to an incoming ball labeled "Ball-shevism." That tribute appeared shortly after a deadly clash in Centralia, Washington, between Legionnaires and members of the Industrial Workers of the World (IWW). On the anniversary of the Armistice in November 1919, Legionnaires paraded past the IWW headquarters. Gunfire killed four of them. A mob castrated and lynched one IWW member. Anxieties about a Bolshevik uprising subsided when none had occurred by May Day 1920.[40]

During the Red Scare, suspicion spread widely to socialists, including journalists and public officials. Five Socialist assemblymen were suspended by the New York legislature. A political cartoon in the socialist *New York Call* suggested that the legislature was so autocratic and dictatorial that it would rather welcome the German Kaiser, the Emperor Nero, and the Spirit of the Inquisition. When Carl Sandburg returned in 1918 from a trip to Sweden, federal authorities accused him of supporting the Bolsheviks in Russia. His association with socialists had made him a security risk. Before the war he had been a labor organizer for the

Wisconsin Social-Democrats, a journalist at the *Milwaukee Leader*, a participant in the presidential campaign of Eugene V. Debs, and secretary to the Socialist mayor of Milwaukee. He had married Lillian Steichen, a fellow socialist and the sister of photographer Edward Steichen, and published articles in the *International Socialist Review*. During the war he was a European correspondent for the Newspaper Enterprise Association, returning home in 1919 to join the staff of the *Chicago Daily News* for 13 years.

That summer Sandburg covered the Chicago race riot. It was one of at least 20 separate outbreaks of rioting and racial violence in 1919 including those in Washington, D.C.; Omaha, Nebraska; Knoxville, Tennessee; Lexington, Kentucky; and Elaine, Arkansas. Some traced the racial tension to whites' reactions to the rising postwar aspirations of 380,000 black servicemen, 140,000 of whom had served in France to make the world "safe for democracy." The massive demobilization of the army occurred at the same time as a postwar slump in employment.[41]

Chicago's racial tensions had been growing since a massive migration of blacks from the South had provided labor for wartime industries and the stockyards. The city's black population more than doubled as thousands in the South, terrorized by a wave of lynchings, responded to the civil rights appeals in the black newspaper, the *Chicago Defender*. Its founder and publisher, Robert Abbott, challenged blacks to leave the oppressive South for jobs and freedom. "Chicago is a receiving station that connects directly with every town or city where the people conduct a lynching," Sandburg wrote in 1919. So serious was the wartime labor drain in the South that some localities banned the *Defender*. The *Atlanta Constitution* editorialized that blacks would be disappointed in Chicago or Harlem. Rumors circulated that Northerners were preventing blacks from returning to the South.[42]

The Chicago riot started when blacks allegedly crossed an imaginary line at a segregated lakefront beach. The dispute escalated into a violent stone-throwing fight. One black swimmer, Eugene Williams, stayed in the water as stones flew in his direction, lost his grip on a railroad tie, and drowned. Anger and rumors about his death brought out mobs of whites who attacked trolleys and homes, beating and shooting blacks. Blacks fought back. Outnumbered police were reinforced when the mayor mobilized soldiers with bayonets. After five days in a "swirling maelstrom," as jurors later called it, 38 people were dead—23 blacks and 15 whites—and 291 were wounded. Sandburg's series of stories concluded that "the race question is national and federal. There must be cooperation between states. And there must be federal handling of it." Walter Lippmann, in the preface to Sandburg's 1919 book, concluded that the "race problem as we know it is really a by-product of our planless, disordered, bedraggled, drifting democracy."[43]

Countering the wave of racism, the National Association for the Advancement of Colored People held its 1920 conference in the South, in Atlanta. Edward Bernays, who had honed his skills in the wartime Office of Public Information, was hired to publicize the conference. Bernays focused on the importance of blacks to the economic development of the South. "This approach was based on an appeal to their [whites'] fear of losing profits if migration of workers persisted," Bernays said. Despite some threats, the conference was held without incident, and stories appeared in several newspapers, including the Atlanta papers, the *New York Globe,* New York's *Evening Post,* and the *Chicago Daily News.* In what was also a landmark for the new profession of public relations, Bernays noted that, "For the first time in the history of the country, under the dateline of the South's industrial metropolis, news was published throughout the country alerting the people of the United States that whites and Negroes alike were seeking new status for the Negro."[44]

While Sandburg and most other war correspondents settled into domestic journalism after the war—he was assigned to review motion pictures—U.S. newspapers and news agencies continued to commit resources to covering postwar Europe. Some Americans who had experienced war, like Ernest Hemingway, returned to Europe. Newcomers, among them women such as Dorothy Thompson and Anne O'Hare McCormick, went either as staff writers or freelancers.

In Paris, the press faced unexpected political obstacles in reporting news from the peace conference. Walter Lippmann, still serving President Wilson, noted enormous confusion about the American peace effort. Because the Germans had surrendered on the basis of Wilson's Fourteen Points, the British and Italians wanted the points explained, and Lippmann wrote detailed memoranda. In January 1919, shortly after the U.S. peace commission arrived in Paris, Lippmann resigned and returned to the *New Republic,* where he joined his fellow editors in opposing ratification of the Versailles Treaty for, as one memoirist recalled, "breaking faith with Germany and [violating] our moral obligations to the world."[45]

Wilson had said the peace would be "openly arrived at," but he conceded to secret sessions. News was to be released through Wilson's designated press agent, the former muckraker Ray Stannard Baker. George Seldes concluded that Wilson allowed the host, French Prime Minister Georges Clemenceau, to "fool him into agreeing that the sessions should be secret." Seldes, Herbert Bayard Swope (the Pulitzer Prize winner), and hundreds of other journalists who crowded the Paris hotels "were outraged at having to work through keyholes rather than in the open," wrote historian Frederic Paxson.[46]

Frustrated by the secrecy, William Allen White concluded that the treaty's architects created "the formula of destruction which was to shatter the world." He had asked Lippmann to intercede at the White House so he could be a member of the president's peace party. Failing at that, White received a hard-to-get passport and, as a working journalist earning $1,000 a month plus some expenses, he cabled stories three times a week to the McClure Syndicate, attending the American, British, and French press conferences, and working six to eight hours a day. In the late afternoons he walked along the banks of the Seine with Colonel House, though White "did most of the talking." White mingled with Baker and other wizened correspondents, most of whom smelled doom, among them the publisher of the *Nation*, Oswald Garrison Villard, who had opposed America's entry into the war, and "the wisest of all," Frank Herbert Simonds. An associate editor of the Republican *New York Tribune*, Simonds was a military specialist and strongly anti-Wilson. White thought Simonds "was beginning to know the truth. But he was such an inveterate pessimist that I could not believe the truth when he told it to me."[47] White, a lifelong optimist, eventually concluded that "I did not know the truth and that few, if any, of the American correspondents knew it. Ray Baker was illuminating when he talked and most obliging when we asked questions…. For no one knew the truth. I doubt now if Wilson did; and if Clemenceau and [British Prime Minister] Lloyd George suspected it they did not reveal it."[48] By July 1919, Wilson had compromised, gaining his League of Nations covenant but conceding to British, French, and Italian demands to assign responsibility for the war—"war guilt"—to Germany and punitive reparations arrived at without negotiation with the German delegation. Summoned to the signing, the Germans appeared to Swope as condemned men, giving off "the same feeling as in court when the judge pronounces sentence of death of a murderer."[49]

In the United States, the press mirrored a growing political opposition to the treaty and to involvement in postwar Europe. In July 1919 Wilson came home somewhat exhausted to find Progressives disenchanted with the treaty and Republicans opposed. Pleading for ratification, he traveled the nation until he suffered a debilitating stroke. Led by Republicans, who in the 1918 election had won control of Congress, the Senate in November 1919 rejected the treaty and, with it, the League of Nations. As the Senate reconsidered, there were reports that in Europe the treaty was "repudiated today by those forces of labor and liberalism to whom the future government of Europe belongs." In March 1920, the Senate again rejected the treaty, leaving the matter of peace unresolved. In the summer of 1921, the new Republican president, Warren G. Harding, signed a treaty with Germany that officially ended the war with no provision for a League of Nations.[50]

When Wilson was in France, it was thought that his exhaustion was caused by an attack of the Spanish influenza then spreading around the world. In the United States, news of the epidemic demonstrated how the nation's press grappled rather ineffectively with a subject that dealt with clearly public issues—public health and public policies. From June 1918 into the early months of 1920, newspapers and magazines published thousands of stories as the scope and nature of the menace spread from Europe, infecting about one-fourth of the U.S. population of 105 million and killing 675,000. As it grew from epidemic to pandemic, it claimed between 50 million and 100 million lives worldwide, becoming the deadliest plague in history.[51]

In this public role, the press reported information that was often contradictory, in part because of the inexperience and ineptitude of U.S. public health authorities. In a study of media coverage of the influenza pandemic, Debra Blakely has found four recurring ways by which the media framed the issue: "the importance of the problem, the impact, the strength of the evidence, and the cause." Early stories indicated that the disease was limited to Germany and attributed the epidemic to the malnutrition of its blockaded wartime population. The *New York Times*, which prided itself as the public's newspaper of record, downplayed the relevance to its readers by placing the stories on inside pages.[52]

As daily newspapers day by day reported more deaths, Sunday editions and magazines attempted to give a broader picture of the epidemic after it spread to American troops and then to the United States. By December 1918, when the first wave was peaking with staggering death tolls, *Science* magazine surveyed the "epidemic." *Survey* sought a "program to combat influenza." *Literary Digest* asked, "Is the influenza a Chinese plague?" and published a series about prevention and care through behavioral responses that were recommended or required by public health authorities. Citizens were urged to live healthy lives, seek vaccinations, quit spitting in public, and—in line with the Anti-Saloon League campaign—abstain from liquor.[53]

Panic about the plague strengthened the League's postwar crusade for Prohibition. During the war, temperance crusaders celebrated when Congress proposed a Constitutional Amendment for Prohibition, partly because of the wartime pressure to use grain for food rather than alcohol and partly because of sentiment against brewers, many of whom were German. In January 1919, the Anti-Saloon League's newspaper, the *American Issue*, proclaimed victory. In the midst of the influenza epidemic, the Eighteenth Amendment had been approved by the required three-fourths of the states in less than 13 months, with 23 states voting yes in the first 16 days of 1919. Congress then passed the Volstead Act, prohibiting all manufacture, distribution, and sale of alcoholic beverages, to take effect on January 17, 1920. Influenza victims objected that the law kept them from treating their illness with whiskey. Front-page stories and editorials in the *New York Times* mentioned epidemic victims' need for whiskey for medicinal purposes. Congress responded by making an exception for influenza. Acceptance of Prohibition was expected to be less fervent in the big cities such as New York. Anticipating this, the Anti-Saloon League rallied upstate clergymen to sign a petition to New York City churches "demanding that they not only acquiesce in but show enthusiasm for up-state views on prohibition."[54]

Brewers also sought exemptions. The proposal to allow the sale of beer and light wines became a hot issue during the 1920 election campaign. Its defeat was attributed in part to the Nineteenth Amendment, which in August 1920 gave women the right to vote. According to the *American Issue*, the powerful new women's vote ensured the election of a dry Congress that would not support such an amendment. House drys outnumbered wets by 250–73 in passing the Willis-Campbell antibeer bill prohibiting doctors from prescribing beer or liquor for medicinal purposes.[55]

Predictions that women would vote as a bloc were soon debunked. Months before victory, the convention of the National American Women Suffrage Association divided into Republican and Democratic camps, each claiming that their party had done the most to promote the right to vote, although it had been Theodore Roosevelt's renegade Bull Moose Party in 1912 that first put the women's vote in its national platform. "Suffragists Split by Party Politics," read a headline in the *New York Times.* After passage in August of the Nineteenth Amendment, a *Times* editorial declared that although "a vast, united force has been let loose," it was "doubtless true that women will divide much as men have done among the several parties. There will be no solid 'woman vote.'" However, the editorial predicted, it was "inconceivable" that "political issues and leaders should continue to be merely man-made."[56]

Another influence on the 1920 presidential election was the expanded use of the newsreel as a mass medium. Newsreels had been made during the 1912 election, and Theodore Roosevelt was especially good at exploiting them. In 1916, Democrats claimed that director Tom Ince's antiwar picture, *Civilization*, depicted the horrors of war so effectively it inadvertently complemented President Wilson's reelection slogan, "He Kept Us out of War."[57] In 1920, a rising young political campaign manager, Will Hays, determined to use the screen advantageously for his Republican presidential candidate, Warren Harding. Befriending the film industry, Hays gave "the news reels the same recognition as the press," wrote the contemporary film historian Terry Ramsaye. "Harding posed willingly and often…. The air was full of news reels, and the news reels were full of Warren G. Harding." The "return to normalcy" campaign, promising a retreat from wartime concerns about international affairs, proved far more acceptable to voters than Democrat James. M. Cox's support of American entry in Woodrow Wilson's League of Nations.[58]

For the first time, the presidential-election outcome—Harding's victory—was broadcast on radio. On November 2, 1920, the Westinghouse Corporation's station KDKA in East Pittsburgh, using a rooftop transmitter built for the occasion by engineer Frank Conrad, sponsored the first scheduled radio programming. The station played music and announced the election results telephoned from the *Pittsburgh Post*. A local audience estimated in the hundreds, many of them gathered in meeting places and churches, listened to radio sets provided by Westinghouse, which aimed to generate sales. That first scheduled broadcast demonstrated radio's potential as a mass medium with social and commercial value, setting the stage for a decade of debate over radio's regulation.[59]

After Harding's landslide victory, Hays became the fledgling motion-picture industry's friend in the cabinet. Shortly afterward, the industry leaders, led by Lewis J. Selznick, lured Hays into their business. Hays had served less than a year as postmaster general—countering the threat of a national rail strike with plans to employ the whole U.S. Army—when the screen industry's leaders, desperate to combat scandal and new censorship laws, offered him $100,000 a year to become an all-powerful industry czar. In 1922, Hays became the head of the Motion Picture Producers and Distributors of America and set out to clean up the movie industry and restore profits at the box office.[60]

The fervor for censorship coincided with another restrictive movement to limit immigration. The anti-immigration impulse dated from the 1880s and was driven largely by economic concerns. The 1882 Chinese Exclusion Act was passed to protect jobs in California, and a 1907 executive order by President Roosevelt halted migration of Japanese laborers from Hawaii and Mexico. Shiploads of immigrants regularly arrived in America, totaling almost nine million in the peak year of 1900. In 1915 and again in 1917, Wilson had vetoed a literacy test for immigrants—as had President Cleveland in 1891 and Taft in 1913—on the grounds that "the opportunity of education" was "one of the chief of the opportunities" immigrants sought. In 1917, with strong backing from Senator Henry Cabot Lodge and the Immigration Restriction League, Congress overrode the veto and passed the literacy test for immigrants over the age of 16.[61]

Postwar anti-immigration sentiment, inflamed by domestic bombings and the Red Scare of 1919–1920, increased the clamor to forbid immigrants who did not accept American values. The debate over immigration restrictions stirred passions concerning race, radicalism, and religion. In the context of Walter Lippmann's assessment that domestic disorders reflected a "planless, disordered, bedraggled, drifting democracy," anti-immigration advocates in Congress pushed strongly for adoption of their plan to stop the "drift." In 1919 they urged expulsion of suspected anarchists. "Free speech in the United States is ours, not theirs; free speech is ours, not theirs," declared Congressman Albert Johnson of Washington State, sponsor of West Coast and U.S. immigration restrictions.[62]

As pressure mounted for a major anti-immigration law, newspapers and magazines reflected the focus on aliens, Reds, anarchists, and socialists. The imbalance of stories and editorials advocating immigration restrictions and deportations suggested a media bias. Shortly after the Armistice, Hearst's *Boston American* had excoriated the campaign to "slander" Bolsheviks in Russia. His editorial writer urged Americans to be patient with the revolution that had overturned the ancient autocracy of czars. Antialien bias leaped into headlines. The *New York Times* front page framed a police roundup in the metaphor of a successful deer hunt, linking in the same story the push for sedition legislation: "50 Reds Bagged in Night Raids Here...House Gets Sedition Bill with Teeth; Friend of Trotzky Is Taken." Acts of violence appeared to bias journalists toward stronger law enforcement. Two days after the bomb was detonated at Attorney General Palmer's home, a *New York Times* editorialist wrote that the Constitution should not "be permitted to become the bulwark of defense of a lot of miscreants, foreign born or foreign bred and taught, who seek the overthrow of American institutions." The nation's first tabloid newspaper, the New York *Daily News*, sparked discussion through large photographs. On the day after a bomb went off on Wall Street, the *Daily News* gave over its full front page to a photo of the twisted remains of the wagon that carried a bomb. Some papers featured sensational headlines. The *Boston Herald* screamed, "Bolshevist Plan for Conquest of America!" and "Bride Thinks Reds Kidnapped Missing Groom." One historian concluded that the press legitimized Palmer's raids on alleged anarchists through "biased news coverage laced with inaccuracies, fabrications, exaggerations, sarcasm and ridicule."[63]

In 1920, a major study criticized most U.S. press coverage of the Russian Revolution and its aftermath as "a disaster" that had misled the American public. Writing for the *New Republic,* Walter Lippmann and Charles Merz, an associate editor of the *New York World,* concluded that "the news about Russia is a case of seeing not what was, but what men wished to see." News was guided not by facts but by "hope and fear in the minds of reporters and editors." Using unidentified sources and swayed by editorial policies, the press had circulated rumors rather than facts. The Lippmann-Merz findings, based on more than 3,000 stories in the *New York Times* from 1917 to 1920, noted major shifts in reporting based on emotional shifts. At first, an optimistic press handled news of the revolution "in a rather uncritically pro-Bolshevik fashion." After the new Soviet government made peace with Germany "the tone and quality of the news changed radically," influenced by "organized propaganda" and fear of the "Red Peril." They concluded that "certain correspondents are totally untrustworthy because their sympathies are too deeply engaged." Other "improperly trained men have seriously misled a whole nation." The *Times* editors "profoundly and crassly influenced their news columns... both as to emphasis and captions." As a solution to "growing distrust," Lippmann and Merz recommended reform of journalistic standards within the profession.[64]

In the wake of the Red Scare, the federal government acted on anti-immigration legislation. On June 5, 1920, Congress amended the Immigration Act to allow deportation of anarchists and aliens advocating terrorism.[65] That fall, the election of Harding with his call for "normalcy" seemed to underscore the need to identify "normal" American values and suspicion of foreign-born radicals. If anything, antialien bias was strengthened in May 1920 when alleged Italian anarchists, Niccola Sacco and Bartolomeo Vanzetti, were arrested in Massachusetts for the armed robbery of a factory payroll during which two men were shot. Sacco and Vanzetti were alleged to be associated with an anarchist antiwar publication. The government had halted publication in 1917 and deported its editors to Italy in 1919.[66]

In this atmosphere of fear and isolationism, Congress in 1921 passed a new form of immigration restriction: the national-origins quota system. Secretary of State Charles Evans Hughes provided Congress with country-by-country immigration lists and comments from officials seeking restrictions, although the State Department insisted Hughes made no recommendations. Nevertheless, one official report sent by Hughes recommended that the U.S. "restriction on immigration should be so rigid that it would be impossible for most of these people to enter the United States." In Congress, some objected to officials' references to Jews, Persians, and Armenians as being "unfit." Other critics defended immigration as an American policy, embodied in the Statue of Liberty and Emma Lazarus's welcoming verses: "Give me your tired, your poor, / Your huddled masses yearning to breathe free, / The wretched refuse of your teeming shore."[67]

Advocates of "emergency" restrictions won the debate in the House of Representatives. Congressman Lucian Walton Parrish, Democrat of Texas, urged, "We should stop immigration entirely until such a time as we can amend are immigration laws and so write them that here-after no one shall be admitted except he be in full sympathy with our Constitution and laws, willing to declare himself obedient to our flag, and willing to release himself from any obligations he may owe to the flag of the country from which he came." The quota system limited admissions from each European country to three percent of each foreign-born nationality in the prewar 1910 census. The law favored Northern Europeans at the expense of Southern and Eastern Europeans. Most Asians continued to face exclusion.[68]

Even so, the law did not satisfy the anti-immigration movement, partly because the quotas were linked to the 1910 census, which included peak years of immigration.[69] The media reflected this discontent, indicating that stronger measures were needed. The war's chief American propagandist, George Creel, raised his voice in two articles. Creel asked, "Melting Pot or Dumping Ground?" and answered with "Close the Gates! The Way to Shut a Door Is to Shut It." On New Year's Day 1922, the featured front-page picture in the New York *Daily News* showed immigrants streaming into Ellis Island. Six months later, the *Daily News* front-page caption noted that seven steamships carrying 7,000 people, including "these steerage passengers aboard the Conte Rosso," arrived at Ellis Island "after a race in fog and rain to be the first to land passengers on July 1, 1922, the start of a second fiscal year of sharply reduced immigration quotas."[70]

Domestic events thus seemed more often linked to those in Europe, increasing the demand for news from the Continent. Journalists overseas tracked the results of the peace treaties and reported on elections, public demonstrations, eruptions of violence, and the emergence of new political regimes. Recovered from his wound, Floyd Gibbons returned to Europe as chief of the *Chicago Tribune*'s foreign news service, editor of its Paris edition, and a reporter of various conflicts, disasters, and exotica. Rheta Dorr stayed on as a foreign correspondent from Prague, which became the capital of the new nation of Czechoslovakia. Seldes also wrote for the *Chicago Tribune*, first in London and then as its chief European correspondent, reporting from the Communist Soviet Union and from Benito Mussolini's Italy.

After his Russian adventures, Carl Ackerman settled in London in 1920 as head of the foreign service for the *Philadelphia Ledger*. There he took long walks in Hyde Park with Colonel House, estranged now from Wilson because the president "never forgave me...because when I returned [to Washington] I immediately wrote [Senator] Lodge offering [to] give him all information I had about peace [conference]." Gravitating toward conflict, Ackerman went to Ireland, seeking to interview the leader of the armed rebellion against British rule. One meeting in August 1920 with Michael Collins gained Ackerman a second meeting in April 1921 at Collins's hideout. From Dublin, Ackerman traveled secretly to "A 'sub-headquarters' of the Irish Republican Army. Somewhere in Ireland." There he probed the goals of the rebellion.

"What about peace?" I asked. "What are your terms for settlement?"
    Collins, who was seated at my right beside a small table dropped his head for a few seconds and then replied: "Our terms have been often and clearly stated. The right of this country is to complete independence. The people have decided in favour of the Republican form of government. You will recall that when we spoke on this point at our previous meeting I told you that Mr. Lloyd George had

an opportunity of showing himself a great statesman by recognizing the Irish Republic. He has that chance still."

"Do you mean a republic within the British commonwealth of Nations or outside?" ...

"I mean an Irish Republic."

Thus again, Michael Collins, Ireland's national hero reiterated in two words the aspirations of the Irish people—an "Irish Republic." ...

"The terror the British wanted to instill in this country has completely broken down.... It's dreadful, of course, but we must go on until we are finally rid of these demons."

The interview, which appeared in the *Philadelphia Ledger* on April 2, helped the British Foreign Office shape strategy for Irish independence and allowed Ackerman to claim some credit for the birth of the Irish Free State.[71]

NOTES

1. The election was so close that it was undecided until the Far West sided with Wilson, giving him 277 electoral votes to 254 for Charles Evans Hughes.

2. Woodrow Wilson, "A Flag Day Address," in *April 7–June 23, 1917,* vol. 42 of *The Papers of Woodrow Wilson,* ed. Arthur S. Link (Princeton, NJ: Princeton University Press), 499. The Zimmerman telegram, sent by German Foreign Minister Arthur Zimmerman, was decoded by the British and channeled to Wilson; Zimmerman sought to engage Mexico and Japan in the war against the United States, promising Mexico the return of former Mexico territory in the western United States. British Foreign Secretary Arthur Balfour called the telegram "one of Germany's extraordinary blunders which she is always making." Arthur Balfour, *Papers of Woodrow Wilson,* 42:332.

3. Wilson, "Flag Day Address," 500. Wilson justified his harsher response to the Germans because, he said, their submarines took lives while the British blockade took replaceable property. For discussions of American neutrality policy, see John W. Coogan, *The End of Neutrality: The United States, Britain and Maritime Rights, 1899–1915* (Ithaca, NY: Cornell University Press, 1981), 235; and Jurg Martin Gabriel, *The American Conception of Neutrality After 1941,* rev. ed. (New York: Palgrave Macmillan, 2002), 26–27.

4. "Letter to the President," from the Secretaries of State, War, and the Navy, April 13, 1917, container 1, George Creel Papers, Collection MSS17210, Manuscript Division, LOC. Executive Order, container 1, Creel Papers.

5. Ibid.

6. Executive Order, container 1, Creel Papers.

7. "Letter to the President."

8. The appointment of Creel and the subsequent censorship disappointed some Progressives, among them Walter Lippmann. On February 19, 1917, Lippmann, whose editorials in the *New Republic* were respected by Wilson, advised the president that in case of war he should place any censorship under

"civilian control, under men of real insight and democratic sympathy" and recommended Interior Secretary Franklin K. Lane. Walter Lippmann to Woodrow Wilson, February 6, 1917, in *Public Philosopher: Selected Letters of Walter Lippmann,* ed. John Morton Blum (New York: Ticknor & Fields, 1985), 61.

9. Stephen Koss, *The Twentieth Century,* vol. 2 of *The Rise and Fall of the Political Press in Britain* (Chapel Hill: The University of North Carolina Press, 1984), 5, 53, 161; Harold D. Lasswell, *Propaganda Technique in World War I* (Cambridge, MA: MIT Press, 1971), 31, 33. Comparing British and U.S. appointments, Lasswell concluded that "the balance on the scale on this particular matter inclines toward the American practice."

10. Biographical information in container 1, Creel Papers; see also John J. Pauly, "George Creel," in *Biographical Dictionary of American Journalism,* 146.

11. Granville Hicks, *John Reed: The Making of a Revolutionary* (New York: Macmillan, 1937), 143.

12. In 1915 Creel was a speaker and member of the Campaign Committee for the New York State Men's League for Woman Suffrage. Container 4, Creel Papers.

13. Stephen Ponder, "Presidential Publicity and Executive Power: Woodrow Wilson and the Centralizing of Government Information," *American Journalism* 11 (3): 258; see also Stephen Vaughn, *Holding Fast the Inner Lines: Democracy, Nationalism, and the Committee on Public Information* (Chapel Hill: University of North Carolina Press, 1980); and James R. Mock and Cedric Larson, *Words that Won the War: The Story of the Committee on Public Information, 1917–1919* (Princeton, NJ: Princeton University Press, 1939).

14. Woodrow Wilson to George Creel, August 24, 1918, container 1, Creel Papers. Wilson usually signed his editing notes "Cordially and Faithfully Yours" or "Faithfully yours." Creel explained the editing process: "When I spoke at public gatherings, it was always with the President's permission and sometimes at his request. In every instance I showed him what I meant to say, and as can be seen...he went over each of them with painstaking care." Although Wilson typically made minor corrections, he made a major deletion on August 24, 1918. As the war was nearing its end, Wilson deleted Creel's reference to a controversial indemnities condition for peace that Wilson had specifically eliminated ("We seek no indemnities for ourselves ...") in his April 1917 war message to Congress. Now he edited Creel's sentence to delete the struck-through words: "We are not fighting merely to compel the return of captured provinces, the payment of indemnities, the restoration of ruined lands, or the rehabilitation of conquered peoples." July 29, 1917, container 1, Creel Papers.

15. Woodrow Wilson, "Preliminary Statement to the Press," May 17, 1917, typed draft in container 1, Creel Papers. The statement echoed Lippmann's advice to Wilson: "It will be more important to control untruth than it will be to suppress truth as is done so much in Europe. In case of war the protection of a healthy public opinion in this country will be of the first importance." Lippmann to Wilson, February 6, 1917, in *Selected Letters,* 60–61.

16. "Censorship and Suppression," *Nation,* April 12, 1917, 424–25.

17. George Creel, "Preliminary Statement to the Press," May 17, 1917, container 1, Creel Papers.

18. Fredric L. Paxson, "The American War Government, 1917–1918," *American Historical Review* 26 (October 1920): 55.

19. "The Committee on Public Misinformation," *New York Times*, July 7, 1917, 7.

20. Ibid., 75–76.

21. George Creel, "Press Regulations," July 30, 1917, box 1, Elmer Earle Roberts Papers.

22. Michael S. Schudson, "Journalism," in *Oxford Companion to United States History*, ed. Paul S. Boyer (New York: Oxford University Press, 2001), 411; see also Michael Schudson, *Discovering the News: A Social History of American Newspapers* (New York: Basic Books, 1978). See also Wm. David Sloan, "The Media in Trying Times," in *Perspectives on Mass Communication History* (Hillsdale, NJ: Lawrence Erlbaum, 1991), 283–99,

23. James D. Startt, "American Propaganda in Britain During World War I," *Prologue: Quarterly of the National Archives and Records Administration* 28 (1): 17–33; James D. Startt, "American Film Propaganda in Revolutionary Russia," *Prologue: Quarterly of the National Archives and Records Administration* 30 (3): 167–79.

24. Elmer Davis, *History of the "New York Times,"* 355–56; "Success of Allied Propaganda," *Literary Digest*, October 5, 1918, 19–20; George Creel, "Flashing Democracy Around the World," *World Outlook*, November 8, 1918, 8.

25. "Conscription Adopted by Congress," *Survey*, May 5, 1917, 120; W. B. McCormick, "Emergency Army Law and the Citizen," *Review of Reviews*, June 8, 1917, 606–8; "Draft Made Really Selective," *Literary Digest*, November 3, 1917, 10; "Politics in Draft Exemptions," *Literary Digest*, July 14, 1917, 9–10; "Selective Draft Law Declared Constitutional," *New York Times*, February 6, 1918; "Oklahoma's Draft Resisters," *Literary Digest*, August 18, 1917, 11–12; "What Each One of Us, According to Incomes, Should Contribute to the Cost of the War," *Literary Digest*, April 20, 1918, 100–3; G. D. Strayer, "War Savings Campaigns in the Public Schools," *Review of Reviews*, August 1918, 169–71; "Mass Saving as a War Resource," *New Republic*, August 25, 1917, 92–94; "Wage Earners as Government Bond Buyers," *Literary Digest*, August 4, 1917, 64; "What to Plant in Your Back Yard," *Illustrated World*, June 7, 1917, 493–97.

26. Robert V. Hudson, "William Henry Irwin," in *Biographical Dictionary of American Journalism*, 366; Larry L. Adams, *Walter Lippmann* (Boston: Twayne Publishers, 1977), 60.

27. Startt, "The Media and Political Culture," *The Significance of the Media in American History*, 204.

28. William E. Leuchtenberg, *The Perils of Prosperity, 1914–1932* (Chicago: University of Chicago Press, 1972), 45. President Wilson intervened to have the ban lifted in four days. Startt and Van Tuyll, "The Media and National Crises, 1917–1945," 325. Gompers joined Wilson's Advisory Commission, forming his own labor committee, which was supported by the American Federation of Labor and "designed to counteract the antiwar activities of certain of the Socialist labor leaders." Paxson, "American War Government," 57–59.

29. "Mr. Hearst's Loyalty," *Literary Digest*, May 25, 1918, 12–13.

30. "The Case of Mr. Hearst and His Newspapers," *Current Opinion*, July 1918, 5–8.

31. Floyd Gibbons, *Chicago Tribune,* February 26, 1917, in Pickett, "The Sinking of the *Laconia,*" *Voices of the Past,* 239–41; Edward Gibbons, *Floyd Gibbons, Your Headline Hunter* (New York: Exposition Press, 1935); Douglas Gilbert, *Floyd Gibbons: Knight of the Air* (New York: R. M. McBride, 1930); Robert L. Hoskins, "Floyd Gibbons," in *Biographical Dictionary of American Journalism,* 268–69.

32. Tom Clark, *The World of Damon Runyon* (New York: Harper & Row, 1978); Kahn, *Swope,* 178–179; Patricia Ward D'Itri, *Damon Runyon* (Boston: Twayne Publishers, 1982); Jean Wagner, *Runyonese: The Mind and Craft of Damon Runyon* (Paris: Stechert-Hafner, 1964); John J. Pauly, "Damon Runyon," in *Biographical Dictionary of American Journalism,* 614–15.

33. Harold Ross, "How a Soldier Should Behave while on Leave," *Stars and Stripes,* February 28, 1918; Franklin P. Adams, "An Ode to Ice Cream Soda," *Stars and Stripes,* April 19, 1918; Alexander Woollcott, "A Famous Story about a Marine and a Dog," *Stars and Stripes,* June 14, 1918, all reprinted in Pickett, *Voices of the Past,* 244–49; see also Brendan Gill, *Here at the "New Yorker"* (New York: Random House, 1975); Dale Kramer, *Ross and the "New Yorker"* (Garden City, NY: Doubleday, 1952); James Thurber, *The Years with Ross* (New York: Little, Brown, 1959); Harris E. Ross, "Harold Wallace Ross," in *Biographical Dictionary of American Journalism,* 603–4; Samuel Hopkins Adams, *Alexander Woollcott* (Freeport, NY: Books for Libraries Press, 1970); Wayne Chatterton, *Alexander Woollcott* (Boston, 1978); Dwight Jenson, "Alexander Woollcott," in *Biographical Dictionary of American Journalism,* 759–60; Grantland Rice, *The Tumult and the Shouting: My Life in Sport* (New York: A. S. Barnes, 1954); Rice obituary, *New York Times,* July 14, 1954; Laura Nickerson, "Henry Grantland Rice," in *Biographical Dictionary of American Journalism,* 587–88; Franklin P. Adams, *Something Else Again* (Garden City, NY: Doubleday, Page, 1920); Franklin P. Adams, *The Diary of Our Own Samuel Pepys* (New York, 1935); Adams obituary, *New York Times,* March 24, 1960; Harris E. Ross, "Franklin Pierce Adams," in *Biographical Dictionary of American Journalism,* 9.

34. Richard O'Connor, *Heywood Broun: A Biography* (New York: Putnam, 1975); Dale Kramer, *Heywood Broun: A Biographical Portrait* (New York: Current Books, 1949); Heywood Broun obituary, *New York Times,* December 19, 1939; Harris E. Ross, "Heywood Broun," in *Biographical Dictionary of American Journalism,* 81–84. See also Heywood Broun, *It Seems to Me* (New York: Harcourt Brace, 1935); Heywood Broun, *The Collected Edition of Heywood Broun* (New York: Harcourt, Brace, 1941); Sam G. Riley, *The American Newspaper Columnist* (Westport, CT: Praeger, 1998), 83. Broun's reputation as an outsider had surfaced earlier at Harvard University, where he was turned away by the staff of the *Harvard Crimson.* He did not do well academically, and after he failed French he did not graduate. Nonetheless, he was part of one of Harvard's "golden ages," and his classmates included two other future journalists, Walter Lippmann and John Reed, the poet T. S. Eliot, humorist Robert Benchley, authors Conrad Aiken and Stuart Chase, future New Deal Secretary Francis Biddle, and historian Samuel Eliot Morison. Adams, *Lippmann,* 18.

35. Sadie L. Mossler, "They Call Me the Hen Editor: The Story of a Small-Town Newspaper Woman," *Woman's Home Companion,* October 1918, 32; Rheta Childe Dorr, *A Woman of Fifty* (New York: Funk & Wagnalls, 1924); Dorr obituary, August 9, 1948, *New York Times*; Startt and Van Tuyll, *The Media in America: A History,* 323.

36. George Seldes, *Can These Things Be!* (1931), reprinted in Randolph T. Holhut, *The George Seldes Reader* (New York: Barricade Books, 1994), 47–56.

37. The other three reporters were Cal Lyon, Lincoln Eyre and Herbert Corey. George Seldes, *You Can't Print That: The Truth Behind the News, 1918–1928* (Garden City, NY: Garden City Publishing, 1929), in Holhut, *The George Seldes Reader,* 57–68. Seldes subsequently regarded his Hindenberg scoop as "the biggest story in the world" because of Nazi claims in the 1930s that Germany lost the war not on the battlefield but when the civilian government gave the Army a "stab in the back."

38. Carl W. Ackerman to C. V. Van Anda, August 30, 1918, "*New York Times* Correspondence 1918–1919," box 122, Ackerman Papers. Van Anda's assistant noted on the letter: "Accepted for the *New York Times* by C. V. Van Anda, Managing Editor"; Carl W. Ackerman, 1918, "Siberia Notes, Memoranda, Fragments," box 141, Ackerman Papers; Carl W. Ackerman to Mr. Van Anda, December 29, 1918, box 122, Ackerman Papers; Carl W. Ackerman to Col. Edward M. House, 1919, "House, Edward M.," box 29, Ackerman Papers.

39. William Allen White, *Autobiography* (New York: Macmillan, 1946*)*, 611; Elmer Davis, *History of the "New York Times,"* 259; "Bombing at Washington, D.C. Home of Attorney-General Palmer," *Literary Digest,* June 14, 1919, in Leo Robert Klein, "Red Scare (1918–1921): An Image Database," William and Anita Newman Library, Baruch College, City University of New York; Walter Lippmann, *Public Opinion* (New York: Macmillan, 1938), 14; David E. Kyvig, *Daily Life in the United States, 1920–1939: Decades of Promise and Pain* (Westport, CT: Greenwood Press, 2002), 5.

40. Ding Darling, "Where Public Sympathy Gets Off," *New York Tribune,* reprinted in *Literary Digest,* November 22, 1919; "Step by Step," *New York Evening Telegram,* reprinted in *Literary Digest,* November 1, 1919; "The Gauntlet Flung Down," *Brooklyn Eagle,* reprinted in *Outlook,* May 21, 1919; "Bomb-erang," *Baltimore American,* reprinted in *Literary Digest,* June 21, 1919; and "Sock It Hard," *Portland (OR) Telegram,* reprinted in *Literary Digest,* November 29, 1919. All from Klein, "Red Scare"; Kyvig, *Daily Life in the United States,* 5.

41. Lee E. Williams and Lee E. Williams II, *Anatomy of Four Race Riots* (Hattiesburg: University and College Press of Mississippi, 1973); Becky Givan, "Global Mappings: Knoxville, TN, Race Riot of 1919," Political Atlas of the African Diaspora, Institute for Diasporic Studies, Northwestern University, http://diaspora.northwestern.edu/cgi-bin/WebObjects/DiasporaX.woa/wa/displayArticle?atomid ? 604

42. Carl Sandburg, *The Chicago Race Riots,* (July 1919; repr., New York: Harcourt, Brace, and World, 1969), 31, 53, 60; Black Holocaust Society, http://www.blackwallstreet.freeservers.com/

43. Eugene Williams (coroner), "Verdicts Rendered by Coroner's Jury on the Race Riot Cases," 27, "Deaths, Disturbances, Disasters, and Disorders in Chicago: *The Race Riots: Biennial Report, 1918-1919*," eds. Ellen O'Brien and Lyle Benedict, Chicago Public Library, www.chipublib.org/004chicago/disasters/riots_race; Sandburg, *Race Riots: Biennial Report,* 79; Lippmann, in *Race Riots: Biennial Report,* xix.

44. "1920 NAACP Conference in Atlanta: Civil Rights Action through the Media," Museum of Public Relations, New York, http://www.prmuseum.com/bernays/bernays_1920.html

45. "Joy among the Philistines; What the Peace Treaty Teaches," *New Republic,* June 7, 1919, 169–70. Robert Morss Lovett, *All Our Years* (New York: Viking, 1948), cited in Adams, *Lippmann,* 60.

46. George Seldes, *World Panorama* (1933), reprinted in Holhut, *The George Seldes Reader,* 70; Frederic L. Paxson, *American Democracy and the World War: Postwar Years: Normalcy, 1918–1923* (Berkeley and Los Angeles: University of California Press, 1948), 16.

47. White, *Autobiography,* 546–47, 500, 554–55, 558. Simonds "saw the rocks and the wreck ahead. He wrote it to his papers. And much thanks he got for it. The President became bitter against him and he lost caste and standing as men always do who proclaim the unpleasant and terrible truth." One day in February 1919, Simonds showed White his cable with the lead sentence: "The League of Nations is dead. The treaty of peace is impossible." White said Simonds "felt that without a common police force to implement the treaty of peace and to make good the decisions of the League of Nations, the League would fall into a political mechanism to promote the balance of power, the old organ of European political stability. He also was sure that without an international police force, the terms of the treaties soon would be violated." See also F. H. Simonds, "Mr. Simonds on the Treaty," *New Republic,* March 3, 1920, 30–31.

48. William Allen White, *Selected Letters of William Allen White,* ed. Walter Johnson (New York: Henry Holt, 1947), 195; White, *Autobiography,* 550. Among his confidants, Villard, a grandson of the abolitionist editor William Lloyd Garrison, was uncompromising in his views against America's participation in the war and alienated patriotic readers.

49. Seldes, *World Panorama,* in Holhut, *Reader,* 79–80; "German Peace Treaty; Full Text of the Historic Document Signed at Versailles on June 28, 1919," *Current History,* August 1919, 285–68.

50. C. Nagel, "Moral Objections to the Treaty," *Nation,* August 9, 1919, 172–73; G. Frank, "Has Wilson Failed? An Examination of the Liberal Outlook," *Century,* August 1919, 506–20; "Case against the Treaty," *Nation,* July 12, 1919, 62; "America's Abandonment of Europe," *Literary Digest,* December 6, 1919, 21–22; "Defeat of the Treaty," *New Republic,* February 25, 1920, 371–72.

51. John M. Barry, *The Great Influenza: The Epic Story of the Deadliest Plague in History* (New York: Viking, 2004). The U.S. Census for 1920 recorded 105,710,620 residents.

52. Debra E. Blakely, "Social Construction of Three Influenza Pandemics in the *New York Times,*" *Journalism and Mass Communication Quarterly* 80 (4): 887–88; "Vienna Racked by Bread Riots: German Hunger Spreads Disease,"*New York Times,* June 21, 1918, 7; "Germans with Fever Drop in Their Tracks," *New York Times,* July 9, 1918, 10; "Epidemics in Germany," *New York Times,* July 26, 1918, 20.

53. "Is the Influenza a Chinese Plague?" *Literary Digest,* December 7, 1918, 26–27; "How the Flu Mask Traps the Germ," *Literary Digest,* December 21, 1918, 21; "Expert Medical Advice on Influenza," *Literary Digest,* December 28, 1918, 23; "Vaccination against Influenza," *Literary Digest,* December 28, 1918, 25; "Program to Combat Influenza," *Survey,* December 28, 1918, 408–9; "Influenza Epidemic," *Science,* December 13, 1918, 594; Blakely, "Influenza Pandemics," 890.

54. "U.S. Is Voted Dry! 36th State Ratifies Dry Amendment Jan. 16," *American Issue,* January 25, 1919, 1. The *American Issue* was the publication of the Anti-Saloon League. Eventually, 46 of 48 states ratified (the two exceptions were Connecticut and Rhode Island). Digital Archive of the Anti-Saloon League Archive and Temperance Collection of the Westerville Public Library, Westerville, Ohio; Blakely, "Influenza Pandemics," 890; "Country against City," *New York Times,* January 19, 1920, 8.

55. *American Issue,* November 13, 1920, 1, cited in Meg Lamme, "Snatching Defeat from the Jaws of Victory: Communications of the Anti-Saloon League of America, 1920–1933," *Atlanta Review of Journalism History* 4 (Fall 2003): 1–49; "Pass Anti-Beer Bill in House 250 to 93," *New York Times,* June 28, 1921, 1. A dry Congress won reelection in 1922 and in 1924 resisted wet efforts for the beer and wine amendment.

56. "Suffragists Split by Party Politics; Mrs. Bass Attacks Republican Women Who Spread Propaganda at Convention," *New York Times,* February 13, 1920; "The Woman of Thirty," *New York Times,* August 29, 1920.

57. Ramsaye, *Million and One Nights,* 728.

58. Ibid., 813.

59. Kyvig, *Daily Life in the United States,* 62; George H. Douglas, *The Early Days of Radio* (Jefferson, NC: McFarland, 1987); Robert L. Hilliard and Michael C. Keith, *The Broadcast Century: A Biography of American Broadcasting* (Boston: Focal, 1992); Harding won by a landslide, receiving 60 percent of the popular vote and 404 electoral votes to 114 for Cox and his vice presidential running mate, Franklin D. Roosevelt. Radio stations soon multiplied. By 1923 there were 556.

60. Ramsaye, *Million and One Nights,* 813–18. Legal film censorship had begun as early as 1907 in Chicago and 1908 in New York City and had led to statutes in other cities and states. In hiring Hays, the motion picture producers followed the lead of professional baseball owners after the Black Sox betting scandal in the 1919 World Series. On November 12, 1920, baseball owners had installed an all-powerful commissioner of baseball, the stern federal judge Kennesaw Mountain Landis, to send the message that the sport would be cleared from the clutch of gamblers. In 1921, using his dictatorial control to restore the game's reputation, Landis banned "Shoeless" Joe Jackson and the seven other implicated Sox players from baseball forever.

61. "A Historical Look at U.S. Immigration Policy: Number of Immigrants to the U.S. Per Decade, 1820–1990," U.S. Bureau of the Census, 1993. Lodge said that in the 20 years since 1886, the United States had admitted 1,829,320 immigrants who admitted they could not read or write in any language.

62. Kristofer Allerfeldt, *Race, Radicalism, Religion, and Restriction: Immigration in the Pacific Northwest, 1890–1924* (Westport, CT: Praeger, 2003); "House Passes Bill to Curb Red Aliens," *New York Times,* December 21, 1919, 3, in Sue D. Taylor, "Casting Radicals upon the Waters: Press Support of the Deportation Campaign of 1919–1920," paper presented to the History Division, Association for Education in Journalism and Mass Communications, Chicago, 1998. "50 Reds Bagged in Night Raids Here…House Gets Sedition Bill with Teeth; Friend of Trotzky Is Taken; Gregory Weinstein, Co-Editor of Soviet Leader, Now on Ellis Island; Communist Leader Held;…Foreign Papers Seized," *New York Times,* January 6, 1920, 1.

63. "50 Reds Bagged in Night Raids Here," 1. Other stories on the front page that day were headlined: "Nation has 3,000 'Perfect Cases' Behind Bars"

and "Begin Procedure to Deport Reds." Gerald MacFarland, *Boston American*, December 26, 1918, in Nasaw, *The Chief*, 273–74. MacFarlane wrote, "For all we can say positively the Bolsheviki leaders may be saints or crooks or just ordinary men. But we can say this with certainty, that the great majority of people keep them in power, and that for more than a year there has been a vast conspiracy to slander them, and that there is a good ground for suspicion that men who have to be lied about continuously in order to make them appear bad are not so very bad after all." "The Bomb Conspirators," *New York Times*, June 4, 1919, 14; photograph by Ed Jackson, *New York Daily News*, September 16, 1920, 1, http://www.dailynewspix.com/; Paul Sann, *The Lawless Decade: A Pictorial History of a Great American Transition from WWI Armistice and Prohibition to Repeal and the New Deal* (New York: Crown Publishers, 1957); Taylor, "Casting Radicals upon the Waters."

64. Walter Lippmann and Charles Merz, "A Test of the News," *New Republic*, August 4, 1920, 1–42.

65. After President William McKinley was assassinated by a Polish anarchist, Congress enacted the Anarchist Exclusion Act, which allowed immigrants to be excluded on the basis of their political opinions.

66. *Cronica Sovversiva* was believed to be the most influential anarchist journal in America.

67. "Hughes Asks Rigid Immigration Ban. Calls Restriction of Aliens Imperative; Siegel, in Reply, Condemns Listing of Armenians, Jews and Persians as Unfit," *New York Times*, April 20, 1921, 1; "Hughes Sent Files, Not Views on Races; Official Denial Is Made that Secretary Gave Opinion in Immigration Curb," *New York Times*, April 21, 1921, 1.

68. House of Representatives Debate, April 20, 1921, Document Archive, American Civil Rights Review, http://www.americancivilrightsreview.com/docs-immigration1921.htm.

69. Immigration peaked around 1900 when almost nine million entered the United States. In 1910, the number decreased to about 5.7 million. In 1890, the total was around 5.4 million. By 1930, immigration restrictions reduced the number to about 600,000. "A Historical Look at U.S. Immigration Policy," U.S. Bureau of the Census, 1993.

70. George Creel, "Melting Pot or Dumping Ground?" *Collier's*, September 3, 1921; Creel, "Close the Gates! The Way to Shut a Door Is to Shut It," *Collier's*, May 6, 1922; "Immigrants Arriving at Ellis Island," *New York Daily News*, January 1, 1922, 1; Seven steamships carrying 7,000 people," *New York Daily News*, July 1, 1922, 1.

71. Carl W. Ackerman, June 23 and 24, 1920, in "London Notes, 1920–1921," Diary, box 1, Ackerman Papers; Prime Minister David Lloyd George referred to the interview on April 25 in the House of Commons as reported in the British press: "Michael Collins Interviewed; No Compromises; Sinn Fein Victory Assured," *London Morning Post*, April 26, 1921; "Irish Freedom Born at Conference between Lloyd George and Glynn; So Declared Carl W. Ackerman at Banquet Last Night," *Albany Times-Union*, March 18, 1922, 1. Glynn was former New York Governor Martin H. Glynn. Box 1, Ackerman Papers.

5

Rise of Professionalism

A journalist who uses his power for any selfish or otherwise unworthy purpose is faithless to a high trust.
—American Society of Newspapers Editors, Code of Ethics, 1923

During Harding's term, news coverage of the presidency expanded to the mutual benefit of the president and the Washington press corps. As a newspaper publisher[1] who welcomed journalists and understood their usefulness, Harding resumed the practice of holding regular White House press conferences, normally twice a week, as Wilson had done during his first two years. Like Wilson, Harding acknowledged the value to all parties of institutionalizing the president-press relationship. The regularity of press conferences induced Washington correspondents and their employers to depend upon them for stories, increasing the flow of news from the White House.

At the same time, Harding's staff, building upon wartime techniques for managing news and shaping public opinion, sought to advance Harding's agenda and present an image of an active, healthy president. With the postwar growth of the White House press corps—it would grow from only a dozen reporters to 150 during Harding's term—attendance now became a privilege regulated by the president's staff, which administered formal rules for accreditation, attendance, and conduct. While the credentialed journalists valued their White House access and the regularity of stories, some complained that the president used the conferences to manipulate the press and public opinion. As the press corps came to realize, management of news, developed by Wilson's

wartime administration, had been adopted for peacetime domestic purposes. Journalists now had to acknowledge the influence of the relatively
new practice of public relations.[2]

Beyond the press conferences, Harding's media savvy set a precedent
for the press-presidency relationship. He continued to appreciate the
impact of newsreels that had helped him win the presidency. As
magazines and newspapers, especially tabloids, now featured more
photographs, Harding cheerfully posed with White House guests or in
public. Continuing Wilson's practice of speaking at press society meetings of journalists and publishers, Harding spoke at the National Press
Club, the American Newspaper Publishers Association, the American
Society of Newspaper Editors, and the White House Correspondents
Association, the new organization created to regulate attendance at his
press conferences. His friendly, likeable approach to the press helped
shield him from the scandal that began to surface in the press during his
second year.[3]

The policies that guided Harding's relationship with media were also
indicating how corporate America could manage press relations and
influence media messages. This development had been anticipated first
by Ivy Lee, an 1899 graduate of Atlanta's Emory University and often
cited as the "father of public relations." In the prewar years, Lee had
handled media relations effectively for the Pennsylvania Railroad and
for the beleaguered John D. Rockefeller. During the war, George Creel
and his staff in the Committee on Public Information adopted and developed techniques for managing the news and mobilizing public opinion.
In the postwar years, the ranks of public relations counselors increased
as some of Creel's staff, notably Edward Bernays, served clients in the
expanding corporate world. Bernays wrote the first book on public relations, designating it a field of communication study and practice. Others
with experience in journalism found even better-paying careers as public
relations counselors, among them Carl W. Ackerman. In 1921, after six
years overseas as a distinguished foreign correspondent, he returned to
the United States and built a national clientele that included the Eastman
Kodak Company. On the whole, these counselors heralded a new trend
in management of media relations. They introduced a methodology for
planning and shaping public information, including models for staging
press conferences and spectacles to attract attention, as well as advance
planning to deflect negative publicity during business crises.

The Republican campaign slogan promising a return to "normalcy"
presumed that America had once been normal or that there were identifi-
able norms that could and should be achieved and maintained. A good
deal of the energy and press attention during the 1920s was devoted to
such identification and enforcement of norms. Amid Prohibition, the
Anti-Saloon League underscored obedience and enforcement, as well

as resistance to legislative loopholes. Allied in spirit to Prohibition were those who wanted to clean America of hostile aliens. Akin to that, religious revivalism, notably in the South, began to blur the lines between church and state in efforts to outlaw the teaching of evolution. Allied with the idea of "normalcy," the prevailing antisocialist, antianarchist advocates were pressing in Congress for stricter immigration limits to add to the "emergency" legislation of 1921. At the same time in the South, the impulse for order nurtured an especially aberrant strain of normalcy, reviving membership in the outlawed Ku Klux Klan, which resorted to social control of Negroes through lynchings and terror.

The Harding administration soon evidenced its eagerness to shift the country's priorities toward domestic concerns, one of which was to prevent involvement in another European war. Having rejected membership in the League of Nations, the United States acted unilaterally as an independent world power that sought to keep the other powers in check. Harding's most significant achievement, judging from press coverage, was the three-month Washington Conference treaty by which the United States, Britain, Japan, France, and Italy agreed to limit warships.

Domestically, the Harding administration set the tone for the decade by supporting conditions favorable to the expansion of business ventures. Buoyed by their 1920 election landslide, Republicans reversed some Progressive Era reforms, cutting taxes to benefit large corporations and encourage business expansion, sometimes in the extreme. In one scandalous case, Harding's Interior Department invited corporations to exploit public oil reserves to meet the rising demand from automobile owners. As the press revealed, Harding's men had given private oil companies leases to exploit two U.S. naval petroleum reserves established by Wilson during the war. In April 1922, the *Wall Street Journal* disclosed this leasing of national reserves to private companies as a "notable departure on the part of the government." The *Journal* noted that Secretary of the Interior Albert Fall had leased the huge naval reserve at Teapot Dome, Wyoming.[4]

Subsequently, Hearst's newspapers emphasized these allegations of corruption. A Senate investigation into the "Teapot Dome scandal" revealed that Harding, who appointed Fall, had authorized the transfer of the oil reserves from the navy, entrusting them to Fall. Investigations incriminated Fall for accepting a bribe; he was sentenced to prison. The inquiry also implicated another Harding appointee, Attorney General Harry Daugherty, who resigned. Under Harding, one historian later noted, "corruption, always more or less normal in state and municipal politics, moved to Washington." William Allen White came away from an interview with Harding in the White House "feeling that it was the scene of a terrific struggle....[Harding] was deeply fond of his friends the grafters—the petty politicians in every state, who were looking for pickings."[5]

Harding was also deeply fond of journalists. As he confided to White, Harding pined for the simpler, daily thrill of publishing his hometown newspaper, the *Marion Star*. So good was his rapport with the press that the fallout from the Teapot Dome scandal did not harm his reputation while he lived. After his sudden death in office in August 1923, the trade journal *Editor & Publisher* said no president before him had such "mutually frank and satisfactory contacts with the reporters." The correspondents who controlled congressional press accreditation adopted a resolution that "no finer contact of genuine understanding and sympathy ever was established between an American president and the newspapermen."[6]

Harding's death catapulted his vice president, Calvin Coolidge, into the presidency. In the view of press pundits, Coolidge gave the Republicans an even stronger chance to hold the presidency. In the East, Walter Lippmann confided privately that, "Coolidge looks to me an absolute certainty to the Republicans. Not only has he all the strategic advantages which come from control of the Federal patronage, but he has proved himself a very shrewd politician." In the Midwest, William Allen White appreciated Coolidge's talent as "a tremendous shock absorber. His emotionless attitude is an anesthetic to a possible national conviction of sin." White envisioned that the nation would eventually be "shocked out of its materialism," a logical conclusion to the "sordid decade."[7]

Acknowledging the utility of Harding's successful press relationships, Coolidge kept Harding's chief publicity officer and continued to meet twice weekly with reporters and frequently with photographers. Coolidge, however, frustrated the White House press corps. Accustomed to Harding's news-conscious approach, journalists soon found that the new president provided far less useful material. Despite the complaints, Raymond Clapper of the United Press acknowledged that the correspondents still attended the press conference and were "willing to endure occasional irritations rather than give up a good source of news.'" Even when signing important legislation, Coolidge's comments were pedestrian at best. In 1924, he signed the Johnson-Reed immigration law, which was even more discriminatory than the 1921 act, underscoring the principle of preserving America's "racial" composition. "America," Coolidge said tersely, "must be kept American." The president could chat and tell stories, but his silence on White House politics encouraged the press to call him "Silent Cal," a nickname that seemed to encourage more of the same. As one historian noted, the strongest dissent came from *Baltimore Sun* correspondent Frank R. Kent, who contended that Coolidge was unfit to be president and that the White House correspondents should quit playing along with his silent charade.[8]

Kent's critical dissent was published not in his newspaper but in one of the new generation of magazines appealing to postwar Americans. The monthly *American Mercury*, launched in 1924 by the Baltimore journalist

Henry Louis Mencken, welcomed such political commentary on postwar America as well as social and literary criticism. As such, the iconoclastic Mencken was at odds with numerous magazines that focused on what Harding had called "normalcy"—notably the mainstream *Saturday Evening Post*, the covers of which now frequently featured Norman Rockwell's paintings depicting scenes of domestic tranquility. In 1922, *Better Homes and Gardens* capitalized on Americans' domestic focus. Also that year, DeWitt Wallace published the first issue of his monthly *Reader's Digest*, appealing to the expanding and busy middle class by condensing other magazines' articles. Addressing the needs of readers too busy to keep up with daily newspapers, as well as those who sought interpretation of events, Henry Luce and Briton Hadden in 1923 introduced the first U.S. newsmagazine. Their *Time* met an apparent postwar need for encapsulation of current events. In 1925, Harold Ross, the wartime editor of the military *Stars and Stripes*, aimed to reach an audience of sophisticated readers with his weekly the *New Yorker*, a brilliantly edited showcase for talented writers of fiction, nonfiction, and poetry, as well as artists, whose humorous cartoons commented on big-city life.

Magazines and newspapers, while focusing on domestic topics, nonetheless carried some news of postwar Europe and rising tensions in Asia. In the postwar years, news agencies and larger newspapers maintained a slimmed staff of correspondents abroad, who reported on political and economic ramifications of the peace treaties, disarmament conferences, and economic summits. For the *New York Times*, Walter Duranty reported from Moscow about the political and social reforms dictated by the Communist regime of the USSR, the Union of Soviet Social Republics. Edwin Ware Hullinger with the United Press got an exclusive interview with the former Milan newspaper publisher, Benito Mussolini, who had emerged as a strongman to snuff out communists in postwar Italy. Some Americans contracted to work as freelancer journalists, among them Ernest Hemingway from Paris and Dorothy Thompson from Vienna.

Back home, few names in 1920s journalism attracted more attention than Henry Louis Mencken. Before launching the *American Mercury*, he had developed his social and political views as a newspaper journalist, war correspondent, and social critic for Baltimore's *Evening Sun*. At the same time he co-edited with George Jean Nathan the journal *Smart Set*, writing for the "civilized minority" of "normal, educated, well-disposed, unfrenzied, enlightened citizens." While Nathan usually confined his attention to theater and literature, Mencken unearthed hypocrisy and wartime greed. In the column he and Nathan shared, Mencken castigated hoglike businessmen who during the war had made "gigantic and wholly unearned fortunes" while others were "doing the fighting and paying" a $30 billion war debt, mostly to profiteers. In the context of socialist criticism, Mencken wanted "to prevent capital from making such an unmitigated hog of itself that even a people so docile as the Americans will rise up and destroy it."[9]

Mencken fashioned himself as a "destructive critic," regarding "constructive critics" such as Walter Lippmann and Herbert Croly as confused or disillusioned by the rejection of the Treaty of Versailles and most of Wilson's Fourteen Points. In his 1922 book, *Public Opinion*, Lippmann sharply revised his optimistic view of the public role in democratic politics, wavering between hope and despair. On one hand, he worried that, "The number of human problems on which reason is prepared to dictate is small." On the other, willful critics of falsehoods gave Lippmann hope. During the war, he said, "There was huge lying. There were men with the will to uncover it." In this vein, Mencken pledged that his monthly would "devote itself pleasantly to exposing the nonsensicality of all such hallucinations, particularly when they show a certain apparent plausibility."[10]

At the *Mercury,* Mencken pledged to battle what he considered the lunacies and "boobs" of the decade, taking up social and political criticism. His targets were many. He frequently criticized the press for cowardice, notably for its general acquiescence in the postwar Red hysteria. He had battled A. Mitchell Palmer and continued to fight the nativist, antialien movement. He ridiculed "idiotically utopian" ideas, including those of the Anti-Saloon League and Prohibition, religious fundamentalists, and antievolutionists. Regarding Washington, he scowled at light punishments meted out in the oil scandal to Attorney General Daugherty and "thugs and perjurers" in public office, noting that "A Congressman with his ears cut off, you may be sure, would not do it again."[11]

His iconoclasm attracted and offended readers and writers around the nation. In 1926, by his own count, he inspired more than 500 editorials, most of them jabbing back. Readers often responded with demeaning comments, sometimes likening him to lower creatures. Mencken relished the attention and mocked the criticism by publishing it with attributions. "I will content myself with the bald statement that he is a weasel," said one. Another described him as "this maggot, this ghoul of new-made graves, this buzzard." An editorial writer questioned Mencken's journalistic ethics, noting that "he seems above and beyond the cardinal principles enunciated by newspaper men recently in Washington, namely, 'truth, decency and fairness.'" Others, however, respected "the sage of Baltimore" for his erudite battle against hypocrisy. He especially inspired college students. Even in the South he had adherents, among them the budding journalist Ralph McGill, then a student at Vanderbilt University in Nashville. "Henry Mencken was of course our knight in shining armor who each month slew the dragons of dullness in the pulpits of Washington, the governor's office, the legislature and in the seats of the mighty generally."[12]

Mencken generally denigrated the South, populated in his mind by Confederates with a culture as barren as the Sahara. Segregation, he asserted, suppressed an authentic culture, that of the Negro. The *Uncle Remus* tales, Mencken contended, should be credited to African folk tradition rather than to their popularizer, *Atlanta Constitution* journalist Joel Chandler Harris. Take away those tales, said Mencken, and Chandler would be a fifth-rate author. Mencken recognized at least one oasis in the South's cultural desert. In praising the literary magazine, the *Fugitive*, published from 1922 to 1925 at Vanderbilt University in Nashville, he said it "constitutes, at one moment, the entire literature of Tennessee." A Vanderbilt student noted that the *Fugitive* staff publicized the laurel, but the comment "brought forth cries of rage and protest from a number of papers and critics outside Nashville."[13] Certainly among Mencken's harshest critics in the South were those sympathetic with or acquiescent about one of his targets, the lynch-mad Ku Klux Klan.

Although the Northern press led the fight against the Klan, at least three Southern newspapers in Tennessee, Georgia, and Alabama broke the silence common in the region's press with investigations that won them Pulitzer Prizes. In 1923, the *Commercial Appeal* in Memphis documented the Klan's nefarious activities with front-page stories together with J. P. Alley's cartoons of hooded Klansmen. The Klan's defeat in the 1923 city elections was credited in part to the newspaper. In 1925, Julian and Julia Harris at the *Columbus Enquirer-Sun* won the Pulitzer for their relentless anti-Klan efforts in Georgia. In 1927 the *Montgomery Advertiser* conducted a campaign against the Klan on its editorial pages. Occasionally an individual journalist took on the Klan, as did Ralph McGill at the *Nashville Banner*. All followed the lead of the *New York World*. There, executive editor Herbert Bayard Swope, turning to in-depth stories to compete with the *Times*, invested men and resources in a monumental crusade against the Klan. The *World* stories written by Roland Thomas were syndicated to more than two million readers of 18 daily papers, including one in the South, the *New Orleans Times-Picayune*. The series won the Pulitzer in 1921. While the series helped stop the Klan in New York City, some said the crusade helped the Klan recruit in the West and Midwest.[14]

Meanwhile, the passage of the Nineteenth Amendment encouraged women to seek political office. In West Virginia in 1922 and again in 1924, Izetta Jewell Brown Miller became the first woman south of the Mason-Dixon Line to run for the U.S. Senate. In 1924 she became the first woman to second the nomination of a presidential candidate, John W. Davis of West Virginia, at the Democratic national convention. Newspaper coverage of her Senate campaigns focused on the novelty of a widow running for national office. Brown underscored the gender issue by purposely emphasizing women's issues and a campaign theme of "mother-love in politics." "It sounds odd doesn't it," she said in 1922.

"But I am just old-fashioned enough to believe that the spirit of mother-love will never hurt a community, a state or a nation."[15]

The growth of the weekly black press in the 1920s reflected urgent social, economic, and political needs among the increasing urbanization of African Americans. As massive migration of blacks continued to populate the communities of the North and the segregated cities of the South and Midwest, the "race" weeklies focused on community news that was almost completely ignored by white-owned dailies. "The Negroes assert with reason that many injustices and many terrible events are often suppressed," wrote press critic and civil rights advocate Oswald Garrison Villard. The South's nine million Negroes, he underscored, "have no means of getting unbiased news to the American people," except through their own newspapers, which whites seldom read. "The only Negro, they declare, who can reach the first page of he great dailies is the Negro criminal; if there is occasional recognition of a great Negro musician or scientist, it is usually with surpassing condescension, as one admires a reading horse or a trained seal."[16]

Most of the race weeklies were in the North, but some were in border states, the South, and the Midwest. The oldest ongoing paper was the *Baltimore Afro-American,* joined by the *Chicago Defender,* the *Pittsburgh Courier,* the *Amsterdam News,* the *Norfolk Journal and Guide,* the *Kansas City Call,* and in 1928, the *Atlanta World,* which in 1932 became for one generation the nation's only Negro daily. Financed largely by advertising from the growing Negro commercial and professional communities, the weeklies' pages became a forum for the communities' social, religious, and educational developments as well as coverage of racial injustices. The black weeklies, augmented by the Associated Negro Press national service, carried the most complete stories about lynchings, Ku Klux Klan terror, and the political initiatives by the NAACP.

In the mainstream press, competitive forces accelerated the trend toward building media empires through mergers, consolidations, and cross-media ownership. Throughout the 1920s, numerous newspaper closings were criticized as the consequence of "a thirst for monopoly." In 1923, a critic in Oswald Garrison Villard's the *Nation* noted that two recently closed Pittsburgh newspapers, the *Dispatch* and the *Leader* had been victims of "newspaper cannibalism"—"purchased for the purpose of extinction by the five remaining dailies, on the avowed ground that there were too many newspapers in Pittsburgh for the successful conduct of all." The five remaining dailies were "practically under one control" of the family of Secretary of the Treasury Andrew Mellon.[17]

As the practice of buyouts became more common, so too did the deaths of familiar newspapers and layoffs of journalists. In 1924, Frank Munsey sold the *New York Herald,* which had been founded in 1835 as one of the first Penny Press newspapers. When the *Herald* was merged with Ogden Reid's *New York Tribune,* Villard mourned "the disappearance of an historic newspaper, the throwing out of work of hundreds of journalists and printers and the further narrowing of the field of metropolitan journalism."[18] The *Nation* in 1923 had vilified Munsey as having "the original patent on killing newspapers."[19] In his 1928 book, *The Disappearing Daily,* Villard, the *Nation's* editor, lamented what he saw as a steady decline in the vitality of American journalism, signaled by fewer newspapers owned by large groups; a lack of individuality; growing conformism dictated by media magnates; increasing preoccupation with entertainment, comics, and feature stories; and growing influence of advertising departments over editorial and news decisions.[20]

The economic advantages of media mergers inclined newspaper owners to buy radio stations or start new ones. By 1924, several news papers operated stations, notably in the Midwest, Southwest, and South, in Chicago, St. Louis, Detroit, Kansas City, Minneapolis, Dallas, Fort Worth, and Atlanta. The *Chicago Daily News* radio editor contended that the station resulted in "good will, that intangible, yet nevertheless invaluable asset for quasi-public institutions, such as newspapers." Direct profit was not the primary motive, he said. "Dollars may not directly follow from the pleasures experienced by listeners to programs broadcasted by newspapers, but the feeling of friendliness is there, and the friendship of the masses makes strength for the newspaper."[21]

While radio's advantage as a medium for news was underscored by coverage of election results and special events, most radio stations presented little regular news coverage. Without an investment in a news staff, broadcasters usually read from newspapers. In 1922, however, the *Atlanta Journal's* WSB gained national attention when an entertainment announcer, Lambdin Kay, interrupted concert music to announce news of a fire two blocks from the *Journal's* downtown building. The broadcast rallied firefighters. "This is probably the first time in the history of radio in the South," the *Journal* declared, "that news of a fire was broadcast from a station little more than a hundred yards from the flames itself." The *Literary Digest* amplified the historic significance. "The extent to which radio has invaded the newspaper world is illustrated in the reports from newspapers of widely scattered cities hundreds of miles from Atlanta."[22]

Less optimistic about radio's financial prospects, some newspapers retreated from broadcasting, including the *Chicago Tribune,* the *Minneapolis Tribune,* and the *Atlanta Constitution,* rival of the *Atlanta Journal.* The *Constitution* editor, Clark Howell, said his paper "quit broadcasting because, after we installed a station at great expense and operated it for a year, we reached the conclusion that the novelty had worn off."[23]

However, press attention to the novelty of radio accelerated its diffusion during the 1920s. Newspapers and magazines reported on every nuance and published listings of stations' programs and features about people in the emerging industry. "Much of the radio's popularity," one critic noted in 1923, "is due to the way the newspapers have been playing it up." He estimated that "without these published programs the broadcasting stations would be seriously handicapped."[24]

Magazine stories kept radio in the public discourse as a growing subject both fascinating and controversial. Many articles focused on audiences. In 1924 the new trade magazine *Radio Broadcast* reported the astonishment of cowboys who heard broadcasts over a simple radio set up at the rim of the Grand Canyon. *School and Society* magazine stressed the educational benefits, predicting that 15 million young people would be reached when the Radio Corporation of America in 1928 began weekly broadcasts of youth concerts "through a chain of twenty or more stations."[25]

The economic boom in the 1920s benefited newspapers and magazines and eventually radio stations and networks. In the first years, radio advertising was experimental and increased slowly until advertisers were persuaded of the extent of the unseen audience. There was as yet no method for measuring how many people listened to any one station at any one time. Another drawback was that these uncounted audiences were divided among hundreds of small stations. Stations interfered with each other's programs, which sometimes were indecipherable amid static.[26]

The movement to introduce commercials became controversial, meeting resistance from those who conceived of the airwaves as a "public medium" in which commercials were intruders. In 1922 one critic noted, "Driblets of advertising, most of it indirect so far, … are floating through the ether every day …. More of this sort of thing may be expected." Another wrote in 1923 that he was "opposed to the scheme principally because it is against good public policy." In 1925, Commerce Secretary Herbert Hoover asserted that "service to the listener" should be Congress's primary concern.[27]

Critics who valued programming criticized commercials. One objected to advertising on grounds of "public policy," arguing that people "should not be forced" to listen to advertising. Practically speaking, commercial interruptions would be self-defeating to advertisers: "An audience that has been wheedled into listening to a selfish message will naturally be offended."[28] While radio's advocates competed to emphasize diversity in programming—educational, religious, and classical music—many viewed advertising as a nuisance or a danger. "The woods are full of opportunists who are restrained by no scruples when the scene of profit comes down the wind," warned a broadcast enthusiast in 1922 as he urged national legislation to restrict commercials.[29]

Legislation was in the works. After chairing the Fourth National Radio Conference in 1925, U.S. Commerce Secretary Herbert Hoover made a radio broadcast to report the results. His talk presaged the direction of federal legislation. Responding to complaints about radio interference and static, he forecast fewer and better stations, each to be licensed by the federal government after demonstrating "that [the] operation will serve in the public interest .... The ether is a public medium and its use must be for a public benefit."[30]

The national debate culminated in the Radio Act of 1927, which essentially settled the major questions of ownership and content, including advertising. The act officially privatized radio broadcasting, which would now be licensed and regulated by a commission. The Radio Act established the ideal standard of serving the public interest. The licensing process aided the major broadcasters, who by the mid-1920s "saw that they would have to kick the educational and other non-commercial squatters off the valuable spectrum spaces which they occupied. In the process, public space created in radio would be collapsed in order to expand the technology's commercial applications." Entertainment, enshrined in variety shows, came to dominate programming, especially as the act eliminated numerous small, interfering stations serving what the press termed "special interests"—religion, education, or high culture.[31] Whereas several hundred broadcasters had operated nonprofit stations, the majority of them affiliated with colleges and universities, the Radio Act led a historic transition from nonprofit stations to commercial-driven national networks.

Radio's viability as a mass medium came as the public invested in radio receivers. The Radio Corporation of America (RCA), incorporated in 1919 with nearly all the assets of the Marconi Wireless Telegraph, enjoyed rapid growth with the advent of scheduled programming. From 1921 to 1923, RCA's gross income skyrocketed from $5 million to $26 million, including more than $22 million from the sale of radio apparatuses. In addition to this fortune, sales of receivers built a potential mass audience ripe for advances in programming. In 1926 RCA launched the first national radio network, the National Broadcasting Corporation (NBC).[32]

During the decade, as publishers watched warily, radio gained a significant share of national and local advertising dollars. After 1926, the linking of independent local audiences into the national networks of NBC and the Columbia Broadcasting System (CBS) further threatened to erode the financial base on which newspaper fortunes were built. Rather than battle radio, many publishers bought stations. At the network level, radio programmers competed fiercely to sign contracts with singers who would do well on radio, notably the mellow and romantic Harry Lillis "Bing" Crosby and the nightclub jazz of jiving "Hi De Ho" Cab Callaway from Harlem's Cotton Club.

Radio's innovators occasionally scored a coup in news coverage. In July 1925, WGN, owned by the *Chicago Tribune,* made the first live broadcast of a trial from a courthouse in Dayton, Tennessee, where a football coach and biology teacher, John Scopes, was being prosecuted for teaching Charles Darwin's theory of evolution. Equipped with rented AT&T cables that stretched from Chicago to Dayton, announcer Quinn Ryan and his broadcast crew were instant celebrities, permitted to locate four microphones to best advantage in the courtroom. For more than a week, about 200 journalists in the Rhea County Courthouse feasted on what H. L. Mencken called the "monkey trial," a first-rate showdown between evolutionists and "enlightened" Christians on one side and creationists on the other—or, more simply, between science and old-time religion.[33]

The test case had been arranged by Dayton citizens, in cooperation with the American Civil Liberties Union with teacher John Scopes, who agreed to become the challenging defendant. The citizens' group, hoping to attract tourists to their economically strapped town, succeeded mainly in gaining national attention from political, religious, legal, and press celebrities. The trial focused largely on William Jennings Bryan, the three-time Democratic presidential candidate who joined the prosecution team, and on Clarence Darrow, the famous criminal defense lawyer from Chicago.

Bryan had become the chief spokesman for "fundamentalist" Christians who maintained their belief in the biblical account of the six-day creation.[34] With Bryan's high-profile advocacy—his syndicated column was published widely in the South—fundamentalists in 1922 nearly passed such a law in Kentucky, losing by one vote. In 1923, Florida did pass an antievolution law. A similar Georgia bill died in 1924 after opposition from the publishers of the Columbus Enquirer-Sun, Julia and Julian Harris. H. L. Mencken later wrote to Julia Harris that "If you had not put up a battle against it, the chances are that it would have gone through with a bang."[35] In 1925, Tennessee's Butler Act banished the theory of evolution from public schools and colleges, outlawing "any theory that denies the story of the Divine Creation of man as taught in the Bible, and to teach instead that man has descended from a lower order of animals."[36]

Press and radio covered the trial as a spectacle. When Bryan walked into the courtroom on the first day, Ryan commented, "Here comes William Jennings Bryan. He enters now. His bald pate like a sunrise over Key West." H. L. Mencken called it "the Tennessee Circus." Characteristically biased and entertaining, Mencken got to the heart of what disturbed antievolutionists—the teaching of the descent of man from nonhuman primates, or simply monkeys. Taking that cue, Hearst's Atlanta Georgian editors sent reporter Mildred Seydell with a picture of a monkey's hand to compare it with the hands of Bryan, Darrow, and the Bible-toting judge, John T. Raulston. A Chicago Tribune cartoon portrayed monkeys supporting a proposition that "man is not related to the monkey.... The proposition would get a lot of support if monkeys could vote on it." A cartoon in the Dallas News portraying a wizened organ grinder whose monkey's cup was overflowing with coins of publicity suggested that Dayton was capitalizing on the trial "for all it's worth." [37]

Mencken labeled Bryan a "fundamentalist pope" and correctly predicted the trial's outcome after the jury was packed with admitted antievolutionists. Comparing Bible Belt fundamentalists with Red Scare anticommunists, he concluded, "It will be no more possible in this Christian valley to get a jury unprejudiced against Scopes than it would be possible in Wall Street to get a jury unprejudiced against a Bolshevik." Ultimately he concluded that Daytonians were even more offended that he wrote about the agitated and, to him, ludicrous religious rites of fundamentalists that he spied in the mountains—"the orgies of the Holy Rollers." As Mencken forecast, Scopes was convicted and fined $100, although an appeals court reversed both his conviction and fine. After the trial, the mob of journalists evacuated Dayton, missing a dramatic endnote when Bryan died days later. Mencken thought it sad that only one or two reporters remained, so that the obituary for the great orator, statesman, and presidential aspirant was "badly mishandled. If the old boy had died while the trial was going on he'd have been turned off much more competently, for many virtuosi were then on hand."[38]

The extent of the trial's media coverage acknowledged the importance of the religious and moral movement that had fostered Prohibition and aimed to regulate more aspects of American life. The creationism-versus-evolution debate, however, sprang from deeper sources. The general moral impulse now extended to mass media, evidenced by a growth of religious broadcasting, especially of Sunday services, Bible studies, and commentary. Inevitably, moral commentary targeted practices of the press.

The trustworthiness of journalists had been undermined by a number of internal and external factors. Partisanship, sensationalism, and yellow journalism had taken a toll over time, fueling doubts about accuracy and fairness. During and since the war, government propaganda and self-serving publicity had eroded reliability, as Mencken contended. The increasing impact of public-relations counselors raised questions about bias and the suppression of news unfavorable to clients and advertisers. There were allegations that journalists took bribes as well as criticism that publishers, amassing fortunes and chains of newspapers, were primarily mercenary. Had the remarkable growth of the press as a business enterprise been achieved at the expense of the development of professionalism and truth?

Certainly politicians recognized the political impact of the newspaper chains. In 1930, Franklin Roosevelt, as Democratic governor of New York, kept in touch with publishers in both parties. On one hand, he corresponded with James M. Cox, the Ohio newspaper publisher and 1920 Democratic presidential candidate, Roosevelt's running mate. On the other hand, Roosevelt was corresponding with Frank E. Gannett, the publisher of a string of Republican newspapers in upstate New York. Since 1906, Gannett had been buying and merging newspapers, notably Rochester's *Evening Times* and *Union and Advertiser*, which he merged into the *Times-Union*. Together with his development of both the Teletypesetter and faster and cheaper engraving, he was wealthy and politically active when Roosevelt wrote to deny a request, ask a favor, and invite Gannett to the capital to "talk over many things." After several riots in state prisons had focused press and public attention on poor conditions, Gannett's papers requested access to interview prisoners. Roosevelt told Gannett that previous requests by Hearst's papers, Pulitzer's *New York World*, the *New York Times*, and the *Daily Graphic* had been denied because "it would be very unwise" to "talk with the prisoners themselves." Instead, Roosevelt said he "would be delighted to have you run a series of articles telling about actual prison conditions. The more plain and unvarnished truth that can be told, the better. By doing this we shall the sooner get better prison accommodations, and at the same time get improvements in the present laws." A key reason for not allowing prisoner interviews, he explained, was his distrust of newspaper sensationalism when "prisoners take great delight in filling reporters full of all sorts of gory details."[39]

Critics of newspaper and broadcasting ethics had begun urging the adoption of industry-wide codes, not unlike those being adopted by professional baseball after the 1919 World Series fix and, more recently, by Hollywood's besieged moviemakers. The unregulated content of movies and risqué misconduct by movie stars had led to organized public opposition demanding restrictions on the industry. Filmdom's leaders, aiming to avoid government regulation, responded in 1922 by founding an industry oversight agency, the Motion Picture Producers and Distributors of America (MPPDA). Following the baseball owners' lead in hiring a rock-honest judge to houseclean the sport of gamblers and co-conspirators, the moviemakers chose a president esteemed for his religious and political credentials. The new "decency czar" was Will Hays, who had been a national lay leader in the Presbyterian Church, a Republican national chairman, and was now President Harding's postmaster general. His "Hays Office" held the last word on content and could prevent a Hollywood movie from being released. The industry leaders hoped its code of ethics would, as one historian has noted, "project an image of professionalism that would make additional regulation by outsiders appear to be unnecessary." Like baseball club owners, movie moguls also regarded self-regulation as insurance for continued box-office profits.[40]

Like their counterparts in Hollywood, newspaper publishers preferred their own industry solution rather than risk government meddling with the First Amendment. In 1923, criticism of the press rose to the level of the White House as President Harding addressed the issue of journalistic ethics with the American Society of Newspaper Editors (ASNE). At the same time that his administration was defending against accusations of corrupt practices, the president took the offensive, urging the editors to adopt the code of ethics already under consideration. That year, the ASNE approved the Canons of Journalism, declaring it was "an effort to raise the standards of journalism." The canons first addressed responsibility: "A journalist who uses his power for any selfish or otherwise unworthy purpose is faithless to a high trust." The other six sections addressed freedom of the press, independence, sincerity, truthfulness and accuracy, impartiality, fair play, and decency. However, ASNE, which was comprised of daily newspaper editors in cities above 50,000 in population, did not provide for enforcement and specific penalties. Editors relied instead on the "hope that deliberate pandering to vicious instincts will encounter effective public disapproval or yield to the influence of a professional condemnation." Critics noted that the society was "powerless—and by its own decision—to expel the blackest criminal who might have found his way into its membership."[41]

At national and state levels, organizations and codes of conduct indicated an impulse toward standardization and professionalism. The Washington press corps, grown larger in the postwar years, tended to police its ranks more carefully. In Washington, following the lead of the White House Correspondents Association, which screened reporters, a News Photographers Association admitted only accredited photographers. Excluded from the men's organizations, women maintained their own. In 1922, revitalized by the arrival of women's suffrage, women founded the Women's National Press Club as a successor to the Women's National Press Association founded in 1882. In 1926, the Society of Professional Journalists, founded in 1908, adopted the ASNE code of ethics. State press associations multiplied. After the first in Kansas in 1910, Missouri and Texas followed in 1921, South Dakota and Oregon in 1922, and Washington in 1923.[42] "One of the agreeable spiritual phenomena is the soul-searching now in progress among American journalists," H. L. Mencken wrote in 1924, a year after the ASNE adopted its code of ethics. He credited the rise in virtue to increased prosperity and financial independence, dating from profitable coverage of the terrible war. With incomes raised, reporters were less inclined to pad their salaries by taking bribes. And as businesses competed for space, business managers were less likely to suppress news distasteful to advertisers. As a result, Mencken asserted, "The liberated journalist, taking huge sniffs of free air, began to think of himself as professional man."[43]

Part of this impulse toward professionalism favored the development of a generation of better-educated journalists. The movement for structured journalism education, accelerated by Pulitzer, had by 1930 reached into more than 200 colleges and universities, financed in part by the publishers' fortunes to which Mencken alluded.[44] Income in the millions was no longer unusual. In 1926, the *New York Times* reported its gross annual income at $25 million with a yearly payroll of $7 million.[45] The schools' graduates increased in both quantity and quality. In 1924, the University of Missouri's School of Journalism graduated its largest class, 90 students. The University of Oregon's school proudly announced that one of its journalism seniors won a Rhodes Scholarship to Oxford.[46] By 1930, the *New Republic* noted, "Every up-and-coming American university nowadays has a department of journalism, and some of them possess full-fledged schools, housed in handsome edifices of their own." It reported that in an ASNE survey asking editors if the schools were making "better journalists," 75 editors replied yes, 12 no, and 15 were uncommitted.[47]

Critics who had scoffed at Pulitzer's vision for journalism schools were still active in 1930. "What we want is men who are not so mechanically perfect as to have lost all individuality, initiative, and independence," one editor stated. The *New Republic* writer sided with critics who still argued that journalism did not meet the test for a true profession and that a liberal education prepared a man better than "journalistic technique."[48] "What ails these schools of journalism," concluded the acerbic Mencken, was that they were "simply trade schools" and were "seldom manned by men of any genuine professional standing, or of any firm notion of what journalism is about."[49] Some educators agreed. Amid "widespread and well-founded opinion that all is not well with the thousands of students receiving journalism instruction," the Pulitzer School's director called for a national inquiry.[50]

The professoriate, responding to critics, were banding together nationally to differentiate themselves from technique-centered schools by supporting higher standards for journalism education. The Association of American Schools and Departments of Journalism (AASDJ), formed in 1917, and the allied American Association of Teachers of Journalism (AATJ) had by 1924 grown into a substantial cadre of academics concerned with improving the discipline's quality. The 1924 AASDJ conference in Chicago was led by Willard Grosvenor Bleyer of the University of Wisconsin, an influential pioneer in the schools movement who would soon publish his history text asserting the interdependency of journalism education, journalism, and democracy. The two associations banded together to publish their proceedings, as well as a bibliography of current books and articles about journalism. The premier 1924 *Journalism Bulletin* included the AATJ convention guest presentation by the noted foreign correspondent of the *Chicago Daily News*, Edward Price Bell, on his specialty, "The Interview."[51]

The associations stressed their preeminence over trade schools. At its 1924 meeting the AASDJ resolved that education for the proper practice of journalism was as important as preparation for careers in law or medicine. The well-rounded curriculum in the university schools would prepare the journalist to report events in a context that would promote understanding. That year the academic associations won the profession's endorsement of university curriculum and "against courses in journalism not a part of a school of journalism." At the ASNE convention, a committee of editors declared that academic and professional training for journalism should be part of a "complete course at a university school of journalism leading to a degree" or take place at "a summer school of journalism maintained by a recognized institution of learning and supplementing the regular college course." The ASNE also endorsed graduate schools "to the end that their educational standards shall be on a par with those maintained at the best schools of law and medicine."[52]

The inclusion of journalism in university curricula encouraged the development of methodical research about America's mass media. In the short span of a decade, dozens of scholars began research in journalistic practices, history, propaganda, and public relations. Others studied the diffusion of visual communication through newsreels and photographs. The soaring popularity of talkie films also accelerated the dissemination of national and international news through newsreels shown in the theaters. Tabloid newspapers' use of photographs in greater numbers and sizes encouraged a new generation of photographers to depart from the traditional model of the art photograph.

Coverage of murder trials, witnesses, and defendants provided tabloids with profitable photographic opportunities. In January 1928, Tom Howard strapped a camera to his left leg and got the sensational photograph of convicted murderess Ruth Snyder as the current jolted her body in the electric chair at Sing Sing, a picture that sold an extra 500,000 copies of the New York *Daily News*.[53] During the 1926 trial of Florence Hall for the murder of her husband and his mistress, the *Daily News* in 20 days published almost as many column inches of pictures (2,138.5) as news stories (2,991.5). "The *News* plunged knee-deep into the story with unblushing gusto," wrote Silas Bent in the *New Republic*. Hearst's competing New York *Mirror* took on a quasi-detective role, finding witnesses and gathering "practically all the evidence on which the prosecution relied." By contrast, the *New York Times* published few pictures (209.5 column inches), but the most news (4,893), "squeezing in more words to the column inch than any of its competitors."[54] Hidden cameras also invaded the sanctuaries of the elite. Notable was the use of the triggered camera to gain a glimpse of European diplomats during one of many secret conferences. Magazines also used photographs inventively, as in *Vogue*'s displays of fashions.

Several of the new magazines catered to the Jazz Age appetite for openness in sexual matters. "Prudery lies slain, false modesty has expired," media critic Oswald Garrison Villard observed in 1926, referring sarcastically to "the rise of a great new American literature, 'throbbing with personality,' 'baring the human soul in all its elemental passions,' letting in the light upon all mysteries of sex, and serving its country by brushing aside the last of our mid-Victorian reserves, reticences and retirements."[55]

One ruler in the regime of new magazines was the publishing millionaire Bernarr Macfadden, whose publishing empire was headquartered in a six-story building at 1926 Broadway. Banking on the success of his *Physical Culture* magazine, Macfadden launched in 1919 the monthly *True Story*, followed by *Movie Weekly, True Romances, Dream World, Fiction Lovers, Dance Lovers, Radio Stories, True Detective Mysteries,* and *Modern Marriage,* all selling by his accounts in the tens or hundreds of thousands of copies. He also acquired newspapers in Philadelphia, Detroit, and other cities and in 1926 launched a new tabloid newspaper, the New York *Evening Graphic.* His tabloid traded in eye-catching front-page headlines: "Pretty Girl Has Three Hubbies"; "Cop Dying, 4 Bandits Shot"; and "Heiress Penniless in Cell as Check and Jewel Crook." Villard conceded that the "true story" genre "succeeds because there was a real need of simple, straightforward—if you please, melodramatic—stories." Like it or not, the new Macfadden publications and their imitators represented "a readers' revolt against the conventional and sophisticated story which ornaments the pages of the more sedate and conservative magazines."[56]

Tabloid journalism and radio broadcasting did much to popularize jazz and jazz musicians and underscore the characterization of the decade as the Jazz Age. The mainstreaming of jazz on the radio legitimized and nationalized the music, despite mixed feelings toward the music, which was usually associated with Prohibition-era speakeasies and dives serving illicit liquor. While some segments of society revered the music, others objected to the musicians' morals. In Cincinnati, a jazz club was deemed a nuisance when it tried to locate near a home for girls. Teachers of classical piano frequently lamented that pupils wanted to play jazz riffs rather than sonatas.

In the African American community, disagreement was sharp. Few elites accepted improvisational jazz as having redeeming musical or social value. Carter G. Woodson, who as founder of the *Journal of Negro History* and Negro History Week was a cultural arbiter, considered jazz—and associated behaviors of drinking and dancing—so deleterious to the image of the Negro race that the music ought to be silenced. "Persons who are concerned with social progress then must take steps to restrict jazz and stamp it out as an evil," he wrote from Paris in October 1933 in his syndicated column published in the Baltimore *Afro-American.*

Woodson conceded that "Hitler, in spite of his otherwise questionable acts, achieved well when he drove the jazz element from Germany." Woodson prayed that jazzmen be put to death: "Would to God that [Hitler] had the power...to round up all jazz promoters and performers of both races in Europe and America and execute them as criminals." Even those who might tolerate the playing of jazz could hardly condone the lifestyles associated with illicit drinking in speakeasies and night clubs, promiscuous women, erotic dancing, and related vices assumed to involve bootleggers and mobsters.[57]

Woodson targeted the African American press for encouraging such behavior. Throughout the 1920s, these urban weekly newspapers featured the lifestyles of Negro jazzmen, especially celebrities who had gone to play to appreciative audiences in London and Paris. Beginning in 1919, trumpeter Sidney Bechet, then 22, scored triumphs in London with the Southern Syncopated Orchestra and in 1925 arrived in Paris. "It seems bizarre," wrote his biographer, "that Sidney Bechet had to travel to Europe to receive the sort of expert acclaim that was worthy of his vast talents." In 1928 the Noble Sissle Band, playing at the Ambassadeurs in Paris, was so popular that it "was held over indefinitely." Sissle's "blue-book" of autographed plaudits "is the talk of European social circles." Some African American women also found an appreciative audience. In 1925, the gorgeous Josephine Baker arrived in Paris with the Revue Nègre, in which Bechet was playing. Within months, Baker left the group to gain fame singing and dancing in the Folies Bergère and in time chose to become a French citizen. Her experience, declared the *Chicago Defender*, "shows the democratic spirit of the French people who always recognize beauty and merit wherever they find it."[58]

Celebrity watching was a new phenomenon in African American society, and the press and the public seemed appreciative. Editors capitalized on the exploits of entertainers who were finding a way to make a living and seemed to be breaking some of segregation's color barriers. They tracked the successes of Louis "Satchmo" Armstrong and the rise of Ethel Waters from a dishwasher and waitress to a singer at Harlem's famous Cotton Club, on the radio, and on Broadway. By the late 1920s the newspapers grouped jazz stories on designated entertainment pages such as the Baltimore *Afro-American*'s "Looking at the Stars" or the *Norfolk Journal and Guide*'s "Trailing the Stars—Radio—Screen—Stage."[59]

African American newspapers also had serious concerns. On a more-or-less regular basis these papers reported hundreds of lynchings in the Southern states. As recorded by the Tuskegee Institute in Alabama, the NAACP, and others, more than 2,800 persons, most of them black, were killed by lynch mobs from the 1880s through the 1920s. More so than the white press, the African American newspapers reported graphic details. Such publicity was building support for another federal antilynching law such as the one that Congress had not passed in 1919, the year after 60 blacks were lynched.[60]

While the black press struggled to maintain its voice, the establishment press continued the trend toward mergers and monopolies. In the Midwest, the former gas-company executive and congressman Ira Clifton Copley had been acquiring newspapers in Illinois since 1905. In 1928, at the age of 63, he challenged the record-setting buying sprees of Munsey and Hearst. As his biographer recorded, Copley concluded "one of the greatest mass newspaper purchases ever made.... Probably no publisher has acquired so many newspapers in so short a time as Colonel Copley did in the first half of 1928." He extended his Illinois chain to the West Coast, purchasing the morning San Diego *Union* and the San Diego *Evening Tribune* from the estate of John D. Spreckels, who died in 1926, as well as control of 16 other California dailies. Since 1905, he had bought 24 newspapers in the two states. In moving into San Diego, Copley became a part of a new generation of newspaper owners following the colorful era when Speckles's papers had dueled with the dailies of E. W. Scripps.[61]

NOTES

1. Harding purchased the *Marion Daily Star* in Marion, Ohio, in the 1880s. He and his wife, Florence Kling Harding, increased circulation and made the paper influential. Harding was elected a state senator in 1899, served as lieutenant governor from 1903 to 1905, and was defeated in a bid for governor in 1910 but won the election to the U.S. Senate in 1914. In 1920, Harding became the first sitting senator to be elected president, after which he sold the newspaper in the late winter or early spring of 1923.

2. Stephen Ponder, "That Delightful Relationship: Presidents and the White House Correspondents in the 1920s," *American Journalism* 14 (2): 166, 174–75. See also Elmer C. Cornwell Jr., *Presidential Leadership of Public Opinion* (Bloomington: Indiana University Press, 1965); J. Frederick Essary, *Covering Washington: Government Reflected to the Public in the Press* (Boston: Houghton Mifflin, 1927); James K. Pollard, *The Presidents and the Press* (New York: Macmillan, 1947). During the first month of Harding's administration, his friendly attitude toward journalists was reported in the new trade journal *Editor & Publisher.*

3. Ponder, "That Delightful Relationship," 171–72.

4. "Sinclair Consolidated in Big Oil Deal with U.S.; Contract Signed with Government and Sinclair Oil Interests for Development of Teapot Dome in Wyoming; Dome Estimated to Contain 150,000,000 to 200,000,000 Barrels of High-Grade Oil," *Wall Street Journal*, April 14, 1922, 1. Payoffs to Interior Secretary Albert Fall were revealed later.

5. B. Noggle, *Teapot Dome Oil and Politics in the 1920s* (New York: W. W. Norton, 1965); James Leonard Bates, *The Origins of Teapot Dome: Progressive Parties and Petroleum, 1909–1921* (1963; repr., Westport, CT: Greenwood Press,

1978); Hasia Diner, "Teapot Dome, 1924," in *Congress Investigates: A Documented History, 1792–1974,* ed. Arthur M. Schlesinger Jr. and Roger A. Bruns (New York: Chelsea House Publishers, 1975); Hofstadter, *The Age of Reform,* 286; White, *Autobiography,* 620.

6. White, *Autobiography,* 618; Ponder, "That Delightful Relationship," 172–73. Harding told White that "every day at three-thirty, here in the midst of the affairs of state, I go to press on the Marion Star. I wonder what kind of layout the boys have got on the first page. I wonder how much advertising there is …. I would like to walk out in the composing room and look over the forms before they go to the stereotyper. There never was a day in all the years that I ran the paper that I didn't get some thrill out of it."

7. Walter Lippmann to S. K. Ratcliffe, November 3, 1923, in *Selected Letters,* 156; White, *Autobiography,* 632.

8. Ponder, "That Delightful Relationship," 174–75. See Frank R. Kent, "Mr. Coolidge," *American Mercury,* August 1924, 385–90.

9. George Jean Nathan and H. L. Mencken, "Repetition Generale," *Smart Set,* March 1921, 40, 42; Edgar Kemler, *The Irreverent Mr. Mencken* (Boston: Atlantic Monthly Press, 1950), 155–64.

10. H. L. Mencken, "Editorial," *American Mercury,* January 1924, 27; Walter Lippmann to Ray Stannard Baker, January 2, 1922, in *Selected Letters,* 143–44; Lippmann, *Public Opinion,* 417–18; Benjamin F. Wright, *Five Public Philosophies of Walter Lippmann* (Austin: University of Texas Press, 1973), 38, 57.

11. Mencken, "Editorial," January 1924, 27; H. L. Mencken, "Editorial," *American Mercury,* June 1924, 155–60; Kemler, *The Irreverent Mr. Mencken,* 156.

12. The three criticisms were attributed to Samuel R. Guard on WLS radio, Eugene L. Pearce in the *Tampa Times,* and an editorial writer in the *Omaha World-Herald;* they are cited in H. L. Mencken, *Menckeniana: A Schimpflexikon* (1928; repr., New York: Octagon Books, 1977), i, 1, 60; Ralph McGill, *The South and the Southerner* (Boston: Atlantic Monthly Press, 1963), 77–78.

13. Marie Hardin, "Georgia Journalism and H. L. Mencken: The Rewards and Perils of 'Southbaiting,'" paper presented at the Association for Education in Journalism and Mass Communication, Southeast Colloquium, Lexington, Kentucky, 5 March 1999; McGill, *The South and the Southerner,* 80.

14. Rodger Streitmatter, "Defying the Ku Klux Klan: Three 1920s Newspapers Challenge the Most Powerful Nativist Movement in American History," paper presented to the History Division, Association for Education in Journalism and Mass Communication, August 10, 1996; Hardin, "Georgia Journalism and H. L. Mencken"; Leonard Ray Teel, *Ralph Emerson McGill: Voice of the Southern Conscience* (Knoxville: University of Tennessee Press, 2001), 35.

15. "Presidential Bee Is Buzzing in Izetta Jewel's Bonnet," *West Virginia Wheeling Intelligencer,* March 31, 1926, 4; "Mrs. Brown in Senate Race," *West Virginia Wheeling Intelligencer,* June 22, 1922, 1. Both are cited in Sharon Wills Brescoach, "The Press and Political Patronization: A Historical Study of the Coverage of Izetta Jewel Brown Miller, 1920s Woman Politician," unpublished paper presented at AEJMC Southeast Colloquium, Lexington, KY, March 4, 1999.

16. Oswald Garrison Villard, "The Press Today: The Associated Press," *Nation,* 16 April 1930, 443–44.

17. "More Newspaper Cannibalism," *Nation,* February 28, 1923, 232.

18. "Munsey Destroys Another Daily," *Nation,* March 26, 1924, 334. In the 1920s, under editor and owner Oswald Garrison Villard, the *Nation* was a leading voice criticizing the decline of diversity in the newspaper field.

19. Oswald Garrison Villard, "Frank A. Munsey: Dealer in Dailies," *Nation,* June 20, 1923, 713. Villard recalled that a cartoon in 1916 in *Life* (predating Henry A. Luce's *Life* magazine) showed "a cemetery of newspapers and magazines slain by Mr. Munsey." The tombstones memorialized four newspapers in New York, one in Philadelphia, and several other publications. Villard added *Godey's* and *Peterson's,* two of America's oldest magazines.

20. Oswald Garrison Villard, *The Disappearing Daily: Chapters in American Newspaper Evolution* (New York: Alfred A. Knopf, 1944).

21. Winfield Barton, "What Broadcasting Does for a Newspaper," *Radio Broadcast,* February 1924, 344–45.

22. "A Newspaper Radio 'Beat,'" *Literary Digest,* October 21, 1922, 27–28.

23. Barton, "What Broadcasting Does for a Newspaper," 344–45.

24. "Shall We Advertise by Radio?" *Literary Digest,* May 26, 1923, 27.

25. Thomas H. McKee, "When Cowboys Heard Bedtime Stories: An Adventure in Receiving at a Grand Canyon Dead Spot," *Radio Broadcast,* February 1924, 338–40; "Radio Educational Program of Walter Damrosch," *School and Society,* August 4, 1928, 138; Walter Damrosch, "Radio and Music Education," *NEA Journal,* November 1928, 11–12.

26. Orange Edward McMeans, "The Great Invisible Audience," *Scribner's,* April 1923, 410–16; "The March of Radio: Real Information on the Size of Radio Audiences," *Radio Broadcast,* April 1924, 468–69.

27. Joseph H. Jackson, "Should Radio Be Used for Advertising?" *Radio Broadcast,* November 1922, 72–76; "Shall We Advertise by Radio?"; "Hoover on the Ether's 'Howls and Growls,'" *Literary Digest,* December 19, 1925, 45; Robert McChesney, "Conflict, Not Consensus: The Debate over Broadcast Communication Policy, 1930–1935," in *Ruthless Criticism: New Perspectives in U.S. Communication History,* ed William S. Solomon and Robert W. McChesney (Minneapolis: University of Minnesota Press, 1993), 224. McChesney cites Edward F. Sarno, "The National Radio Conferences," *Journal of Broadcasting* 13 (2): 189–202, and Carl J. Friedrich and Jeannette Sayre, *The Development of the Control of Advertising on the Air* (New York: Radiobroadcasting Research Project, 1940).

28. "Shall We Advertise by Radio?"

29. Jackson, "Should Radio Be Used for Advertising?" 76; "The Church's New Voice," *Outlook,* May 28, 1924, 131–32; Jennie Irene Mix, "The Listeners' Point of View: How Shall We Get Great Artists to Broadcast?" *Radio Broadcast,* May 1924, 11–17; Robert H. Moulton, "Linking the Farmer with His Market: How the Chicago Board of Trade Brings the Wheat Pit to the Farm," *Radio Broadcast,* July 1924, 261–65; "Radio—the New Social Force," *Outlook,* March 19, 1924, 465–67.

30. "Hoover on the Ether's 'Howls and Growls,'" 45.

31. Elaine Prostak Berland, "'Up in the Air': Re-considering the Cultural Origins of Broadcasting and the Myth of Entertainment During the 1920s," *American Journalism* 9 (3–4): 63–64.

32. John Morrow, "Radio—a New Field for Investment: An Analysis of the Industry and Three Companies Whose Shares Are in the Public Eye," *Radio Broadcast,* September 1924, 373–78.

33. Subsequently, the Scopes case was called the "Trial of the Century." In retrospect, the case provided insights into the media's impact on court cases, the separation of church and state, freedom of speech, the judicial system, regional differences, community standards in developing teaching curricula, reasons for individual or regional economic success, great speeches, and the art of oration. Public Broadcasting System, "The Monkey Trial: Teacher's Guide: Suggestions for Active Learning," 1999, http://www.pbs.org/wgbh/amex/monkeytrial/tguide/index.html.

34. The term "fundamentalist" derived from *The Fundamentals,* a monumental series of 12 volumes of articles written by eminent clergy, theologians, and professors and published between 1909 and 1915 in rebuttal of modernism. To the publishing committee, a "fundamentalist" was a Christian who accepted without compromise the essential doctrines of Christianity. The popularity of the series continued after the committee had distributed the volumes to 300,000 ministers of the Gospel, missionaries, and Sunday school superintendents. The work was continued by the King's Business, a Los Angeles publishing house, and in 1917 the articles were reprinted in four volumes by the Bible Institute of Los Angeles; in 1993, a new edition was published by Baker Books of Grand Rapids, Michigan. Essentially, as one modern critic noted, the articles "laid out the case for Christian orthodoxy, and provided a body of argument for the opponents of modernism." Peter J. Boyer, "The Big Tent: Billy Graham, Franklin Graham, and the Transformation of American Evangelicalism," *New Yorker,* August 22, 2005, 45. See also the Fundamentals home page, http://www.xmission.com/~fidelis.

35. H. L. Mencken, "Editorial," *American Mercury,* September 1925, 16; Ray Ginger, *Six Days or Forever? Tennessee vs. John Thomas Scopes* (Boston: Beacon Press, 1958), 24; H. L. Mencken to Julia Collier Harris, August 4, 1925, in Julian La Rose Harris Collection, Special Collections, Robert W. Woodruff Library, Emory University, Atlanta, Georgia, cited in Hardin, "Georgia Journalism and H. L. Mencken"; Charles Pekor, "An Adventure in Georgia," *American Mercury,* August 1926, 410.

36. "The Tennessee Anti-evolution Act (1925)," in *Education versus Creationism: The Public Education Controversy,* ed. J. Peter Zetterberg (Phoenix, Arizona: Oryx Press, 1983), 386.

37. Ryan Quinn, WGN transcript, Public Broadcasting System, "The Monkey Trial: People and Events: WGN Radio Broadcasts the Trial," 1999, http://www.pbs.org/wgbh/amex/monkeytrial/peopleevents/e_wgn.html; H. L. Mencken, "The Tennessee Circus," *Evening Sun* (Baltimore), June 15, 1925; Fred Hobson, *H. L. Mencken: A Life* (New York: Random House, 1994), 256; Mildred Seydell, "Hands Never Lie," Mildred Seydell Papers, Special Collections, Robert W. Woodruff Library, Emory University, Atlanta, Georgia, cited in Marie Hardin, "Mildred Seydell" (MA thesis, Georgia State University, 1995), 22–23. Other cartoons can be found on Douglas O. Linder, "Famous Trials,": http://www.law.umkc.edu/faculty/projects/ftrials/scopes/SCOPES.HTM

38. H. L. Mencken, *Evening Sun* (Baltimore), July 9, 1926, reprinted in *D-Days at Dayton,* ed. Jerry R. Tompkins (Baton Rouge: Louisiana State University Press, 1965), 37; Hardin, "Georgia Journalism and H. L. Mencken"; H. L. Mencken, *Thirty-five Years of Newspaper Work: A Memoir,* ed. Fred Hobson, Vincent Fitzpatrick, and Bradford Jacobs (Baltimore: Johns Hopkins University Press, 1994), 141–42. Although the Tennessee appeals court reversed the conviction, it upheld the Butler Act.

39. Franklin D. Roosevelt to Frank E. Gannett, January 4, 1930, in *F.D.R.: His Personal Letters,* ed. Elliott Roosevelt (New York: Duell, Sloan and Pearce, 1947–1950), 3:99–100. Throughout the 1930s, Gannett's chain strengthened, largely by his creation of the Gannett Foundation. He became nationally prominent as an opponent of President Roosevelt's New Deal, was nominated for New York governor in 1935, and became a candidate for the Republican presidential nomination in 1940. "Portrait," *World's Work,* February 1932, 53; "Gannett Chain Gets Eighteenth Link," *News-Week,* May 19, 1934, 29; "Publisher Insures Future of His Newspaper Chain," *News-Week,* October 5, 1935, 34–35; Frank E. Gannett, "America's Future," *Vital Speeches,* June 1, 1939, 497–500; "How Much Press freedom? Controversy over Debate between Gannett and Ickes," *New Republic,* January 25, 1939, 329.

40. "The Will Hays Papers," ed. Douglas Gomery and John O'Connor, University of Maryland, Cinema History Microfilm Series, http://www.lexisnexis.com/academic/2upa/Apc/WillHaysPapers.asp; Wm. David Sloan, "Historians and the American Press, 1900–1945: Working Profession or Big Business?" *American Journalism* 3 (3): 154; John P. Ferré, "Codes of Ethics: Efforts to Promote Image of Professionalism," in *History of the Mass Media in the United States,* ed. Margaret A. Blanchard (Chicago: Fitzroy Dearborn, 1998), 144–45. The professional baseball club owners chose Judge Kennesaw Mountain Landis, who promptly banned without parole all Chicago White Sox players allegedly involved with gamblers in fixing the World Series.

41. Harding's address to the ASNE was newsworthy for his denial of wrongful conduct with bankers. "No Banker Swayed Him, Says Harding," *New York Times,* April 29, 1923, 1, cited in Ponder, "The Delightful Relationship," 172; "Canons of Journalism, Adopted by the American Society of Newspaper Editors, April 1923," *World's Work,* November 1924, 45; Willis J. Abbot, "The A.S.N.E. and Its Ethical Code," *New Republic,* May 22, 1929, 15–16.

42. Ponder, "The Delightful Relationship," 170–71; Ferré, "Codes of Ethics," 145.

43. H. L. Mencken, "Editorial," *American Mercury,* October 1924, 155.

44. Among the donors after Pulitzer were the Tribune Company in Chicago, which supported Northwestern University's Medill School; the *Minneapolis Tribune* publisher William Murphy, who bequeathed $350,000 to the University of Minnesota; and Ward Neff, whose gift made possible a separate journalism building at the University of Missouri. Brad Asher, "The Professional Vision: Conflicts over Journalism Education, 1900–1955," *American Journalism* 11 (4): 306.

45. "Statistics of the *New York Times,*" *New York Times,* 75th anniversary number, May 12, 1926, 34.

46. "Notes on the Schools: Missouri's Largest Class," and "Another Rhodes Scholar," *Journalism Bulletin* 1 (1924): 9.

47. "Why Schools of Journalism?" *New Republic*, October 9, 1930, 283–84.

48. Ibid.

49. Mencken, "Editorial," October 1924, 158.

50. "Why Schools of Journalism?" 283.

51. Edward Price Bell, "The Interview," *Journalism Bulletin* 1 (1924): 13–18; The same issue (p. 8) recorded the town-to-gown movement of former journalists into academe: One now headed the journalism department at the University of North Dakota, Grand Forks, and a former newspaperman from Indiana, John E. Stempel, was in charge of journalism at Lafayette College in Easton, Pennsylvania, where "courses in copy reading and feature writing have been added."

52. "Profession Approves Schools," *Journalism Bulletin* 3 (1926): 17.

53. Simon M. Bessie, *Jazz Journalism: The Story of the Tabloid Newspapers* (New York: E. P. Dutton, 1938), 117.

54. Silas Bent, "The Hall-Mills Case in the Newspapers," *New Republic*, December 8, 1926, 581.

55. Oswald Garrison Villard, "Sex, Art, Truth and Magazines," *Atlantic Monthly*, March 1926, 388, 390, 396.

56. "Bernarr Macfadden, the Father of Physical Culture," http://www.bernarrmacfadden.com; Villard, "Sex, Art, Truth and Magazines," 396.

57. Carter G. Woodson, "Has Jazz Been a Help or a Hindrance to Racial Progress?" *Afro-American* (Baltimore), October 14, 1933, 18; see also Leonard Ray Teel, "The Jazz Rage: Carter G. Woodson's Culture War in the African-American Press," *American Journalism* 11 (4): 348–50.

58. John Chilton, *Sidney Bechet: The Wizard of Jazz* (New York: Oxford University Press, 1987), 35–40; "Sissle and Band Will Remain at Ambassadeurs," *Amsterdam News*, August 29, 1928, 7; "Negro Entertainers in Europe," *Amsterdam News*, September 2, 1928, 6; "Chooses France," *Chicago Defender*, July 23, 1932, 20; Chilton, *Bechet*, 73–77; "French Mannequin," *Chicago Defender*, July 17, 1932, 1.

59. During the Depression, Waters was earning a fabulous $7,000 a week. "Ethel Waters Wins Laurels in New Show; Star of Palais Royal Floor Show in New York," *Norfolk Journal and Guide*, February 10, 1934, 14; "Ethel Waters at a Mere Trifle of $7,000 per Week," *Norfolk Journal and Guide*, February 24, 1934, 13; Ralph Matthews, "Looking at the Stars," Baltimore *Afro-American*, 21 October 1933, 18; Allan McMillan, "Chicago Nite Life," Baltimore *Afro-American*, October 21, 1933, 19.

60. Leonard Ray Teel, "The African-American Press and the Campaign for a Federal Anti-lynching Law, 1933–34: Putting Civil Rights on the National Agenda," *American Journalism* 8 (2–3): 84–107.

61. Swanson, *The Thin Gold Watch*, 1, 114, 120–21, 128; Julia Crain Zaharopoulos, "Ira Clifton Copley," in *Biographical Dictionary of American Journalism*, 133.

6

Reprogramming the Media Market

The character of American journalism had been radically transformed from
what the founding fathers visualized.
　　　　　　　　　—Leo Rosten, *The Washington Correspondents*, 1937

In stark contrast to the raucous, escapist mood of the 1920s, sobering
economic situations in the 1930s forced Americans to question the foundations of their way of life. It was as though a carefree shopping spree
had ended and the spenders now faced staggering debt. Soon newspapers
would be blamed for giving little warning about the fragile economy and
the impending collapse of values in the stock market. Even after the stock
market's downturn in September 1929 and the sudden plunge in October,
journalists, for the most part untrained in economic theory and practice,
seemed slow to understand the broad consequences of the financial and
economic dislocation of 1929 that would eventually be called the Great
Crash. In a short time, the disastrous corporate and personal losses in the
New York Stock Exchange would emanate shock waves touching every
American. In the meantime, the national press continued to report the
insistence of President Herbert Hoover and others in high places that the
economy was still on "a sound a prosperous basis."[1]

While Hoover, through most of his four-year term, maintained his
publicly optimistic outlook, resisting major changes in his conservative
approach to government, the media played a central role in stimulating
a national conversation about economic and political ramifications in
America and overseas. In news reports, the press began to offer a statistical analysis of an epidemic of unemployment as the national economy

became mired in the Great Depression. By 1933, when the Depression seemed to reach bottom, industrial layoffs and business failures left one in every four workers desperately jobless.[2]

The crash and the ensuing Depression ushered in an era of grave doubts. Many icons of business and industry whose optimistic speculations had often been quoted in the press were now exposed as little better than greedy liars, at worst, or blind fools. No longer would much value be placed upon the optimism of such important capitalists as John J. Raskob, a director of General Motors. The "magic of his name," the *New York Times* reported in March 1929, boosted General Motors stock 12 points in just a few days and triggered a wider surge of investment. As one historian of the crash noted, "the mightiest of Americans were, for a brief time, revealed as human beings.... On the whole, the greater the earlier reputation for omniscience ... the greater the foolishness now exposed." Things "concealed by a heavy façade of dignity now stood exposed, for the panic suddenly, almost obscenely, snatched this façade away."[3]

Sensing an appetite for serious analysis, the press offered an array of thoughtful editorialists and columnists who commented on aspects of the political, economic, and social situation and often offered solutions. As such, newspapers' opinion pages became a new "marketplace of ideas." It was in this marketplace that some editors tried to explain the sudden disappearance of prosperity. "Where is our money?" asked an editorialist in Iowa. "The answer is not difficult.... We spent it." As a solution, another Midwest editor recommended cutting federal taxes and reducing the size of government bureaucracies, opposing sharply the competing notion that the government should *increase* both services and taxes to aid the unemployed. At issue was the traditional commitment to a balanced budget, together with a fear of inflation, and the belief that an "avoidance of borrowing ... protected people from slovenly or reckless public housekeeping."[4]

As the Depression deepened, the press reflected widespread doubts about the American political and economic system. Some critics questioned whether the capitalist system could revive and return the country to prosperity. Others urged the national government to take responsibility and exercise emergency powers in dealing with hunger and homelessness. Correspondents' reports of seemingly successful autocratic economic experiments in the Soviet Union, fascist Italy, and Nazi Germany made some people wonder if a powerful leader could deal more urgently in meeting extreme national needs.

Critics and blame seekers meanwhile targeted the mass media. The press was criticized at best for not emphasizing warning signs, and at worst for deluding Americans into believing that prosperity was unending. Walter Lippmann, America's popular mass-media philosopher, acknowledged that the inability to notice the "treacherous conditions" leading to the crash had been a "marvel."[5] Even as stock values fell in 1929, optimists at the *Wall Street Journal* scolded pessimists and interpreted the decline as "a major advance temporarily halted for technical readjustment."[6] The *Journal's* shortsightedness has since been blamed on editors who narrowly conceived their mission as reporting, not analysis. Trained at the wire services, reporters focused on events rather than on underlying causes and trends.[7]

Some press critics were relentless and unforgiving. George Seldes, who in the 1920s reported on Europe's economic troubles, concluded that press coverage of the U.S. economy had maintained a false sense of security as it "furnished the lies and buncombe of the merchants of securities."[8] The socialist and muckraker Upton Sinclair blamed the "blindness and greed of ruling classes" for propagating "ignorance and prejudice, deliberately created and maintained by prostitute journalism."[9] In fact, newspapers had offered inadequate economic information. In a survey of Washington correspondents, 91 of 107 (86.6%) agreed that their newspapers failed to give "significant accounts of our basic economic conflicts."[10]

For American media, the economic downturn presented enormous financial problems that accelerated the trend of failures and mergers and affected even long-established newspapers and magazines. In 1931, Ralph Pulitzer sold his father's monumental *New York World* to media magnate Roy Howard, head of the growing Scripps-Howard newspaper chain. Howard killed the evening and Sunday editions and merged the morning *World* with his *New York Telegram*. The chains increased their reach and power so much that critics of the press worried about the danger of media domination by a few so-called press lords.[11] The "disappearing dailies" left many cities with few, if any, competing newspapers.[12] Some newspapers were rescued and remained independent. The *Washington Post* was losing $1 million a year and was nearly bankrupt in 1933 when it was bought at auction by financier Eugene Isaac Meyer.[13] One of the nation's new media scholars, Willard Bleyer, noted in 1933 "the constant reduction in the number of daily newspapers by consolidations, in accordance with the prevailing monopolistic character of present-day capitalism."[14]

Journalism and the newspaper industry faced serious challenges. Criticized regularly for inaccuracy and advocacy, editors placed new emphasis on the professional standards and ethics articulated in the Canons of Journalism adopted in 1923 by the American Society of Newspaper Editors. While reporters were urged to report facts accurately, they faced an increasing challenge in dealing with divergent sets of "facts" distributed by public relations agents seeking, as Walter Lippmann had cautioned, to "manufacture" public opinion. "The work of reporters," Lippmann wrote, "has thus become confused with the work of preachers, revivalists, prophets and agitators." What the public in a democracy required, he insisted, was a "steady supply of trustworthy and relevant news." To correct reporting's "grosser evils" Lippmann advocated basic reforms—identifying the newspaper's staff, documenting articles, identifying sources of information, and "more successful analysis." Further, he challenged schools of journalism to turn "newspaper enterprise from a haphazard trade into a disciplined profession."[15]

Economic distress concerns trouble both reporters and publishers. Spurred by layoffs and reduced paychecks during the Depression, journalists sought better wages and working conditions. Some banded together to establish their first labor organization, the Newspaper Guild. Publishers worried over network radio's increasing audience and advertising share. The prospect of a declining economy thrust the issue to center stage. By the end of the decade, the "talking box" of the early 1920s had matured from a communications craze for a mechanical minority to an industry with about 200,000 employees serving as much as a third of the population. Radio claimed a space in American living rooms and a place in the daily culture, making, as one scholar in 1929 noted, "a contribution of the most far-reaching nature to the solidarity of the people served."[16] As academics praised the *range* of programming, including drama and literature, executives leading the networks catered to larger audiences interested in popular entertainers, collegiate and professional sports, and news.[17]

Direct competition in news reporting developed more slowly, in part because of the expense of developing a news organization. By 1929 local and network radio news announcers had progressed little from the practice of having announcers read newspaper stories and wire-service bulletins. Even so, the broadcast of radio bulletins frequently "scooped" the newspapers, which would not be delivered until hours later. As radio's share of advertising increased, newspaper owners acknowledged the potential of the new medium and responded with various competitive strategies.

Publishers responded by offering content still unavailable on radio. More space was devoted to interpretative reporting and commentary on politics and the economy. With the growth of the national government during the Depression, a new breed of Washington-based columnists secured an audience. Through national syndication, newspapers' equivalent to radio networks, the intellectual insights of Walter Lippmann and the gossipy insider disclosures of Drew Pearson were read at breakfast tables across America.[18]

Economic chaos also created opportunities. Some magazine publishers found new, receptive audiences. The need to make a serious inventory of the nation's economic health stimulated interest in business publications. *Business Week* debuted in 1929, and Henry Luce's *Fortune* magazine in 1930. The success of Luce's weekly newsmagazine *Time,* launched in 1923, became a model for two competing weeklies starting in 1933. On

February 17, the first foreign-news editor of *Time,* Thomas J. C. Martyn, published the first issue of *News-Week,* which mimicked *Time's* sectional layout. Washington journalist David Lawrence converted his *United States Daily* newspaper, begun in 1926, into the weekly *United States News.* A third weekly launched that year, on October 28, was *Today,* headed by Raymond Moley, who resigned as assistant secretary of state to become editor. Somewhat different in format, *Today* promised a mix of literature and politics including stories by Sherwood Anderson and nonfiction about the New Dealers in Washington, among them Roosevelt's choice for secretary of agriculture, the Republican Henry Wallace.[19]

In the 1930s the innovative Luce was fast becoming one of the century's most influential media voices. *Time* had been earning profits since 1927 with its formula of "downgrading dull fact and upgrading color, entertainment or message." His *Fortune* had been a work in progress in 1928, when he hired a group of writers, editors, and photographers to create a dummy of a luxurious magazine aimed at well-to-do readers and advertisers—tycoons of the world of business, industry, and the stock market. *Time's* business section was too brief to treat what Luce saw as "the struggle, excitement, romance, wealth, and power" of businessmen and industrialists, the nation's royalty. "Our best men are in business," he claimed in the prospectus. His partner, Briton Hadden, disliked the idea and thought it unlikely to succeed but did not block money for the experiment. After Hadden died in 1929, Luce went ahead with his plans.[20]

In February 1930, undeterred by the stock market crash, Luce (at age 32) launched *Fortune.* The large-format magazine (11.25 by 14 inches) weighed more than two pounds and sold for $1 a copy ($10 a year), with advertising based on 30,000 subscriptions. Its projected circulation for 1931 was 40,000. The first issue contained 184 pages, with about 120 pages of ads. Keyed to a wealthy audience, ads displayed the "first showing" of the "silent gear-shift" Pierce-Arrow five-passenger sedan; Crane bathrooms to please "even Sarah Bernhardt"; the nationwide chain of Curtiss-Wright airports, leasing space "to executives of any type"; and gentlemen's clothes "for Southern and tropical resort wear."[21]

Fortune was distinguished by its focus on business and its lavish illustrations. The inaugural art cover featured a female muse. Full-length features romanticized American industry and were illustrated by color art and by photographs, some by a talented 26-year-old woman who specialized in industrial scenes, Margaret Bourke-White. Stories in the first issue gloried in the achievements of industry's giants, including the once-maligned $3 billion-a-year meat-packing industry. Far from scandalizing meat packers as muckraker Upton Sinclair had done in *The Jungle* in 1906, *Fortune* personified Swift and Company as an American model—"butcher for 20,000,000 persons.... Standing astride the Mississippi, he reaches with his right hand into the great agricultural states, producing two-thirds of all U.S. livestock, and with his left hand hurls $3,000,000,000 worth of steaks and chops and hams toward the huge population centers of the East." Bourke-White's photographs of pigs alive and butchered were a forerunner of the photographic essay. The first issue also surveyed American banking and finance in 10,000 words. Another feature credited "David Sarnoff, the Puck of radio," with outwitting British radio competitors. A gallery of "Living Rothschilds" heralded the legendary family of financial wizards. For exotica, the staff went offshore to visit industrial age "Island Kingdoms" of the wealthy—mansions and castles of the giants of steelmaking, hotels, chocolates, Wesson salad oil, and Wrigley's chewing gum.[22]

Critics responded with praise and displeasure. Social historian Frederick Lewis Allen noted how *Fortune* was written for the conservative rich by teams of liberals: the staff had "trimmed its sails so skillfully to the winds of conservatism" through "a brilliant [technique] of team-research and team-authorship" shaped mainly in New York offices.[23] A critic in the *Nation* regretted that *Fortune* had not lived up to its prospectus in 1928, which promised to "inquire with unbridled curiosity." The result instead glorified tycoons and was "saluted by boards of directors."[24]

Outside the mainstream press, Americans sought information and meaning in alternative publications. The ongoing migration of African Americans seeking industrial jobs in Detroit and other cities, together with increasing literacy and racial awareness, provided an expanding market of readers. Weeklies flourished among the burgeoning African American communities in Harlem, Pittsburgh, Chicago, New York, Baltimore, and Norfolk. The outspoken editors of African American papers in the North often enjoyed influence beyond their metropolitan areas, their publications circulating even in the legally segregated South, where opinions about civil rights had few forums.

The African American press also thrived in the urban South, partly because readers and advertisers were clustered together in segregated neighborhoods. In Atlanta, an enterprising advertising genius, William Alexander Scott II, capitalized on a surge of rural migration to the cities in the 1920s, caused in part by an epidemic infestation of boll weevils in the cotton fields. Scott had been a champion debater at Atlanta's Morehouse College, and in 1927 he put that talent to work in Jacksonville, Florida, soliciting advertisements for an African American directory of businesses for the densely settled segregated areas of the city. In 1928, the same technique worked successfully when he compiled a directory of African American businesses in the segregated neighborhoods around and beyond Atlanta's Auburn Avenue. Having established a solid business base, he followed up on a suggestion to start a newspaper. As such, his weekly paper, the *Atlanta World*, started with a solid advertising base; it also benefited from the support of Scott family employees, including his brother, C. A. Scott, in the press room.

Scott envisioned publishing a daily paper and expanded the *World* in manageable steps. By 1930, despite the stock market crash, he published the paper twice a week. In 1931, although the Depression had deepened, he established the Scott Syndicate, which banded together publishers of numerous African American weeklies and semiweeklies across the South and beyond to Iowa and Ohio. That same year, he went to Chicago searching for an editor capable of helping him launch the daily. Scott found Frank Marshall Davis, who in 1927 had edited the *Evening Bulletin*, an African American daily that had lasted five months in Chicago. Scott saw in the 25-year-old newspaperman the necessary confidence and determination. For his part, Davis's desire to manage a daily overcame his reluctance about moving South. Although he worried about living under segregation, Davis recalled years later that "economically, it [Atlanta] was almost like Paradise, in comparison with Chicago of that day."[25]

Committing to daily publication had been troublesome in other cities. At least nine African American dailies had started and failed in Northern cities after the World War, despite the mass influx of African Americans from the South. Nevertheless, Scott and Davis moved ahead to the next step, publishing three times a week. Then, as Davis recalled, Scott "comes in one day and—he calls everybody 'Doc.' He says, 'Doc, let's put out a daily.'"[26] On March 14, 1932, Scott proudly published the first edition of the *Atlanta Daily World*—"the only daily newspaper published anywhere in the world by Negroes."[27]

Under Davis, the *World*'s opinion page had a notably bolder voice. Davis articulated a deep resentment of segregation and injustice. More outspoken in his columns than African Americans who had lived under segregation, Davis sometimes made Scott uncomfortable enough to advise moderation. Scott once told him, "Doc, you know you're in the South now. You can't say things like you're saying…. Take it easy."[28] Davis recalled how his columns would "calm down" for three or four issues then "get back to my old stride … against the mores of the South."[29]

Davis attacked the social system that tolerated lynchings. As a boy in Kansas, he had a personal experience with lynching when a group of boys who had read about lynching experimented by putting a noose around his neck. Lynchings haunted his editorials and the poetry he wrote regularly and concealed in a desk drawer, to be published when he left Atlanta. Davis challenged the official statistics that showed lynchings decreasing, arguing that "anybody with the mind of a moron has every reason to believe that many Negroes are killed yearly in isolated parts of the South with no news of these murders ever reaching print, and that many recorded murders have all the elements of lynching." He argued that the white Southern judges were guilty of "legal lynchings." In 1931 he opposed the execution of a 14-year-old boy caught burglarizing the home of a white family. In 1932 he argued that murders and lynchings would not stop until people of both races were certain of swift punishment.[30]

Davis's reputation spread among journalists in the African American press. In 1931, he turned down an offer to be managing editor of the *Kansas City Call* when Roy Wilkins left to become head the New York office of the National Association for the Advancement of Colored People, editor of its journal, the *Crisis,* and eventually national executive director. Davis's courage became legendary and inspired a generation of journalists. Lerone Bennett, who made his reputation at *Ebony* magazine, started at the *World*, where reporters retold stories of Davis's courage.[31]

The news and views Scott and Davis published were almost entirely neglected by mainstream newspapers, which was precisely why African Americans supported their "race" papers. The *World* and a host of weeklies highlighted accomplishments of African Americans while championing political, economic, educational, and legal reforms. During the Depression, these editors banded together more closely to support efforts to gain civil rights and legal protection. They underscored the example of Mahatma Gandhi's nonviolent freedom crusade in India and urged African Americans to give a dollar in support the NAACP for such causes as a federal antilynching law.[32]

African American women made significant contributions in the race press during the 1930s. In the Midwest, Lucile Bluford, a 1932 graduate of the University of Kansas, worked briefly with Davis at the *World* before going to the *Kansas City Call,* where she demonstrated courage in the coverage of lynching and eventually became editor and publisher and was esteemed as the "conscience of Kansas City." In New York, Marvel Cooke started in 1925 at the NAACP's *Crisis,* editing and writing under the supervision of W.E.B. DuBois. With that solid background in race politics, she joined the *Amsterdam News* in Harlem, where she soon became a spokesperson for employees' grievances, organized the first Newspaper Guild unit at an African American paper, and stood in the picket line during a successful 11-week strike. "I was very disappointed in the *Amsterdam News* after I came to work there," she recalled years later. "I left there because of a headline ["Killed Sweetheart. Slept with Body"] which, to me, is very typical of what the black press will do, and I understand it, you know, for circulation…. I mean, to get subscriptions, they went into the murders, the off-beat social conditions. You know, the black press, to me, has never lived up to its potential, except for very few exceptions—maybe the *Afro-American,* maybe *Pittsburgh Courier.*" After she left the *News,* Cooke worked in Harlem as managing editor of the *People's Voice,* owned by Adam Clayton Powell. Finally quitting the race press, she had the distinction of becoming the first African American to be hired by a white-owned daily, the New York *Compass.*[33]

In the male-dominated, white-owned press, women made notable progress against traditional gender barriers. At the *Chicago Tribune,* Genevieve Forbes Herrick, 35, bucked the tradition that kept women from reporting serious subjects and was becoming one of the best-known front-page female reporters of crime and politics. Another of the country's first front-page newspaperwomen during the early 1930s, Lorena Hickok of the Associated Press, persuaded First Lady Eleanor Roosevelt to begin holding women-only press conferences. In New York City, Ishbel Ross, 34, was at the peak of her career as the city's best female reporter for the *New York Tribune* and later the merged *Herald Tribune.*

Crises in Europe provided reporting opportunities overseas for women. In 1929, Mary Marvin Breckinridge was beginning a career as a filmmaker, would lead into photojournalism and reporting from Europe for CBS.[34] Women in the 1930s were building reputations that eventually would win them professional honors. *New York Times* reporter Anne O'Hare McCormick was on her way to becoming the first woman to win a Pulitzer Prize (1937) for overseas correspondence. By 1931, 38-year-old Dorothy Thompson had been living in Europe and writing freelance journalism for 11 years. Thompson had come to Europe on her own and found work covering trouble spots and winning the respect and friendship of the overseas press corps. As early as 1923 she tried to interview Adolf Hitler, who, with his four-year-old Nazi party, had attempted unsuccessfully that November to overthrow the German government and establish a right-wing nationalist one. Subsequently, the public fascination with Hitler's tactics as he reemerged in German politics generated a multitude of stories, but most American correspondents glimpsed the *Führer* only at mass rallies or in motorcades. Thompson persisted until December 1931, when, after Hitler's Nazis had become the second-largest party in Parliament, she was granted an interview that also made *her* famous. Hitler's press chief arranged the meeting at the Adlon Hotel, the gathering place for American correspondents in Berlin. Hitler would not answer her questions but instead spoke "always as though he were addressing a mass meeting.... He gives the impression of a man in a trance. He bangs the table." Hitler said he would "get into power legally. I will abolish this parliament.... I will found an authority-state." Face to face with the rising political leader, Thompson was unimpressed. Hitler seemed "inconsequent and voluble, ill-poised, insecure ... the very prototype of the Little Man," an unlikely leader of the sophisticated German people.[35]

As the Depression lingered, newspaper publishers recognized readers' appetite for vigorous political commentary on a national level. A new generation of commentators who had come of age during the Progressive Era included several whose political views had been seasoned by the World War and by travel in postwar Europe. By 1931, Lippmann, at 42, was a liberal political sage, writing mostly unsigned editorials as editor of the Pulitzer family's Democratic *New York World.* That year, the *World* failed financially, and Lippmann accepted an offer to write a personal, syndicated column for Ogden Reid's conservative Republican *New York Herald Tribune.* The announcement in the Republican newspaper promised that Lippmann, "the brilliant spokesman of liberalism," would "express freely his opinions on such subjects as he may select." Meanwhile, Lippmann's classmate at Harvard, columnist Heywood Broun, had been fired by *World* publisher Ralph Pulitzer in 1928 after he criticized the paper's "fear of shocking any reader." A year later, at the age of 41, Broun became a $30,000-a-year columnist for Scripps-Howard's *New York Telegram.* Drew Pearson, 50 in 1929, was observing Washington politics from his perch on the nearby *Baltimore Sun.*[36]

Other print journalists transitioned from print to radio news and commentary. Radio encouraged the sudden emergence of so many commentators on the airwaves that one critic, referring to the sheer numbers, called them "excess prophets." By 1929, Hans Von (H. V.) Kaltenborn, at 51, had been associate editor of the *Brooklyn Eagle* and a once-a-week broadcaster for six years. That year, with the launch of CBS, he quit print journalism to become a regular commentator for a respectable salary of $100 a week.[37] Another print convert to CBS, Elmer Davis, a former *New York Times* foreign correspondent of Lippmann's generation, replaced Kaltenborn during the late 1930s.[38]

Within the media, self-criticism spurred a trend toward more commentary on politics and economics. The American Society of Newspaper Editors concluded that newspapers could best serve the "average reader" by offering more "explanatory and interpretive news." This sanction validating and encouraging interpretation of the news was justified, the ASNE declared, because events were "complex" and "moving more rapidly than at any other period in the recent history of the world."[39] The interpretative reporting and opinion writing that characterized European journalism now became mainstays of American journalism, though usually segregated on clearly marked opinion pages. The most provocative and stimulating opinion columns were circulated nationally through syndicates. Such were Lippmann's hundreds of columns. The first, on September 8, 1931, discounted President Hoover's optimism as a "dangerous illusion," warning that "we are in the midst, not of an ordinary trade depression, but of one of the great upheavals and readjustments of modern history." Between 1931 and 1937, Lippmann's "Today and Tomorrow" daily column for the *New York Herald Tribune* was syndicated to 155 newspapers.[40]

In Washington, where the nation now looked hopefully for economic recovery, Lippmann was not optimistic. By 1931 he denounced "all the front page prophets" who continually predicted "the turn was at hand," and who encouraged Americans "that the magical force of the business

cycle would bring everything back to normal." It was "a fatal misunderstanding ... to suppose that the economic cycle proceeds regardless of
human decisions."[41] Lippmann concluded that Hoover was confused and
had "no well-considered conception of his office and of his own purposes"
and advised him to clear his mind—"read fewer newspapers and ... care
less what journalists say."[42] In the summer of 1931, *Washington Merry-
Go-Round*, an anonymously authored best-selling book (five printings in
July alone) was so critical of Hoover that it seemed libelous. Hoover asked
for an investigation, and the Washington press corps speculated for weeks
about the authors until they were identified as Drew Pearson and Robert
S. Allen. Allen was fired by the pro-Hoover *Christian Science Monitor*, and
Pearson lost his job the next year when their second book came out.[43]
Pearson and Allen soon contracted to write a syndicated "Washington
Merry-Go-Round" column for an audience eager to read unauthorized
"leaks" and insider gossip that often enough proved to be true. It was
"the beginning of a new era in news-styles from the capital."[44]

Pearson and Allen disregarded traditional limits accepted by the
Washington press corps for criticism of presidents, Congress, and their
own press colleagues. In *Washington Merry-Go-Round* they contended that
Hoover's policy amounted to "suppression and inaction" and misrep-
resentations, meaning Hoover did "not do or say anything that would
reveal the truth about the great catastrophe." They claimed that Hoover
failed as president because of his autocratic personality, a trait that he had
exhibited in China, where for years he had been a businessman "ruthless"
enough to chain a laborer to a stake in the hot sun or steal a man's mining
property. Nor would relief from the Depression come from the House of
Representatives, which Pearson and Allen called "the Monkey House,"
where members were "the lowest common denominator of the ignorance,
prejudices and inhibitions of their districts."[45]

Their final chapter criticized the press, particularly the capital press
corps. Breaking the gentlemen's agreement not to criticize colleagues, they
portrayed the press as selling their services to government, of spreading
propaganda, of suppressing antigovernment news, and of lying and bias.
Washington correspondents "write not what they know but what the
viciously partisan and reactionary policy of their employer dictates....
The American press is stifling and thwarting what little idealism and
honesty still exists in its ranks."[46] Publishers' "dictates," the authors
asserted, were suffocating the free press.[47]

Press critics found much wrong with the patterns of ownership of the
press that had developed after 1900 as press lords accumulated chains of
papers and magazines. Those concerned with the role of diverse voices in
a democracy warned that the accelerating trend of mergers and consolidations threatened the public interest by eliminating newspaper competition, discouraging the organization of labor, and reducing the number of

independent outlets. Publishers' purchases of radio stations set off more alarms as critics envisioned an irreversible trend.[48]

Added to this, media critics alleged, often justifiably, that advertisers controlled content to the extent that newspapers and news agencies suppressed stories for financial advantages. Oswald Garrison Villard accused the Associated Press of "wholesale lying and crass misrepresentation," notably in reporting racial injustice in the South, but also in coverage of labor strikes. The underlying problem, Villard stressed, was that the news agency depended upon its member newspapers. In the South, reporters seldom reported lynchings fairly. In Arkansas, the Associated Press amplified local racial troubles as a "Negro rebellion ... possibly planned for the whole South." On labor issues, member newspapers usually sided with employers, as in the Pittsburgh steel strike in 1919. "The misfortune remains that in labor matters the Associated Press is too often dominated by the class tendency of its members."[49]

Critics found numerous ethical flaws in the press. A target of continual scorn was the press's resort to sensationalism pandering to base reader tastes, often by invasion of privacy. The Chicago press came in for special condemnation after the murder in 1930 of *Tribune* reporter Jake Lingle. The investigation revealed "startling" evidence that Lingle was not an innocent victim of gangland warfare but had profited from a second career in the criminal underworld as "a crook, a blackmailer, a peddler of illicit favors, and close friend of high and low police officers not all of whom were or are above suspicion." The case raised questions whether other newsmen crossed over to racketeering and besmirched Chicago journalism much as Chicago's "Black Sox" scandal in 1919 had tarnished professional baseball.[50]

No critic targeted the media more accurately than George Seldes. Seldes had perceived the newspapers' flaws from inside, first as a young reporter in Pittsburgh when his story about the son of a prominent businessman was suppressed to get more advertising. After the war he served as chief European correspondent for the *Chicago Tribune,* the newspaper that Washington correspondents in the 1930s ranked "least fair and reliable."[51] Seldes's first book, *You Can't Print That* (1928), examined censorship of foreign news in the U.S. press, tracing the practice of suppression and distortion to the publishers of newspaper empires.

Seldes had outstanding models for his probative methods. He admired Lincoln Steffens's muckraking, and as a cub reporter in Pittsburgh, Seldes had been inspired by the press criticism of Will Irwin. Carrying on the muckraking tradition, Seldes targeted journalism's faults in the style of a prosecutor persuading a jury.[52] In *Lords of the Press* (1938), he charged that most of the faults came down from the top, the owners. He called Joseph Medill Patterson of the New York *Daily News* the "Lord of Tabloidia." He welcomed the declining fortunes of Hearst, the "Lord of San Simeon."

Seldes called Scripps's successor, Roy Howard, "the Light That Failed," alleging that Howard subverted the Scripps newspapers to seek "loot, and not laurels." Seldes accused his former boss, publisher Colonel McCormick of the *Tribune*, of printing whatever "rumor and gossip" supported his views. "It used to be said in our Paris office that the colonel had one of the finest minds of the seventeenth century."[53]

American publishers, Seldes argued, extolled a free press while systematically suppressing news at variance with their views. He agreed with critics who blamed the stock market crash on "the failure of our newspapers to inform us honestly and accurately about the economic situation from 1927 to 1929."[54] He claimed newspapers shared that blame because Washington correspondents had become "servile" to publishers and editors at the expense of facts. "Correspondents," wrote Seldes, "know that they cannot write contrary to the social, political and economic prejudices or philosophies of their bosses and get away with it for long."[55] To publishers who pleaded ignorance of the stock market's weakness, Seldes cited the decline of investigative reporting. Some of the vast amounts of money spent on ballyhooing murder trials of the 1920s could have been diverted to investigate economic claims. "Obviously there was no desire or intention to do so," he argued. If owners contended that they withheld negative information about the economy in the hope of preventing panic, Seldes countered, "Obviously just as stores and corporations are the sacred cows of certain smaller newspapers, so Big Business is the great Sacred Golden Bull of the entire press." As for protecting the public from panic, Seldes reminded them of a motto of Charles Dana, past editor of the *New York Sun:* "What the good Lord lets happen I am not ashamed to print in my paper."[56]

At the heart of this latter-day muckraking was the traditional democratic ideal that the American press should serve the public. By the twentieth century, Leo Rosten observed in his 1937 survey of the Washington press establishment, "The character of American journalism had been radically transformed from what the founding fathers visualized." Newspapers had always been "properties ... dedicated to the making of profit," but modern publishing required enormous investments, "an enterprise which is no longer accessible except to the wealthy." He concluded that "newspapers get the type of reporting which they encourage ... and the public receives Washington correspondence of a character which newspaper publishers, and ultimately they alone, make possible." Rosten noted that publishers cannot be curbed when they abuse freedom of the press, although a doctor or a maniac is subject to prosecution. "But a newspaper publisher can give criminal advice, lie to the public, poison its intelligence, and conduct campaigns against civil liberties, decent morals, and the democratic system itself without being held accountable for his conduct."[57]

Against such attacks, publishers mounted a defense. By the 1930s, owners appreciated the newly flourishing practice of public relations and the importance of answering criticism publicly. Carl Ackerman soon emerged as an articulate spokesperson for the press. A wartime foreign correspondent, Ackerman left journalism to advise corporations in public relations and rose to become assistant to the president of General Motors. In 1931 the Columbia University Graduate School of Journalism, from which Ackerman had graduated in the first class in 1917, chose him as dean.

Addressing the American Society of Newspaper Editors in 1933, Ackerman launched a three-pronged counterattack. He acknowledged some of journalism's shortcomings, rebutted other accusations, and skillfully questioned the credibility of press critics. Ackerman contended that critics were utopians who wanted "an ideal quite beyond human realization." He glossed over criticism that publishers concealed profits and power agendas, admitting that "there are owners of newspaper properties whose motives can be questioned," though he did not name anyone. He directed attention to "many important newspaper publishers and editors ... who have no outside financial or personal interest."[58]

Facing questions about the 1929 crash, Ackerman conceded that the press had erred but was now more reliable. He admitted that newspapers could not escape blame for both advertising that was misleading and for financial news that was "promotional rather than informative." Citing Wall Street as a "paradise of promoters," he noted that most financial writers "rode the wave of financial promotions and accepted ... the optimistic and extravagant opinions of so-called financial and business leaders." Ackerman concluded that the public, now with eyes wide open, was understandably concerned about the management of newspapers, but that readers still "look to the press as their reliable and incorruptible friend and counsellor."[59]

As the 1930s began, newspaper publishers dominated American journalism. After two decades of mergers, their numbers had diminished, leaving some owners controlling many media outlets. At the head of the world's largest newspaper chain, William Randolph Hearst, now in his mid-60s, could influence the choosing of presidential candidates. Colonel McCormick, in his late 40s, had built the *Chicago Tribune* into the leading newspaper of the Midwest. McCormick's cousin, Eleanor "Cissy" Medill Patterson, nearing 50, was breaking into the publishers' circle, seeking to buy Hearst's *Washington Herald*. Always reluctant to sell, Hearst persuaded her to become editor and publisher until, in 1939, she bought it. In 1929, Alicia Patterson, a great-granddaughter of Joseph Medill, was 23 years old and writing for magazines in New York. By 1940 she would found *Newsday* on Long Island and build it into one of the nation's most successful and influential newspapers. When E. W. Scripps died in 1926, his protegé, Roy Howard, then in his early 60s, set out to bring more newspapers into the Scripps-Howard chain. On the West Coast, Harry Chandler, in his mid-60s, had established a power base as publisher of the *Los Angeles Times* and was acknowledged as one of the elite when his peers elected him president of the American Newspaper Publishers Association (ANPA).

On occasion, publishers banded together to guard against government suppression that threatened a free press. In a notable case, the ANPA helped to expand press freedom nationally by intervening to overturn a Minnesota case that closed a newspaper that Minneapolis officials attacked as a nuisance. The issue at the heart of the case—prior restraint, censorship that suppressed publication—had lingered since 1690, when the Massachusetts governing council in Boston banned the colonists' first newspaper, *Publick Occurrences.*

The landmark case involved the Minneapolis publisher of the *Saturday Press,* a small weekly that frequently printed scandal and bigotry. The publishers, Jay Near and Howard Guilford, accused the county attorney and other public officials of permitting Jewish racketeers and illegal whiskey traders to operate freely in the city. The publishers were blatantly anti-Semitic. After Guilford was shot while driving to the office, Near charged, "It was a Jew who employed Jews to shoot down Mr. Guilford." Recovering in the hospital, Guilford wrote that the county attorney, Floyd Olson, was a "Jew lover." The county attorney won a court order closing the *Saturday Press* under the state Public Nuisance Law, passed in 1925.[60]

When the Minnesota Supreme Court upheld the ruling of the Minneapolis judge, the case escalated in importance as a precedent. In New York, the founder of the new American Civil Liberties Union recognized the Minnesota nuisance law as "a new device for previous restraint of publication ... a menace to the whole principle of freedom of the press." In Chicago, the Minnesota case outraged the *Tribune*'s McCormick. He prodded the ANPA to vote its moral support for a fight to the U.S. Supreme Court. "If we don't do something, free press in this country would disappear," he wrote to ANPA President Chandler, publisher of the *Los Angeles Times.*[61]

The *Saturday Press* issue divided publishers. Chandler initially did not want the ANPA to risk widening the effect of a law that existed in only one Midwestern state. "If we go to the Supreme Court now and that tribunal upholds the Minnesota court," Chandler replied to McCormick, "we will have stirred up the matter to a point strongly conducive to similar legislation in other states."[62] Minnesota publishers did not want to appeal, and some Eastern publishers questioned the wisdom of defending Near's scandal sheet. A *Christian Science Monitor* editorial asked if the real threat to freedom was elsewhere—"a menace which comes from the unscrupulous within the ranks of the profession." The weekly *Literary*

Digest worried that an attack might lead to more-dangerous laws. But the Republican *New York Herald Tribune* and other newspapers backed McCormick. With McCormick agreeing to pay most of the cost, the ANPA in 1930 voted 254–5 to appeal to the U.S. Supreme Court.[63]

The ANPA won narrowly. In 1931, the Supreme Court ruled 5–4 that the Minnesota "gag" violated the Constitution's Fourteenth Amendment protecting citizens from state laws that impaired Constitutional rights, including the First Amendment right of freedom of the press. Chief Justice Charles Evans Hughes said the Minnesota law could lead from widespread suppression of press freedom by the legislation, "to a complete system of censorship." For the first time, the Supreme Court invalidated a state law because it denied press freedom. *Near v. Minnesota* demonstrated that newspaper publishers acting in their own self-interest might also act as guardians of Americans' liberties. The *New York Times* wrote that the ruling "will amply reward those who saw from the first the peril that lay in the Minnesota law."[64]

The victory for freedom of the press, however, did not raise hope in the business offices. Facing undeniable competition from radio, publishers considered strategies to cut their losses. As the Depression deepened, the ANPA headed toward a showdown with radio networks focused on competition for diminished advertising income. By 1932, the stage was set for what became known as the press-radio war. [65]

The two national networks—NBC and CBS—dominated the airwaves. Since its start in 1926 as a division of the Radio Corporation of America, NBC set the pace. After 1928, the Columbia Broadcasting System successfully challenged NBC's monopoly, stimulating creativity in network programming for entertainment and news. By 1931, with David Sarnoff directing NBC and William Paley guiding CBS, the two networks accounted for nearly 70 percent of American broadcasting.[66] Paley transformed the failing United Independent Broadcasters chain of stations by renegotiating contracts and acquiring more affiliate stations. In one year he converted the balance sheet from a loss of $179,000 to a net profit of $474,000, and in 1931, despite the deepening Depression, CBS produced a profit of $2.35 million.[67]

The two network giants, both sons of recent immigrants, had proved to be every bit as ingenious, inventive, and competitive as the newspaper publishers. Sarnoff's family, persecuted in Russia, had emigrated to New York in 1900, when he was nine. Paley was born in 1901, the son of an Eastern European immigrant who accumulated wealth in Philadelphia as a cigar manufacturer. In contrast with Sarnoff's rags-to-riches story, Paley was born into wealth and used family money to jump-start his career.[68] Sarnoff understood earlier than others the commercial possibilities of radio technology. At NBC he placed his confidence in the network's technical facilities and in its superior sound, backed by the vast resources of

RCA's manufacturing. Paley's expertise was in management. He focused on creating innovative programming and on hiring outstanding talent—stars. On a cruise to France in 1931, he heard a recording of a singer whose voice he immediately wanted for CBS. He cabled his office, "Sign up singer Bing Crosby."[69]

Sarnoff the engineer and Paley the salesman managed their empires differently, largely because they headed corporations with fundamentally different structures. RCA had created NBC to stimulate the sales of RCA radio equipment, so NBC was accountable to RCA, not directly to stockholders.[70] Sarnoff managed NBC for RCA, not for himself. By contrast, CBS sold programming, not radio sets, and its profits and losses were scrutinized directly by its investors, including Paley's father. Because Paley was manipulating money he had created, he was permitted to be more flexible. The multiplying profits confirmed his investment decisions, including awards of large contracts to attractive stars.

Sarnoff, far more austere, acted like a guardian of the treasury at NBC. Even after he became head of NBC's parent corporation, RCA, Sarnoff often let a star go rather than pay more than a predetermined limit. Sarnoff "deplored the extravagant excesses of the Hollywood movie colony, with its wild parties, its ostentatious homes and its glittering lifestyles" and did not socialize with NBC's talents. By contrast, Paley was "eager, to spend time with them, to hear their complaints, to share their frustrations, to enjoy their company."[71]

The networks focused mainly on entertainment, taking cues from national ratings. The first national ratings in 1930, based on telephone interviews, were devised by marketing pioneer Archibald Crossley. Crossley soon identified audience favorites: Cantor, Ed Wynn, Jack Pearl, Burns and Allen, and, beginning in the fall of 1929, NBC's *Amos 'n' Andy*, the blackface vaudeville act by the vaudevillian performers Freeman Gosden and Charles Correll. By the mid-1930s, Benny and Bergen had the highest ratings.[72]

Network competition for talent led them to raid each other's lineups, a common practice among publishers. Paley had given Jack Benny and George Burns and Gracie Allen their start on CBS in 1932. "Everyone laughed at Jack Benny's stinginess and scratchy violin, at Gracie Allen's lost brother," Paley recalled. Benny and Burns and Allen switched to NBC, but Paley eventually lured them back, and with them came Red Skelton and Edgar Bergen with his wooden dummy, Charlie McCarthy. During one raid in 1935–1936, Paley signed NBC's vaudeville stars Eddie Cantor and Al Jolson. He also lured Major Bowes's *Amateur Hour*. That show succeeded, Paley believed, because "listeners loved to empathize with the amateur performers and to try to second-guess who would win the competition for the most applause and who would get the gong that cut short the performance."[73]

With comedy, drama, music, and audience-participation shows, radio broadcasting became an oasis of prosperity during the Depression. Sales increased steadily for evermore sophisticated radios. In 1930, slightly more than a third (35%) of American families owned radios. By 1935, that figure had almost doubled to 65 percent, and radio was established as a mainstay of American life.[74] As the audience widened, radio's income from advertising multiplied. By the early 1930s, a member of the Federal Radio Commission noted that commercials provided "the lifeblood of the industry." The growth in income from minimal amounts in 1928 to $72 million by 1934 was astonishing. In media economics, that was an unprecedented phenomenon.[75]

Radio's dramatic commercial success eroded the advertising monopoly enjoyed by newspapers and magazines. Furthermore, this success paralleled the worst years for newspaper advertising. Although the new medium attracted new advertising money, it also drained unmeasured sums that probably would have been paid to newspapers and magazines. The competition for scarce dollars spread from the big Eastern cities to the South and Midwest. While newspapers still drew more advertising nationally, radio revenues from 1930 to 1935 rose by $83.5 million—more than the combined increases of newspapers ($39.4 million) and magazines ($30.7 million). Between 1928 and 1933, radio's share of advertising placed in the major media increased from 2 percent to 10 percent, much of it taken from newspapers.[76]

Aside from their advertising woes, publishers worried about radio's forays into the delivery of news. By the 1930s, the networks and most stations had yet to develop their own serious news coverage—what one historian called the "dimension that would eventually define its importance and legacy as much as the entertainment programs." As radio programs competed with movies as the most popular pastime across the country, networks, content with the practice of reading news items published in dailies or acquired from national newswire services, invested little in developing news staffs. .[77] Typically, listeners heard bulletins, or newsbreaks, about important events, as when Charles Lindbergh landed in France in 1927 on his heroic flight across the Atlantic. Networks also hired announcers to discuss the day's news. NBC in 1930 offered the first daily news program, 15 minutes of commentary anchored by "world traveler" Lowell Thomas, a discussion format soon copied by others.

After relegating news delivery to the newspapers for a decade, radio suddenly made major strides into the news business. In 1932, the broadcasting of "breaking" news gained sudden popularity first in the reporting of the kidnapping of Lindbergh's infant son and later during the presidential campaign.[78] That year as well radio added 15-minute newscasts, spot coverage of sports, public service announcements, elections returns, and reports of major disasters and crimes. Partly because communication technology was becoming more sophisticated, broadcasters often beat newspapers with the first information on stories, thus multiplying radio audiences for short periods of time. Some stations developed independent news gathering. In 1930, a station in Beverly Hills, California, began the first sustained news broadcast. In 1931, an Illinois broadcaster used a remote unit in an airplane to follow a bank robber's car for 100 miles until police stopped the car. In 1932, the CBS network affiliate in New York broadcast the first news of the kidnapping of Charles A. Lindbergh's infant son. Continuing, almost-nonstop coverage of the Lindbergh family boosted the profile of news broadcasters.[79]

Phenomenal competition from radio news led publishers to consider schemes of control. Some justified control because they felt network news broadcasts threatened the existence of newspapers. The AP had begun selling its news to radio stations, at an extra charge, largely because increasing numbers of its members were publishers who had bought radio stations. This practice was opposed by publishers who were members of AP but had no holdings in radio. They sought to ban from all radio stations the frequent AP news bulletins and delay all AP news until their newspapers were off the press. In 1932, the ANPA passed a resolution favoring "an attempt to curtail broadcasting of AP news."[80]

Late in 1932 the controversy quickened, triggered by CBS's decision to report the November 1932 Roosevelt-Hoover presidential election during prime time (7 P.M. to 11 P.M.). For access to news of the election results, CBS contracted with the United Press agency, but UP canceled the contract a few days before the election under pressure from their main clients, the newspapers. CBS President William S. Paley later considered the episode a "comedy of errors," although publishers suspected a conspiracy. Managers of UP's competitor, the Associated Press, claimed they did not know about the cancellation of the CBS-UP contract and offered CBS its election news service. On election night, UP learned about AP's arrangement, and suddenly the UP teletype machine at CBS "began chattering in the election returns." That night, the competing International News Service also installed a machine at CBS, and CBS "devoted the whole night to the election and capped it by broadcasting words of the new president-elect live from Hyde Park, New York." Weeks later, CBS radio also beat newspapers on February 15, 1933, in broadcasting news from Miami of an attempt to assassinate the president-elect.[81]

The wire services backed down under pressure from their main clients, the publishers without radio holdings. A survey showed the AP that a great majority of member newspapers responding—826 of 1,049—did no broadcasting, leading the AP to restrict use of its news. At its annual meeting in April 1933, the AP voted to cut off news dispatches to any radio network or chain. UP and INS did the same. In response, NBC retreated from newscasting, but rival CBS formed its own Columbia News Service, buying the Dow Jones newswire from Washington, contracting with overseas news services, and arranging for more than 800 stringers in U.S. cities with populations of 20,000 or more. Out of necessity, Paley created broadcast journalism's first independent news-gathering agency.[82]

Pressure from publishers continued. Paley claimed that Kent Cooper, AP's general manager, "tried to frighten me into making peace with the publishers … [Cooper] predicted dire consequences for CBS if we did not agree to limit the amount of news we would broadcast." Publishers suggested that they might go to Congress, which was then considering a new federal communications law governing broadcasting that conceivably could include restrictions on radio broadcasting, or even government ownership. Some newspapers threatened to stop publishing CBS's program listings. In 1933 CBS was denied access to the U.S. Congress press galleries, which were reserved for press and wire services.[83]

While publishers sought to suppress radio news, they had not worried as much about the networks' expansion of news commentary. Commentators who discussed the news became radio's "talkie" version of print journalism's columnists. During the early 1930s, the numbers of radio commentators multiplied, helping to generate a national discourse on serious domestic and international events. As the nation's focus turned on Washington amid a growing nationalization of American life, readers and listeners seemed eager, if not desperate, to understand the ramifications of the Depression and the actions being taken by the president and Congress. Then, too, despite a largely isolationist population, there was growing concern about international political and military conflicts.

Network news commentators could become as popular as entertainers. By 1933 NBC's Lowell Thomas had inspired a trend. Other networks soon hired competing personalities, often from among print journalists with radio voices and style. CBS hired H. V. Kaltenborn, who had news-broadcasting experience while an editor at the *Brooklyn Eagle*, and a new Mutual Network of smaller stations hired the freelance writer Gabriel Heatter. At NBC, Thomas, greeting listeners with a warm "Good evening, everybody," became so popular that, as one biographer noted, he was credited with "instilling the habit of turning to the radio as a source of news."[84] In this context, the battle for audience and advertising between newspapers and radio set the stage for a showdown.

NOTES

1. Seldes, *Freedom of the Press*, 148.

2. Arthur M. Schlesinger Jr., *The Politics of Upheaval*, vol. 3 of *The Age of Roosevelt* (Boston: Houghton Mifflin, 1960), 3, 571.

3. *New York Times*, March 24, 1928; John Kenneth Galbraith, *The Great Crash, 1929* (Boston: Houghton Mifflin, 1961), 3.

4. Edwin P. Chase, "Where Is Our Money?" *Atlantic News-Telegraph*, December 2, 1934, reprinted in Wm. David Sloan and Laird B. Anderson, *Pulitzer Prize Editorials: America's Best Writing, 1917–2003*, 3rd ed. (Ames: Iowa State Press, 2003), 51–55; Henry J. Haskell, "Too Much Government," *Kansas City Star*, March 25, 1932, reprinted in Sloan and Anderson, *Pulitzer Prize Editorials*, 49–50; Galbraith, *The Great Crash*, 189.

5. Walter Lippmann, "To-day and To-morrow: Magical Prosperity," *New York Herald Tribune*, September 8, 1931, 19.

6. Galbraith, *The Great Crash*, 74, 91–92.

7. Edward E. Scharff, *Worldly Power: The Making of the Wall Street Journal* (New York: Beaufort Books, 1986), reviewed by James L. Baughman, *Journalism Quarterly* 63 (1986): 863–64.

8. Seldes, *Freedom of the Press*, 149.

9. Upton Sinclair, *The Brass Check*, rev. ed. (New York: Albert and Charles Boni, 1936), 428.

10. Lee C. Rosten, *The Washington Correspondents* (New York: Harcourt, Brace, 1937), 345.

11. George Seldes, *Lords of the Press* (New York: Julian Messner, 1938). Seldes called the American Newspaper Publishers Association the "House of Lords of our press."

12. Oswald Garrison Villard, *The Disappearing Daily*.

13. J. Douglas Tarpley, "Eugene Isaac Meyer," in *Biographical Dictionary of American Journalism*, 484; Meyer bought the *Post* for $825,000 shortly after he resigned as governor of the Federal Reserve Board. He outbid, among others, V. V. McNitt, of the McNaught Syndicate, which was unwilling to pay more than $552,000. *Editor & Publisher*, September 2, 1933.

14. Willard Grosvenor Bleyer, "Journalism in the United States, 1933," *Journalism Quarterly* 10 (1933): 300.

15. Walter Lippmann, *Liberty and the News* (New York: Harcourt, Brace and Howe, 1920), 8, 11, 78, 100.

16. Laurens E. Whittemore, "Development of Radio," *Annal of the American Academy*, supplement, 7 March 1929, 1, 7; By 1928, network programming was available coast to coast, broadcasts were clearer, and radio sets were less expensive. Christopher H. Sterling and John M. Kittross, *Stay Tuned: A Concise History of American Broadcasting*, 2nd ed. (Belmont, CA: Wadsworth Publishing, 1990), 112.

17. Bruce J. Evensen, "Jazz Age Journalism's Battle over Professionalism, Circulation and the Sports Page," *Journal of Sport History* 20 (3): 229–46. Between 1900 and 1930, newspapers increased space for sports coverage by 50 percent. During the 1920s, even more space was devoted to sports icons such as the New York Yankees' slugger Babe Ruth and golfing great Bobby Jones. Jack Dempsey's heavyweight boxing matches sold more newspapers than any other sporting event.

18. Robert S. Lynd and Helen Merrell Lynd, *Middletown in Transition* (New York: Harcourt, Brace, 1937), 375–76, quoted in Rosten, *The Washington Correspondents*, 140; By 1936 newspaper and magazine publishers noted an increase in their total advertising. "Added Ads Cheer Publishers; Assembling for Convention, They Are Pleased by Higher Lineage in Their Newspapers. Magazines Also Gain 13%," *Business Week*, April 18, 1936, 14.

19. *Today*, financed by Averill Harriman, Vincent Astor, and Harriman's sister, Mrs. Mary Rumsey, merged in 1937 with *News-Week*, which then was renamed *Newsweek*. Mary E. Stewart, "Sherwood Anderson and William C. Stewart at *Today*," Memoir, Department of Journalism, University of Richmond, online at http:// journalism.Richmond.edu/studentvoice/mary_stewart1.htm

20. John Kobler, *Luce: His Time, Life, and Fortune* (New York: Doubleday, 1968), 80; W. A. Swanberg, *Luce and His Empire* (New York: Scribner's Sons, 1972), 74–75, 151.

21. *Fortune*, February 1930, 2, 8, 28, 34; Kobler, *Luce*, 81–82.

22. *Fortune*, February 1930, 26, 28, 34, 36, 54–55, 60, 66, 82–84, 99; Vicki Goldberg, *Margaret Bourke-White* (New York: Harper & Row, 1986), 108; Theodore M. Brown, "A Legend that Was Largely True," in Margaret Bourke-White, *The Photographs of Margaret Bourke-White*, ed. Sean Callahan (New York: Bonanza Books, 1972), 10–11.

23. Allen, *Since Yesterday*, 220.

24. Milton St. John, "True Stories de Luxe," *Nation*, March 4, 1931, 239–40.

25. Frank Marshall Davis, interview with Carol Oukrop, Honolulu, March 29, 1984, transcript, 3, Kansas State University, Manhattan, Kansas.

26. Teel, "W. A. Scott," 158–71; Davis, interview with Oukrop, 2.

27. W. A. Scott, "Publisher's Note," *Atlanta World*, March 14, 1932, 1.

28. Davis, interview with Oukrop, 24–25.

29. Ibid.

30. Frank Marshall Davis, "Touring the World," *Atlanta World*, February 17, 1932, 6; Davis, interview with Oukrop, 25; Frank Marshall Davis, "Kansas Joins," *Atlanta World*, April 20, 1932, 6. Davis did not publish the poems he wrote about lynching and other aspects of the South until after he returned to Chicago in 1934 to become managing editor for the Associated Negro Press. His first book of poetry, *Black Man's Verse*, was published by Norman Forge's Black Cat Press in 1935. In 1937, Black Cat Press published Davis's second book of verse, *I Am the American Negro*.

31. Davis, interview with Oukrop, 6; Rodger Streitmatter, "African American Women Journalists: Breaking the Double Barriers of Race and Gender," paper presented to the Association for Education in Journalism and Mass Communication, April 1991, 15; Lerone Bennett, telephone interview with Leonard Ray Teel, April 1989.

32. Teel, "The African-American Press and the Campaign for a Federal Anti-lynching Law, 1933–34," 84–107.

33. Marvel Cooke, interview with Kathleen Currie, October 4–6 and October 30, 1989, transcript, 18, 31, 51–54, Women in Journalism Oral History Project of the Washington Press Club Foundation, in the Oral History Collection of Columbia University and other repositories, http://npc.press.org/wpforal/cook3.htm; Rodger Streitmatter, "An African-American Woman Journalist Who Agitated for Racial Reform," paper presented to the Association for Education in Journalism and Mass Communication, Boston, August 1991.

34. Maurine H. Beasley, "Mary Marvin Breckinridge Patterson: Case Study of One of 'Murrow's Boys,'" paper presented to the Association for Education in Journalism and Mass Communication, Boston, August 1991. See also David H. Hosley and Gayle K. Yamada, *Hard News: Women in Broadcast Journalism* (New York: Greenwood Press, 1987), 1–24.

35. Marion K. Sanders, *Dorothy Thompson: A Legend in Her Time* (Boston: Houghton Mifflin, 1973), 166–68; Peter Kurth, *American Cassandra: The Life of Dorothy Thompson* (Boston: Little, Brown, 1990), 160–63; Ishbel Ross, *Ladies of the Press: The Story of Women in Journalism by an Insider* (New York: Harper & Brothers, 1936), 360–66; Dorothy Thompson, *I Saw Hitler!* (New York: Farrar & Rhinehart, 1932), 12–18; Georg Bernhard, "Tactics of Hitler," *New York Times,* December 13, 1931, sect. 3, 1, 8.

36. "Walter Lippmann," advertisement, *New York Herald Tribune,* September 2, 1931, 10; Adams, *Lippmann,* 52; Donald A. Ritchie, *Press Gallery: Congress and the Washington Correspondents* (Cambridge, MA: Harvard University Press, 1991), 215–16.

37. H. V. Kaltenborn, *Fifty Fabulous Years, 1900–1950: A Personal Review* (New York: Putnam, 1950), 109–15; David G. Clark, "Kaltenborn's First Year on the Air," *Journalism Quarterly* 42 (1965): 378–79, quoted in David Holbrook Culbert, *News for Everyman: Radio and Foreign Affairs in Thirties America* (Westport, CT: Greenwood Press, 1976), 70.

38. Irving E. Fang, *Those Radio Commentators!* (Ames: University of Iowa Press, 1977), 4, 10. Commentator Quincy Howe made the remark.

39. Schudson, *Discovering the News,* 148.

40. Ibid., 150; Lippmann, "To-day and To-morrow: Magical Prosperity," 19.

41. Lippmann, "To-day and To-morrow: Magical Prosperity," 19.

42. Walter Lippmann, October 1, 1931, in Walter Lippmann, *Interpretations, 1931–1932,* ed. Allan Nevins (New York: Macmillan, 1932), 67–68.

43. Charles Fisher, *The Columnists* (New York: Howell, Soskin, 1944), 235. The second book also had no authors' names: *More Merry-Go-Round* (New York: Liveright, 1932). See also Oliver Pilat, *Drew Pearson: An Unauthorized Biography* (New York: Harper's Magazine Press, 1973), 22.

44. Rosten, *Washington Correspondents,* 139.

45. Robert S. Allen and Drew Pearson, *Washington Merry-Go-Round* (New York: Liveright, 1931), 63–64, 74, 217.

46. Ibid., 321, 365.

47. Douglas A. Anderson, "The Muckraking Books of Pearson, Allen, and Anderson," *American Journalism* 2 (1): 16.

48. Already by 1920, in more than half (57%) of newspaper cities, one publisher controlled the local daily or dailies. At least 559 dailies disappeared through consolidation or merger between 1909 and 1950. Royal H. Ray, "Concentration of Ownership and Control in the American Newspaper Industry" (PhD diss., Columbia University, 1951), cited in Harvey J. Levin, "Competition Among Mass Media and the Public Interest," *Public Opinion Quarterly* 18 (1954): 62.

49. Oswald Garrison Villard, "The Press Today: The Associated Press." *Nation,* April 16, 1930, 443–44; David M. Rubin, "Liebling and Friends: Trends in American Press Criticism, 1859–1963," paper presented to the Association for Education in Journalism, Ottawa, 1975, 3, cited in J. Herbert Altschull, *From Milton to McLuhan: The Ideas Behind American Journalism* (New York: Longman, 1990), 277–282.

50. "Newspaper Criminals in Chicago," *Nation,* July 23, 1930, 88.

51. Rosten, *Washington Correspondents,* 196.

52. As a cub reporter, Seldes had been inspired a generation earlier by the press criticism of muckraker Will Irwin (1873–1948).

53. Seldes, *Lords of the Press*, 20, 227, 99, 53. The term "House of Lords" had been used before to refer to publishers. Charles E. Merriam wrote in 1931 that newspaper owners had become an informal and irresponsible House of Lords. See Charles E. Merriam, *The Making of Citizens: A Comprehensive Study of Methods of Civic Training* (Chicago: University of Chicago Press, 1931), 213; the sarcastic reference to McCormick was published years later. George Seldes, *Even the Gods Can't Change History: The Facts Speak for Themselves* (Secaucus, NJ: L. Stuart, 1976).

54. George Seldes, *Freedom of the Press*, 151.

55. Seldes, *Lords of the Press*, 294.

56. Seldes, *Freedom of the Press*, 151–152.

57. Rosten, *Washington Correspondents*, 278, 304, 301–2.

58. Carl Ackerman, "The Challenge to the Press," in *Killing the Messenger: 100 Years of Media Criticism*, ed. Tom Goldstein (New York, Columbia University Press, 1989), 159–68.

59. Ackerman, "The Challenge to the Press," 159–168.

60. Fred W. Friendly, *Minnesota Rag: The Dramatic Story of the Landmark Supreme Court Case That Gave New Meaning to Freedom of the Press* (New York: Random House, 1981), 47–48. Historically, Minneapolis had been plagued by municipal corruption. In his "Shame of the Cities" series in 1904, muckraker Lincoln Steffens documented how the mayor turned the city over to criminals; the mayor was run out of town, but bribes and payoffs still flourished.

61. Ibid., 63, 88.

62. Ibid.

63. Ibid., 63, 88–91.

64. John Lofton, *The Press as Guardian of the First Amendment* (Columbia: University of South Carolina Press, 1980), 207, 209–10.

65. *Broadcasting* magazine headlined its coverage of the 1933 ANPA convention "AP and ANPA Declare War on Radio." William S. Paley, *As It Happened: A Memoir* (Garden City, NY: Doubleday, 1979), 125.

66. Robert W. McChesney, "Strange Days Indeed! Louis G. Caldwell, the American Bar Association, the American Legal Community and the Changing Attitude Toward Federal Regulation of Broadcasting, 1928–1938," paper presented to the Association for Education in Journalism and Mass Communication, Minneapolis, Minnesota, August 1990, 7.

67. Lewis J. Paper, *Empire: William S. Paley and the Making of CBS* (New York: St. Martin's Press, 1987), 28; Donald L. Shaw, "The Rise and Fall of American Mass Media," Roy W. Howard Public Lecture (Bloomington: Indiana University, 1991), 17; Erik Barnouw, *Tube of Plenty: The Evolution of American Television*, rev. ed. (New York: Oxford University Press, 1982), chapter 2.

68. Philip T. Rosen, *The Modern Stentors: Radio Broadcasters and the Federal Government, 1920–1934* (Westport, CT: Greenwood Press, 1980), 147.

69. Paper, *Empire*, 40.

70. John W. Shaver, "Radio's N.B.C.: A Manufacturing Enterprise with 50,000,000 Final Inspectors," *Factory and Industrial Management*, January 1930, 59–61.

71. Ibid., 116.

72. Lichty and Topping, *American Broadcasting*, 453.

73. Paley, *As It Happened*, 70, 108; Paper, *Paley*, 18, 42, 116–17.

74. Ibid.

75. McChesney, "Strange Days Indeed!" 7.

76. Levin, "Competition among Mass Media and the Public Interest," 62–79, in Lichty and Topping, *Broadcasting*, 246–49, 256; Sterling and Kittross, *Stay Tuned*, 133.

77. Gerd Horton, *Radio Goes to War: The Cultural Politics of Propaganda during World War II* (Berkeley and Los Angeles: University of California Press, 2002), 13.

78. Sterling and Kittross, *Stay Tuned*, 122.

79. Sammy R. Danna, "The Rise of Radio News," Lichty and Topping, *Broadcasting*, 339–340; Rudolph D. Michael, "History and Criticism of Press-Radio Relationships," *Journalism Quarterly* 15 (1938): 179.

80. Allen Raymond, "The Follies of Radio," *New Outlook*, 162 (2): 38–41; Michael, "Press-Radio Relationships," 179; Paley, *As It Happened*, 123.

81. Ibid., 124.

82. Raymond, "The Follies of Radio," 38–41; Sammy R. Danna, "The Press-Radio War," in *American Broadcasting: A Source Book on the History of Radio and Television*, ed. Lawrence W. Lichty and Malachi C. Topping (New York: Hastings House Publishers, 1975), 345.

83. Ibid., 126; Danna, "Radio News," 342.

84. John P. Freeman, "Lowell Jackson Thomas," in *Biographical Dictionary of American Journalism*, 696–97.

7

Focus on Big Government

I want to talk for a few minutes with the people of the United States.
— President Franklin Roosevelt, first fireside chat, 1933

The honeymoon between the president and the press was sweet but short. Soon after President Roosevelt had taken office in April 1933, he began advancing legislation intended to relieve the economic blight of the Depression. His New Deal envisioned a dramatic departure from "balanced budget" government—an unprecedented program of direct federal relief and economic regulation. At the outset, some newspaper editorial writers and publishers, among them William Randolph Hearst, congratulated the president for an industrious start at solving problems left by Hoover. Humor columnist Will Rogers expressed the country's mood after Roosevelt's first week in office: "The whole country is with him, just so he does something."[1]

Within weeks, as the legislation took shape, much of this cautious press support vanished, replaced by critical opposition and occasional hostility. Some publishers attacked the New Deal plan to raise taxes and redistribute wealth. To many it seemed to mimic remedies espoused by socialists, or by the communist regime in the Soviet Union. Opponents in the press also claimed that rapid expansion of federal government agencies threatened press freedom. Hearst soon took a leading role among a cohort of anti-Roosevelt publishers. Ironically, Hearst was responsible for Roosevelt's winning the Democratic nomination and the presidency. At the Democratic convention in 1932, it was Hearst who, at a critical juncture, supported Roosevelt despite the fact that one of his earlier Front-page editorials branded Roosevelt a "sinister" internationalist. Hearst made the turn when his own favorite, U.S. House Speaker John Nance Garner of Texas, failed to win the nomination. After hurried phone calls and conversations, Garner withdrew and the Texas and California delegations switched to Roosevelt.[2]

During 1933, Roosevelt relied on cooperation from the press and the business community. However, the government's increasing debt to deal with unemployment provoked muttering among businessmen during 1934. After Roosevelt's Democrats won a large majority in the 1934 midterm Congressional elections, conservatives pressed Roosevelt to set limits on spending. Channeling questions from their publishers, White House reporters questioned Roosevelt at his press conferences. In January 1935, one reporter asked whether the president saw a limit to the national debt. Roosevelt answered by asking what the reporter would do about people who were starving.

"Would you let them starve in order to keep the public debt from going beyond a specific amount?"
"Of course not, Mr. President."
"There you are. I don't know."[3]

As early as November 1933, Hearst began labeling Roosevelt's National Recovery Act (NRA) the "No Recovery Allowed" law. Hearst insisted that industry could not recover from the Depression if it had to hire a million more people at higher wages and shorter hours. In Chicago, Colonel Robert McCormick's *Tribune* consistently published stories and editorial cartoons opposing the New Deal's redistribution of wealth.[4] Hearst and other publishers, including publishers who had built fabulous fortunes, criticized Roosevelt's New Deal, which subverted their financial holdings. The president's spending policies unbalanced the budget with increasing deficits, notably when he asked early in 1935 for $4.8 billion in work-relief payments. By then his tax policies and his "punitive" rhetoric about redistributing the wealth alarmed businessmen and wealthy Americans, who claimed Roosevelt aimed to "soak the rich." The president's speeches, wrote Raymond Moley, a New Deal insider and journalist, "signalized the adoption of a policy of reform *through* taxation, of taxation for reform."[5] As historian Arthur Schlesinger observed, the New Deal aroused many to believe that such an expansive national government "was destroying American freedom." The hiring of bright young people in order to expedite new federal programs often seemed arbitrary, argued Hearst, who called the New Deal "government by personal whim."[6]

Newspaper tycoons were criticized in turn. Among their harshest critics were writers who sided with the labor union movement or otherwise identified with the goals of the New Deal. Leo Rosten, whose book was critical of publishers' hold over the Washington press, acknowledged his support for the New Deal.[7] Press critic George Seldes was ardently pro-union and a friend of New York columnist Heywood Broun, who in 1933 founded the journalists' union, the Newspaper Guild.[8] Social critic Frederick Lewis Allen observed in the 1930s that newspapers had become capital-intensive businesses concentrating power into fewer and fewer hands. Publishers had become capitalists "on a considerable scale, and their influence was likely to be exerted on behalf of property rights, of big business, of the interests of important advertisers."[9]

Most alarming to the wealthy was Roosevelt's surprising tax reform, announced in June 1935. In his message to Congress, which was received with cheers and applause, Roosevelt targeted inequities in the income tax of 1913, notably loopholes that permitted tax evasion and accumulations of wealth. "Our revenue laws have operated in ways to the unfair advantage of the few," he told Congress. In the context of the Depression and deficit spending, the president insisted that the wealthy pay more toward the national debt. He aimed to tap protected corporate earnings as well as inheritances of more than $10 million. As justification, he noted that "vast personal fortunes" had been built not only by luck but "because of the opportunities for advantage which government itself contributes." One Senate supporter said the president merely wanted a "share-the-burden-of-government" program. Critics termed the plan a "soak-the-rich" proposal or a "share-the-wealth" program such as had earlier been advocated by Louisiana Senator Huey Long. In fact, the *Times* reported, the new taxes were intended to "force partial redistribution of large fortunes" to produce $340 million—$200 million from inheritances, $100 million from individuals, and $40 million from corporations.[10]

The 1935 Congress, which endorsed the president's principle of raising taxes on the wealthy, had "thrown the business community into paroxysms of fright," Moley wrote. Publisher Roy Howard, another Roosevelt supporter, agreed, counseling the president that "any experienced reporter will tell you that throughout the country many businessmen who once gave you sincere support are now not merely hostile, they are frightened ... that you fathered a tax bill that aims at revenge rather than revenue—revenge on business." Hearst likened Roosevelt to Lenin. In April 1935, Hearst told Edmond D. Coblentz, the supervising editor of his newspaper chain, "The distribution-of-wealth policy is nothing but the plunder of the worthy well-to-do, a policy pursued to the limit by Lenin.... We have practically a dictatorship now."[11]

By 1935, an estimated 60 percent of U.S. newspapers opposed the New Deal. Hearst and other elite "Roosevelt bashers" controlled about one-fifth of the daily national newspaper circulation. In many of them hostility toward Roosevelt resembled hatred. Schlesinger contended that the vitriol "was an emotion of irrational violence, directed against Roosevelt's personality rather than his program, incoherent in its argument, scandalous in its illustrations, sometimes scatological in its imagery."[12] Roosevelt claimed that 85 percent of newspapers opposed his policies. An analysis of 167 editorials in newspapers that Roosevelt read found that 33 percent were favorable, 36.5 percent were unfavorable, and the other 30.5 percent in neither category.[13]

The stage was set for a dramatic showdown between the publisher and the president, characterized by a year of backroom political maneuvers and public blasts and counterattacks. With the 1936 election in his sights, Hearst, feeling betrayed and vengeful, charged ahead to lead the effort to unseat the "socialist" in the White House. When his idea for a "Jeffersonian Democratic" third party proved fruitless, Hearst changed his political affiliation to the Republican party, aiming to handpick the Republican nominee.[14]

Whomever Hearst chose would be guaranteed editorial support from the greatest publisher in terms of holdings. His empire reached into every region with 28 newspapers and a daily circulation of six million copies read by as many as 20 million Americans. Added to this were his magazines; his newspaper syndicate, which recirculated stories; his news agency; and his radio stations, which used Hearst-agency news and broadcast Hearst's talks. He had built, biographer David Nasaw noted, "the nation's first media conglomerate by extending his newspaper empire horizontally into syndicated feature, photo, and wire services; magazines; newsreels; serial, feature and animated films; and radio." Given Hearst's unyielding control, his editors—who nicknamed him "Chief"—had long been "regarded with contempt by most other newspaper people as well-paid but voiceless slaves."[15]

By late 1935 Hearst was still undecided about whom to support when Coblentz told him over the phone that Republicans were talking about the governor of Kansas, Alfred M. Landon.

"Where is he from?"
"He is from Kansas."
"Is he a good man?"
"I understand he is a good man."
"How can he be good and come from Kansas?"[16]

From then on, Hearst's papers supported Landon. As one of the few Republicans who survived the Democratic landslide in 1934, Landon appealed to Hearst as an "America first" politician, unlikely to get Americans tangled in foreign affairs. At home, Landon had balanced his state's budget, reduced taxes despite the Depression, and opposed Roosevelt-style taxes that Hearst and big business called "class legislation" that was "confiscatory." To publicize Landon, Hearst launched a media blitz. In September 1935, in a statement syndicated by the North American Newspaper Alliance, which was owned by the *New York Times,* Hearst declared that Landon could beat Roosevelt. On a radio broadcast from his California castle at San Simeon, he attacked Roosevelt's "foreign, Fascist ideas of personal dictation." By November, Hearst's editors were devoting "columns of praise to Landon."[17]

Hearst's magazines strove to give the Kansas governor a national profile. Adela Rogers St. Johns wrote about Landon for *Good Housekeeping.* Hearst's magazine division head, Richard Berlin, dispatched Damon Runyon, one of his most talented writers, to the capital in Topeka. The popular Broadway columnist wrote a lengthy magazine article intended to "present Landon acceptably, both to the unsophisticated reader and to the hard-headed money crowd in the East."[18]

Runyon was a prime example of a talent Hearst had nurtured. By 1935, he was at the peak of his popularity and financial success. He had written for Hearst's *New York American* since 1911 as a sportswriter, crime reporter, war correspondent, and columnist. Through the Hearst syndicate, Runyon reached far more readers than most American journalists. Two Hearst agencies, King Features and the International News Service, circulated his stories across America. By the 1930s, Runyon's most popular beat, far from national politics, was the life of Broadway. His "tales of showgirls, touts, crapshooters, and thugs" appeared in Hearst's *Cosmopolitan* and other magazines. He earned as much as $5,000 a story, and up to $10,000 for movie rights. He was also busy bringing out book collections of his Broadway stories. *Guys and Dolls* (1931) was followed in 1934 by *Blue Plate Special* and in 1935 by *Money from Home.* That same year he was finishing a Broadway play, *A Slight Case of Murder.*[19]

Emerging from this world of glitter and glamour, Runyon put everything aside, spent time with the obscure corn-belt conservative, and wrote fast. Very likely Hearst chose or approved Runyon's theme—the "Horse and Buggy Governor"—to praise traditional virtues as a contrast to Roosevelt's "socialism." Months earlier, Roosevelt had used that very phrase in criticizing the Supreme Court majority that ruled his National Industrial Recovery Act unconstitutional. Convinced, as Moley later wrote, that "the Court majority was the implacable enemy of all change," Roosevelt told a press conference on May 31 that the Court had a "horse-and-buggy" interpretation of interstate commerce. Roosevelt's public disrespect for the Supreme Court "provoked a storm of denunciation more violent than any other during Roosevelt's administration—denunciation that went on day after day through early June."[20]

Unofficially, the campaign to nominate Landon began in November when *Cosmopolitan* introduced "the horse and buggy governor." "He likes to get out among the people of the corn belt and talk over practical farming…. He is a baseball fan, likes football and nearly all other forms of

sport.... He is a family man, a clean man, and withal a wholly sane man."
Runyon quoted Landon's matter-of-fact political pragmatism: "A man
who succeeded Roosevelt in 1936 would have a tough job." Parlaying that
bare fact into a political challenge, Runyon editorialized: "We gather that,
tough as it might be, Alf M. Landon wouldn't shrink from the job if called
upon to take it." One critic noted that Runyon's article was "an index of
what Hearst believes the American public will swallow."[21]

Runyon's portrait launched a national media conversation. Because
so little had been written about Landon, Runyon's article "became the
source of background material for all Republican papers, whose files
were devoid of any 'color' material, or any other material, about him."
Hearst kept media attention on Landon by paying the governor a visit. In
December 1935 Hearst and his mistress, actress Marion Davies, left New
York, traveling by private train coach to Hearst's California home with
a media entourage that included his longtime New York editor Arthur
Brisbane, his publisher friend Paul Block, and editor-publisher Eleanor
"Cissy" Patterson, who was transforming Hearst's *Washington Herald* into
a moneymaker. In Kansas, Hearst, Block, and Brisbane lunched with the
plain-spoken, efficient, tax-cutting governor. Afterward, Hearst declared,
"I think he is marvelous."[22]

In the absence of effective competition, the "horse and buggy" gov-
ernor won the Republican nomination in July 1936. Consistent with
Hearst's political aims, Landon launched a campaign emphasizing
criticism of the New Deal and pledging not to "outpromise" Roosevelt.
In the Midwest his attacks on the president's Agricultural Adjustment
Act farm aid seemed unlikely to win farmers, "who have benefited from
AAA checks and are sticking by President Roosevelt." Roosevelt's camp
considered Landon's speeches "schoolboyish." Interior Secretary Harold
Ickes, whom Hearst's papers branded a communist, discredited Landon
as a stooge for Hearst. Ickes's friend Cissy Patterson, publisher of Hearst's
Washington Herald, conceded to Ickes that "Landon would not have been
heard of if it had not been for the Hearst build-up." Despite his debt to
Hearst, Landon tried to distance himself somewhat from the publisher as
Hearst's constant anti-Roosevelt bashing became excessive and seemed
to backfire.[23]

Given Hearst's role in the Landon ascendancy, there was talk among
Roosevelt's advisers about counterattacking. As early as February,
Roosevelt himself seemed "about ready to turn someone loose on" Hearst
but spoke of the matter only privately, Harold Ickes noted. By July, before
Landon's acceptance speech, Ickes and Postmaster General James A. Farley
agreed that they should make the publisher "one of the main issues in the
campaign." During August Roosevelt seemed reluctant to fight Hearst,
partly because of suggestions that Hearst might agree to a truce. A friend
of Hearst's, whom Roosevelt did not identify, suggested that because of

declining advertising Hearst might welcome a truce if Roosevelt sent an emissary. Ickes advised against negotiations. "You are the President of the United States and Hearst has been attacking you. The move should come from him." Eventually, the president favored a strategy of counterattack as Hearst and other anti-Roosevelt publishers printed stories, editorials, and cartoons containing distortions, suppressions, smears, and innuendoes, and often alleging socialist and communist ties.[24]

A center of Roosevelt bashing was in Chicago. Landon's Republican vice presidential running mate, Colonel Frank Knox, published the *Daily News*; Hearst had two Chicago papers, the *American* and the *Herald and Examiner*; and McCormick directed the *Tribune*. "If there is one American publisher who dislikes Franklin Roosevelt more than William Randolph Hearst, it is Robert Rutherford McCormick of the *Chicago Tribune*," *Time* magazine noted. The *Tribune*'s political cartoons regularly savaged Roosevelt's New Deal economic policies. One depicted the employees' entrance to American industry boarded up and marked "Closed by Roosevelt's Attack on Business." Another pictured a laboring taxpayer working hard to benefit "self-pitying minorities" and undeserving "drones" who sit idly and complain.[25]

All three publishers used their papers to allege that the Soviet Communist Party supported Roosevelt. His orders came directly from Russia, according to an August 9 *Tribune* story from its Northern European correspondent in Riga, Latvia, Donald Day, which was then circulated by the Republican National Committee. By August 28, the rival *Chicago Daily Times* had alleged the *Tribune* story was "a hoax" and offered $5,000 for any proof. The *Daily Times* investigation showed that Day erred by attributing to the Soviet Communist Party a speech broadcast in Chicago on May 29 by American Communist Earl Browder that was simply reprinted in a Soviet journal, Day's source. Nonetheless, on September 1, Knox's *Daily News* contended that Soviet Communists sought to "play up to other radical groups and to defeat Landon and Knox."[26]

Hearst then amplified the same accusations. On September 21, Hearst's papers, including the *Chicago Herald and Examiner* and the *New York American*, declared in an eight-column editorial, "Moscow Backs Roosevelt," and claimed the existence of "a vicious plot on the American republic." Two days earlier, after Roosevelt's campaign learned about the forthcoming editorial, his press secretary, Stephen T. Early, counterattacked. Early accused "a certain notorious newspaper owner" of trying to "make it appear that the President passively accepts the support of alien organizations hostile to the American form of government. Such articles are conceived in malice and born of political spite ... fake issues which no patriotic, honorable, decent citizen would purposely inject into American affairs." In Europe, Hearst ordered his papers to print his response. "I do not say and I never have said ... that he willingly receives support of the

Communists…. I have simply said and shown that he does receive the support of these enemies and that he has done his best to deserve the support." *Time* quoted U.S. Communist Party presidential candidate Earl Browder's response: "It is no longer news that Hearst is a liar." However, *Time* noted that U.S. communists "are this year hoping & praying for the re-election of Franklin Roosevelt. Their declaration for him has been delivered obliquely in the form of statements by Nominee Earl Browder and other Red leaders that the No. 1 Communist objective in the current campaign is to 'defeat the Landon-Hearst-Liberty League reaction.'"[27]

Roosevelt contended that Hearst "has done more harm to the cause of Democracy and civilization in America than any three other contemporaries put together." He confided to Harold Ickes that he still held Hearst "responsible for an absolutely unjustifiable war with Spain and that he had been responsible, too, for the assassination of a president"—referring to McKinley." The prejudices of publishers, Roosevelt asserted, corrupted news. Washington bureau chiefs "write what the owner of the newspaper tells them to write, and they leave out half the truth." Money—"the checkbook and the securities market"—was what counted for publishers, who were out of touch with the ordinary person. Some writers were simply misinformed, as when in December 1935 the *New Republic* "was in ignorance of some very important facts" about the Works Progress Administration. One exceptional writer from the White House view was Raymond Clapper for the Scripps-Howard chain. Early in 1936 he was "doing the most worth-while work … a liberal who keeps his feet firmly on the ground."[28]

At Hearst's newspapers, Arthur Brisbane and other editors worried that the anti-Roosevelt campaign could lose readers by the millions. In July, a public opinion survey commissioned by Henry Luce's *Fortune* magazine concluded that 43.3 percent of Americans who were polled considered Hearst's influence on politics as bad, with 10.5 percent saying it was good. The remaining 46.2 percent with no opinion, according to *Fortune*, included those who lived in areas where there were no Hearst papers.[29]

This relatively new practice of measuring public opinion was becoming popular for metropolitan newspapers and national organizations, although sampling methods were often unreliable. In 1936, methods of "straw polls" varied so much that two weeks before the election many pollsters and pundits thought the election would be close. In reality Roosevelt's victory trumped his enemies. He received 61 percent of the popular vote and 98 percent of the Electoral College votes, 523–8. Landon won only Maine and Vermont. His own Kansans preferred Roosevelt.[30]

Four of the most prominent national pollsters were "baffled and surprised by the overwhelming character of the Democratic victory." Such was the analysis in January 1937 in the first issue of the *Public Opinion*

Quarterly, a new journal published by Oxford University Press. Furthest from the mark was the *Literary Digest;* this became a factor that contributed to that publication's ultimate demise. In predicting winning margins in 1928 and 1932, the *Digest* had been off the mark by 12 percent and 6 percent, respectively. In 1936, it was embarrassingly far off the mark, forecasting that Landon would win with 32 states. Postmortems revealed faulty sampling practices. In Chicago, where Roosevelt won 2 to 1, the *Digest* based its prediction of a slight Landon win on a mailed survey of 100,000 voters registered by March, not the October voter lists with "new voters who evidently supported Roosevelt in larger numbers than Landon." Also, the *Digest* poll was "overloaded with persons in the higher income groups" who were more likely to be pro-Landon. They were also more likely to return the mailed survey in contrast to numerous working-class voters, who "were not interested in sending back the ballots."[31]

All four national polls—by the *Digest*, Crossley, Gallup, and *Fortune* magazine—were less accurate on state-by-state predictions than some of the metropolitan newspaper polls. On the overall national vote, *Fortune* made the best estimate, in part by luck since it polled only 4,500 people nationwide (75 in Chicago). *Fortune* predicted Roosevelt would receive 62 percent of the popular vote, 1 percent more than he actually got.[32]

The Gallup poll achieved "relative success," bettering the Crossley poll, and setting the stage for decades of profitable success for George Gallup's Institute for Public Opinion. Although Gallup underestimated the Roosevelt win by about 6 percent, analysts credited Gallup with the best measurement methods. In an article, Gallup stated that he sought "a representative sample rather than a huge one"—a total of about 100,000 from a mail survey supplemented by personal interviews—and used "a system of weights for the different classes."[33]

The 1936 election was Hearst's last great effort to select a president. He had misjudged the appeal of Landon's character and ability as well as the power of the anti-Roosevelt press. The "lack of influence of the newspapers," Ickes concluded, was the "outstanding thing about the campaign." In defeat, Hearst immediately tried to cut his losses by conceding to Roosevelt indirectly. Roosevelt said his son-in-law, John Boettiger, had received a call on election night from Marion Davies. "We know a steamroller has flattened us out," she said, "but there are no hard feelings at this end." Then Hearst took the phone and confirmed her statement. Hearst then published an editorial "in which he slobbered all over the president," noted Ickes, who unlike Hearst still had hard feelings and hoped the president would limit access by the Hearst wire services.[34]

Roosevelt's White House, and the president himself, managed the media better than any previous administration. In establishing a pattern for press relations, Roosevelt certainly benefited from the experience of his distant cousin, Theodore Roosevelt, whom historians credit as the first president to use newspapers effectively "as a means of reaching the people."[35] Theodore had cultivated favorite reporters, whom he charmed "to build an extensive positive reputation."[36] Franklin, while President Wilson's assistant secretary of the navy, witnessed the first regular presidential press conferences and then held his own press conferences at the Navy Department. It helped that he had college experience as a reporter and editor-in-chief of the *Harvard Crimson*, and that he "liked reporters, and, in the main, respected the job they had to do." He could call them by name, discuss their stories, ask for ideas, and "kid them about their hangovers."[37] Further experience as the 1920 Democratic vice presidential candidate, as a New York legislator, and as a governor guided Roosevelt in developing a complex White House communications strategy for managing media. With the assistance of a full-time presidential press secretary, he revived the practice of holding press conferences that had been regarded as worthless and almost abandoned during the Coolidge and Hoover administrations. Roosevelt's news conferences were intended to be friendly and informal, dominated by his charming personality. Unlike cousin Theodore, Franklin cultivated the Washington press corps as a whole—not only favorite reporters.

Roosevelt took advantage of modern ideas and technology. He benefited from the state-of-the-art public relations and publicity practices developed in the postwar period and first canonized in the 1920s. He made controlled use of photography and newsreels and conversed directly with the American public through the most *unmediated* political medium—radio.

In the White House, Eleanor Roosevelt played the greatest media role ever for a first lady. With the help of Associated Press reporter Lorena Hickok, Mrs. Roosevelt arranged Monday morning press conferences for female correspondents only, attended at first by more than 30 women. This special access to the White House helped secure the women's jobs during the Depression and encouraged other news operations to hire women. Emma Bugbee of the *New York Herald Tribune* wrote that the press conferences "soon became a channel for [Mrs. Roosevelt's] crusades in the field of social welfare ... by pressing at every opportunity for the measures she considered important." On her travels, Mrs. Roosevelt encouraged some female reporters to accompany her—among them Bugbee, Bess Furman of the Associated Press, Dorothy Ducas of the International News Service, Ruby A. Black of the United Press, and Kathleen McLaughlin of the *Chicago Tribune*.[38] Mrs. Roosevelt also wrote radio speeches and articles for newspapers and magazines, including a column, "My Day," which was syndicated to 135 newspapers by 1940. She was a favorite subject for editorial cartoonists. Jerry Doyle of the *Philadelphia Record* drew Mrs. Roosevelt looking up from the typewriter as the president entered a room with photographs showing his accomplishments and boasting, "*My* day."[39]

The president made his press conferences the keystone of his communications policy. In contrast with previous presidents, he held them frequently and expanded attendance to include more Washington correspondents, seldom fewer than 100, frequently more than 200. By conducting the sessions with an air of informality, Roosevelt tried to establish a rapport with the press while dispensing news and views. In his first term, he held press conferences twice a week, 337 by his count, wherever he was.[40]

Roosevelt communicated his philosophy at his first press conference four days after inauguration. The president explained that he wanted to continue "the kind of very delightful family conferences" he had held as governor in Albany. "I am told that what I am about to do will become impossible, but I am going to try it." Dispensing with the post-Warren Harding practice of requiring written questions in advance, he would answer as many impromptu questions as time allowed. "There will be a great many questions, of course, that I won't answer." Some questions "I do not want to discuss, or I am not ready to discuss, or I do not know anything about." He almost never responded to hypothetical questions.[41]

In exchange for this access and candor, the president limited the journalists' use of what he said. He continued his Albany practice of talking about confidential information "off the record"—asking not to be quoted. He made it "perfectly clear" that "I do not want to be directly quoted." Further, he insisted that reporters keep "off the record" information secret from "your own editors" and from "your associates who are not here." Roosevelt cautioned, "There is always the danger that, while you people may not violate the rule ... the other party may use it in a story." He also provided reporters with "background information"—"material which can be used by all of you on your own authority and responsibility, not to be attributed to the White House."[42]

The actual news releases—which journalists using derogatory slang called "handouts"—were issued by the nation's first official presidential press secretary. To bridge the gap between presidency and the press, Roosevelt chose an experienced journalist and personal friend, Stephen Early. With more than 20 years experience in journalism and Washington politics, Early seemed specifically groomed for the new job. After starting with a Washington newspaper and then working for United Press, he had moved on to the Associated Press in Washington when Roosevelt was heading Wilson's Navy Department. In 1920, he left journalism briefly to assist Roosevelt's vice presidential campaign and was credited with teaching Roosevelt the techniques of Washington publicity. In 1927, Early switched to a new medium with the fast-growing Paramount Newsreel Company.[43]

As press secretary, Early became the voice of the New Deal. Roosevelt explained that Early would be "available at all times to answer questions from the press." Early also scheduled time each morning to give out "background"—the "White House slant"—which Roosevelt considered important "to keep correspondents from printing inaccurate stories."[44] To respond with corrections and rebuttals, he installed a wire service tele-type in his office. Over the years Early gained a reputation as ingenious and hardworking, though sometimes short tempered and grouchy. Historian Arthur Schlesinger Jr. described Early as "tough, hard-driv-ing, profane." He cultivated the press's goodwill by keeping reporters' interests in mind—insisting on his own access to the president for press inquiries—but he often strained relations with reporters because of his loyalty to Roosevelt.[45]

Early's talent for public relations served the president in other ways. Inside the White House, he helped resolve disagreements among New Dealers, who quarreled about projects and jurisdictions and contradicted each another in public.[46] Realizing the New Deal needed to be explained, Early focused government publicity on the new agencies' emergency proj-ects and beneficiaries. With Early coordinating a team of publicists, this massive information project by the end of 1933 was producing about 1,000 news releases a month. With the goal of winning approval of New Deal programs, the publicists selected facts that presented a positive picture, constructing what media critic Richard Steele called propaganda.[47]

While news handouts streamed to Washington reporters, Early aimed to send a "sympathetic portrait of the New Deal" to relatively isolated citizens. Roosevelt valued small-town newspapers that were beyond the influence of urban press lords—about 6,700 newspapers published weekly or less frequently. In 1933, more than 17.5 million Americans received all or most of their printed news from these papers, and other millions depended on small city dailies.[48] Many editors with small staffs accepted well-written news releases uncritically, often printing them without revision, especially when the news and feature stories, ques-tion-and-answer columns, and government cartoons sometimes arrived in press-ready plates impossible to edit. This "massive spoon feeding of the press," devised by the Creel committee during the World War, was perfected by New Deal publicists, many of them former reporters.[49]

Applying public relations to audio and visual media, Early framed Roosevelt's image in newsreels and photographs. He had joined Paramount in 1927, the year it entered the newsreel business and the year when sound was added, and his expertise helped Roosevelt become "the most compelling presidential personality of the sound era." At W. French Githens's Embassy Newsreel Theatre in New York City, audiences did not sit silently as they watched newsreels of Roosevelt's New Deal events and fireside chats. Githens recalled how anti-New Dealers would "hiss."[50]

Early succeeded in enforcing a White House ban on visuals that reminded Americans of the president's handicap. In newsreels and pho-tographs the president was never to be shown "walking with his crippled gait or being pushed about in his wheelchair."[51] In his 1932 presidential campaign, Roosevelt alerted the press at a California stop, "No pictures of me getting out of the car, boys."[52]

Roosevelt used electronic communication effectively. In the face of increasing opposition to his New Deal programs, the president relied on radio to bypass the filter and bias of newspaper editors. By eliminating middlemen between the messenger and the message, Roosevelt intended "to restore direct contact between the masses and their chosen leaders." As governor of New York he had bypassed the state's partisan press by taking "an issue directly to the voters by radio, and invariably I have met a most heartening response."[53]

Amid the despair of the Depression, he had a mass audience from coast to coast. The networks' affiliated stations in large and small cities created a web of urban and rural listeners that rivaled the reach of the great newspaper chains. Wherever people gathered around radios, in living rooms or public places, they received the message as individuals. Roosevelt's radio style seemed to appreciate the individual listener. Schlesinger observed that he "seized on the radio as a revolutionary new medium of person-to-person communication."[54]

The president's use of radio was exemplified by eight fireside chats in his first term—28 in his four terms. Roosevelt cast himself "as a man at ease in his own house talking frankly and intimately to neighbors as they sat in their living rooms."[55] While radio transported him to America, it also seemed to "bring the people right into the White House.... Washington was no farther away than the radio receiving sets in their living rooms."[56] The first fireside chat, broadcast on March 12, a Sunday evening eight days after Roosevelt's inaugural address, and after he had ordered the closing of banks, conveyed his "firm belief that the only thing we have to fear is fear itself." His chat's opening words—"I want to talk for a few minutes with the people of the United States"—set a conversational tone intended to calm a nation mired in joblessness and bankruptcies. "I want to tell you what has been done in the last few days, why it was done, and what the next steps are going to be."[57] Speaking calmly about the crisis, the president said banks would soon reopen. Will Rogers said Roosevelt explained banking so that everyone, even bankers, understood.[58] Ratings showed that 30 percent of the radio audience heard the first chat.[59]

In broadcasting these chats directly to Americans, the president established a direct medium for regularly communicating New Deal elements he knew would be controversial. Experience as governor of New York and in the Wilson administration had led him to regard powerful newspapermen as important allies who could also be potent adversaries. In 1932, as governor and presidential hopeful, Roosevelt, stung by criticism from the widely read philosopher-columnist Walter Lippmann, complained to a friend that Lippmann was ill informed such that "in spite of his brilliance, it is very clear that he has never let his mind travel west of the Hudson or north of the Harlem!" While columnists, reporters, publishers, or the new breed of radio commentators might misunderstand, misinterpret, or distort his forthcoming program, Roosevelt, taking the microphone into his own hands, could make his pitch plainly and, if necessary, correct the record to his satisfaction. After his second chat eight weeks later, he observed, "I think I made clear to the country various facts that might otherwise have been misunderstood and in general provided a means of understanding which did much to restore confidence."[60]

Analysts agreed that the president's personable manner and informal format combined charismatically so that "for the first time in American history the people of the nation were made to feel that they knew their President personally and that they were receiving inside information first hand on important events."[61] Roosevelt clearly benefited, as his sociability and active agenda contrasted starkly with the public memory of Hoover's cautious aloofness.

The president's frequent radio broadcasts, intended to break newspaper publishers' near monopoly over dissemination of information and opinion, also had the effect of strengthening the radio industry's hold on its audience. Ever sensitive to the competition, newspaper executives had continued to survey ascendancy of radio as well as newspaper readers' preferences. One survey among women by the University of Chicago's School of Business advised Louisville's *Herald-Post* that women liked the front-page cartoons (83%) best, followed by fashion pictures (78%), comic strips (68%), health features (48%), and letters to the editor (47%). Least liked were bridge lessons (11%) and foreign news (8%). [62]

During 1933 publishers determined to take strong measures to suppress the intrusion of radio networks into the news business. In a major move, the publishers, who controlled the Associated Press, United Press, and International News Service, banded together to deny radio stations access to news on those wires. That action occurred at a time when Congress was considering a new federal communication law that would address the phenomenal growth of private networks since passage of the Radio Act of 1927, which was vague about regulating networks and advertising, "the two dominant elements of the unfolding broadcasting industry."[63] This was partly because Congress was trying to regulate an industry whose future could only be imagined. Not until 1928 did the radio industry become an effective advertising-driven medium.[64] There was also a pre-1929 reluctance to legislate federal regulation of big businesses, especially booming ones.

The prospering commercial-broadcasting industry had soon triumphed over weakly organized critics and reformers. Under the 1927 act and its governing Federal Radio Commission, nonprofit stations dwindled from 253 to 65. Alleging monopoly and overcommercialization of broadcasting by the major networks, reformers wanted to reserve 25 percent of channels for educational or other nonprofit organizations, or to create a national nonprofit network like the British Broadcasting Corporation. With a strong commercial industry lobby opposing such ideas, Congress placed no further restraints on the commercial-broadcasting industry. Behind the scenes, Roosevelt seemed to side with this decision. The president was enjoying success in using commercial radio and wanted to "maintain cordial relations" with broadcasters.[65] Roosevelt "felt pressed to create a sympathetic regulatory agency to ensure his ready access to the airwaves."[66] Since 1927, the networks had succeeded, as one historian noted, in winning over Congress, the White House, and the newly formed Federal Radio Commission to their view that broadcasting by network-controlled chains, with financial and engineering resources, was consistent with the American free-enterprise system and in the best interests of the public. Paley and Sarnoff hoped to avoid reopening the issue of private versus government ownership in a pitched battle against the influential publishers together with other opponents seeking government ownership or at least more public access. Amid these developments, the networks, through the National Association of Broadcasters, sought an accommodation with the American Newspaper Publishers Association.[67]

Negotiations led to a truce, the Biltmore Agreement. In December 1933, the parties convened a press-radio summit meeting at the Biltmore Hotel in New York. In the resulting agreement, CBS, NBC, and the ANPA reached a compromise that addressed the main grievance of publishers and the main economic goal of the networks. As the journal *Broadcasting* reported, radio "concedes to journalism that news-gathering is merely incidental to radio's prime function of entertaining and educating, and radio secures from the press a plainly implied acceptance of the fact that sponsor-support is the proper American way of broadcast operation." Paley agreed to abandon his fledgling Columbia News Service. The networks also agreed to cut back 15-minute newscasts to only five minutes—to be broadcast only after morning and afternoon newspapers were on the street. For those five-minute newscasts, the publishers offered a Press-Radio Bureau, which would supply not the standard news reports but news *summaries* from the wire services. Again, to protect newspapers' advantage, these Press-Radio Bureau summaries would be restricted to 30 words or less. Radio commentators were appalled. CBS's H. V. Kaltenborn said the agreement represented "the complete defeat of radio." The publishers did grant a major exception; they conceded to radio, consistent with its licensed duty to broadcast in the "public interest," the right to announce news bulletins immediately on any news of "transcendent importance." Because broadcasters themselves would decide what news was so important it could not be withheld, this exception was a loophole in the agreement.[68]

Very likely, the network executives knew that the Biltmore Agreement could not suppress radio news for long. Paley later on acknowledged its fragility. Realistically, the networks had been free for too long to be contained. Some CBS and NBC affiliates, independent stations, and regional networks made arrangements to break the embargoes. By March 1, 1934, when the Press-Radio Bureau was ready to issue its sanitized news bulletins, "no one was paying much attention to any of the provisions of the so-called agreement.... Almost all spot news was being supplied to the radio stations as news of 'transcendent importance.'" In practice, the Press-Radio Bureau could not meet increasing demand for news. By 1935, UP and INS were selling news to radio stations, and the ANPA relaxed its opposition to advertising sponsorship of newscasts. Ultimately, Paley wrote, "radio could not be held back from performing its vital role of bringing the news to listeners faster than any other medium." Radio's tycoons had faced the newspaper barons and "won full-fledged recognition ... co-equal with newspapers in the dissemination of news. Radio would never be controlled or dominated by the print media."[69] In 1935, Edward R. Murrow would join CBS as director of radio discussions and within two years launch CBS's shortwave international broadcasting from Europe of such events as the coronation of Britain's King George IV.

With the passage of the Federal Communications Act of 1934, confirming private ownership of radio networks, the networks were free to expand, and publishers had to adjust to the established mediascape. The Communications Act of 1934 had streamlined government regulation of communications without changing the basic principles of the 1927 Radio Act. The five-member Federal Radio Commission was replaced by a seven-member Federal Communications Commission appointed by the president. The law gave the FCC broader authority to regulate all forms of interstate and foreign communication, including the telephone industry.

If nothing else, the press-radio conflict confirmed to newspaper publishers the futility of suppressing the new medium, leading them to reconsider profitable strategies. Having lost at beating radio, they might now invest more heavily in radio. One contemporary scholar noted that the relaxed attitude of the press toward radio could be traced "to those leaders who saw the power of radio and were acquiring, even while the war was going on, broadcasting stations of their own." Many recognized the possibilities for profit. Some publishers with stations began to "roll their own" news programs. Ironically, when publishers sought to sell their self-styled newscasts to news-hungry radio operators, the Associated Press, which supplied radio news, stepped in to rein in the publishers.[70]

The accelerating trend toward newspaper buyouts and mergers now extended to broadcasting, establishing even larger media corporations. During the 1930s, publishing companies came to own or control about 30 percent of radio stations, a trend that would accelerate until a handful of cross-media owners garnered more than half of the money spent on local radio. In 1930, 91 publishers either owned or cooperated in the management of radio stations. By 1937 listings showed that the same number of publishers owned or controlled 208 stations of the 717 stations with regular channels. In several states, newspaper ownership of stations topped 40 percent—in Texas it was 24 of 49 stations, Minnesota 8 of 19, and Oregon 7 of 16—arousing the FCC's fear of monopoly of radio by newspapers.[71]

By 1935, despite the Depression, the radio industry enjoyed the beginning of its golden age. Radio matured as America's second *national* medium (magazines being the first), carrying news, entertainment, and advertising coast to coast. Radio manufacturers, led by RCA, had placed 30 million sets in American homes. Industry employment, while relatively small, had grown to 11,000. More than 600 stations were licensed to broadcast, of which 300 were economically significant and 200 constituted "the backbone of the medium."[72]

Another outcome of cross-media activity was that networks often broadcast commentary from guest newspaper correspondents and columnists. In December 1935, Edgar Ansel Mowrer, home briefly from Paris, where he was the correspondent for the *Chicago Daily News,* spoke on NBC for 10 minutes on Italian aggression against Ethiopia. Some journalists quit newspapers for a successful career in broadcasting, as did Elmer Davis, switching to CBS from the *New York Times.*[73]

Radio's expansion of "name" commentators in turn stimulated newspapers to publish more columnists, resulting in the creation of print's own cadre of personality pundits. Walter Lippmann, who had moved to Washington to be closer to the political adventures of the era, was perhaps the most widely read columnist. His "Today and Tomorrow" in the *New York Herald Tribune* from 1931 onward was syndicated to hundreds of newspapers nationally and overseas. Arthur Krock, the *New York Times'* Washington bureau chief starting in 1932, wrote "In the Nation" and in 1935 won the Pulitzer Prize for his coverage of the New Deal.

Some managed to have dual careers in newspapers and radio. Dorothy Thompson of the *New York Herald Tribune* rose to prominence in 1934 when Hitler expelled her from Germany, likely because of her unflattering article about him, and her subsequent book, *I Saw Hitler!*[74] By 1936, she was writing about world and national affairs in her column "On the Record." Thompson was equally comfortable with radio and had an NBC audience estimated at five million, making her America's most influential female radio commentator.[75]

Ultimately, the end of the press-radio war spurred the development of expansive network news gathering. The popularity of news commentators stimulated the development of serious news-gathering staffs. At CBS, Paley took the lead, investing millions in news gathering at home and overseas, eventually under the leadership of the ambitious and talented Washington State University graduate, Murrow, who started as director of talks.

Concurrent with their dispute with radio, newspaper publishers were also fighting a challenge from organized labor within their own newsrooms. For decades, reporters had grumbled about low pay and long hours. Talk about organizing increased as newly unionized newspaper-production employees, who operated typesetters and presses, were earning at least 30 percent more than reporters. In 1933, news reporters established their first labor organization, the Newspaper Guild.

The newsroom union movement started in the big cities. In Chicago in 1901, Hearst had stopped a budding union effort. In Boston after World War I, news writers actually formed a union; again it was Hearst who ended it by firing all the union members and importing workers from California and Chicago. Hearst, who owned more newspapers in more cities than any of his colleagues, became the foremost union buster, quashing still more attempts in San Francisco and elsewhere. In 1934, the 71-year-old Hearst told a reporter that he opposed editorial unions because they would deprive journalists of their "romantic" character. More likely, as one biographer noted, the publisher resented any constraint on the autocratic power he had wielded since 1887. Hearst and other publishers argued that reporters' unions would lead reporters to slant news to a pro-union bias and thus impair freedom of the press.[76]

The architect of the Newspaper Guild was the Scripps-Howard columnist for the *New York World-Telegram,* Heywood Broun. Broun was a bundle of contradictions. He had a privileged background (at Harvard he had been a classmate of Walter Lippmann) but became a liberal critic of the privileged class and was for a time a socialist. His first wife, the ardent feminist Ruth Hale, was credited with urging him into controversies and liberal causes, at least until they were divorced in November 1933. By 1933, Broun was 44, had been writing a column for more than a decade, and was living comfortably in a penthouse, earning $30,000 annually as one of the nation's best-paid syndicated columnists. From this comfortable perch he sympathized with newspaper reporters, who, during the Depression, were losing jobs or suffering pay cuts. He often devoted his column to finding them jobs. In early August, he lunched at New York's exclusive Club 21 and, after a couple of drinks and a hearts-of-palm salad, borrowed the typewriter in the club office and in 25 minutes tapped out the column that launched the guild. "A Union of Reporters" appeared on August 7, 1933, but caused very little anxiety among publishers.[77]

Broun had talked about unionizing since 1931 when the Pulitzers sold the *World* and several of Broun's friends lost their jobs. Some knew Broun as one who started things but didn't finish them; perhaps because of this, he gave himself a deadline of seven weeks to start the "newspaper writers' union," for which he felt there was an urgent need. "Beginning at nine o'clock on the morning of October 1," Broun promised, "I am going to do the best I can to help in getting one up." Among the obstacles were reporters' own prejudices against unionization. For too long, news-room employees, because of their strong individualism and sense of status, believed unions were for "dopes like printers, not for smart guys like newspapermen," he wrote, quoting a letter from an unemployed reporter. Yet printers enjoyed far more job security and better wages. Another obstacle was the publishers' insistence, stated at hearings on the National Recovery Act's Publishers Code, that editorial staffs were "professional employees," thus excluded from NRA wage-and-hour regulations. Ultimately, Broun hoped that the NRA would end the six-day work week; a five-day work week would require newspapers to hire more reporters.[78]

Broun's 58th Street penthouse became headquarters for the union movement. As one biographer portrayed the scene, "Broun presided from behind his cluttered kidney-shaped desk…. Others sat on the daybed or on piles of books or on the floor." The journalists compromised on a more refined "guild" rather than a "union," planned other branches around the nation, established the *Guild Reporter* newspaper, and compiled a series of demands—a five-day, 40-hour work week, a minimum-wage scale (many had been paid only $15 a week), and the right to bargain with publishers.[79]

When the guild was launched in New York in November and elsewhere in the following months, it roused mixed reactions. While some publish-ers warned that reporters' demands would raise publishing costs and cut profits, some welcomed the guild, among them Joseph M. Patterson of New York's *Daily News* and David Stern of the *New York Post.* Some were undecided; some hid their opposition.

Hearst, through his editors, fought the union openly. Guild members were targeted. The *Lorain Journal* in Ohio locked out guild employees. Twenty-three reporters for Hearst's *New York American* publicly resigned from the union. In Chicago, the chapter dwindled from more than 100 to fewer than 10. In San Francisco, where Hearst worried less about competition, staffers at the *Examiner* and the *Call Bulletin* were fired or transferred to demeaning assignments. A veteran music critic was sud-denly reassigned to report on celebrities arriving at hotels.[80] A standoff in Seattle led to a strike in 1936 that closed the *Post-Intelligencer* and put 650 employees out of work. Hearst blamed American communists.[81] American Communist Party members allegedly infiltrated some local chapters, especially where moderate Newspaper Guild leaders were unable to negotiate with publishers. Radical factions schemed to extend guild meetings for hours then passed their own rules after moderates had gone home. As national president, Broun used his personal appeal to prevent the moderates and communists from splitting the union, always striving to keep his brainchild alive.[82]

The first constitutional test resulted in victory against the Associated Press. The AP under general manager Kent Cooper refused to recognize the guild spied on guild meetings, threatened its employees, and fired several. In April 1937, the U.S. Supreme Court rejected the AP's "freedom of the press" defense and ordered the wire service to reinstate reporter Morris Watson, who had been the national guild vice president.[83]

As national president, Broun traveled widely promoting the guild and occasionally showing up in a line of picketing reporters. In Toledo, Ohio, state police attacked a picket line with tear-gas grenades. Broun ran but was arrested. When an officer referred to him as a "rich New York Communist," Broun corrected him: "rich New York *columnist*." Enjoying his added celebrity status, he conceded that he was "subconsciously an exhibitionist. And not so very subconsciously at that."[84]

Broun played a symbolic role in the first successful guild action in New York City. It occurred in the fall of 1935 at New York's *Amsterdam News,* an African American newspaper founded in Harlem in 1909. The staff, enthusiastic about being included in a labor movement, was set to strike when their African American publisher locked them out. Pickets were encouraged when Broun joined them on several occasions. Marvel Cooke, a beginning journalist, watched as Broun "tried his best to get arrested on that line ... but he never made it. He was very disappointed." Cooke recalled that Broun "seemed a very human person, very large, over six feet, and very heavy, and quite sloppy looking.... He was there every day. He was quite an inspiration to us." After 11 weeks, the lockout ended in victory. Cooke's salary almost doubled from $18 to $35. Before the strike she had been the society editor's flunky; now she became a reporter. The guild had established itself, although publishers subverted some of its gains. "They [the *Amsterdam News*] never really accepted the union," Cooke noted. "They got rid of us one by one ... saying (our) work wasn't up to standard or they'd find some flaw.... I would have been fired from there, too, but I got saved by the bell, by being able to resign."[85]

During the Depression, Broun also belonged an elite group of New York newspaper journalists, magazine writers, and playwrights who invigorated the city's literary life. Their unofficial though famous gathering place was the lounge of the Algonquin Hotel. Along with Broun, the regulars were Franklin P. Adams, Alexander Woollcott, James Thurber and E. B. White of Harold Ross's *New Yorker,* the sportswriter Grantland Rice, Robert Benchley, Dorothy Parker, and Ben Hecht, who wrote the play *Front Page,* which spawned a genre of screenplays about journalists. In that oasis, lubricated by post-Prohibition cocktails, this literary elite shared their experiences and generated ideas soon to be amplified in newspapers, the theater, and magazines. Some were noted for their humor, expressed in spoofs and cartoons, especially welcome during the Depression. White in 1934 spoofed the unreality of the fashion magazines *Vogue* and *Harper's Bazaar,* whose stories and photographs of society personalities portrayed "surcease from the world's ugliness, from disarray, from all unattractive things ... a world in which there was no awkwardness of gesture, no unsuitability of line, no people of no importance.... How barren my actual life seems."[86]

In fact, the world of magazine publishing was thriving despite the Depression. The *New Yorker* continued to gain a loyal following among urban sophisticates for its mix of wry humor, commentary, criticism, and Thurber's cartoons depicting, as Dorothy Parker surmised, a world of desperate, hapless people. DeWitt and Lila Wallace's *Reader's Digest* had by 1929 reached a circulation of 250,000 people eager to save time by reading condensed, simplified material from other publications.

Even more dazzling in the magazine world were the multiple successes of Henry Luce, whose editorial teams adapted to changing times and tastes. As the Depression deepened, *Fortune* challenged the traditional secrecy of tycoons, some of whom might be held responsible for investors' losses. The public, Luce said, "has a right to know how business works." In 1934, *Fortune* writer Eric Hodgins exposed profiteering by Europe's war-munitions manufacturers, leading to the U.S. Senate investigation of American "merchants of death."[87]

Luce's publishing empire, centered in New York's architecturally stunning Chrysler Building (photographed by Margaret Bourke-White), attracted a host of talented writers. Luce hired poet Archibald MacLeish, economist John Kenneth Galbraith, and James Agee, who at 25 in 1934 published his first work, a book of poetry. At *Fortune,* Agee's subjects were as diverse as the Tennessee Valley Authority, vacation cruises to Havana, and the orchid industry. He began an article on cockfighting with, "You are a gentleman. You have a taste for sport (most likely horses), leisure to indulge it, and an estate." In the storytelling tradition, he began his piece about roadsides by introducing his characters: "this American continent; this American people; the automobile; the Great American Road, and—the Great American Roadside." Agee's piece on the one-month season at Saratoga race track starts with the contrast of the town out of season: "Eleven solid months of every year the small strange city of Saratoga Springs or Saratoga, or The Springs, or The Spa, is as dead a home of 13,700 people as you can locate."[88]

In the summer of 1936, *Fortune*'s editors gave Agee an assignment with more scope. They sent him and photographer Walker Evans to gauge the depth of the Depression in the Deep South, especially among poor tenant farmers who worked land they did not own. In 1936, Roosevelt's concern for this landless class of farmers in the Depression led him to appoint a Committee on Farm Tenancy. In Alabama, Agee and Evans stayed with tenant farmers who were near the bottom of America's economic ladder. In words and pictures they portrayed the daily struggles and oppressive reality of life for three families—the Gudgers, the Woods, and the Ricketts. In New York, however, the *Fortune* editors decided not to publish the work. Ultimately, Agee and Evans expanded the material and published it as a book, *Let Us Now Praise Famous Men,* in 1941.[89]

Luce was meanwhile planning America's first weekly magazine devoted to photography. *Life* intended to capitalize on advances in photographic technology—from faster film and smaller cameras to improved technology in photoengraving. Then, too, he was impressed by a new generation of innovative photographers, among them the first generation of photojournalists. Evidence suggested that photographs would have a large, appreciative audience. The camera craze, as Allen called it, produced a public appetite for pictures, nurturing a new generation of photographers. "We have got to educate people to take pictures seriously," Luce wrote. *Life*'s prospectus claimed the weekly picture parade would help people "to see life; to see the world; to eyewitness great events; to see strange things; ... to see and to take pleasure in seeing; to see and be amazed; to see and be instructed." In 1935 he assembled the staff to produce the prototype of *Life.*[90]

Bourke-White moved to the *Life* staff as one of its first four photographers. By 1936 she had established a national reputation after two trips to Russia and widely disseminated photographs published in two books and numerous magazines. Fellow photographer Carl Mydans, whose pictures documented the Depression in the gaunt faces of Dust Bowl farmers, admired Bourke-White for being "obsessed by the excitement of what she and the camera could do together." Luce assigned her to go West and photograph President Roosevelt's New Deal flood-control dams being built on the Columbia and Missouri rivers. She found a human interest story there as well and a few days before deadline telegrammed: "Think Fort Peck night life will be very good of several bar scenes crowds watching bowling billiards taxi dancers at work two or three hard snaps of prostitutes."[91] *Life*'s first issue, November 23, 1936, featured one of those dams on the cover. Inside, Bourke-White's pictures told a story of the new Wild West of hard work and saloon life and dime-a-dance girls in the frontier shanty-towns around the dams. This achievement typified her later career.[92]

Sales of the first issue nearly doubled the expected 250,000 on which advertising rates were based. It quickly sold out—466,000 copies. Sales soon exceeded one million, but because ad rates were so low the magazine lost $6 million before it began to make handsome profits. Luce had also won a race, publishing America's first picture magazine six weeks ahead of his nearest competitor. In January 1937 Gardner Cowles Jr., who claimed he had been planning a picture magazine since 1933, published *Look.*[93]

The weekly African American press also registered significant gains in circulation and influence despite the Depression, particularly in the Northeast and Midwest but also in the South. Amid the economic chaos, the race newspapers became evermore important as forums for expression of dissent as well as hope for African Americans, who were routinely ignored by mainstream establishment media. Minority entrepreneurs and reporters met the unserved needs of millions. Some weeklies circulated outside their regions and gained national influence, notably the Baltimore *Afro-American* (founded in 1892), the *Chicago Defender* (1905), the *Pittsburgh Courier* (1910), and Norfolk's *Journal and Guide* (1910). Other weeklies influenced decision makers in their communities or regions, among them New York's *Amsterdam News* (1909), the *St. Louis Argus* (1912), and the *Kansas City Call* (1919). The *Atlanta World* remained the only African American daily.[94]

By 1933, opposition to lynching widened into a national crusade. The campaign was spurred by a dramatic increase in killings, reported most fully and criticized most effectively in African American newspapers. In October 1933, the *Baltimore Afro-American* calculated that "since August 27 we have averaged one lynching a week." Late in 1933, after two lynchings in Alabama and Maryland, *Pittsburgh Courier* editors argued, "We have the plainest proof that action by the federal government is needed if lynching is to be stamped out."[95] The NAACP organized and led a campaign for a federal antilynching law, an effort that the African American press supported, encouraging readers to join the NAACP.

Entrenched opposition to antilynching legislation arose in the United States Senate. Southern senators, arguing that such a law represented another attempt of the federal government to dictate to the South, threatened to stall President Roosevelt's New Deal legislation. Meanwhile, progressive white Southerners in the 1930s, citing the general decline in lynchings in the decades since 1900, maintained that an antilynching law was unnecessary because social pressure would eliminate lynching. In the *Atlanta World*, Davis challenged the official statistics that showed lynchings decreasing, arguing that "anybody with the mind of a moron has every reason to believe that many Negroes are killed yearly in isolated parts of the South with no news of these murders ever reaching print, and that many recorded murders have all the elements of lynching."[96]

While Southern senators stifled the antilynching bill in Congress, the campaign publicity raised the nation's level of awareness and possibly helped reduce the frequency of lynchings. As the terroristic practice continued, the African American press led in documenting the crimes. In 1942, Lucile Bluford, then a daring reporter for the *Kansas City Call*, decided to drive to Sikeston in southeast Missouri to investigate the lynching of Cleo Wright, who had been charged with burglarizing a home and threatening two women. He had been shot by a policeman and was in jail when a mob took him, tied him to a truck, dragged him through town, and burned his body. "We found out that the lynching could have been prevented," said Bluford, who later became the *Call*'s editor, publisher, and majority owner. She wrote that law enforcement officers "knew ahead of time" and were "telling the black folks to get off the street" because someone was "going to have a little 'fun.'" No action was taken, but Bluford believed that the stories and the NAACP efforts "resulted in lessening of the lynchings. They finally disappeared."[97]

African American reporters covering the South for Northern newspapers faced a special danger. In the spring of 1933, the *Amsterdam News* noted that its reporters in Decatur, Alabama, had "been assured of protection from the mob" as they covered the trial of the Scottsboro Boys, nine African Americans who were charged with raping two white women. For this effort, the *News*, the Baltimore *Afro-American*, the *Journal and Guide*, and other black newspapers joined to form Co-operative Publishers. Member newspapers received reports on the lynchings from William N. Jones, managing editor of the *Afro-American*, and P. Bernard Young Jr., managing editor of the *Journal and Guide*.[98]

African Americans in the Midwest often migrated to pursue publishing opportunities in Chicago. Frank Marshall Davis returned to Chicago in 1934 and became managing editor of the Associated Negro Press. Davis's circle included John H. Johnson, a bright young man whose mother had sacrificed to bring him from Arkansas so he could go beyond the eighth-grade limit. In Chicago, Johnson had graduated as president of his high school class, edited the school newspaper, and for six years worked as director of publicity for an insurance company before beginning his career as publisher of *Negro Digest* and *Ebony* magazine.[99]

During the 1930s leadership of the civil rights movement passed from the pulpit to the pages of newspapers as the African American press seized the initiative. Editors, rather than preachers, became the most outspoken voices on behalf of racial justice. Not since the abolitionist press before the Civil War had so many African Americans articulated the need for urgent changes. The press of the 1930s resumed what has been called the African American "jeremiad," the continuing discussion of the American promise, warnings about broken promises, and hopeful prophecy about fulfillment of that promise.[100] Robert Abbott of the *Chicago Defender* outlined a 10-point plan for racial progress, emphasizing economic opportunity. P. B. Young Sr., publisher of the *Journal and Guide*, underscored the need for educational opportunity and promoted Black History Week. Carl Murphy of the *Baltimore Afro-American* and Robert S. Vann of the *Pittsburgh Courier* (who in 1933 became the nation's first African American special assistant U.S. attorney general) championed legal rights. While at the *Atlanta World*, Davis warned readers not to be beguiled by promises from the American Communist Party.

World news relating to African Americans' struggles for justice received attention, particularly on the opinion pages. In India, Mahatma Gandhi's passive resistance to British rule became a heroic model. The *Defender's* editors admired how Gandhi mobilized his people through spiritual force to achieve social, economic, and political goals. They hoped for an American Gandhi. "Are there no Gandhis among us? Are we to remain a Race without a policy? What we need in America is a Gandhi who will fight the cause of the oppressed."[101] Jones of the *Afro-American* noted that Gandhi, "starving himself in India to call the world's attention to the manner in which white England is exploiting the working masses of that vast country, may yet win his victory. Colored citizens in America might well become interested in India.... Let us hope that some Gandhi will develop in America."[102]

The African American press related its problems to the race edicts of Adolf Hitler in Germany and Nazi suppression of civil rights for Jews and other minorities. "This is extreme racialism and nationalism gone mad," the *Courier* declared. "We would be criminally negligent to assume that Americans of color would fare better under a Fascist government here than the colored citizens of Germany."[103] When a Jews-only theater was licensed in Berlin, the *Afro-American* called Hitler "Germany's chief Ku Kluxer" and remarked that he "has evidently studied the Southern U.S.A. system of Negro baiting. It is the old story. No part of the world is safe from oppression so long as oppression is practiced in any part of the world."[104]

The political turmoil in Europe and Asia became hard for Americans to ignore. By the mid-1930s, news of the extraordinary international events pervaded American society, intruding even into movie theaters, where every week 70 million Americans, seeking escape from the Depression, viewed newsreels shown between features. A new media genre, newsreels were part documentary, part Hollywood. They presented dramatically diverse stories, from light interlude features to attention-grabbing news reports with stunning, memorable footage of people and events, some photographed by lucky cameramen and others "re-created" after the event.[105] Some audiences feasted on the genre. In New York's Embassy Theatre, a theater that showed only newsreels, film of Roosevelt's fireside chats provided "the greatest single attraction" in the 1930s, but audiences saw for the first time other world leaders—Mussolini, Hitler, Joseph Stalin, Chiang Kai-shek, and Winston Churchill. "Each had his adherents in the city, who flocked to the Embassy Theatre when their favorite was on the screen."[106]

In 1935 Henry Luce's *The March of Time* documentary newsreels showed controversial and disturbing footage. The Japanese invasion of China provided what one critic called "some of the grimmest but most spectacular footage" of the 1930s. On August 14, 1937, three newsreel cameramen for

The March of Time, Hearst's *News of the Day,* and Universal were filming in Shanghai when the Japanese bombed two hotels, a department store, and a residential neighborhood. In the midst of the expansion of movie palaces, one critic, the owner-editor of the *Motion Picture Herald,* claimed that such violence violated the sanctuary of the theater. Martin Quigley complained that the documentary product of Louis de Rochemont "is calculated to destroy the theatre as the public's escape from the bitter realities, the anguishes and the turmoil of life." Despite industry critics, the 1935–1936 productions won a Special Academy Award in 1937 for "significance to motion pictures and for having revolutionized one of the most important branches in the industry—the newsreel."[107]

More than other newsreels, *The March of Time* chronicled, with editorial bias, the economic and political developments in the Soviet Union, Nazi Germany, and Fascist Italy. One segment titled "Moscow!" featured progress of the Communists' economic five-year plan and progress in producing coal. Another titled "Japan!" looked inside the imperial country that had invaded China. Footage gave audiences their only glimpses of the era's prominent dictators—Joseph Stalin, Adolf Hitler, and Benito Mussolini. "While film producers in other newsreel studios eschewed controversial political and military items," historian Raymond Fielding noted, "*The March of Time* stubbornly paraded the faces and deeds of the world's most controversial figures."[108]

The content of newsreels, often perceived as biased or disturbing, provoked criticism and suppression. Footage that week after week focused on the military and war caused Oswald Villard, editor of the *Nation,* to observe in 1934 that "not in a year have I seen a newsreel which did not play up the military or navy." He singled out Hearst newsreels for "deliberate propaganda." More-militant critics picketed movie houses that showed Hearst newsreels, leading some theaters to refuse them. In the context of private and public criticism, editors frequently cut a photographer's proudest work if it showed "moments of violence and accident … either just before the moment of impact or before the reality of death or injury became apparent to the audience."[109]

At the same time, a growing clamor over sexual content in Hollywood films aroused a renewed effort to control corporate and independent moviemaking. Social and religious critics had long expressed concerns about the impact of film on morals, especially among the young. These concerns led religious organizations to boycott offensive movies and to pressure state governments to legislate film censorship. In April 1934 the Catholic Church launched the Legion of Decency, which gained support from other faiths. Although federal regulation failed to pass, six states had enacted film censorship laws that extended to newsreels and movies. The public outcry, together with a fear of further legislation, motivated filmdom to censor itself. The Motion Picture Producers and Distributors of America (MPPDA) turned the problem over to its president, Will Hays, who had governed as decency czar since 1922. In 1934, as some motion picture companies were going bankrupt and religious leaders' attacks on immorality in films threatened to keep millions from going to the movies, the Hays Office acted quickly.[110]

Hays and the MPPDA board on July 12, 1934, strengthened its Production Code Administration. *Variety,* the movie-industry magazine, reported that the Hays Office was "supreme pontiff of picture morals from now on." In deference to Catholic opinion, Hays placed a "fighting Irishman" in charge of enforcement. The press portrayed Joseph I. Breen, a former newspaper editor, as "umpire of the movies, assigned to preview every picture and to order the product cut, remade, or discarded." Henceforth, no company was to exhibit any picture not approved by Breen. Producers balked at some of Breen's judgments, but he was not reversed.[111]

The code covered everything related to morals. The industry's guiding principle stated that "No picture shall be produced which will lower the moral standards of those who see it.... Correct standards of life ... shall be presented. Law, natural or human, shall not be ridiculed." Censorship would apply to portrayal of crimes, sex, vulgarity, obscenity, profanity, costume, dances, religion, locations (such as bedrooms), national feelings, and titles. In 1935, the MPPDA established a $25,000 fine for any movie distributed without approval from the Production Code Administration.[112] Praise came from the Vatican. In July 1936 Pope Pius XI issued an encyclical concerning motion pictures, commending Hollywood's Production Code Administration as a model. In November, Hays visited Rome and was received by the pope.[113]

While filmdom was protecting morality in movies and shielding viewers from horrific war scenes from newsreels, newspapers, magazines, and radio emphasized "disturbing" news and controversy. As the focus of news shifted from the 1920s conferences on peace and armaments control to the 1930s outbreaks of hostilities and threats of a wider war, publishers channeled more money, space, and airtime for reports from the scenes of European and Asian crises.

Amid international political and military crises, a generation of American overseas correspondents earned a measure of prominence. After the war, adventuresome journalists had migrated to Europe, one historian has observed, "as part of a broader post-war exodus of young American writers, artists, and intellectuals." Journalists who settled in Europe learned the languages, cultures, and politics. During the 1920s and 1930s some freelanced stories to U.S. newspapers that retained no offices in Europe or had cut staffs during the Depression. This vanguard of internationalists was well ahead of most Americans in appreciating the increasing interdependence of nations and the probability of another war.[114]

Dictators seized the nation's attention and, in some cases, won admiration for their expediency in dictating what appeared to be economic progress. In Italy, Benito Mussolini's fascist administration had triumphed over communists as well as other opposition parties, impressed tourists by making the trains run on time, and cleared malarial swamps. In the Soviet Union, Joseph Stalin's communist dictatorship seemed from press reports to be miraculously converting the landed peasant class into a classless society in collective farms and urban industries. By 1938 Luce's *Time* magazine chose Hitler as its Man of the Year because, more than any other man, he had influenced world events "for better or worse." As each dictator controlled the press within his country, the means to these ends were often overlooked or downplayed. Mussolini, while destroying democratic institutions, proclaimed that fascism was the highest form of democracy.[115]

The public fascination with Hitler and Germany during the 1930s generated a multitude of stories. By January 20, 1933, Hitler had manipulated the electoral process sufficiently to be appointed chancellor by president Paul von Hindenburg. Following Mussolini's precedent in Italy, Hitler by March secured a change in the Constitution enabling him to rule by decree for four years. In the same month he expelled Dorothy Thompson. "She had been given twenty-four hours to get out," wrote William L. Shirer, who arrived in Berlin an hour or two later, now as a reporter for Hearst's Universal News Service after a short stint in Vienna with the *Chicago Tribune*. "It was a rather surprising judgment for so veteran and astute a Berlin correspondent." Like Thompson, Shirer underestimated Hitler's support and will to rule. Even after Hitler was named chancellor, Shirer felt that Germans would "soon seen the light, and that would be the end of this once-Austrian vagabond."[116]

Simultaneously, the Soviet Union and Stalin's "Five Year Plan" received increasing treatment from a small corps of Moscow correspondents. Some were sympathetic with Stalin's reforms, at least until the mid-1930s. Louis Fischer, who had gone there to live in 1922 at the age of 26, earned a reputation as an expert on the Soviet Union, writing for the *Nation* and publishing four books between 1930 and 1935, including a two-volume study called *The Soviets in World Affairs* (1930). In 1936 he left for the war in Spain to report and fight briefly on the side of the Republican antifascists.[117]

Contemporary with Fischer, one of the most trusted Americans analyzing the Communist regime from Moscow was the *New York Times* correspondent Walter Duranty. After covering the war and the Paris Peace Conference, he settled in Moscow in 1922. His analyses of momentous developments in Soviet politics and economic reform, together with his interviews with Stalin, gained him a reputation as an expert on Soviet affairs and, in 1932, the Pulitzer Prize for international reporting.

Afterward, however, contemporaries discredited his reports, claiming he was deceived by Stalin and Soviet propaganda, notably in underreporting the devastating famine and starvation induced by Stalin's Five Year Plan, which decreed collectivized agriculture, dismantling private farming. As the winter of 1932 approached and famine threatened to starve the peasantry, Duranty conceded that the Five Year Plan "has run against an unexpected obstacle—the great and growing food shortage in town and country alike." But he differed with reports of famine, asserting: "There is no famine or actual starvation, nor is there likely to be." The *Times,* in a subsequent apologetic explanation, noted that "Duranty's cabled dispatches had to pass Soviet censorship, and Stalin's propaganda machine was powerful and omnipresent. Duranty's analyses relied on official sources as his primary source of information, accounting for the most significant flaw in his coverage—his consistent underestimation of Stalin's brutality…. Taking Soviet propaganda at face value this way was completely misleading, as talking with ordinary Russians might have revealed even at the time." As an instance, the *Times* noted:

Describing the Communist plan to "liquidate" the five million kulaks, relatively well-off farmers opposed to the Soviet collectivization of agriculture, Duranty wrote in 1931, for example: "Must all of them and their families be physically abolished? Of course not—they must be 'liquidated' or melted in the hot fire of exile and labor into the proletarian mass."

The Pulitzer Prize board twice declined to revoke his prize because it found "no clear and convincing evidence of deliberate deception." Duranty left Moscow in 1934 and, like Fischer, covered the Loyalists in the Spanish civil war.[118]

That fighting in Spain attracted a cadre of American war correspondents. At one time or another, Fischer and Duranty were joined by Floyd Gibbons, Herbert Matthews, Webb Miller, Ernest Hemingway, and Martha Gellhorn. Some had traversed the globe from war to war. Miller, with the United Press, had covered hostilities in Ireland and Morocco and Mahatma Gandhi's resistance to British rule in India. Gibbons reported alternately for NBC radio and Hearst's International News Service and was frequently the voice heard on U.S. newsreels. After losing an eye while covering the war in France, he reported Japan's war in China and met up with Miller and Matthews during the Italian war in Ethiopia.[119]

Hemingway signed up with the North American Newspaper Alliance to apply his talents to reporting for newspapers and magazines and gathering material for a novel that became *For Whom the Bell Tolls.* His dispatches from the front, like those of some other American correspondents, sympathized with the elected leftist Republic, the Loyalists, fighting the fascist forces of General Francisco Franco. At Teruel, Hemingway wrote of the bravery of a Loyalist force that in "zero weather" disrupted Franco's plans by "forcing the enemy to fight…. So, regardless of whether Teruel is captured, the offensive has achieved its purpose of forcing Franco's hand and breaking up plans for simultaneous Guadalajara and Aragon offensives."[120] By contrast, Gellhorn had no war experience when she arrived at the height of the war in 1937 and reported for *Collier's*. Partly with Hemingway's mentoring, Gellhorn became a seasoned correspondent, writing sensitively about the terror inflicted by the bombing of urban populations, the very fact that inspired Picasso's horrific painted images in *Guernica*.

Meanwhile, the war in China was reported continuously by an outstanding early graduate of the first journalism school, at the University of Missouri, Edgar Snow. At 23 in 1928, Snow went to China and became assistant editor of *China Weekly Review*, later settling in Beijing and, during the war, writing for the *Saturday Evening Post*, the *New York Sun* and the *Chicago Tribune*. In 1936, he scored a coup, interviewing the leaders of the revolutionary Chinese Red Army.

By the late 1930s, news agencies, major newspapers, and eventually radio networks led by CBS, increased the number of correspondents in Europe. As news organizations reassessed commitments to foreign coverage, journalists often shifted from one employer to another. Some, like William Shirer, left the press for radio, joining Edward R. Murrow's CBS European broadcast team in Berlin in 1937. Murrow saw in Shirer the continental rival to NBC's Max Jordan, who was getting news scoops because of NBC's contract with Germany's state-monopoly radio system. Shirer had learned on the job since joining other expatriates in Paris in 1925. In 1927, when Shirer was 23, the *Chicago Tribune* foreign news service sent him to India to cover Gandhi's movement, then sent him to Vienna. In 1932, after a dispute with *Tribune* publisher Robert McCormick over a minor story, Shirer was fired and quickly hired by Hearst's Universal News Service and sent to Berlin. When Hearst dissolved UNS in 1937 to cut his losses, Shirer accepted the offer from Murrow, the new CBS European director in London, to become the correspondent for Europe. Although Shirer failed the "trial broadcast" for CBS executives, Murrow interceded, arguing that he was a great reporter.[121]

Shirer soon saw enough of Hitler to understand his "astounding success." His "first glimpse" was of Hitler riding "like a Roman emperor" through Nuremberg's narrow streets decked with "tens of thousands" of swastika flags. The 30,000 who packed the hall suddenly grew quiet, and Hitler made his entrance, striding "slowly down the long centre aisle while thirty thousand hands were raised in salute…. He is restoring pageantry and colour and mysticism to the drab lives of twentieth century Germans."[122] He coped with Nazi censors, who had to approve all broadcast scripts and frequently ordered changes. The Nazi foreign-press chief, Shirer noted, warned the overseas press corps "to report on affairs in Germany without attempting to interpret them. History alone can evaluate the events now taking place here under Hitler." "I was not willing to wait that long," Shirer said. "But I soon learned to watch my step. All through my years in Berlin I was conscious of walking a real, if ill-defined, line." One after another of his colleagues were expelled, and he learned that he was suspected of spying. When war began in 1939, Nazi censorship became more severe, and much of what Shirer saw could be mentioned only to friends and his diary.[123] After covering Nazi conquests in Czechoslovakia, Poland, and France, he left Berlin in December 1940 for a visit to the United States, nervously concealing in his luggage his diary, which in 1941 would become his first book, *Berlin Diary.* Shirer did not return until after the war.

Visiting journalists who did not remain in Germany were freer to offend the Nazis. Ralph McGill, 39, soon to be editor of the *Atlanta Constitution,* was in Vienna on April 9, 1938, to witness an ecstatic Hitler whip up public fervor for the next day's plebiscite on unification with Germany. On April 10, one month after German troops invaded Austria, 99.75 percent of voting Austrians voted *Ja* to approve. McGill mailed his articles to Atlanta, where they were published two weeks after he left Nazi jurisdiction. He wrote candidly, revealing his loathing of the Nazi "madness." He noted the penetration of Nazi propaganda—leaflets dropped from airplanes and messages blared from street loudspeakers—the suppression of opposition newspapers and labor unions, Nazi lies that nobody dared dispute publicly, and throngs of youths and the unemployed whose "hysterical, fanatical" shouting pressured voters and terrorized the Jews. In defiance, he delivered to a Jewish family "a memorized message about the location of certain papers which were to be burned lest they fall into Nazi hands."[124]

McGill was alarmed by how fast the Austrian democracy had collapsed. Businessmen and mobs of the unemployed had cooperated with the Nazis and now worshipped "the god of the German nation." "Vienna learned quickly," he wrote. "All the shopkeepers greet each customer as he enters and leaves with 'Heil Hitler.' I sat there stirring my coffee and wondered what the opponents of Mr. Roosevelt, who think him a dictator, would do if they had to say, 'Heil Roosevelt' every time they purchased a collar or a pack of cigarets." McGill thought Austria's surrender—to "a terrible form of government and one which crushes out most that is decent in its people"—signaled coming disaster. He perceived Hitler's strategy and envisioned a Nazi takeover of Czechoslovakia. "Hitler will get what he wants without war. England will not fight. Not yet, at any rate. And Hitler, who doesn't want war, will go ahead."[125]

Expression of such opinions was discouraged at CBS. As a matter of policy, CBS and NBC executives wanted correspondents to appear neutral while reporting confrontations among European nations. During the Nazi takeover of Czechoslovakia in the autumn of 1938, Murrow told his American audience the ideal of radio news: "We are trying to provide material on which an opinion may be formed, but we are not trying to suggest what that opinion should be." Despite such restrictions, Murrow's network broadcasts had, one biographer estimated, "more influence upon America's reaction to foreign news than a shipful of newspapermen."[126]

By July 1939, when war seemed probable, Murrow again expanded his staff. He found 26-year-old Eric Sevareid working two jobs in print journalism, by day for the Paris edition of the *Herald Tribune* and by night for United Press. When Sevareid also failed his test broadcast for CBS executives, Murrow assured him, "That's all right. I'll fix it. Quit your other jobs anyway and don't worry about it." Sevareid recalled that friends advised he would be "crazy to follow his advice.... I knew Murrow only slightly ... but there was something about him that evoked a feeling of trust." When the job came through, Sevareid reported the outbreak of war.

I faced the prospect of speaking each night to a new and frighteningly large audience, through a new and frighteningly personal medium, about the event we had known would happen, which had obsessed our minds for years, which came now, almost as a relief after so much tortured suspense, at the beginning of September.[127]

Murrow and other correspondents would soon play a major role in the debate over American involvement in Europe's hostilities.

NOTES

1. Arthur M. Schlesinger Jr., *New Deal*, vol. 2 of *The Age of Roosevelt*, (Boston: Houghton Mifflin, 1958), 13.

2. Arthur M. Schlesinger Jr., *The Crisis of the Old Order, 1919–1933*, vol. 1 of *The Age of Roosevelt* (Boston: Houghton Mifflin Co., 1957), 286, 289, 304, 307–8; W. A. Swanberg, *Citizen Hearst: A Biography of William Randolph Hearst* (New York: Scribner's Sons, 1961), 435–38; Kenneth S. Davis, *FDR: The New York Years, 1928–1933* (New York: Random House, 1979), 267, 261; Michael Barone, *Our Country: The Shaping of America from Roosevelt to Reagan* (New York: Macmillan, 1990), 53–54, 682 n8.

3. Franklin Delano Roosevelt (hereafter FDR) Press Conference No. 172, January 5, 1935, cited in Schlesinger, *The Politics of Upheaval*, 264, 270.

4. Swanberg, *Hearst*, 440, 474.

5. Raymond Moley, *After Seven Years* (New York: Harper & Brothers, 1939), 208, 280. Moley was an original member in 1932 of Roosevelt's "Brain Trust" and in October 1933 became an editorial columnist for the new weekly newsmagazine *Today*, renamed *Newsweek* in 1937. He also contributed articles for a newspaper syndicate.

6. Schlesinger, *New Deal*, 476.

7. Taking a point from public relations practice, Rosten suggested that newspapers not "over-emphasize the errors" of the New Deal to aid in "buttressing its prestige." Rosten, *Washington Correspondents*, 299.

8. Seldes said his criticism was neglected by the press because few wanted to hear about lies, propaganda, half-truths, and hidden agendas. See Pamela A. Brown, "George Seldes and the Winter Soldier Brigade: The Press Criticism of *In Fact*, 1940–1950," *American Journalism* 6 (2): 101. During his long career he inspired a range of critics from A. J. Liebling to I. F. Stone to consumer advocate and presidential candidate Ralph Nader.

9. Frederick Lewis Allen, *Since Yesterday: The Nineteen Thirties in America* (New York: Bantam Books, 1961), 218.

10. "Roosevelt Asks Inheritance Taxes and Other Levies on Big Fortunes; Tax Move a Big Surprise; The President Proposes Money Be Segregated to Pay National Debt; Concentrated Riches Hit; Points in Tax Message," *New York Times*, June 20, 1935, 1; "Borah Goes to Aid of the President on New Tax Plan; 'Absurd' to Call It a 'Soak-the-Rich' or 'Share-Wealth' Program, He Says," *New York Times*, June 24, 1935, 1; "New Tax Program Pressed Despite a Revolt in House; Yield Is Put at $340,000,000; Tentative New Tax Rates," *New York Times*, June 26, 1935, 1. While in the Senate in 1934, Huey Long gained a large following through his advocacy of a "share-our-wealth" plan. By imposing high taxes on the rich, he promised to provide every family with a $5,000 homestead allowance and a guaranteed annual income of at least $2,000. His popularity rose to the point that he was considered a possible third-party candidate to oppose the New Deal. On September 8, 1935, Long was shot at the Louisiana Capitol Building in Baton Rouge by Dr. Carl Weiss, the son-in-law of a political enemy, Judge Benjamin Pavy. Long died on September 10.

11. Moley, *Seven Years*, 317–17; Edmond D. Coblentz, *William Randolph Hearst: A Portrait in His Own Words* (New York: Simon & Schuster, 1952), 170–71.

12. Schlesinger, *New Deal*, 565.

13. Robert E. Herzstein, *Roosevelt & Hitler: Prelude to War* (New York: Paragon House, 1989), 85; Graham J. White, *FDR and the Press* (Chicago: University of Chicago Press, 1979), 73–77, in Richard W. Steele, *Propaganda in an Open Society: The Roosevelt Administration and the Media, 1933–1945* (Westport, CT: Greenwood Press, 1985), 53.

14. Nasaw, *The Chief*, 516–17, 227.

15. Nasaw, *The Chief*, xiii–xiv; Herzstein, *Roosevelt & Hitler*, 85; Swanberg, *Hearst*, 476.

16. Coblentz, *Hearst*, 181.

17. Coblentz, *Hearst*, 181; "Tax Plan Assailed as 'Confiscation'; Executive Committee of Board of Trade Calls Proposal Class Legislation," *New York Times*, June 28, 1935, 2; Swanberg, *Hearst*, 474; Donald R. McCoy, *Landon of Kansas* (Lincoln: University of Nebraska Press, 1966); Harold Ickes, November 13, 1935, Diary, reel 1, page 1237, Harold Ickes Papers, Manuscript Division, LOC.

18. Ferdinand Lundberg, *Imperial Hearst: A Social Biography* (New York: Equinox Cooperative Press, 1936), xii–xiii; Nasaw, *The Chief*, 516.

19. John Pauly, "Damon Runyon," in *Biographical Dictionary of American Journalism*, 614–15.

20. Moley, *Seven Years*, 306–8.

21. Damon Runyon, "Horse and Buggy Governor," *Cosmopolitan*, November 1935, 5–6; Lundberg, *Hearst*, xii–xiii.

22. *New York Times*, December 10, 1935, 6; "Kansas Candidate," *Time*, May 18, 1936, 15; "Landon: Little Known Man Who Captured the Front Page," *News-Week*, June 13, 1936; "The Landon Build-Up," *Nation*, June 27, 1936, 833.

23. "Landon Prepares Crucial Speeches; Aides Expect 'Make or Break' Farm and Social Security Declarations This Week; Won't 'Outpromise' Rival; Will Say This in Des Moines and Milwaukee Talks—Trade Pack to Be Hit in Minneapolis," *New York Times*, September 20, 1936, 1; Harold L. Ickes, *The First Thousand Days, 1933–1936*, vol. 1 of *The Secret Diary of Harold Ickes* (New York: Simon & Schuster, 1953), 665–666.

24. Harold Ickes, February 4, 1936, Diary, reel 1–2, Ickes Papers; Ickes, *First Thousand Days*, 633; Ickes, August 10, 1936, Diary, reel 2, Ickes Papers. The truce with Hearst had been suggested earlier. While chairman of the Securities and Exchange Commission in November 1935, Joseph Kennedy also handled finances for Hearst and tried "to reconcile the President with Hearst," Ickes noted. "The President told me that he said to Kennedy that in his opinion there was no man in the whole United States who was as vicious an influence as Hearst." Ickes, *First Thousand Days*, 472. Two months, later press secretary Steve Early noted that the Hearst papers were no longer calling the New Deal the "Raw Deal" and said he heard from a drinking partner of Marion Davies that "Hearst's attitude toward the administration was mellowing." Ickes, January 18, 1936, Diary, reel 1, pp. 1360–61, Ickes Papers.

25. W. Cameron Meyers, "The Chicago Newspaper Hoax in the '36 Election Campaign," *Journalism Quarterly* 37 (3): 356–64; "President Beats Gun Denying Publisher's Red Blast," *Time*, September 26, 1936; "American Industry Closed by Roosevelt's Attack on Business," *Chicago Tribune*, February 15, 1936; "The Worker and the Drone," *Chicago Tribune*, February 26, 1936.

26. Donald Day, "Moscow Orders Reds in U.S. to Back Roosevelt," *Chicago Daily Tribune*, August 9, 1936; Richard Finnegan, "Prove *Tribune* Story—$5,000," *Chicago Daily Times*, August 28, 1936, 1; *Chicago Daily News*, September 1, 1936; Finnegan, "Editorial," September 2, 1936, *Chicago Daily Times*.

27. "White House Hits 'Malice' in Attack; Charges 'Notorious Newspaper Owner' Is Framing People by False Tales; Believed to Mean Hearst; His Aides Here Answer by Giving Out Proofs of Article Appearing Today," *New York Times*, September 20, 1936, 1; "Moscow Backs Roosevelt," editorial, *Chicago Herald and Examiner*, September 21, 1936; "President Beats Gun," *Time*, September 28, 1936, 14; Meyers, "The Chicago Newspaper Hoax," 356–64.

28. Schlesinger, *New Deal*, 567; Ickes, October 9, 1937, Diary, reel 2, p. 2368, Ickes Papers; Ickes, December 30, 1935, Diary, reel 1, p. 1320, Ickes Papers; Ickes, March 9, 1936, Diary, reel 1, p. 1426, Ickes Papers.

29. Ickes, *First Thousand Days*, 492, 669, 684; "The Hearst Issue," *Time*, 7 September 1936, 9; "Fortune Quarterly Survey: Hearst Papers' Influence on National Politics," *Fortune*, July 1936, 148.

30. Archibald M. Crossley, "Straw Polls in 1936," *Public Opinion Quarterly* 1 (1937): 24.

31. Hadley Cantril, ed., "Technical Research: How Accurate Were the Polls?" *Public Opinion Quarterly* 1 (1937): 97, 100, 102–3. Metropolitan newspaper polls that came closer than the Gallup poll in predicting Roosevelt majorities in their

states were the Baltimore *Sun* (64% in Maryland), the *New York Daily News* (65% in New York), and the *Chicago Daily Times* (58% in Illinois).

32. Ibid.

33. Cantril, "Technical Research: How Accurate Were the Polls?" 104; George Gallup, "Putting Public Opinion to Work," *Scribner's*, November 1936, 38. Gallup claimed his Institute of Public Opinion would be able "to predict figures accurate within three points for all doubtful states and for all other states that have sizeable populations."

34. Concerning Landon's lack of appeal, Ickes noted that "the people pretty generally got the impression that he had neither the character nor the ability that a President of the United States ought to have." Ickes, *First Thousand Days*, 702; Ickes, November 7, 1936, Diary, reel 2, p. 1820, Ickes Papers.

35. Schlesinger, *New Deal*, 561.

36. Betty Houchin Winfield, *FDR and the News Media* (Urbana: University of Illinois Press, 1990), 1, 4, 81–82, 238–39.

37. Schlesinger, *New Deal*, 560.

38. Richard Lowitt and Maurine Beasley, eds., *One Third of a Nation: Lorena Hickok Reports on the Great Depression* (Urbana: University of Illinois Press, 1981), xxix, xxxiv; Emma Bugbee, "Mrs. Roosevelt: Portrait of a Beloved Woman," *New York Herald Tribune*, November 8, 1962, in Barbara Belford, *Brilliant Bylines: A Biographical Anthology of Notable Newspaperwomen in America* (New York: Columbia University Press, 1986), 175, 186.

39. Jess Flemion and Colleen M. O'Connor, eds., *Eleanor Roosevelt: An American Journey* (San Diego: San Diego State University Press, 1987), 191.

40. Franklin D. Roosevelt, "The First Press Conference," *The Year of Crisis, 1933*, vol. 2 of *The Public Papers of Franklin D. Roosevelt*, ed. Samuel I. Rosenman (New York: Random House, 1938), 39–40. See also Theodore G. Joslin, "President Meets the Press," *Washington Sunday Star*, March 4, 1934, reprinted in ibid., 40–45. From 1933 to 1945 Roosevelt held 998 press conferences.

41. Roosevelt, "The First Press Conference," *Year of Crisis*, 30–31.

42. Ibid.

43. The term "handout" came from "the phrase originally used for a bundle of stale food handed out from a house to a beggar." Daniel J. Boorstin, *The Image: A Guide to Pseudo-Events in America* (New York: Harper & Row, 1964), 18; Judith A. Serrin, "Stephen Tyree Early," in *Biographical Dictionary of American Journalism*, 209–10.

44. Franklin D. Roosevelt, "Note," *Year of Crisis*, 39; see Stephen E. Schoenherr, "Selling the New Deal: Stephen T. Early's Role as Press Secretary to Franklin Roosevelt" (PhD diss., University of Delaware, 1973).

45. Serrin, "Early," 208; Steele, *Propaganda*, 11; Schlesinger, *New Deal*, 516.

46. Ickes, *First Thousand Days*, 230–35, 405.

47. Steele, 15.

48. Ibid., 14–16.

49. Ibid.

50. Raymond Fielding, *The American Newsreel, 1911–1967* (Norman: University of Oklahoma Press, 1972), 173, 184, 201.

51. Ibid., 280. Similar editing courtesy was extended to King Victor Emanuel of Italy, who was "only slightly taller than a midget ... to avoid showing him being

lifted onto his horse or seating himself on his special elevated chair at the Opera House in Rome."

52. Winfield, *FDR*, 10.

53. Schlesinger, *New Deal*, 559.

54. Ibid.

55. Ibid.

56. Waldo W. Braden and Earnest Brandenburg, "Roosevelt's Fireside Chats," *Speech Monographs* 22 (5): 302, cited in Lichty and Topping, *Broadcasting*, 302; Russell D. Buhite and David W. Levy, eds., *FDR's Fireside Chats* (New York: Penguin Books, 1993).

57. Roosevelt, *Year of Crisis*, 61. The chats were devised by CBS Washington office manager Harry C. Butcher. Schlesinger, *New Deal*, 559.

58. Will Rogers, *Sanity Is Where You Find It*, ed. Donald Day (Boston: Houghton Mifflin, 1955), cited in Schlesinger, *New Deal*, 13.

59. Ratings were compiled by the Cooperative Analysis of Broadcasting (CAB, or Crossley), begun in 1929 as the first significant effort to measure national audiences listening to a sponsor's show. CAB employees telephoned listeners in 30 cities. J. Fred MacDonald, *Don't Touch That Dial: Radio Programming in American Life, 1920–1960* (Chicago: Nelson-Hall, 1979), 34, 40. Roosevelt delivered the last fireside chat on June 12, 1944.

60. Lippmann had accused Roosevelt of being politically vague about utility and power matters. Franklin D. Roosevelt to Llewellyn Cooke, January 18, 1932, in *F.D.R.: His Personal Letters*, 3:254; Franklin Roosevelt to James M. Cox, March 9, 1933, in *F.D.R.: His Personal Letters*, 3:337; after the 1932 election, as his concern about Germany increased, Roosevelt offered Cox the ambassadorship, but he declined; MacDonald, *Don't Touch That Dial*, 160.

61. Lichty and Topping, *Broadcasting*, 302.

62. "Topics of the Day: What Women Like to Read in Newspapers," *Literary Digest*, May 12, 1934, 9.

63. Frank J. Kahn, ed., *Documents of American Broadcasting*, 4th ed. (Englewood Cliffs, NJ: Prentice-Hall, 1984), 40–41, 47–48, 50, 53.

64. John W. Spaulding, "1928: Radio Becomes a Mass Advertising Medium," *Journal of Broadcasting* 7 (1): 31–44, in Lichty and Topping, *Broadcasting*, 219–28.

65. Robert W. McChesney, "Franklin Roosevelt, His Administration, and the Communications Act of 1934," *American Journalism* 5 (4): 207, 228, 229; "President Roosevelt's Message to Congress," February 26, 1934, in Kahn, *Documents*, 105–7.

66. Philip T. Rosen, *The Modern Stentors: Radio Broadcasters and the Federal Government, 1920–1934* (Westport, CT: Greenwood Press, 1980), 174.

67. Robert W. McChesney, *Telecommunications, Mass Media and Democracy: The Battle for Control of U.S. Broadcasting, 1928–1935* (Oxford: Oxford University Press, 1993), 170.

68. "Peace with the Press," *Broadcasting*, January 1, 1934, 22; McChesney, *Telecommunications*, 171; Giraud Chester, "The Press-Radio War: 1933–1935," *Public Opinion Quarterly* 13 (1949): 252; Louise Benjamin, "Radio Comes of Age," in *The Media in America: A History*, ed. Wm. David Sloan, 6th ed. (Northport, AL: Vision Press, 2005), 361; Sterling and Kittross, *Stay Tuned*, 178.

69. Paley, *As It Happened*, 128–29.

70. Sterling and Kittross, *Stay Tuned*, 259; William Safire, "Media Quiet about Own Power," *Atlanta Constitution*, 20 January 2003, A9; "Added Ads Cheer Publishers," 14; Michael, "Press-Radio Relationships," 181.

71. Karl L. Bickel, *New Empires* (Philadelphia: J. B. Lippincott, 1930); Michael, "Press-Radio Relationships," 182.

72. Herman S. Hettinger, "Some Fundamental Aspects of Radio Broadcasting Economics," *Harvard Business Review* 14 (Autumn 1935): 14–18, in Lichty and Topping, *Broadcasting*, 235.

73. Mowrer's news commentary on the NBC Red Network is shelved at RWB 7211, B4, Library of Congress SONIC Database, a searchable online database offering researchers easy access to documentation on more than 100,000 broadcast recordings in the Library of Congress's NBC Radio Network Collection, from 1931 through 1986. http://www.midcoast.com/~lizmcl/links.html. The National Archives and Records Administration also holds a substantial collection of broadcast recordings dating to the 1920s. Highlights include the David Goldin collection of discs from WOR, New York, and recorded copies of the complete Milo Ryan Phonoarchive from the University of Washington—which includes a near-complete run of CBS morning newscasts from 1939 through the mid-1940s, as recorded at KIRO, Seattle. Most of the radio material is found in Record Group 200. New listings are being added to this database regularly. Audio copies of much of the material may be obtained by researchers. See also Sterling and Kittross, *Stay Tuned*, 122; Robert L. Hoskins, "Dorothy Thompson," in *Biographical Dictionary of American Journalism*, 699.

74. Thompson had been outspoken against Nazi treatment of the Jews. She called Hitlerism "a revolt against the whole of modern civilization ... a sort of social activism, a return to the darker side of the Middle Ages." With the critic Benjamin Stolberg, a German refugee, she authored "Hitler and the American Jew," *Scribner's*, September 1933, 136. After her expulsion, she continued to criticize the Nazis. Dorothy Thompson, "Good-by to Germany," *Harper's*, December 1934, 43–51; Kurth, *American Casandra*, 163.

75. Morrell Heald, *Transatlantic Vistas: American Journalists in Europe, 1900–1940* (Kent, Ohio: Kent State University Press, 1988), 49.

76. Lundberg, *Imperial Hearst*, 196–97; Kramer, *Heywood Broun*, 244; Rosten, *Correspondents*, 282–83; Swanberg, *Hearst*, 440–41.

77. Kramer, *Heywood Broun*, 243–44.

78. Heywood Broun, "A Union of Reporters," August 7, 1933, *New York World-Telegram*, reprinted in *Collected Edition of Heywood Broun*, 295–97; O'Connor, *Broun*, 180–81; Harris E. Ross, "Heywood Campbell Broun," in *Biographical Dictionary of American Journalism*, 81–83.

79. Kramer, *Heywood Broun*, 245; O'Conner, *Broun*, 184–84.

80. Lundberg, *Hearst*, 197–98; Kramer, *Heywood Broun*, 26.

81. Swanberg, *Hearst*, 477.

82. O'Connor, *Broun*, 186–87.

83. Villard, *The Disappearing Daily*, 48, 56; O'Connor, *Broun*, 186.

84. O'Connor, *Broun*, 186–87.

85. Marvel Cooke, interview with Kathleen Currie, Women in Journalism Oral History Project of the Washington Press Club Foundation, October 31, 1989, transcript 68–69, 77.

86. E. B. White, "Dusk in Fierce Pajamas," *New Yorker,* 1934, reprinted in *Fierce Pajamas: An Anthology of Humor Writing from the "New Yorker,"* ed. David Remnick and Henry Finder (New York: Modern Library, 2002), 8–9.

87. Kobler, *Luce,* 82–83.

88. James Agee, *Selected Journalism,* ed. Paul Ashdown (Knoxville: University of Tennessee Press, 1985), 1, 19, 42, 63, 97, 114, 139.

89. James Agee and Walker Evans, *Let Us Now Praise Famous Men* (1941; repr., New York: Ballantine Books, 1960). The first printing in 1941 sold fewer than 600 copies to Depression-weary and war-distracted readers. But in 1960, five years after Agee died at 55, and two years after his autobiographical novel, *A Death in the Family,* posthumously won the Pulitzer Prize, Houghton Mifflin reissued *Let Us Now Praise Famous Men.* It was called "the most famous unknown book in contemporary letters" and earned its place among American nonfiction classics, inspiring a generation of literary journalists. One, John Hersey, introduced the 1988 edition, asserting that Agee's work became a "kind of Bible" for young people navigating "the troubled sixties." The government study emphasized the importance of the Agee and Evans's book. The Committee on Farm Tenancy reported in February 1937 that half the farmers in the South—and almost a third of farmers in the North, and a fourth of Western farmers—did not own the land they worked. These figures, accompanied by reports of great suffering and stark poverty, led to the enactment of the Bankhead-Jones Farm Tenancy Act, which reorganized the Resettlement Administration as the Farm Security Administration, and which included among its purposes assisting enterprising tenants in becoming landowners. Arthur S. Link and William A. Link, *American Epoch: A History of the United States since 1900,* 7th ed. (New York: McGraw-Hill, 1993), 1:309.

90. Allen, *Only Yesterday,* 220; Goldberg, *Bourke-White,* 174–75.

91. Goldberg, *Bourke-White,* 177.

92. Carl Mydans, "A Tireless Perfectionist," in Bourke-White, *The Photographs of Margaret Bourke-White,* 25; ibid., 10–11, 35–38, 107–17; "Carl Mydans, Photographer," obituary, *Atlanta Constitution,* August 18, 2004.

93. Goldberg, *Bourke-White,* 176–77; Swanberg, *Luce,* 144.

94. Davis returned to Chicago in 1934, where he subsequently became managing editor of the Associated Negro Press, and where he published the deeply moving poems written in Atlanta condemning lynching and general racism.

95. "Lynchings Go Up," *Baltimore Afro-American,* October 21, 1933, 16; *Pittsburgh Courier,* November 4, 1933, 2.

96. Davis, "Touring the World," 6.

97. Lucile Bluford, interview by Fern Ingersoll, Women in Journalism Oral History Project of the Washington Press Club Foundation, August 26, 1989, transcript 79–81, 169. Her story was headlined, "Writer's Investigation Shows Officials Could Have Prevented Killing." In 1939, Bluford had applied to attend graduate school at the segregated University of Missouri School of Journalism. She was turned away.

98. "Amsterdam News Correspondents Were Protected," *Amsterdam News,* April 12, 1933, 2.

99. Davis, interview with Oukrop, 20–21; "Ebony with Pictures," *Newsweek,* September 24, 1945, 86.

100. David Howard-Pitney, *The Afro-American Jeremiad: Appeals for Justice in America* (Philadelphia: Temple University Press, 1990), 6–8.

101. "Will a Gandhi Arise?" *Chicago Defender,* November 5, 1932, 14.

102. William N. Jones, "Day by Day," *Baltimore Afro-American,* October 1, 1932, 6. As Jones expressed his hope for an American Gandhi, Martin Luther King Jr. was three years old. Jones earned a national reputation for his coverage of the rape trial of nine young men, the so-called Scottsboro Boys, in Decatur, Alabama.

103. "Germany's Six Hundred," editorial, *Pittsburgh Courier,* February 17, 1934, 10.

104. "Jim Crow for Jews Now," *Baltimore Afro-American,* October 14, 1933, 16.

105. Despite early ethical complaints and allegations of fraud, reenactment, sometimes blended with actual footage, became "a fairly common practice." Fielding, *The American Newsreel,* 149–50.

106. Fielding, *The American Newsreel,* 201; *Film Facts 1942* (New York: Motion Picture Producers and Distributors of America, 1942), 11; "Vatican over Hollywood," *Nation,* July 11, 1936, 33, in Paul W. Facey, *The Legion of Decency: A Sociological Analysis of the Emergence and Development of a Social Pressure Group* (New York: Arno Press, 1974), 169.

107. Fielding, *The American Newsreel,* 207, 222, 233; "Japan-China!" in "Trouble Beyond Our Shores: 1935–1936," pt. 3, *The March of Time,* 1937. This segment on Japan and China, narrated by Westbrook Van Voorhis and produced by de Rochemont, was subtitled "Manchukuo, the Japanese Puppet State in China, Celebrates Its Fourth Anniversary Amidst International Uproar of the Japanese Occupation."

108. Ibid., 231; "Moscow!" in "Trouble Beyond Our Shores: 1935–1936," pt. 3, *The March of Time,* 1937. In the midst of the Depression, this segment looked at the Soviet Union's second five-year economic plan, focusing on "the plan's most important contributor, Alexei Stakhanov, who discovered a method for speeding up coal production among his fellow coal miners."

109. Ibid., 266, 280.

110. Raymond Moley, *The Hays Office* (Indianapolis, Indiana: Bobbs-Merrill, 1945), 15, 87.

111. *Variety,* June 15, 1934, in Olga J. Martin, *Hollywood's Movie Commandments* (New York: H. W. Wilson, 1937), 35; "A Fighting Irishman Comes to Hollywood," *Terre Haute (IN) Star,* July 17, 1934, in ibid., 34, 37.

112. Moley, *Hays Office,* 241–42; Shirley Biagi, *Media/Impact: An Introduction to Mass Media,* 2nd ed. (Belmont, CA: Wadsworth Publishing, 1992), 211.

113. Ibid., 87–88. Enforcement of the code did not lead the Legion of Decency to disband or relax. Church leaders felt that some films might slip past the code. Between 1936 and 1943, the Legion's "C" mark condemned 53 pictures—Howard Hughes's *The Outlaw,* plus 52 low-budget independent and foreign films. In 45 of these, "suggestive sex" was cited as a reason for condemnation. *Smashing the Vice Racket* (1940) was condemned because it showed "prostitution and white slavery" and because of "immodest dress and costume; double meaning lines; obscene dancing and implications." In the 1942 French film *Le Roi,* "crime is presented as attractive; virtue is ridiculed and adultery is condoned." Legion of Decency Films Reviewed, November 1939–November 1940, 30, in Facey, *Legion of Decency,* 93,

95; Legion of Decency Films Reviewed, November 1940–November 1941, 29, in ibid., 94.

114. Heald, *Transatlantic Vistas,* xii–xiii, 228–29. This "wave" of American journalists included Dorothy Thompson, John Gunther, Vincent Sheean, William L. Shirer, Leland Stowe, H. R. Knickerbocker, Negley Farson, Herbert L. Matthews, Edgar Ansel Mowrer, and Louis Lochner. Ernest Hemingway, part of this wave, quit journalism after his fiction became profitable but returned to reporting during World War II.

115. Giorgio Bertellini, "Duce/Divo: Masculinity, Racial Identity, and Politics among Italian Americans in 1920s New York City," *Journal of Urban History* 31 (2005): 685–726; "Man of the Year," *Time,* 2 January 1939, cover; Raymond J. Sontag, *A Broken World, 1919–1939,* in *The Rise of Modern Europe: A Survey of European History,* ed. William Langer (New York: Harper Torchbooks, 1971), 144.

116. William L. Shirer, *The Nightmare Years, 1930–1940,* vol. 2 of *20th Century Journey: A Memoir of A Life and The Times* (Boston: Little, Brown, 1984), 59, 118n.

117. See Louis Fischer Papers, Department of Rare Books and Special Collections, Princeton University Library, http://libweb.princeton.edu/libraries/firestone/rbsc/finding_aids/fischer.html

118. Walter Duranty, "The Crisis in the Socialisation of Agriculture," *New York Times,* November 24, 1932. At the same time, an experienced Welsh reporter in the Russian countryside reported famine among peasants because grain for bread as well as milk and potatoes had been collectivized and "carted away and sent to the towns." Gareth Jones, "Will There be Soup? Russia Dreads the Coming Winter," *Western Mail* (Cardiff, Wales), October 15 and 17, 1932; Gareth Jones, "Famine Rules Russia, The 5-year Plan Has Killed the Bread Supply," *Evening Standard* (London), March 31, 1933, 1. http://www.colley.co.uk/garethjones/soviet_articles/famine_rules_russia.htm; "*New York Times* Statement about 1932 Pulitzer Prize Awarded to Walter Duranty," *New York Times* Web site, http://www.nytco.com/company-awards-pulitzer-note.html.

119. When Gibbons died, *Time* magazine remarked on his adventurous career: "Floyd Gibbons, who was torpedoed on his way to London on the S. S. *Laconia* in 1917, then lost an eye at Château Thierry, saw Italy's war in Ethiopia, Japan's war in China. But last week in Pennsylvania, as it must to every man, Death came to Floyd Gibbons." "Fair-Haired Boys," *Time,* October 2, 1939, 54.

120. Ernest Hemingway, "The Loyalists," *New Republic,* 1938, in *The Mammoth Book of Journalism,* 224.

121. William L. Shirer, *Berlin Diary: The Journal of a Foreign Correspondent, 1934–1941* (New York: Alfred A. Knopf, 1941), 13–14; William L. Shirer, *The Start, 1904–1930,* vol. 1 of *20th Century Journey: A Memoir of A Life and the Times* (New York: Simon & Schuster, 1976), 321, 492. Shirer, *The Nightmare Years 1930–1940,* vol. 2 of *20th Century Journey; A Memoir of A Life and The Times,* 44–46, 54–55; Shirer, *Berlin Diary,* 77–80, 559; A. M. Sperber, *Murrow: His Life and Times* (New York: Freundlich Books, 1986),103–4; Robert J. Landry, "Edward R. Murrow; *Scribner's* Examines a Radio Foreign Correspondent ... His Technique, Rivals, and Influence on American Opinion ... His Tactics in Columbia's Battle Abroad with NBC," *Scribner's,* December 1938, 10.

122. Shirer, *Berlin Diary,* 18–19.

123. Shirer, *Nightmare Years,* 138–39.

124. Ralph McGill, "McGill in Vienna; Orgy of Adulation Accorded Hitler, the 'Build-Up' of Herr Goebbels Described in Dramatic Detail by Writer," *Atlanta Constitution*, April 28, 1938, 1; "McGill Foils Nazi Terror to Aid Refugee; Writer Brings Memorized Message to Vienna Victims," *Atlanta Constitution*, May 2, 1938, 5; William L. Shirer, *The Rise and Fall of the Third Reich: A History of Nazi Germany* (New York: Simon & Schuster, 1960), 347–50.

125. Ralph McGill, "McGill in Vienna; Hitler Invests Salute to Viennese with Pompous Drama," *Atlanta Constitution*, April 29, 1938, 1; Ralph McGill, "McGill in Vienna; Only a Fool Will Deny Hitler Hasn't Done Much for Germany and Will Do Much for Austria, Writer Declares," *Atlanta Constitution*, May 4, 1938, 7; Ralph McGill, "McGill in Vienna: People of Austria Were Skillfully Coerced into Voting 'Ja' in Humorless Plebiscite with Fine Goebbels Touch," *Atlanta Constitution*, May 1, 1938, 9K.

126. Landry, "Edward R. Murrow," 7–8.

127. Paley, *As It Happened*, 135–36; Eric Sevareid, *Not So Wild a Dream* (New York: Atheneum, 1976), 106–8.

8

The Debatable Peace

That the nation is face to face with the gravest crisis since the Civil War
hardly admits of dispute. Within the next few months ... there seems certain
to be decided the tremendous issue, whether this country will face Germany
and the future with allies or without them.

—*New York Herald Tribune*, 15 January 1941

After September 1939, the war in Europe, Africa, and Asia increasingly
engaged U.S. media at home and overseas. Domestically, newspapers followed the critical debate over the U.S. role as domestic policy and practice
wavered between military "preparedness" on one hand and intervention
on the other. Overseas, correspondents covered the first two years of the
war as neutrals, as they had from 1914 to 1917. The journalists stationed
overseas were soon joined by reporters, photographers, magazine writers,
and even novelists, among them John Steinbeck and Ernest Hemingway.
To get close to the fronts, the Americans developed paramilitary skills,
blended in with uniforms, developed soldierly instincts and nerves, and
demonstrated both courage and a willingness to take risks. For many,
among them broadcaster William Shirer, the chaos and danger would
be the high-water mark of their journalistic careers; for others, notably
Edward R. Murrow and Eric Sevareid, Europe's war provided a passport
to further prominence.

Neutral journalists occupied a special position in the warring countries,
where they were treated with privilege and regarded with suspicion.
Germany, by offering neutrals lodging and extra rations of food and
gasoline, attracted more than 100 journalists to Berlin, where they could

be watched. German officials monitored news dispatches and reacted harshly to unfavorable reports by harassing the journalists, disconnecting their phones, issuing warnings, or detaining and jailing them. A United Press reporter, Richard C. Hottelet, was jailed for a month before a charge of espionage was dropped.[1]

Shirer was in Berlin when Hitler invaded Poland on September 1, 1939. In his diary he noted what he could not express in his broadcast, that Hitler tried to camouflage the invasion as a "counterattack." "It's a flagrant, inexcusable, unprovoked act of aggression." His military censor permitted Shirer little commentary, but he was permitted to drive into Poland to witness "the hopeless position for the Poles." Just before Shirer left Berlin in 1940, a friend at Broadcasting House warned him that the Nazis suspected him of spying and that the Gestapo had increased surveillance. He became so fearful he "dared not confide" names to his diary.[2]

The war improved opportunities for women. Murrow hired CBS's first female staff correspondent, Mary Marvin Breckinridge. In making her one of "Murrow's Boys," Murrow disregarded the networks' prejudice against women's voices broadcasting important news. As with Shirer and Sevareid, Murrow was concerned more with reporting ability than with conventional broadcast requirements. NBC hired Margaret Rupli to broadcast from Amsterdam and shortly after added Helen Hiett to its Paris staff. NBC in 1937 had broken the gender barrier, outbidding CBS to sign Dorothy Thompson to comment on the news for 13 minutes each week on the *General Electric Hour,* reaching an estimated five million listeners. Before and during the war Thompson became "an American oracle" who told people "what to think."[3]

Breckinridge had made her reputation as a documentary filmmaker and photographer. In London, she was freelancing her photographs through the Black Star agency, which sold her work to *Life.* One evening she had dinner with old friends, Murrow and his wife, Janet. "I had been doing stories on an English village preparing for war, the evacuated children, and things like that. He asked if I would go on the air that Saturday night … and tell about them." Murrow advised, "Keep your voice low." She turned out to be a natural broadcaster as well as a skilled reporter.[4]

Murrow soon asked her to represent CBS in Amsterdam, where the Dutch were hoping to escape invasion. He instructed her to "give the human side of the war, to be neutral, to be honest, to talk like myself, a typical American." Shirer soon invited her to visit Berlin to "do the 'women's angle.'" There, she visited one of nine schools where Nazi brides-to-be learned the urgency of producing children for the Reich. She also wrote a number of stories that went well beyond Shirer's gender guidelines. She covered one of Hitler's speeches. She discovered that German clergymen were wearing paper collars because of a shortage of laundry soap, and that the Nazis had banned burning coal in churches and other institutions. She reported that about half the Jewish population remaining in Germany was on the American consulate's waiting list to go to America. Back in Amsterdam, she rode the last train to Paris before the German army invaded on May 10, 1940. From France she reported the panicked flight of refugees, and on May 28, she broadcast news of the fall of Belgium.[5]

In the spring of 1940, American correspondents joined the stream of refugees. In Paris, Edgar Mowrer of the *Chicago Daily News* hurriedly left his top floor office at 23 rue de la Paix "as the Germans were coming in," recalled the journalist who reopened the office four years later and found that a copy of Mowrer's last piece was "lying on his desk and when you picked it up the blotter was a different color underneath. The place was very dusty—absolutely untouched." Eric Sevareid evacuated his wife and newborn twin sons while continuing to report. CBS instructed him "to move out, if and when the French government moved." The slack would be picked up by Shirer, who was traveling across France *with* the German army. At Bordeaux, Sevareid joined a "crowd of press reporters, representing the great agencies and newspapers all over Britain and the neutral world." There he was the first to broadcast to America that the French government had capitulated rather than fight. Sevareid felt he "had no heart to carry on reporting from the kind of France this would be." As he sailed with refugees to London, "somebody flipped the radio on, and a calm, collected and very familiar voice was speaking very slowly and clearly. It was Bill Shirer."[6]

In the States, others wanted to go to war. Syndicated columnist Ernie Pyle had longed to go overseas before Hitler invaded Poland, rather than write more of the travel pieces he had been publishing since 1935. "Things are so black in Europe we can't think of anything else," he wrote. In 1940, Pyle asked his Scripps-Howard editor, Lee G. Miller, to send him to Europe. "Europe is out," Miller told him. "Good God, there won't be any Europe in a week or two."[7]

London, Hitler's next target, became a sanctuary for refugees and journalists. "Never before has there been such a concentration of journalists in such a small area," observed Janet Murrow, who cooked extra meals for some of them. By summer and fall of 1940, her husband had seized center stage as he reported the bombing of London and the Battle of Britain. "There is something unreal about this air war," he told listeners." Much of it you can't see." More than any other correspondent, he understood the impact of broadcasting news of war *as it was happening*.[8]

The bombing of London drew Murrow up to the rooftops, in contrast to Sevareid, who felt more comfortable in shelters. "Once you start going into shelters you lose your nerve," Murrow told an associate. He roamed the city fearlessly, explaining that he wanted to be among "the little people who live in those little houses, who have no uniforms and get no decoration for bravery." His risk taking inspired others, notably photographers.[9]

By late September, Murrow gained Ministry of Information approval to broadcast during a bombing raid. On the night of September 21, Americans tuning in to *London After Dark* heard Murrow describing the war before his eyes—the searchlights and explosions and "that faint, red, angry snap of antiaircraft bursts." He was back there the next night, reporting, "I'm standing again tonight on a rooftop looking out over London, feeling rather large and lonesome." His sky had one feature Americans could relate to—"a three-quarter moon riding high." Apart from that, "there was one burst of shellfire almost straight in the Little Dipper." Night after night he returned to his distinct vantage point. "This is a race," he broadcast, "the bomb squad trying to take away the bombs that have already fallen, before the next consignment comes down. But the milk and morning papers continue to arrive." He had created, as biographer A. M. Sperber observed, "broadcasting's first living-room war" and in the deed had become an American media icon.[10]

Murrow's broadcasts and reports from other correspondents clustered in the besieged city aroused sympathy for nations resisting Nazi forces and may have tilted U.S. political opinion away from isolationism toward providing material support to Britain. Certainly the correspondents "supplied a valuable source of initiative, background information, and perspective," press critic Morell Heald observed. Some, Dorothy Thompson among them, were "early advocates of American resistance to the totalitarian threat." The reality of aggression by Hitler and his allies, Heald concluded, "did the most to arouse Americans from the dream of isolation."[11]

The wall of historic American isolationism withstood increasing pressure from interventionists. Americans as a whole seemed unpersuaded that their national interests required them to fight and die in another European war reminiscent of the bloodbath of 1914–1918. Isolationism was also the announced policy of a number of American publishers and editors. In the Midwest, McCormick of the *Chicago Tribune* maintained a staunch isolationism, reflecting what he perceived to be a majority of public opinion in America's heartland, farther removed from Europe. In the alternative press, Dorothy Day's monthly *Catholic Worker* maintained her bedrock devotion to the poor by continuing to advocate Christlike pacifism. "And now the whole world is turning to 'force' to conquer," Day had lamented in 1936 during the Spanish civil war. Hearst, who in 1930 had been expelled from France after his papers published terms of the secret Anglo-British Naval Agreement, opposed any effort by Roosevelt to involve America in the war. During the early years of the First World War, Hearst was accused of being anti-British to the point that some thought him pro-German. During the 1930s, Germany won admiration from influential Americans who admired the resurgence under the Nazis, among them Hearst and aviator hero Charles Lindbergh, who in 1940 became a leading spokesman for anti-interventionists. During the 1940 presidential campaign, while Britain was besieged, Roosevelt pledged he was seeking peace and promised in Boston on October 29, 1940, "Your boys are not going to be sent into any foreign wars."[12]

The press, radio, and newsreels documented the internal conflict between isolationists and interventionists. As the debate advanced into 1940 and 1941, news media expanded coverage of the debate over home-land defense. During the bombing of London, Shirer noted from Berlin that the Nazis were "hoping that our isolationists and our Lindberghs will keep us out of the war." Three months after the invasion of France, isolationists rallied to the cause of an "America First" committee founded by a group of Yale University law students committed to an "impregnable defense for America" and "keeping out of the European war." Lindbergh, having returned from living in Europe and viewing the formidable German army and air force, was by 1940 a leading voice against interven-tion. On August 4, 1940, the Mutual Network broadcast his speech stating that the war was not about issues that concerned America—democracy or Christianity—but about historically European matters—"the division of territory and wealth between nations. It has caused conflict in Europe since European history began." On October 30, he spoke at Yale, beginning his association with the America First movement.[13]

The public discourse, amplified by the media, intensified early in 1941 as Congress considered the Lend Lease Act to authorize the president to transfer armaments to any country and defer payment. As debate began, Roosevelt gained an ally in the staunchly Republican *New York Herald Tribune:* "This newspaper believes firmly that aid to Britain is the only possible means to avoid war." On the other side, the administration's crit-ics accused Roosevelt of covering up a secret plan to enter the war, one of many such allegations of secrecy and lying. In the heat of the debate, Republican Senator Robert Taft of Ohio blamed warmongering on "the business community of the cities …, the radio and movie commentators, the Communists, and the university intelligentsia." Nazi propagandists in the United States circulated the view that Jews were behind the effort to make America go to war. In Hollywood, Jewish movie producers feared an anti-Semitic backlash if they produced anti-Nazi films but by 1940 gathered the courage to produce "war movies" that sympathized with victims of the Nazis. Lindbergh agreed that "the Jewish" were one of three groups responsible for leading America into the war. On September 11, 1941, in an America First speech titled "Who Are the War Agitators?" Lindbergh declared, "If any one of these groups—the British, the Jewish, or the administration—stops agitating for war, I believe there will be little danger of our involvement." America First activists accused anti-Nazi groups of being "warmongers" on the fringe of American public opinion. Lindbergh's critics, who had called him a Nazi sympathizer, now accused him of anti-Semitism.[14]

As rhetoric intensified, some journalists stepped forward with new information that focused the public discourse. In September 1941, the popular syndicated political columnist Raymond Clapper, just returned from England, revealed what the British government was not saying publicly: the $7 billion U.S. Lend Lease Act had in six months failed to arm Britain with anything more than "a popgun arsenal." Clapper charged the Roosevelt administration had "covered up" and misled Americans by sending only "token quantities" of planes and food. He blamed bureaucratic delays, which "may give some comfort to Hitler." In conveying the message through Clapper, the British had chosen "America's No. 1 columnist," as the *London Daily Mail* described him in 1940. Given his stature, Clapper's assertions triggered a response from other media. *Life* magazine, owned by ardent interventionist Henry Luce, devoted five pages to challenging the administration's statistics and picturing British plane and tank factories in full production while America's were "still abuilding."[15]

Clapper's revelation may have served the Roosevelt administration's tilt toward intervention by emphasizing besieged Britain's urgent need. By carefully building media support, the president, despite isolationists and America First protectionists, was making persuasive headway. By the summer of 1941, "it was clear that FDR and his interventionist allies were winning the propaganda war," concludes one historian, who credits the Roosevelt administration with "success in shaping the images upon which popular judgements rested."[16]

Certainly by September even media advertisements projected a sense of wartime urgency. Whether to help Britain or defend America, national advertisers linked their products to patriotism and "national defense." Alerting Americans that sources of rubber might be cut off, the Firestone Corporation advised every "loyal American" car owner how to "help conserve rubber" by properly inflating tires. Studebaker sandwiched its new model for 1942 between pictures of planes and trucks, noting that the company "is building an unlimited quantity of airplane engines, military trucks and other materiel for national defense ... and a limited number of passenger cars." Pontiac's car promotion included a statement that it was "proud to be doing our part" to produce for the navy "a new type of automatic cannon." Lockheed Aircraft Corporation noted that its Lodestars "become hard-hitting bombers without major structural changes." Ronson advertised its cigarette lighters for "that soldier or sailor of yours in camp or at sea" because his comfort "depends so much on a good man's smoke."[17]

Into this atmosphere of domestic preparedness, newspapers owned by antiwar opponents of the Roosevelt administration reported on December 4 that the president, while asking Congress for an arms bill for defense purposes, had secretly developed "war plans" for battle in Europe. Robert R. McCormick's *Chicago Tribune* and the affiliated *Washington Times-Herald* had obtained a copy of Roosevelt's top-secret "Rainbow Five" war plan for a 10 million-man army—including five million to fight Hitler's forces in Europe—and the president's letter asking the army and navy to create the plan. Along with its front-page scoop, the *Tribune* published a political cartoon showing Midwesterners in "the Stronghold of Peace," looked warily toward Washington and its "War Propaganda." The news leak shocked members of Congress, some of whom felt betrayed. War Department officials considered the leak an act of unpatriotic disloyalty, and the FBI conducted an investigation. Meanwhile, the news was read with interest overseas, especially in Berlin and Tokyo.[18]

Meanwhile, newspapers and magazines were giving greater coverage to the widening war, illustrating stories with striking photographs. What Murrow accomplished in London with courage and a microphone, a new generation of photojournalists matched elsewhere with their own daring. In June 1941, when the German army invaded Russia, *Life*'s Margaret Bourke-White was the only foreign photographer in Moscow, sent there because her picture editor, Wilson Hicks, had a hunch the Nazis would invade. In July, when German planes bombed Moscow, Bourke-White had the same urge as Murrow to see the bombing from a rooftop and defied government orders to stay in a subway shelter. Atop the American embassy she photographed the night sky—silhouettes of spires against a sky lit by German parachute flares and streaking Russian tracer bullets. Witnessed at that level, the raids "possessed a magnificence that I have never seen matched in any other man-made spectacle. It was as though the German pilots and the Russian anti-aircraft gunners had been handed enormous brushes dipped in radium paint and were executing abstract designs with the sky as their canvas."[19] During two years of war, many other photographers had taken great risks to show the violent struggle for dominance in Europe and Asia. In 1940, *Life* sent Carl Mydans to cover the Russian invasion of Finland and to photograph Mussolini's Italy. His wife Shelley worked with him as a *Life* researcher, covering the aftershocks of the fall of France, wartime England, and the war between Japan and China.[20]

As correspondents dispatched continuous news relating the threatening aggressions by highly centralized totalitarian governments in Germany, Italy, and Japan, Americans grew increasingly anxious and looked for answers from Washington, especially from the president. As one media historian has observed, the rise of totalitarian states in turn "strengthened the American presidency, giving the president leverage which he used not just against the adversary states but against the American public, Congress, and the press, arguing the needs of national security."[21]

NOTES

1. Robert W. Desmond, *Crisis and Conflict: World News Reporting between Two Wars 1920–1940* (Iowa City: University of Iowa Press, 1982), 416; Knightley, *First Casualty*, 240n.

2. Shirer, *Berlin Diary*, 197, 214; Shirer, *Nightmare Years,*: 603.

3. Maurine Beasley, "Murrow's Boys," 22; Sanders, *Thompson*, 230; Kurth, *American Cassandra*, 209.

4. Sperber, *Murrow*, 141–42; Marion Marzolf, *Up from the Footnote: A History of Women Journalists* (New York: Hastings House Publishers, 1977), 139–40; Mary Marvin Breckinridge Patterson, notes for a book never completed, 1952, reel 15, p. 4, Edward R. Murrow Papers, Manuscript Division, LOC, in Beasley, "Murrow's Boys," 9.

5. Mary Marvin Breckinridge Patterson, "Broadcasting from Europe to America," text of speech given at the School of Journalism, Boston University, December 1, 1976, reel 15, p. 6, Murrow Papers, in Beasley, "Murrow's Boys," 11; Shirer, *Berlin Diary*, 277–78, 286, 291–92; Mary Marvin Breckinridge, interview with Beasley, February 28, 1991, in Beasley "Murrow's Boys," 19–20, 24. Soon after the fall of Belgium, Breckinridge, engaged to marry an American diplomat in Germany, resigned from CBS, largely because the U.S. State Department did not like her broadcasting, and she did not want to harm her husband's diplomatic career while the United States was a neutral nation.

6. Helen Kirkpatrick Milbank, interview with Anne Kasper, Washington Press Club Foundation Oral History Project, April 4, 1990, transcript, 2, 75; Sevareid, *Not So Wild*, 144, 152–53, 159; Sperber, *Murrow*, 154.

7. Ernie Pyle to parents, August 24, 1939, and Ernie Pyle to Paige Cavanaugh, May 22, 1940, cited in James Tobin, *Ernie Pyle's War* (Lawrence: University Press of Kansas, 1997), 46, 50.

8. Sperber, *Murrow*, 160, 161.

9. Sperber, *Murrow*, 160–62, 174–75.

10. Sevareid, *Not So Wild*, 169; Kendrick, *Prime Time*, 206, 208; Edward R. Murrow, "This … Is London," September. 22, 1940, in *Voices of the Past*, 325–26.

11. Heald, *Transatlantic Vistas*, 222, 230–31.

12. "William Randolph Hearst and anti-British Propaganda," February 21, 1919, 1–2, report no. 180 from M.I.1.c, New York, to British Intelligence, KV2/824, Public Record Office, London. While these views were expressed after the war, they reflected British views during the war; "The Falsehoods of Hearst; Remarkable Articles in his Pro-German Newspapers; Why He Is Barred," *Daily Express*, October 12, 1916, press clipping in British Intelligence KV2/824, PRO; "Hearst Anti-entente Propaganda," *New York American*, September 4, 1917, press clipping in British Intelligence, KV2/824, PRO; "The Ousting of Hearst," *Outlook*, September 17, 1930; Dorothy Day, "The Use of Force," *Catholic Worker*, November 1936, 4; Thomas Fleming, *The New Dealers' War: F.D.R. and the War within World War II* (New York: Basic Books, 2001), 2.

13. The *New York Times* in November 1941 reported on U.S. tank production but earlier suppressed its discovery of shocking conditions and low morale among recruits in U.S. military training camps; newsreels in 1940 devoted less footage to the war in Europe and more to national defense. Richard W. Steele, *Propaganda in an Open Society: The Roosevelt Administration and the Media, 1933–1941* (Westport, CT: Greenwood Press, 1985, 103, 148; Shirer, *Berlin Diary*, 498; A. Scott Berg, *Lindbergh* (New York: Berkley Books, 1998), 411–13; "Charles Lindbergh's Noninterventionist Efforts and America First Committee Involvement," Charles Lindbergh Web site, http://www.charleslindbergh.com/americanfirst/index.asp. "The Urgent Need of Unity," *New York Herald Tribune*, January 15, 1941.

14. Herzstein, *Roosevelt and Hitler*, 383–85, 396; Berg, *Lindbergh*, 425–29.

15. Raymond Clapper, "U.S. Arms Reaching Britain Called 'a Popgun Arsenal,'" *New York World-Telegram*, September 16, 1941; "Everyman's Columnist," *Time*, July 6, 1942, 40; "Ships Carry a Trickle of Arms to Britain," *Life*, September 29, 1941, 27–31.

16. Steele, *Propaganda in an Open Society*, 97.

17. "An Important Statement about Rubber in National Defense," *Life*, September 29, 1941, 2–3; "Announcing Three New Studebakers for 1942," *Life*, September 29, 1941, 17; "Most Important Announcement Pontiac Has Ever Made!" *Life*, September 29, 1941, 20–21; "Wings of Peace—on Missions of War," *Life*, September 29, 1941, 24; "Something They'll All Go For," *Life*, September 29, 1941, 19.

18. "F.D.R.'s War Plans! Goal Is 10 Million Armed Men; Half to Fight in AEF; Proposes Land Drive by July 1, 1943, to Smash Nazis; President Told of Equipment Shortage," *Chicago Tribune*, December 4, 1941, 1; Fleming, *The New Dealers' War*, 1–12.

19. Goldberg, *Bourke-White*, 236, 240, 241; Bourke-White, *The Photographs of Margaret Bourke-White*, 146–147. Wilson Hicks became picture editor in 1937 after heading the Associated Press News Photo Service. He had nearly full authority over assignments and photographers' lives, often transferring them great distances on short notice. He became executive editor before retiring in 1952 to teach photojournalism at the University of Miami and serve as director of university publications, influencing the choices of editors of the student magazine and newspaper. John Loengard, *Life Photographers: What They Saw* (Boston: Little, Brown, 1998), 19.

20. Shelley Mydans to Lilya Wagner in Lilya Wagner, *Women War Correspondents of World War II* (Westport, CT: Greenwood Press, 1989), 131, 133, 135.

21. David Halberstam, *The Powers That Be* (Urbana: University of Illinois Press, 2000), 13.

9

News of Total War

Anybody who has been in war and wants to go back is a plain damn fool in my book.

—Ernie Pyle, 1944

"Yesterday, December 7, 1941—a date which will live in infamy—the United States of America was suddenly and deliberately attacked by naval and air forces of the Empire of Japan," President Roosevelt said in his address to Congress seeking a declaration of war. That Sunday morning, the attack early upon the U.S. naval base at Pearl Harbor in the Hawaiian Islands had caused "severe damage to American naval and military forces. Very many American lives have been lost." While the Japanese had deceived America "by false statements and expressions of hope for continued peace," they had also attacked a number of targets throughout the Pacific area—Malaya, Hong Kong, Guam, the Philippine Islands, Wake Island, and Midway Island. "I believe I interpret the will of the Congress and of the people when I assert that we will not only defend ourselves to the uttermost but will make very certain that this form of treachery shall never endanger us again." Arthur Krock, whose interviews with Roosevelt had won him two Pulitzer Prizes, noted how quickly the Japanese attack made national unity "an instant consequence," dissipating the antiwar and anti-Roosevelt factions. "You could almost hear it click into place in Washington today." Congress quickly acceded to the president's leadership and approved the declaration of war by 4:09 P.M.[1]

Three days later, when Germany declared war against the United States, Congress also granted the president's declaration of war against

Germany. Military-affairs writer Hanson W. Baldwin noted that the bombers "with the Rising Sun flag of Japan painted upon their black wings" had "merged the Chinese war and the European war into a war of the world."[2]

News organizations urgently sought dispatches from their correspondents in the Pacific. In the Philippines on December 7, Carl and Shelley Mydans sent *Life* their view of the attack, but when *Life* editors cabled for more news about the American defense of the Philippines, Shelley Mydans cabled back the disastrous news through U.S. Army censors: "Bitterly regret your request unavailable here." Soon after, the Japanese captured her and her husband, and for 21 months they suffered "imprisonment, neglect, [and] starvation."[3]

In other ways, the attack on an American territory also challenged media coverage on the home front. New York City was put on a "war footing." The FBI rounded up Japanese and sent them to Ellis Island. On the West Coast, citizens worried about further attacks. In the South, the *Atlanta Constitution* reported that city and the state were taking "swift action in defense efforts." Racial and ethnic groups quickly pledged loyalty to America. But by month's end, Japanese Americans were increasingly suspect as newspapers reported that Japanese spies had aided the attack on Pearl Harbor.[4]

The U.S. entry into the war altered the political and ethical landscape for American reporters, editors, photographers, and filmmakers. Nearly all journalists, at home as well as overseas, could in various ways be involved in reporting the conflict and influencing public opinion. The president's call for unity and patriotism might certainly affect the way in which news was reported. Added to this was the difficulty of reporting a war that was fast paced, highly mechanized, and truly worldwide with theaters in North Africa, Europe, Asia, and the Pacific. No reporter could be expected to see the whole picture. "All of you saw parts of it, vital parts that you reported with truth and accuracy," U.S. General Omar Bradley told the Overseas Press Club after the war. At best, those parts fit together to create what historian Robert Desmond has called a "mosaic" enabling "thoughtful persons ... to gain a reasonable understanding of the war when it was in progress." Many disagreed. Reginald Thompson, a British intelligence officer who in 1944 became a war correspondent for London's *Sunday Times*, concluded that "it was impossible for a general reader of a newspaper to form a balanced view of the progress of the war."[5]

At worst, censors suppressed or altered important pieces. Eleven days after the attack on Pearl Harbor, Congress passed the War Powers Act authorizing President Roosevelt, among other things, to censor communications. Within 48 hours, he established the Office of Censorship, directed as in World War I by a nationally respected newsman, in this case Byron Price. At 50, Price was a veteran professional journalist and an executive news editor of the Associated Press, capable of commanding respect among publishers. When he reported to work, army and navy censors were already on the job, monitoring mail and cables. In time his military and civilian staff grew to 14,462.[6]

Following the model created in 1917, Price articulated a system of voluntary censorship. As in World War I, the voluntary method aimed to achieve the government's goal of suppressing information of value to the enemy through explicit cooperation from the front offices down to the reporters. Ideally, freedom with limitations should gain more acceptance and function more efficiently and cheaply than a bureaucracy of censors as employed in Nazi Germany and fascist Italy. Publicly, Roosevelt told the American Society of Newspaper Editors that government suppression of news and opinion represented the "mortal weapons that dictatorships direct against their own people." He pledged "no government control of news unless it be of vital military information." Sending editors to jail was not an option. Britain and Canada learned from experience that "flagrant violations have gone unpunished because public sentiment would not support punishment."[7]

In the massive effort to inculcate governmental wartime attitudes through newspapers, magazines, radio, and film, the Office of Censorship published guidelines for managing war news, reinforced by oral reminders and revisions. In January 1942, Price published the first edition of the *Code of Wartime Practices*, which covered references to troops, ships, planes, fortifications, production, weather, photographs and maps, casualties, movements of war materials, travels of the president or military leaders, and information about damage inflicted by enemy attacks. As a commonsense guide, he told editors to ask themselves, "Is this information I would like to have if I were the enemy?"[8] Voluntary censorship would infringe on press freedom, Price explained. The war meant that journalism would not be "business as usual," he noted.

It will mean some sacrifice of the journalistic enterprise of ordinary times. But it will not mean a news or editorial black-out.... The columns of American publications will remain the freest in the world, and will tell the story of our national successes and shortcomings accurately and in much detail.[9]

Adopting the British model of involving publishers in the control of war information, the United States invited them to serve in the censorship bureaucracy, usually in an advisory capacity. Some publishers balked. Price persuaded *Miami Herald* publisher John S. Knight to represent the Censorship Office in London, and he appointed others to advise editors across the United States. On April 14–15, 1942, the 40 press executives on this Press Advisory Council met at the Office of Censorship headquarters in Washington. As a first step, they agreed that the Code of Wartime

Practices was reasonable and would forestall "complete military censorship."[10]

Very soon, censorship advisors were dealing with day-to-day questions. As a practical matter, few publishers had read the code, and fewer understood it. In July 1942, E. T. Schultz of the *Deerfield Independent* in Wisconsin wondered if his paper was correct in publishing servicemen's addresses. Wisconsin's new Press Advisory Council member, Donald Wells Anderson, publisher of the *Wisconsin State Journal*, passed Schultz's question to the Washington headquarters. N. R. Howard, assistant director of the Office of Censorship Press Division, found references the enemy would value: a sailor's name with his ship's name, a specific military unit in Panama, air-corps pursuit units located in San Francisco and San Diego. By printing addresses of servicemen, publishers of small weeklies posed the biggest problem for voluntary censorship. In the first eight months, the Office of Censorship handled 3,120 inquiries (390 a month) from newspapermen. News-photo agencies made another 2,216 inquiries. Magazine and book publishers had 883 questions, and several hundred more came from advertising and public-relations agencies.[11]

On the home front, the government gave clearance for magazine stories about the conversion from peacetime to wartime industrial production. Early in 1942 *Life* magazine featured a multipage photo essay on wartime America. One photograph showed the last General Motors automobile coming off the assembly line, a gray Pontiac already adapted to wartime use and economies "with blackout trim" and no spare tire. Other photographs showed that Chrysler Corporation was already producing an "arsenal" of tanks, and Pearl Harbor widows were reporting for work at an aircraft factory.[12]

Censorship of combat filmmaking became nearly absolute. As public interest peaked, and people lined up outside theaters to see weekly newsreels, the military provided at least 80 percent of combat footage, almost always assigning U.S. Signal Corps and Navy cameramen. Civilian cameramen were accredited like correspondents, gave up civilian status, traveled like servicemen with combat units, and were subject to military and naval commands. The footage had to be reviewed in Washington, so that it was often released months after the event—or a year in the case of the attack on Pearl Harbor. According to film historian Raymond Fielding, the "dead and maimed were rarely shown" until near the end of the war in the Pacific. Yet critic James Agee concluded that, "At their weakest, they have things to show which non-record war films, not even the greatest that might be made, could ever hope to show."[13]

One dramatic press report in 1942 spotlighted a gaping hole in voluntary censorship. On June 7, a story in McCormick's *Chicago Tribune* reported the navy's first decisive victory since Pearl Harbor. Around Midway Island in the Pacific, American warships had ambushed and defeated the largest Japanese armada, about 190 ships, eliminating four aircraft carriers and their planes. Alarming to the Office of Censorship, the front-page headline, "Navy Had Word of Jap Plan to Strike at Sea," revealed that the navy had deciphered the Japanese code. The *Tribune*'s Pacific Fleet correspondent, Stanley Johnston, had been returning to Chicago after being rescued during the naval battle one month earlier in the Coral Sea when he learned about the bigger battle in progress. He realized the battle's significance by piecing together an intelligence estimate of the Japanese forces and strategy, his own observations at the Coral Sea, interviews with officers, and details of Japanese warships known to naval experts.[14]

Johnston's Midway scoop did not say the navy had broken the enemy code, which was in fact true, but the story and headline indicated as much. "The strength of the Japanese forces was well known to American naval circles several days before the battle began," Johnston wrote, noting that the navy learned of the force "soon after they put forth from their bases." The story said the navy knew that one Japanese contingent was a decoy toward the Aleutian Islands, intended to conceal the actual target, Midway Island. Johnston's listing of the Japanese ships by class, name, tonnage, and weaponry underscored the story's credibility.[15]

Actually, the story had been approved by naive civilians in the Office of Censorship in Washington but had not been submitted to navy censors, who were intent on concealing details. The commander-in-chief of the U.S. Fleet, Admiral Ernest J. King, concluded that there had been a breach of naval security and was convinced that the Japanese would now realize their code had been deciphered. At the White House, always under attack by *Tribune* publisher McCormick, one of Roosevelt's closest advisors, Interior Secretary Harold Ickes, thought the story was a clear case of "giving aid and comfort to the enemy and therefore a criminal offense" under the Espionage Act of 1917, which went into effect at the start of the war. Ickes knew that Attorney General Francis Biddle respected the First Amendment and opposed sedition laws, but he hoped that Biddle—"if he has any guts"—would indict the *Tribune*. The government did try to bring the *Tribune* to trial but faced the dilemma of having to reveal secrets in making its case to the grand jury. In August, after the secretary of the navy, fearing publicity and further harm, did not reveal the damage done by the story, a grand jury in Chicago refused to indict the *Tribune*. McCormick meanwhile contended that the *Tribune* had been "persecuted" by the Roosevelt administration.[16]

Price revised the code to prevent another Midway-size lapse, closing loopholes such as one that permitted reporting movements or location of "*enemy* vessels in distant waters." By July, he issued new media taboos to prevent giving "aid to the enemy." He now discouraged reports of the sinking of *any* ships, information of enemy sabotage, rumors "spread in such a way that they will be accepted as facts," and "premature disclosure of diplomatic negotiations or conversations." Journalists immediately criticized the additions. Henry Luce's *Time* asserted that "from the new list of 'don'ts' the U.S. people could see how far their news has contracted." The new taboos, *Time* declared, would keep Americans uniformed about the "full seriousness" of the German U-boat campaign and create the "the erroneous impression that sabotage in this war, unlike World War I, is virtually nonexistent." Luce's editors aggressively questioned the government's motives.

The effect of this class of suppression is to extend censorship from its proper military to its improper political sphere, to make it possible for the Government to make important political agreements behind the backs of the public (as in the recent visit of [Soviet Foreign Secretary V. S.] Molotov), to put an end to the ideal of open covenants openly arrived at.[17]

The African American press had widespread problems with censorship officials. When these newspapers emphasized racial discrimination in society and reported flare-ups of race hatred in the military, they raised questions about loyalty. At least eight agencies, including the army, the wartime Office of Facts and Figures, the FBI, the Justice Department, and the United States Postal Service, worried that the stories contributed to racial strife and amounted to negative propaganda. While the post office and FBI investigated throughout the war and recommended legal action, one historian noted that "the black press was in extreme danger of being suppressed" only until June 1942, when Attorney General Biddle "decided quietly that no black publishers would be indicted for sedition during the war." Meanwhile, beginning in February 1942, the *Pittsburgh Courier* triggered in the national race press a "Double V" campaign, inspired by a reader who proposed the "first V for victory over our enemies from without, the second V for victory over our enemies from within." At the same time, one of the leading race papers, the *Norfolk Journal and Guide,* asked African Americans to commit themselves to winning the war because fascists and Nazis were represented "death in its slowest and most excruciating form for American Negroes."[18]

Meanwhile, government and military action against all people of "Japanese ancestry" was swift. In the aftermath of Pearl Harbor, many Californians feared sabotage. As a *Fortune* writer portrayed those days, "Every rumor of Japanese air and naval operations offshore ... helped to raise to panic proportions California's ancient and deep antagonism toward the Japanese-Americans." On February 19, 1942, President Roosevelt signed Executive Order 9066, declaring the three coastal states as a defense area and giving the military authority to remove any civilians. Although California's attorney general, Earl Warren, asserted that "we have had no sabotage and no fifth-column activity since the beginning of the war," others were vehement for punitive action. Hearst's newspapers would later be accused of conducting a "campaign of hate and fear" that "broke all bounds. And, when Hearst called for the removal of all people of Japanese ancestry, he had as allies many pressure groups who had for years resented the presence of Japanese in this country." In March, Roosevelt created the War Relocation Authority (WRA), which supervised the removal and internment of more than 110,000 persons of Japanese ancestry. It was the greatest forced relocation since the 1830s removal of Native Americans from the South. Japanese Americans were required to leave their homes, jobs, and businesses and report to designated military holding areas. Temporary assembly centers were located at fairgrounds, racetracks, and other make-shift facilities, some surrounded by barbed wire, while the WRA over a period of months built 10 internment camps in the West.[19]

Some writers who came in contact with the evacuees sympathized with their plight. Writing in *Survey Graphic*, the self-described magazine of social interpretation, Paul S. Taylor noted that in the days immediately following the executive order, Caucasian witnesses before the House Committee on National Defense Migration were in "almost complete disagreement" about "the appropriate disposition" of the population, 80,000 of whom were born in the United States. However, "once evacuation was decided upon by the military, all groups, whatever their original reluctance, acquiesced." When the WRA hired Dorothea Lange to photograph the camps, she developed a camaraderie with her subjects. In September 1942, she collaborated with Taylor in an article that sympathized with the victims of "a sweeping exodus of people" and provided "glimpses into loyal attitudes among these Japanese." One such photograph showed dozens of children's faces as they pledged a "Salute of Innocence." Eventually Lange contested the WRA's censorship, as many of her photographs were suppressed.[20] By 1944, Eastern critics questioned how long the military would keep "the unwanted minority" from returning to California. Challenging "the Hearst papers and their allies," Luce's *Fortune* insisted that "by continuing to keep American citizens in 'protective custody,' the U.S. is holding to a policy as ominous as it is new. The possibilities of 'protective custody' are endless, as the Nazis have proved."[21]

Despite complaints about censorship, the media generally cooperated in suppressing military and political developments. The Office of Censorship successfully cloaked the Allied landings in Morocco in North Africa in November 1942. In January 1943, Roosevelt kept out of the news as he flew to confer with British Prime Minister Winston Churchill at Anfa, near Casablanca. In April 1943, U.S. forces deciphered a coded message revealing that the commander-in-chief of the Japanese navy, Admiral Isoroku Yamamoto, would be flying over the Solomon Islands. U.S. fliers downed his plane. "It was imperative," a censorship official explained, "that the encounter must appear to have been accidental rather than planned." U.S. reporters learned about the code break, but the Office of Censorship managed to suppress the inside story until the war ended and all U.S. prisoners were returned. Intense media-government cooperation with the British kept secret the date for the D-day invasion of France in June 1944.[22]

While the Office of Censorship became the central "gatekeeper" of war news at home, naval and military censors suppressed information in war zones, especially if the news would boost enemy morale. In October 1944, the Japanese began dispatching kamikaze (suicide) pilots to smash into U.S. warships. More than 100 ships were lost or badly damaged. The navy banned all mention of the incidents to deprive the Japanese of a propaganda weapon, a ban that lasted until mid-April 1945.[23]

Apart from the Office of Censorship, a second executive agency produced and distributed war news, mostly for domestic consumption by the vast majority of newspapers without foreign correspondents. Established on June 13, 1942, the Office of War Information (OWI) was empowered by President Roosevelt's order declaring "the right of the American people and of all other peoples opposing the Axis aggressors to be truthfully informed." In choosing a director, Roosevelt again followed the practice of selecting a respected journalist. At 52, Elmer Davis had experience with newspapers, magazines, and radio. He had established a reputation for accuracy and insight, first as a foreign correspondent for the *New York Times* and then as an essayist at *Harper's* magazine. His analysis of the European crisis in 1937–1938 attracted the attention of CBS. When CBS sent H. V. Kaltenborn to Europe, Davis replaced him. By 1942 he was a familiar voice heard regularly by the CBS audience of more than 12 million.[24]

News that Davis was going into the government elicited congratulations, advice, and even condolences. "I am more sorry than I can say," wrote George Creel, who headed the voluntary censorship in World War I, "that your control over the Army, Navy and [Department of] State is not real in any sense of the word…. While you may think you have established an arrangement that will permit a free flow of the news, just wait until an issue arises." At the *New Yorker*, editor Harold Ross welcomed Davis's condemnation of censorship, "which we here had been shooting off about considerably." From London, Murrow wrote him "a fan letter," and in New York Bill Shirer and others in the CBS "news gang" autographed an irreverent doggerel: "If bureaucrats get you all plastered / When red tape and stuff's in a foment / Please know, that we love you, you [——] / And that's all the news to this moment."[25]

Davis directed two major initiatives. The OWI became both the government's official war-news agency and an instrument of propaganda and psychological warfare. Davis pledged that OWI would "tell nothing but the truth, and we intend to see that the American people get just as much of it as genuine considerations of military security will permit." His workforce, which included many former reporters, gained credibility by adopting a policy of giving some bad news as well as good. Most of its thousands of employees worked in offices in Washington and London, but OWI broadcasters also followed as troops went ashore in North Africa, then Italy and France, and the Pacific islands. Their new 50,000-watt long-wave and medium-wave newscasts were heard in occupied territory far more clearly than the faint short-wave signals sent from American stations. The broadcasts behind enemy lines were part of OWI's second function. The agency engaged in propaganda and psychological warfare in enemy and occupied nations, as well as in neutral and free countries, and at home. Davis said OWI took responsibility for seeing that "the enemy peoples are truthfully informed because we believe the truth is on our side, not only as to the nature and issues of this war, but as to who is going to win it."[26]

At both the Office of Censorship and OWI, the government justified propaganda as self-defense against the enemy's lies and explained that suppression was necessary when battlefield facts hurt morale. The Nazi minister of propaganda, Dr. Joseph Goebbels, who held an information monopoly in Nazi territory, "is still trying hard to fool the American people," Davis said, "through rumors and falsehoods ... using the news itself as a weapon." OWI staffers recast Nazi news items broadcast to the United States, Davis explained, putting Nazi news in "proper relation to the acts of what is going on ... so that the antidote comes along with the poison." He estimated that Germans were spending at least $220 million a year on propaganda. News, Davis concluded, had become another "weapon of war which the enemy uses just as he uses air bombs on people who are closer to him than we are." Referring to the impact of Nazi propaganda, war correspondent Martha Gellhorn concluded that "people will more readily swallow lies than truth."[27]

The OWI also monitored the activities of hundreds of war correspondents, some of whom had been covering the war since the first days in September 1939. By April 1943, the office reported that 600 U.S. correspondents, broadcasters, and photographers had been accredited since Pearl Harbor—400 of them reporting from various war zones.[28] Some had established national reputations. The Scripps-Howard syndicate sent travel columnist Ernie Pyle. Novelist John Steinbeck wrote for the *New York Herald Tribune*. The urbane *New Yorker* assigned A. J. Liebling. From Moscow, *Life* magazine photojournalist Margaret Bourke-White sent stunning photographs after the German invasion of Russia.[29]

With so many African American soldiers in the war, the weekly race papers sent several correspondents to Europe and the Pacific, no longer relying on letters from the front and occasional interviews with returning soldiers. The largest circulating paper, the *Pittsburgh Courier* sent Edgar T. Rouzeau, whose stories were also supplied to smaller papers, including the fourth largest, the *Norfolk Journal and Guide*. Eventually, the Norfolk paper sent its own reporters. Thomas Young, son of publisher P. B. Young, covered the exploits of the Tuskegee Airmen, the first squadron of African American combat pilots, as they regularly debunked the military prejudice that black men could not fly. The third largest of the weeklies, the *Baltimore Afro-America,* dispatched reporters in relays, producing enough stories for a book, *This Is Our War.* In the southwest Pacific with General Douglas MacArthur's staff in 1943 and 1944, Vincent Tubbs personalized the war for African Americans, writing about such noncombat events as a soldier's Christmas in Guinea. Tubbs went home the following December, relieved by Frank Yancey. Earlier, starting in 1942, Ollie Stewart covered the fighting from North Africa to Sicily to Rome and was relieved in December 1943 by Art Carter. Max Johnson went to Italy with the 366th Infantry in March 1944 and joined the invasion of southern France. Elizabeth Phillips became the first African American female overseas war correspondent.[30]

America's war correspondents sometimes stayed longer than planned. Ernie Pyle intended only a six-month tour of combat zones but would end up covering the war almost to its end in Europe and the Pacific. The executive editor at Scripps-Howard, John Sorrells, recognized that Pyle's "homey touches" from England were a relief from battlefront news. "Folks with 'boys' over there are a damned sight more interested in reading the homely, every day, what do they eat and how do they live sort of stuff." Contrasted with the reporting of Liebling, Murrow, and Shirer, Pyle "seldom focused on epic events, great leaders, or grand strategy," wrote military historian G. Kurt Piehler. Nor did he have the literary talent of John Steinbeck or Ernest Hemingway. "Rather, he filled his columns with accounts of the dedication, bravery, and courage of particular privates, sergeants and junior officers. He also dwelt on the mundane and the routine," ascribing value to GI conversations and mail from home. "The front-line soldier I knew lived for months like an animal, and was a veteran in the cruel, fierce world of death," Pyle wrote. "He was filthy dirty, ate if and when, slept on hard ground without cover. His clothes were greasy and he lived in a constant haze of dust, pestered by flies and heat, moving constantly." Pyle "drifted" with troops in North Africa, then to Sicily, Italy, and France. By 1943, as his reports were syndicated in hundreds of dailies and weeklies, *Time* magazine labeled him "America's most widely read war correspondent."[31]

In Algiers, Pyle met his literary hero, Steinbeck, famous since his novel *The Grapes of Wrath.* Steinbeck generally wrote atmospheric pieces, focusing in North Africa on the "bone yard" of wrecked tanks awaiting repair and, in Italy, on the soldiers' rabbits' feet, St. Christopher medals, and other "lucky pieces." Years later, Steinbeck discounted the journalism that he, Pyle, and others wrote as having been "warped and one-sided," blaming military orders, self-preservation, and the correspondents' own invented self-censorship "because there was a huge and gassy thing called the War Effort." They did not report "spectacular liaisons between army Brass" and army women, or "medical discharges for stupidity, brutality, cowardice, and even sex deviation." At General Dwight Eisenhower's urging, correspondents for a time suppressed reports about two incidents in Sicily in August 1943 when Patton, while visiting medical stations, slapped two shell-shocked soldiers he considered cowards, calling one a "yellow bastard" and declaring, "There's no such thing as shell shock. It's an invention of the Jews." British journalist Noel Monks wrote that about 20 correspondents including "big and famous names in American journalism" met and agreed to write nothing, keeping the story quiet until gossip spread to America weeks later. "Ernie Pyle, I remember, was almost in tears as he said his piece." In Washington, Drew Pearson got the story cleared through *domestic* censors, over the objections of the War Department. For his part, Pyle cast the war as a cause so well that he created what biographer James Tobin has called "a modern myth, a way of seeing the chaos and misery that allowed them to make sense of it"—even to feel that, as he'd written of the tent hospital in Sicily, "there was something good about it."[32]

Occasionally, the military permitted female correspondents near the fighting. Marguerite Higgins was attracted to war by her father's stories of 1917–1918 and by Hemingway's novels. She had graduated from Columbia University's Graduate School of Journalism in 1942, and two years later, at 24, she persuaded the *Herald Tribune* to grant her wish "to get to the war before it ended." For *Collier's*, Martha Gellhorn had already covered the "relentless totality of modern war" in Spain, and the wars in Finland and in China before arriving in England for the Second World War. [33]

The military barred women from covering the actual battlefront, but some found a way. After leaving Russia, Margaret Bourke-White in 1943 became the first woman to fly with a U.S. combat mission. Perched in a Flying Fortress four miles up, she photographed the bombing of Tunisia. Also in 1943, Ruth Cowan struggled to get to the battlefront in North Africa. She had been the only female Associated Press reporter in Washington when she persuaded the AP to allow her to cover a "women's angle" in the war—the new Women's Army Corps (WAC) being organized for a mission to London. Overseas, she refused to be limited to covering only women on the English home front. "I wanted to see Patton," she recalled. "I wanted to get upfront and see what he was doing." At the London AP office, she overcame a bureaucratic obstacle in Wes Gallagher, later head of AP, who "wanted to send me back." Soon she was off to North Africa, where she met Patton, in retreat, near the Kasserine Pass in Tunisia.

I heard that there was some action going on up there … so much traffic going back this way when it should have been going that way…. I ran into Patton up there with several other officers and I came up and said, "What's the trouble?" I was the only reporter … and Patton couldn't do much else but sit and talk to me. I think he was so confused by the fact that I was up there.[34]

In the States, the practice of voluntary censorship and news management nettled editors. *Time*'s editors complained when Office of Censorship director Byron Price issued "its new lists of 'don'ts'" banning information about U-boat attacks, acts of sabotage, enemy propaganda, rumors, and "premature disclosure of diplomatic negotiations or conversations." Editors insisted that such censorship "withholds from the U.S. public knowledge of the full seriousness" of the war.[35] The rules sometimes benefited rival newspapers. When an enemy submarine sank a U.S. destroyer near Key West, the morning *Miami Herald* missed a scoop, when it was forced to suppress the story until government censors cleared it, in time for the evening *Miami News* to publish first. *Herald* publisher John S. Knight complained to Price, "We have no quarrel about withholding information in wartime, but it hardly seems fair to release to the afternoon newspapers a story that broke on morning time." Later, when Knight worked for Price's censorship staff in London, the publisher constantly battled military and civilian censors. In a speech in Manchester, England, Knight hoped for a postwar world in which all nations guaranteed a flow of uncensored news, a goal for which he would crusade in 1944 as president of American Society of Newspaper Editors.[36]

Censors silenced reports or discounted speculation about development of a super or "atomic" bomb. In June 1943, Price asked editors "not to publish or broadcast any information whatever" regarding atomic experiments. In January 1945, *Atlanta Constitution* editor Ralph McGill caused "great anxiety" when he predicted in his column that "atomic energy bombs are just around the corner. God help us if Germany comes up with this one. If she really could be first with controlled atomic energy she can conquer the world in two weeks." In a cautionary letter to the *Constitution,* Price's assistant director, Jack Lockhart, noted that because of McGill's credibility as chair of the Freedom of Information Committee of the American Society of Newspaper Editors, "the Germans may well assume that so informed a person as Mr. McGill was speaking from knowledge of our own progress." McGill "clearly indicates that a race is on and that we, too, are engaged in a driving effort to beat the Germans."

No doubt the Germans know that we are devoting some attention to this matter—but by not spotlighting our undertakings we hope we can keep them from learning how extensive our efforts are. Certainly we do not want them to learn, if it is indeed true, that we have progressed to the point where it can be said that the achievement is close at hand.[37]

As the war progressed, media organizations sent more correspondents to Europe and the Pacific. In the spring of 1944 as the military accumulated an invasion force in Britain, more than 500 journalists crowded in London, the greatest such gathering the world had ever seen. Many now came from smaller publications, some reporting the war for the first time, like the *Atlanta Journal*'s managing editor, Wright Bryan. Others had acquired battle credentials. The *New Yorker* relied on Liebling, 39, the urbane stylist who had turned from writing about the underworld of big-city boxers and con men to the bombing of London and the desert war in North Africa. Some were already big names. Ernest Hemingway, then 45 and acclaimed for his novel about the Spanish civil war, *For Whom the Bell Tolls,* arrived by plane on May 17 as special writer for *Collier's* magazine; also writing for *Collier's* was his third wife, Martha Gellhorn, who, in a risky voyage from New York, traveled aboard a ship carrying a cargo of dynamite.[38]

Journalists linked up with the invasion at different stages, some accepting great risk. More than 20 U.S. correspondents went into France with the first troops on the morning of June 6, among them the 30-year-old *Life* photographer Robert Capa, who specialized in getting close to combat. Capa was already known for his Spanish civil war "moment of death" close-up of a soldier reeling backwards (as *Life*'s caption stated on July 12, 1937) "the instant he is dropped by a bullet through the head in front of Córdoba."[39] In the invasion of France, Capa waded waist-deep into the sea, his hands trembling as he changed film. His Contax camera captured the scene of soldiers advancing or dead, though only 9 of his 72 images survived because of overheating in *Life*'s darkroom in London. Farther from shore, Hemingway watched troops on his transport ship, huddled and waiting to go ashore. Through binoculars he saw U.S. destroyers blasting the German positions and lifeless bodies near the beach, then returned to write his story in a London hotel, giving the impression of more personal involvement on "the day we took Fox Green beach." Gellhorn, aboard a hospital ship, managed to get on the beach. Flying in a glider behind German lines, Wright Bryan landed with paratroops and seven other reporters, then managed to get back to England by evening to broadcast to the United States on NBC and CBS. When Bryan returned to France in September, he and two other reporters traveling in a jeep ran into a German gunfire and were captured. Suffering from a gunshot wound in one leg, Bryan was imprisoned in Poland until January, when the Soviet army liberated the camp. With his leg still healing, he set out for Paris on foot, arriving in April. He returned home a hero.[40]

Soon after D-day, hundreds more correspondents arrived in France with waves of troop ships. The morning after D-day, Ernie Pyle landed on a Normandy beachhead where so many had died the day before. Within a day, Liebling landed and was soon elected to the Beachhead Correspondents Committee to deal with communication, censorship, and transportation. One photograph, conveying the reality of an open-air workplace in Normandy, showed Pyle seated at a square table with his typewriter and notes in the midst of an apple orchard. His first dispatch on June 12 ("A Pure Miracle") memorialized the soldiers of the first wave who eventually crossed all barriers to secure the beachhead against entrenched Germans. Many in the first wave were killed by "evil devices" underwater, mines buried in the beach, and barbed wire, concrete gun emplacements, hidden nests of machine guns "with crossfire taking in every inch of the beach." Pyle reported that

The first crack in the beach defenses was finally accomplished by terrific and wonderful naval gunfire, which knocked out the big gun emplacements. They tell epic stories of destroyers that ran right up into shallow water and had it out point-blank with the big guns in those concrete emplacements ashore.

When the heavy fire stopped, our men were organized by their officers and pushed on inland, circling machine-gun nests and taking them from the rear.[41]

Pyle continued throughout the war to describe the experiences of individual soldiers, often suffering, as they did, battlefield fatigue and misery. For days he followed Private First Class Tommy Clayton, 37, who hoped to return to Evansville, Indiana, and open a restaurant. Clayton was an expert rifleman who was luckily missed by three shells on D-day and fought for 37 days without rest. During the advance in August 1944, Pyle wrote:

He was stationed in the bushes at a bend in a gravel road, covering a crossroads only eighty yards ahead of him.

Suddenly three German soldiers came out a side road and foolishly stopped to talk right in the middle of the crossroads. The (Browning automatic rifle) has twenty bullets in a clip. Clayton held her down for the whole clip. The three Germans went down, never to get up.

Weeks later, Clayton was killed. "It saddened me terribly, for I felt very close to him," Pyle wrote. Two months after D-day, Pyle came close to death when Allied pilots accidentally hit his position, dropping "bombs by the hundred, hurtling down through the air above us." In a French farm-yard, Pyle and an officer dashed into the wagon-shed, "squirming like an eel to get under one of the heavy wagons.... You could feel little waves of concussions on your chest and in your eyes." Three days later Pyle learned that the bombs had killed Associated Press photographer Bede Irvin.[42]

Many correspondents took fewer risks, but all experienced discomfort, if not danger. Liebling told his readers about eating "gastronomically despicable" army canned rations ("alleged pork and egg") as he watched out for German snipers. In Normandy, an "Ozark type" colonel advised him that the German snipers didn't have the squirrel-hunting skill of shooting ahead of a moving target. "If you just keep walking," he was told, "they almost always shoot behind you."[43]

Anticipating the liberation of Paris, Hemingway abandoned his role as a correspondent and led a contingent of French guerrillas. At one point, his group encountered German tanks and artillery. In an exchange of shells, the French leader shouted elatedly, "The contact is beautiful." Alarmed, Hemingway told his *Collier's* readers,

It was much too beautiful for me, who had never been a great lover of contact any-way, and I hit the deck as an 88 shell burst alongside the road…. My own war aim was to get into Paris without being shot. I took cover in all the street fighting—the solidest cover available—and with someone covering the stairs behind me when we were in houses or the entrances to apartment houses.

His group of guerrillas, many on bicycles, maneuvered ahead of the cautious French armored division, and Hemingway boasted that he was among the first troops to enter Paris, "the city I love best in all the world." His group entered Paris, cleared some Germans from an apartment build-ing, toasted the liberation with champagne at the Travellers' Club, and claimed to have liberated the Ritz Hotel, where amid the exuberance and kissing of the liberators, he hosted parties with liberated whiskey and champagne.[44]

Liebling and Pyle were not far behind. "I had thought of the whole war as a road back to Paris," Liebling told *New Yorker* readers. As Hemingway had, Liebling and Pyle found the French people kissing and honoring the first liberators. "It was like an entry into Paradise," Liebling wrote, "and all the sweeter because we didn't deserve it." Pyle recalled the first day of Paris's liberation as

one of the great days of all time. Once the jeep was simply swamped in human traffic … we were swarmed over and hugged and kissed and torn at…. Women in white dresses climbed up [tanks] to kiss men with grimy faces. And early the next morning we saw a girl climbing sleepily out of a tank turret.

Pyle, Liebling, and other correspondents were steered by the military to the Hotel Neron. Liebling described the place as "neither dilapidated nor elaborate … a combination of barracks and arsenal, with young men in berets, shirt-sleeves, and pistol belts bounding up the stairs three at a time." He had his first bath since "a swim in a spinachy pond." Pyle found his hotel room "strange after so long in the field…. Sitting there writing within safe walls, and looking out the window occasionally at the street thronged with happy people, it was already hard to believe there ever had been a war."[45]

The military relaxed restrictions against female reporters. By the end of June, six female correspondents had been permitted to visit the Normandy beachhead for three hours. One of the six, Judy Barden of the *New York Sun,* returned to France in July, where she was joined by three others: Dudley Ann Harmon of United Press, Barbara Wace with the Associated Press, and Marjorie Avery of the *Detroit Free Press.* In the fall, Marguerite Higgins of the *Herald Tribune,* among the last wave of journalists to enter Paris, learned war reporting on the job, largely by listening to experienced correspondents. She was surprised at how approachable Hemingway and the others were. Helen Kirkpatrick of the *Chicago Daily News* taught her a lesson in gaining access to military commanders. At lunch at the Hotel Scribe, Kirkpatrick "mentioned proudly that she had been in to see 'The Boss'"—U.S. General Dwight Eisenhower, commander of all Allied forces. Higgins asked for an appointment too, but it wasn't granted until after she had already left Paris. "Having no laurels to rest on, I became a cyclone of energy," she recalled. By spring 1945 Higgins was at the front lines, getting stories with the best. In April, riding in a jeep with Sergeant Peter Furst of *Stars and Stripes,* the military newspaper, she reached the Dachau prison camp ahead of the U.S. Army. Dachau's commander, relieved to see Americans rather than Russians, surrendered to Higgins and Furst. The camp was opened, and Higgins was carried aloft and bruised by "pitifully emaciated" prisoners in a state of "joyful but hysterical frenzy." Higgins's exclusive story helped her win the New York Newspaper Women's Club prize for the best foreign correspondence of 1945.[46]

News of the liberation of Dachau, Buchenwald, and other death camps astonished the world. As early as August 1944, with the liberation of Lublin, Poland, by the Red Army, William H. Lawrence of the *New York Times* reported the discovery of a German concentration camp "for the production of death, in which it is estimated by Soviet and Polish authorities that as many as 1,500,000 persons from nearly every country in Europe were killed in three years." As in other such reports, however, there was little differentiation between Jews and other ethnics or nationals. In November 1944, *New York Times* correspondent John H. Crider, among the first to witness the camp at Auschwitz, quoted the War Refugee Board as declaring that "Germans have deliberately and systematically murdered millions of innocent civilians—Jews and Christians like—all over Europe." In 1944 and 1945, the *Chicago Tribune* published numerous articles about extermination in Europe, rarely mentioning the word "Jew" in a headline and often placing the stories on inside pages. On April 12, allegations of genocide appeared on page 10: "Charges Nazis Slew 5 Million Jews." During the liberation of the death camps in 1945, *Time* magazine mentioned Jews as victims in only one of 16 articles. German prisoners found alive in at Buchenwald were described as "of many persuasions: Communists, Catholic, Socialist, Jew, and some of no particular faith." Mention of Jews was often found in the third or fourth paragraphs. The *Chicago Tribune* reported that the 6th Armored Division had freed 900

Jewish women. By the end of April, however, closer inspections of camp crematoriums and interviews with survivors began to reveal the nature of the extermination process and the Jews as principal victims. Buchenwald was referred to as "an extermination factory."[47]

How could so little have been known about the Nazi program of genocide, the mass gas-chamber executions? Were the media responsible for not publicizing Nazi crimes against the Jews? In fact, journalists had been writing about Hitler's anti-Semitism since his rise to power. In 1933, six months before she was expelled from Germany, Dorothy Thompson warned that Hitler's anti-Semitic laws were disastrous. "Hitlerism," she contended, displayed an "irrationally unmodern Judophobia" and "represented a return to the darker side of the Middle Ages." The American Jewish response was divided: the masses protested, but upper-class Jews with more influence and more investments in Germany reacted with a cautious, diplomatic wait-and-see attitude. From 1933 to 1945, continuous reports and editorials suggested the terror and horror of Hitler's persecution of the Jews. Although the Nazis controlled the German press and manipulated foreign media, a foremost expert of the Holocaust, Elie Wiesel, noted the abundance of reported information before 1945. The problem, Wiesel said, was not information, but persuasion. People simply didn't believe what they read or felt unempowered to act and responded with silence and inaction. [48]

The war in Europe was followed vicariously by the correspondents who had their own war in the Pacific theater. Early in 1945, the uniformed reporters watched from ships or waded ashore as Admiral Chester Nimitz's navy and the U.S. Marines battled from island to island. Robert Sherrod, one of *Time* magazine's 80 worldwide war correspondents, had spent many months at sea before going ashore with the marines at Iwo Jima. The tiny, well-guarded Japanese island and radar center, only eight square miles, was strategically located halfway between Tokyo and the U.S. base on Guam and could become an airfield for the B-29s making bombing raids on Japan. "That first night [February 19] can only be described as a nightmare in hell," Sherrod radioed his editors. The Japanese, surprisingly shielded from days of U.S. air bombardment by a series of tunnels and caves, fired from these positions and pinned down the marines along the volcanic beach in what was described as a blood-bath. With some 21,000 defenders ready to die rather than surrender, it took more than a month to conquer the island. The U.S. death toll was listed as 6,821. "The American struggle to capture Iwo Jima proved to be the bloodiest fight in Marine Corps history," wrote military historian Robert S. Burrell, who claimed that the military overestimated the island's strategic value. What stuck in the minds of the home-front public was Associated Press photographer Joe Rosenthal's picture of six marines planting the American flag atop Mount Suribachi, a feat that had taken four days instead of two. Rosenthal's photograph won a Pulitzer Prize; three of the six marines were killed in action within a month. By June, the military released to first-run theaters its 19-minute color film, *To the Shores of Iwo Jima*.[49]

While the marines were struggling on Iwo Jima, Ernie Pyle was aboard an aircraft carrier in the Pacific. After a few months' rest at home in the fall of 1944, he had acquiesced to the navy's appeal that he give marines in the Pacific the sort of attention he had given army troops in Europe. "Anybody who has been in war and wants to go back is a plain damn fool in my book," he wrote in a column. "I'm going simply because there's a war on and I'm part of it and I've known all the time I was going back." He was cheered by a "Dear Ernie" letter from General Dwight Eisenhower, who had just read *Brave Men*, a compilation of Pyle's war dispatches, which Pyle had sent him. The general said the book "well expresses the reactions of decent people to this bloody business. But the one thing in your book that hits me most forcibly is … where you announce yourself as a rabid, one-man army, gong full out to tell the truth about the infantry combat soldier."[50]

During stopovers in Hawaii and Guam, the navy treated him as a celebrity, underestimating his role as a working journalist on a mission for the individual fighting man. As such the navy angered him when censors deleted servicemen's names from his stories, meaning that "half the columns I write will be thrown out, because they are based on people." After Pyle threatened that he would be "forced to leave the theatre and go on to the Philippines," the censors relented and permitted names. His other problem was that he had seen no fighting while at sea and thought that his stories would remain "uninspired and dull" unless he made some "future Iwo Jima landing, and although I have sworn I would never make another one, I may have to." That opportunity came with the invasion of Okinawa. Ashore on the night before leaving, Pyle spent the hours drinking with *Time*'s Robert Sherrod, at a party with navy officers, hospital ship nurses, and two female Norwegian radio operators. Sherrod recalled, "Ernie was the lion of the party." A few days later, on April 17, a day after the marines landed on Ie Shima, a small island near Okinawa, Pyle joined them. On April 18, the jeep carrying Pyle and three marines was targeted by a sniper firing a machine gun. The four scattered into roadside ditches. Pyle raised his head to look for the others and asked, "Are you all right?" As the soldier beside him reported, "Some shots chewed up the road in front of me and ricocheted over my head." He turned and saw Pyle lying face up, killed by a shot in left temple.[51]

A few days before Pyle's death, the ship's wireless operator had received news of the death of President Roosevelt. The president had died on April 12 at his Southern White House in Warm Springs, Georgia. While sitting for a portrait, he complained of an intense headache, fell unconscious, and died of a cerebral hemorrhage at 4:45 P.M. That afternoon, Vice President Harry Truman, located in the Capitol building, hurried to the White House, where he learned the news and was sworn in as president by 7:09 P.M. The International News Service announced the president's death in a bulletin at 5:45 P.M., followed by the Associated Press and United Press. The four radio networks demonstrated their customary immediacy. Historian David McCullough wrote that, "In New York, CBS interrupted a children's serial about Daniel Boone called 'Wilderness Road,' NBC broke into 'Front Page Ferrell,' ABC interrupted 'Captain Midnight,' and Mutual, 'Tom Mix.'" In stories in various editions, the *New York Times* referred to him as the "War President" and noted the day's good news from the war, that the U.S. Army had crossed the Elbe River and was near Berlin.[52]

One of Roosevelt's last diplomatic messages that morning had been to allay Winston Churchill's concerns about the Soviet army's seizure of Poland. On hearing of the president's death, Churchill said he felt as though he had been "struck a physical blow" and broke down when he relayed the news in a speech to the House of Commons. Pulitzer winner Anne O'Hare McCormick said the photograph of Churchill heading to the Commons was "a revealing picture of what the death of President Roosevelt means to the Allied leaders, particularly in Britain." Most London papers headlined their April 13 editions with "Roosevelt Dead." In Russia, Stalin honored Roosevelt by dictating that newspapers put his picture on the front pages. According to the Japanese agency Domei, Japan's premier, Admiral Baron Kantar Suzuki, expressed his "profound sympathy." Americans had a chance to pay their respects as the train carrying the president's body passed from Warm Springs to Washington and, after the state funeral, to his home in Hyde Park, New York.[53]

While Americans mourned—with flags at half-staff—they expected any day to celebrate "V-E day," victory in Europe. But with the U.S. and Russian armies still engaged in the Battle of Berlin, General Eisenhower at his Advanced Command Post on April 17 declared that V-E day would "not be proclaimed until all important enemy forces pocketed on the western front have been wiped out." On April 25 in Paris, Allied political leaders claimed they, not General Eisenhower, would proclaim V-E day. Each day end's reports seemed to bring the end nearer. On April 28, the *New York Times* noted military-affairs writer, Hanson W. Baldwin, seemed as though he himself were trying to announce V-E day as he reported that the meeting of Russian and American forces on the Elbe River "has brought the war in Europe to a point where anything can happen overnight." The next day, he reported that Berlin was "dying, perhaps with Hitler in its ashes" and that "pockets" of enemy troops might abandon a last-ditch fight. In New York, *Time* magazine was on hold with its end-of-war cover portrait of Hitler's face with a great X across it.[54]

On May 7, the Associated Press's western-front chief, Ed Kennedy, seized the honor of announcing the war's end, and the news that Germany had surrendered unconditionally. Although he and 15 other journalists who witnessed the surrender agreed to wait until General Eisenhower gave clearance to report it, Kennedy called his London office after he learned that German radio had announced the news. "This is Ed Kennedy. Germany has surrendered unconditionally. That's official. Make the dateline Rheims, France, and get it out." In New York, it was 9:36 A.M. when the news came on the AP teletype from London: "Flash. Germany surrenders unconditionally to the Western Allies and Russia." Although Allied leaders proclaimed May 8 as V-E day, the news understandably set off spontaneous celebrations. "London could not wait," the *New York Times* reported. Londoners "danced and pranced in the streets and shot off flares and built great bonfires in the gaping cellars of bombed-out buildings." Neither could New Yorkers wait, massing noisily in the streets and at the Statue of Liberty, streaming into the financial district, and congregating in churches. In Washington, news of the victory came over a special radio apparatus in the House of Representatives as "legislative business proceeded with only minor interruptions." In Chicago, more than 800 policemen were called to duty, and barricades were erected in front of some stores, but the city experienced only a "brief flurry of excitement."[55]

On V-E day, President Truman's broadcast reached a record U.S. radio audience estimated at 36,500,000. The broadcast was part of radio's "greatest show," a round-the-world V-E day celebration that critics said "must have reached vast numbers of listeners in every country on earth." The same day, Treasury Secretary Henry Morgenthau Jr. announced that the U.S. cost of fighting Germany and Japan had reached $275 billion. In London, King George saluted the living and called for a lasting peace.[56]

Apart from the jubilation, there was political concern about the "vital" Russian position in postwar Europe and the continuing war with Japan. The Red Army had continued fighting through the last day of the war, when they captured Dresden, consolidated their hold on Eastern Europe, and won "final-hour victories" in southern German and Austria. At the secret Three-Power talks in Potsdam in late July and early August, Truman, Churchill, and then Churchill's successor as prime minister, Clement Atlee, found Stalin stubbornly resisting or postponing many of their solutions for territorial control in postwar Europe. As for Japan, Stalin pledged that Russia would declare war by August 15. For his part, Truman evidently did not mention that he was planning to force an end to the war before then by authorizing the use of a secret superweapon, the so-called atomic bomb.[57]

Truman had decided to unleash the bomb against Japan's civilian population. Although the project to develop the weapon had been a

closely guarded secret, Truman had learned about it in the summer of
1943 when, as a senator, he inquired about a mysterious expenditure
called the Manhattan Project. Very soon he learned about the cadre of
military leaders, scientists, and industrialists working in secrecy, racing
to beat Nazi experimenters. A year earlier, Winston Churchill had underscored that Allied war plans depended on success in producing "a new
instrument of war for which both sides were avidly groping ... the secret
of the atomic bomb." In July 1943, when a former senator inquired about
a land condemnation in the state of Washington, Truman, despite the
secrecy, told him it was "for the construction of a plant to make a terrific
explosion for a secret weapon that will be a wonder.... I hope it works."
Truman seemed enthusiastic about the potential for the bomb, which was
confirmed in the first test explosion on July 16, 1945, at Alamogordo Air
Force Base in New Mexico. Meanwhile, the air force had achieved nearly
complete access above Japanese cities. As early as March, the bombing by
B-29s had been leaving "a wake of fire no propaganda can conceal from
the Japanese people." By August, air raids had destroyed more than 40
cities, the Japanese later claimed, killing thousands and leaving nearly
nine million people homeless. Still, Japan—neither its military nor its
emperor—did not signal surrender. Some, among them Secretary of State
James F. Brynes, argued that Japan was already beaten and was trying to
make peace without "losing face."[58]

Truman was still aboard the ship returning from Potsdam on August 6
when, at lunch with Secretary Byrnes, an officer delivered a decoded message that the air force had dropped the bomb on Hiroshima four hours
earlier. As his biographer noted, Truman's response was, "This is the
greatest thing in history." A second message reported "complete success,"
and Truman seemed exuberant as he announced the bombing to the crew
around him, adding that it was more powerful than 20,000 tons of TNT. A
day earlier he had briefed newsmen about the bomb and his prepared message to the nation, binding them to secrecy until the bomb was dropped.
Now, as he announced the success, he had "a broad smile on his face,"
recalled United Press White House correspondent Merriman Smith.[59]

To scientists and the military, success meant destruction so devastating to property and lives that unconditional surrender would come
immediately. Based on photographs, U.S. estimates were that the one
bomb's white flash of atomic energy completely "wiped out" 60 percent
of Hiroshima, about four square miles. At first, the stunned Japanese
government said little about the devastation. On August 7, Osaka radio
reported only that train service in Hiroshima had been canceled, but by
August 8, the Japanese admitted to vast ruin.[60] The city's human loss was
at first uncountable. Japan's early estimate of 30,000 dead was revised two
weeks later to 100,000 with the note that over time many more would die
from burns and a new menace called radioactivity.[61]

Subsequent articles in newspapers and magazines explained atomic power and the impact of the bomb on Hiroshima and Nagasaki, citing statistical evidence and referring to the impact on people generally. But, as one analysis demonstrated, "most of these stories steered clear of details that would help readers identify with the dead or the survivors." This was the remarkable difference in John Hersey's *New Yorker* magazine article "Hiroshima." He interviewed six survivors and related their experiences before and after the *pikadon*—Japanese for "flash-boom." Hersey's detailed narrative about the impact of an atomic bomb on these six made it the most important piece published on the subject. The writer Paul Boyer compared Hersey's realism with that in Stephen Crane's *The Red Badge of Courage*.[62] The piece was so long that the *New Yorker* for the first time devoted an entire issue to one subject "in the conviction that few of us have yet comprehended the all but incredible destructive power of this weapon, and that everyone might well take time to consider the terrible implications of its use."[63] One of the survivors who spoke with Hersey, Hatsuyo Nakamura, a war widow and mother, said that, at the moment of the blast, she was standing by a window watching her neighbor, when

everything flashed whiter than any white she had ever seen. She did not notice what happened to the man next door; the reflex of a mother set her in motion toward her children. She had taken a single step ... when something picked her up and she seemed to fly into the next room over the raised sleeping platform, pursued by parts of her house. Timbers fell around her as she landed, and a shower of tiles pummeled her; everything became dark, for she was buried.... She heard a child cry, "Mother, help me," and saw her youngest—Myeko, the five-year-old—buried up to her breast and unable to move. As Mrs. Nakamura started frantically to claw her way toward the baby, she could see or hear nothing of her other children.[64]

The reaction to Hersey's article was dramatic and widespread. Newsstands sold out, and requests for copies were hard to fill. Some publications questioned the editors' judgment in dropping the regular columns subscribers expected. A critic in the *New Republic* regarded "Hiroshima" as "one of the great classics of the war." As the *New Yorker* editors may have expected, the article triggered public questions about the use of the bomb.[65]

As the devastation of Hiroshima was being considered by the Japanese government, another B-29 three days later dropped a second atomic bomb on the port city of Nagasaki. *New York Times* reporter William H. Lawrence, who had become an expert in atomic energy, reported the crew's satisfaction about "good results." Three weeks later he and other reporters were flown at low level to witness the result. "Burned, blasted and seared, Nagasaki looked like a city of death," he wrote. On the day of the blast, smoke—later called the "mushroom cloud"—could be seen from as far as 170 miles. The death toll would eventually be at least 74,000. Nonetheless, Osaka's *Mainichi* daily briefly mentioned that the "new type" of bomb had caused "extremely slight" damage, based on the report of an army post commander distant from Nagasaki. Amid frustration that the Japanese censorship was concealing the seriousness of the bombs, the air force showered three million leaflets warning "the atomic bomb and other explosives would be used again and again to destroy every military resource unless they petitioned the Emperor at once to end the war."[66] Also forcing a quick decision was the fact that Stalin, after the bombing of Hiroshima, surprised Japan and most Americans by declaring war and sending the Red Army against a greatly weakened Japan in what would be called a brief second Russo-Japanese War.[67]

Amid such threats, the Japanese at last surrendered unconditionally. Granted the right to retain Emperor Hirohito, they agreed finally to the U.S. insistence on writing his name into the surrender documents. On August 14, Truman announced the unqualified surrender ending the world war.[68] *Time* magazine, which had drawn an X over Hitler's face for V-E day, refrained from doing the same to the emperor and instead placed the X across the familiar emblem on the Japanese flag, the red rising sun. V-J celebrations were greatest in America, which had been far more involved than any other country in the offensive against Japan. In New York, the revelry was blamed for four deaths. On the sober side, stories reminded that the war's overall toll in six years had created unparalleled deaths and destruction. The end of the war would tax the Allied names and the new United Nations charter. Other stories concerned the nation's economic conversion to peacetime, with assistance from the federal wartime agencies. The *Times'* Hanson Baldwin launched an ongoing debate over the use of the atomic bomb, predicting that the weapon "will long live in the sanguinary history of war" and that its use had sown the "seed of hate."[69]

In Washington, Byron Price had announced that U.S. wartime censorship ended one hour after Truman announced the victory over Japan. Months before that, American newspaper editors had envisioned a peacetime world without censorship and launched an initiative to establish improved flow of news in the postwar world. The elite in the American Society of Newspaper Editors, headed by John S. Knight, argued that openness in news flow worldwide would help "inoculate" the world against the rise of disastrous dictators. Citing the Nazi model of press suppression, the newspaper executives argued that Hitler could not have grown into a menace to civilization if he had not controlled the flow of information. They concluded that guaranteed international freedom of information might be "a strong contribution to the future peace of the world." Knight hoped that such a guarantee would be included in the charter being drafted for the new United Nations. In essence, he wanted to export the First Amendment.[70]

With this stated purpose, Knight in January 1945 dispatched an ASNE delegation on a round-the-world tour to enlist nations' support for a free press. The delegation of three "press missionaries" was headed by the ASNE vice president, Wilbur Forrest, assistant editor of the *Herald Tribune*. The other two were Ralph Emerson McGill, editor of the *Atlanta Constitution* and chair of ASNE's Freedom of Information Committee, and Carl William Ackerman, dean since 1931 of Pulitzer's Columbia University Graduate School of Journalism. They traveled some 43,000 miles, often under hazardous wartime and wintry conditions, and concluded their trip in April 1945 without much assurance of any worldwide agreement. One growing frustration was Soviet opposition to guarantees of international press freedom in the Eastern European nations occupied by the Red Army. Other nations' postwar suspicions effectively prevented a guarantee of press freedom from being included in the U.N. charter.[71] While publishers could envision greater profits in a worldwide news market, radio networks had experienced the most eventful year in 25 years of broadcasting history.[72]

To review the year was a monumental task, but journalists attempted it. Domestically, the press was quickly preoccupied with reporting the "reconversion" to peacetime practices. Most wartime controls on industry had been removed immediately after V-J day. Economists warned of the danger of inflation. Internationally, analysts credited the Western democracies (allied with the totalitarian Soviet Union) with ridding Europe and the Far East of virulent dictatorships, scourges of civilization. The U.S. role in ending history's greatest world war extended into postwar endeavors to assure a lasting peace. While the army was expediting shifts of troops home from Europe, the fact remained that, given the battered and exhausted European nations, the United States and Russia had emerged as the two dominant world powers with major roles in determining the postwar map of Europe, Asia, Africa, and the Middle East. The war had also triggered independence movements in Europe's colonial possessions and protectorates, especially those controlled by England and France, notably India, Egypt, Nigeria, and Algeria. With the motive of establishing a civilian presence around the world, the State Department supported a bill in Congress—a variation of General Eisenhower's postwar vision for mobilizing goodwill journalists like Ernie Pyle—to establish a permanent foreign information service that would spread American information and culture in 62 countries.[73] With all this, together with the U.S. participation in founding the new United Nations, the United States appeared to be committed to a continuing role in international affairs.

NOTES

1. "Franklin D. Roosevelt's Infamy Speech," December 8, 1941; "Congressional Declaration of War on Japan," December 8, 1941; "Congressional Declaration of

War on Germany," December 11, 1941, University of Oklahoma Law Center, http://www.law.ou.edu/hist/html; "Tokyo Bombers Strike Hard at Our Main Bases on Oahu; Naval Based Attacked from Air," *New York Times,* December 8, 1941, 1; Arthur Krock, "Capital Dissensions Fade out in Necessities of Common Cause," *New York Times,* December 8, 1941, 6; Frank L. Kluckhohn, "Guam Bombed; Army Ship Is Sunk; U.S. Fliers Head North from Manila—Battleship Oklahoma Set Afire by Torpedo Planes at Honolulu; 104 Soldiers Killed at Field in Hawaii; President Fears 'Very Heavy Losses' on Oahu—Churchill Notifies Japan that a State of War Exists," *New York Times,* December 8, 1941, 1.

2. Hanson W. Baldwin, "Japanese Attack Merges Conflicts—We Must Not Discount Foe's Strength," *New York Times,* December 8, 1941, 7.

3. Shelley Mydans to Lilya Wagner in Wagner, *Women War Correspondents of World War II,* 131, 133, 135; Shelley Mydans to Jan Haag, November 9, 1991, 2–3; Jan Haag, "Carl Mydans Still Making Photographic History," United Press International, January 15, 1987. In 1944 when U.S. forces recaptured the Philippines, Carl returned and took the famous photograph of General Douglas MacArthur wading ashore. He also went to France, where he photographed Frenchwomen having their heads shaved as punishment for collaboration with the Nazis, then to Japan to photograph the Japanese surrender aboard the battleship U.S.S. *Missouri.* "Mydans, photographer," August 18, 2004. Shelley Mydans also returned to the Philippines and after the war traveled with Carl to write about American troops in Japan. She recalled that she and Carl survived because "we were young and got out of Santo Tomas (inferior and meager rice diet) after less than a year and had some months in [Japanese-occupied] Shanghai before we were interned again and where the diet was based on bread (inferior and meager) rather than rice; we were able to get back to health on the long repatriation voyage on the *Gripsholm.* I, personally, found the Japanese correct in my own dealings with them. Others may not have. And that they could be 'brutal' to military prisoners is a vast understatement." Carl said that in captivity he and Shelley remained a team. "People said to us afterwards, wasn't it a shame that Shelley was caught there too. It wasn't a shame. It was wonderful. We shared it together."

4. "Entire City Put on War Footing; Japanese Rounded up by FBI, Sent to Ellis Island—Vital Services Are Guard," *New York Times,* December 8, 1941, 1; Arthur Krock, "Vulnerability of Hawaii; Deficiencies in Personnel, Equipment and Military System Are Indicated," *New York Times,* December 10, 1941, 5; "City, State Take Swift Action in Defense Efforts," *Atlanta Constitution,* December 9, 1941, 1; Wallace Carroll, "Japanese Spies Showed the Way for Raid on Vital Areas in Hawaii; Arrows Pointing to Objectives Reported Cut in Sugar Cane on Plantations—Data on Ships Was Obtained by Food Dealers," *New York Times,* December 31, 1941, 3.

5. Robert W. Desmond, *Tides of War: World News Reporting 1940–1945* (Iowa City: University of Iowa Press, 1984), 462; Knightley, *First Casualty,* 317.

6. Theodore F. Koop, *Weapon of Silence* (Chicago: University of Chicago Press, 1946), 9–10.

7. Ibid., 164; Wallace B. Eberhard, "Restraining a Free Press in Wartime: Voluntary Censorship at the Grassroots Level," paper presented to the American Journalism Historians Association, University of Kansas, October 1, 1992, 1. Britain and Canada prosecuted only four wartime cases. See also Byron Price,

"What Can and What Cannot Be Printed in War Time," *Congressional Digest*, February 1942, 36–37.

8 Byron Price, *Code of Wartime Practices* (Washington, DC: U.S. Government Printing Office, 1942), 1–4.

9. Ibid.

10. "Memo to Minnesota Publishers and Editors," Donald W. Anderson Papers, Wisconsin State Historical Society, in Eberhard, "Free Press in Wartime," 4–5; Charles Whited, *Knight: A Publisher in the Tumultuous Century* (New York: E. P. Dutton, 1988), 95–109; Desmond, *Tides of War*, 345.

11. N. R. Howard to E. T. Schultz, July 25, 1942, Anderson Papers; and N. R. Howard, Statistical Report of Work of Press Division, April 14, 1942 to January 1, 1943, in Eberhard, "Free Press in Wartime," 2, 5–6.

12. "U.S. Auto Plants Are Closed," *Life*, February 16, 1942, 24, 27.

13. Fielding, *American Newsreel*, 288–95.

14. Stanley Johnston, "Navy Had Word of Jap Plan to Strike at Sea," *Chicago Tribune*, June 7, 1942, 1; Lloyd Wendt, *Chicago Tribune: The Rise of a Great American Newspaper* (Chicago: Rand McNally, 1979), 627–29; Gordon W. Prange, Donald M. Goldstein, and Katherine V. Dillon, *Miracle at Midway* (New York: McGraw-Hill, 1982), 367. Johnston later claimed he did not know until the end of the war that the navy had unscrambled the Japanese machine-enciphered code six months after Pearl Harbor and was eavesdropping on their signals.

15. Johnston, "Navy Had Word," 1.

16. Wendt, *Chicago Tribune*, 632–36; Prange, Goldstein, and Dillon, *Miracle at Midway*, 367; Koop, *Weapon of Silence*, 243; Knightley, *First Casualty*, 283–85; Harold Ickes, Diary, June 14, 1942, reel 5, p. 6716, Ickes Papers; Patrick S. Washburn, *A Question of Sedition: The Federal Government's Investigation of the Black Press during World War II* (New York: Oxford University Press, 1986), 95.

17. "Expanding Don'ts," *Time*, July 6, 1942, 40.

18. Washburn, *A Question of Sedition*, 8–9, 54–55; "Let's Win the War," *Norfolk Journal and Guide*, September 12, 1942, 10; Jinx Coleman Broussard and John Maxwell Hamilton, "Covering a Two-Front War: African-American Correspondents during World War II," paper presented to the Association for Education in Journalism and Mass Communication, Toronto, August 4–7, 2004, 5–6.

19. "Issi, Nisei, Kibei: The U.S. Has Put 110,000 of Japanese Blood in 'Protective Custody,'" *Fortune*, April 1944, 22. A subsequent study of the *New York Times'* coverage of the Japanese during the first four months after Pearl Harbor framed Japanese as the "Other," a people outside the norms of American culture. See Bonnie Brennan and Margaret Duffy, "'If a Problem Cannot Be Solved, Enlarge It': An Ideological Critique of the 'Other' in Pearl Harbor and September 11 *New York Times* Coverage," *Journalism Studies* 4 (1): 3–14.

20. Paul S. Taylor, "Our Stakes in the Japanese Exodus," *Survey Graphic*, September 1942, 375; "Dorothea Lange," in "Journalists, Photographers, and Broadcasters during World War II," http://www.loc.gov/exhibits/wcf/wcf0013.html.

21. "Issi, Nisei, Kibei," 118; see also Brennan and Duffy, "If a Problem Cannot Be Solved, Enlarge It."

22. Wendt, *Chicago Tribune*, 627–29, 632–36; Koop, *Weapon of Silence*, 244; Prange, Goldstein, and Dillon, *Miracle at Midway*, 367; Patrick S. Washburn, "The Office of Press Censorship's Effort to Control Press Coverage of the Atomic Bomb during World War II," *Journalism Monographs* 120 (April 1990): 120.

23. Knightly, *First Casualty*, 297. In Japanese, *kamikazi* means "divine wind."

24. Elmer Davis, *War Information* (Washington, DC: U.S. Government Printing Office, 1943), 9, 11; Lynne Masel-Walters, "Elmer Davis," in *Biographical Dictionary of American Journalism*, 169; President Roosevelt to Elmer Davis, 17 June 1942, Elmer Davis Papers, Manuscript Division, LOC.

25. George Creel to Elmer Davis, August 4, 1942, Davis Papers; Harold Ross to Elmer Davis, July 16, 1942, Davis Papers; Edward R. Murrow to Elmer Davis, September 15, 1942, Davis Papers; News gang to Elmer Davis, June 15, 1942, Davis Papers.

26. Davis, *War Information*, 13; Roger Burlingame, *Don't Let Them Scare You: The Life and Times of Elmer Davis* (Philadelphia: J. B. Lippincott, 1961), 231–32; Desmond, *Tides of War*, 428.

27. Z.A.B. Zeman, *Nazi Propaganda* (London: Oxford University Press, 1964), 176–77; Davis, *War Information*, 15, 19; Martha Gellhorn, *The Face of War* (New York: Simon & Schuster, 1959), 2.

28. Desmond, *Tides of War*, 452.

29. Ernie Pyle, *Ernie's America: The Best of Ernie Pyle's 1930s Travel Dispatches*, ed. David Nichols (New York: Random House, 1989), xi.; Desmond, *Tides of War*, 316, 341; Knightley, *First Casualty*, 276, 298, 308, 320; John Steinbeck, *Once There Was a War* (New York: Viking Press, 1958); A. J. Liebling, *The Most of A. J. Liebling*, selected by William Cole (New York: Simon & Schuster, 1963); Ernest Hemingway, *By-Line, Ernest Hemingway: Selected Articles and Dispatches of Four Decades*, ed. William White (New York: Scribner's Sons, 1967); Leonard Ray Teel, "The Shaping of a Southern Opinion Leader: Ralph McGill and Freedom of Information," *American Journalism* 5 (1): 14–27.

30. Thomas W. Young, "Negro Fliers Bomb Enemy: Engage in Attach on Pantellereia, Italian Air Base, " *Norfolk Journal and Guide*, June 12, 1943, 1; Thomas W. Young, "Flier Downs Nazi Pilot in Fierce Dogfight," *Norfolk Journal and Guide*, July 10, 1943, 1; Introduction to *This is Our War* (Baltimore: Afro-American, 1944), http://www.afro.com/history/OurWar/intro.html; Vincent Tubbs, "Christmas on New Guinea," in *American Journalism, 1938–1944*, vol. 1 of *Reporting World War II* (New York: Library of America, 1995), 761; Broussard and Hamilton, "Covering a Two-Front War," 7.

31. John Sorrells to Walker Stone, November 21, 1942, Lee G. Miller Papers, Ernie Pyle State Historic Site, Dana, Indiana, cited in James Tobin, *Ernie Pyle's War: America's Eyewitness to World War II* (Lawrence: University Press of Kansas, 1997), 67; G. Kurt Piehler in Ernie Pyle, *Brave Men* (Lincoln: University of Nebraska Press, 2004), v, viii, 5.

32. Steinbeck, *Once There Was a War*, xi, xvii, 136–39,195–98; Jackson J. Benson, *The True Adventures of John Steinbeck, Writer* (New York: Penguin Books, 1984), 525–27; Noel Monks, *Eyewitness* (London: Fredrick Muller, 1956), 195–98; Associated Press dispatch from Algiers, November 23, 1943, cited in Knightley, *First Casualty*, 320–21; Tobin, *Ernie Pyle's War*, 139–42.

33. Ruth Cowan [Nash], interview with Margot Knight, 27–28, Women in Journalism Oral History Project of the Washington Press Club Foundation, 21 March 1988; Marguerite Higgins, *News Is a Singular Thing* (Garden City, NY: Doubleday, 1955), 26–27, 55; Gellhorn, *Face of War,* 23.

34. "*Life*'s Bourke-White Goes Bombing," *Life,* March 1, 1943, 17; Cowan [Nash], interview with Knight, 27–28.

35. "The Press: Expanding Don'ts," *Time,* July 6, 1942, 40.

36. Whited, *Knight,* 95, 109; Arthur Krock, "Why Our Newspapers Can't Tell the Truth," *Reader's Digest,* November 1942, 75.

37. Ralph McGill, "V-Bomb Attacks on This Nation?" *Atlanta Constitution,* January 13, 1945, 4; Jack Lockhart to N. S. Noble, January 15, 1945, Record Group 216, file 012 D/4 Atom Smashing, January 1945, National Archives; Patrick S. Washburn, "The Office of Press Censorship's Effort to Control Press Coverage," 120.

38. Carlos Baker, *Ernest Hemingway: A Life Story* (New York: Bantam Books, 1970), 491–92, 496.

39. *Life,* July 12, 1937. The "moment of death" photograph, considered by some to be best war photograph, has nevertheless become controversial. According to those who knew Capa, the photograph could have been authentic or staged. War correspondent John Hersey wrote that Capa told him it was a fortunate shot taken when he "timidly raised his camera to the top of the parapet and, without looking, at the instant of the first machine gun burst, pressed the button." On another occasion, Capa allegedly told *London Daily Express* correspondent O. D. Gallagher that he staged it during maneuvers arranged by a cooperative officer. Two other correspondents, Martha Gellhorn and Herbert Matthews, said they believed Capa's photograph was authentic. Knightley, *First Casualty,* 227–30.

40. Robert Capa Exhibit, National Museum of American History, Washington, DC, September 2004. Capa, born in Hungary, changed his name from Endre Friedmann. *Life* had five other photographers covering D-day—Ralph Morse, George Rodger, David E. Scherman, Frank Scherschel, and Bob Landry. Loengard, *Life Photographers,* 144, 249; Ernest Hemingway, "Voyage to Victory," *Collier's,* July 22, 1944, 11–13, 56–57; Baker, *Hemingway,* 500–1; Desmond, *Tides of War,* 348, 362, 378–79.

41. *Tides of War,* 363, 368; photograph of Pyle by Bert Brandt in Lee G. Miller, *The Story of Ernie Pyle* (New York: Viking Press, 1950), front matter; Ernie Pyle, *Ernie's War: The Best of Ernie Pyle's World War II Dispatches,* ed. David Nichols (New York: Random House, 1986), 275, 278–80.

42. *Ernie's War,* 334–36, 344–47; Ernie Pyle, *Brave Men* (New York: Henry Holt, 1944), 307–9.

43. Liebling, *The Most of Liebling,* 28–29.

44. Ernest Hemingway, "How We Came to Paris," *Collier's,* October 7, 1944, reprinted in Hemingway, *By-Line,* 377, 381; Baker, *Hemingway,* 518–31.

45. Kenneth S. Lynn, *Hemingway* (New York: Simon & Schuster, 1987), 513–14; Hemingway, *By-Line,* 382–83; Ernest Hemingway, *Selected Letters, 1917–1961,* ed. Carlos Baker (New York: Scribner's Sons, 1981), 564–65; Liebling, *The Most of Liebling,* 29–32; Pyle, *Brave Men,* 312–17; Pyle, *Ernie's War,* 351–56, 31–32; A. J. Liebling, *The Road Back to Paris* (Garden City, NY: Doubleday, Doran, 1944); Pyle, *Brave Men,* 312–17; Pyle; Ernie Pyle, *Last Chapter* (New York: Henry Holt,

1946). In 1952, Liebling was awarded France's Legion of Honor medal for his war reporting.

46. Desmond, *Tides of War*, 368; Higgins, *News Is a Singular Thing*, 61–62, 84–95.

47. W. H. Lawrence, "Nazi Mass Killing Laid Bare in Camp," *New York Times*, August 30, 1944, 1, 2; see also *American Journalism, 1944–1945*, vol. 2 of *Reporting World War II* (New York: Library of America, 1995), 267; John H. Crider, "U.S. Board Bares Atrocity Details Told by Witnesses at Polish Camps," *New York Times*, November 26, 1944, 1, 2; see also *American Journalism, 1944–1945*, 553; "Charges Nazis Slew 5 Million Jews," *Chicago Tribune*, April 12, 1945, 10; "Sound Core," *Time*, May 14, 1945, 20; "Tanks Free 1,277 Half Starved Yank Prisoners," *Chicago Tribune*, April 2, 1945, 23; "Congressmen See War Camp Horror," *New York Times*, April 26, 1945, 5; "1,975 Arrive Here from Nazi Prisons," *New York Times*, April 29, 1945, 16; Julia Multinho Simões, "Media Coverage of the Concentration Camps between April and May, 1945: Who Was Liberated?" paper presented at the Southeast Colloquium of the American Journalism Historians Association, Panama City, FL, February 4–5, 2006, 16–23.

48. Thompson and Stolberg, "Hitler and the American Jew," 137–38. See also "Hitler Plans to Destroy European Jews," *Hebrew Christian Alliance Quarterly*, Winter 1943, 25–26; Elie Wiesel, "Solitude and Madness," address given at the annual Bernhard E. Olson Scholars' Conference on the Church Struggle and the Holocaust, New York, March 5, 1975, cited in Robert W. Ross, *So It Was True: The American Protestant Press and the Nazi Persecution of the Jews* (Minneapolis: University of Minnesota Press, 1980), 287. The Nazi model for media control, essential to Hitler's totalitarian state, permitted private ownership of newspapers but required publishers to print information acceptable to the regime.

49. Robert Sherrod, *Time*, February 26, 1945; Robert S. Burrell, "Breaking the Cycle of Iwo Jima Mythology: A Strategic Study of Operation Detachment," *Journal of Military History* 68 (4): 1143–86. The awarding of Pulitzer Prizes for photography began during World War II, in 1942; "Iwo Battle Film Released Today: Navy, Marine and Coast Guard Color Movie to Appear in First-Run Theatres," *New York Times*, June 7, 1945, 25.

50. Pyle, *Brave Men*; Miller, *Pyle*, 391, 399; Tobin, *Ernie Pyle's War*, 236.

51. Miller, *Pyle*, 402–3, 421–25.

52. Miller, *Pyle*, 420; "Roosevelt Is Dead; Truman President; News of Death Stuns Capital; Personal Physician Surprised; Flag at Capitol Lowered," *New York Times*, April 13, 1943, 1; "End Comes Suddenly at Warm Springs; Even His Family Unaware of Condition; Stroke Brings Death to Nation's Leader at 63; All Cabinet Members to Keep Posts; Funeral to Be at White House Tomorrow, with Burial at Hyde Park Home—Impact of News Tremendous," *New York Times*, April 13, 1945, 1; "President Roosevelt Is Dead; Truman to Continue His Policies; 9th Crosses Elbe, Nears Berlin," *New York Times*, April 13, 1945, 1. David McCullough, *Truman* (New York: Simon & Schuster, 1999), 340–45.

53. Fleming, *The New Dealers' War*, 512–14; Anne O'Hare McCormick, "Abroad: The Effect of Roosevelt's Passing on the Big Three," *New York Times*, April 16, 1945, 18; "Tributes in London Press; *Daily Mail* Says, 'Invalid in Strike Turned Forces Against Enemies' … A Leader with Lincoln," *New York Times*, April 16, 1945, 4.

54. "Fall of Reich to Signal V-E Day; Every Important Enemy Force Must Be Erased before We Celebrate, Eisenhower Says," *New York Times*, April 17, 1945,

5; "The Battle for Berlin," *New York Times,* April 21, 1945, 12; "V-E Day to Be Set by Allies' Chiefs; Big Three, Not Eisenhower, Will Announce End of Conflict in Europe," *New York Times,* April 26, 1945, 9; Hanson W. Baldwin, "Nazis Ripe for Collapse; Junction of Allies Ends All Hopes but Futile Resistance May Go On; Party Grip May Relax; V-E Day Looms Nearer," *New York Times,* April 28, 1945, 4; Hanson W. Baldwin, "Quick End of the War in Europe in Sight; Enemy May Decide to Abandon Plans for a Last-Ditch Fight in 'Pockets,'" *New York Times,* April 29, 1945, E5; *Time,* May 7, 1945, cover.

55. "AP Tells the Story of Historic Break; London Office Was 'Sweating Out' Peace News when Call Came from Paris Office; Faulty Connections Hurt; Kennedy's Voice Often Faded as He Dictated Story, Held up Here for 8 Minutes," *New York Times,* May 8, 1945, 4. Ed Kennedy was condemned as unethical by the other European correspondents, and although AP clients used his story, he lost his job. Charles Whiting, *The End of the War: Europe: April 15–May 23, 1945* (New York: Ballantine Books, 1973); Frank S. Adams, "Germany Surrenders: New Yorkers Massed under Symbol of Liberty; Wild Crowds Greet News in City while Others Pray," *New York Times,* May 8, 1945, 1; "25,000 in Financial District Cheer Victory; Thousands Leave Offices to Mill in the Street," *New York Times,* May 8, 1945, 10; "House Limits Halt in Its Day's Work," *New York Times,* May 8, 1945, 4; "Chief Cities Take Victory in Stride; First Bursts of Enthusiasm Are Followed by Return to Work over the Country," *New York Times,* May 8, 1945, 5.

56. "Truman Sets Mark in Radio Coverage; 64.1 Rating of V-E Day Talk Highest on Record—Audience Put at 36,500,000 in U.S.; Many Groups of Listeners," *New York Times,* May 9, 1945, 6; "Victory Cost Set at 275 Billions; Morgenthau Bares Huge Sum in Appeal to Support the Seventh Loan; Contrasts Costs of Wars," *New York Times,* May 9, 1945, 1; "Statement by King George and His Messages on Victory; A Salute to the Living; The Threat of World Tyranny Calls for a Lasting Peace," *New York Times,* May 9, 1945, 8. "Final Soviet Gains End War in Europe; Dresden Taken by Red Army while Tito's Yugoslavs Win Zagreb, Croat Capital; Prague Status Unclear; Scattered German Resistance; Nets Mopped up in Austria, Bohemia, Croatia; Koneff Crashes into Bohemia; Enemy in Prague Yields," *New York Times,* May 9, 1945, 2.

57. Anne O'Hare McCormick, "Effect of V-E Day on Security Conference; More War Ahead; Russian Position Vital," *New York Times,* May 9, 1945, 22; "Final Soviet Gains End War in Europe; Dresden Taken by Red Army While Tito's Yugoslavs Win Zagreb, Croat Capital; Prague Status Unclear; Scattered German Resistance; Nets Mopped up in Austria, Bohemia, Croatia; Koneff Crashes into Bohemia; Enemy in Prague Yields," *New York Times,* May 9, 1945, 2; McCullough, *Truman,* 444–52.

58. McCullough, *Truman,* 289–90; Winston Churchill, *The Second World War: The Hinge of Fate* (New York: Bantam Books, 1962), 3; "Approaches to Japan," *New York Times,* March 5, 1945, 18; "Japan Says Bombs Destroyed 44 Cities, Killed 260,000, Left 9,200,000 Homeless; Most of Mainland Hit; Hardest Hit Cities Named," *New York Times,* August 24, 1945, 3; "Japan Beaten before Atom Bomb, Byrnes Says, Citing Peace Bids; Byrnes Disputes Japan on Defeat," *New York Times,* August 30, 1945, 1.

59. "News of Weapon Electrifies Truman Ship; President Makes Announcement to Crew," *New York Times,* August 7, 1945, 2; McCullough, *Truman,* 453–55.

60. "Atomic Bomb Wiped out 60% of Hiroshima; Shock Awed Fliers; Tokyo Cabinet Meets; Carrier Planes Strike Near China Coast," *New York Times*, August 8, 1945, 1; "Trains Canceled in Stricken Area; Traffic Around Hiroshima Is Disrupted—Japanese Sift Havoc by Split Atoms; Foe Says Massacre Is Aim," *New York Times*, August 7, 1945, 1, 2; "Japan Keeps People in Dark on Nature of New Scourge; Japanese Admit Vast Bomb Ruin," *New York Times*, August 8, 1945, 1.

61. "Japanese Stress Hiroshima 'Horror'; Atomic Bomb 'Radioactivity' Killed 30,000, Says Tokyo—Sympathy Effort Seen; Such Effect Denied Here; Enemy Radio Talks of Toll Still Mounting from 'Burns' Caused by 'Rays' in Area; Japanese Propaganda Aim Noted; Tokyo Builds up Details," *New York Times*, August 25, 1945, 3; John Hersey, "A Reporter at Large: Hiroshima," *New Yorker*, August 31, 1946, 15. The ultimate death toll in Hiroshima has been estimated to be as high as 250,000. Robert Guillain, *I Saw Tokyo Burning* (Garden City, NY: Doubleday, 1981), 242.

62. Paul Boyer, *By the Bomb's Early Light* (New York: Pantheon, 1985), 207, cited in Steve Rothman, "The Publication of 'Hiroshima' in the *New Yorker*," unpublished manuscript, Harvard University.

63. "To Our Readers," *New Yorker*, August 31, 1946, 15.

64. Thomas William McCaskey, "Pikadon (The Flash-Boom): A Study of Press Coverage of the Atomic Bombings of Hiroshima and Nagasaki," *Atlanta Review of Journalism History*, n.s. (1996): 63; Hersey, "Hiroshima," 15, 17.

65. Rothman, "The Publication of 'Hiroshima' in the *New Yorker*."

66. W. H. Lawrence, "2d Big Aerial Blow; Japanese Port Is Target in Devastating New Midday Assault; Result Called Good; Foe Asserts Hiroshima Toll Is 'Uncountable'—Assails Atrocity," *New York Times*, August 9, 1945, 1; "Dead Nagasaki Seen from a B-17; Atomic Bomb Wiped out Center," *New York Times*, August 27, 1945, 1. Lawrence won a Pulitzer Prize for his reporting. "Atom's Smoke Pall Seen 170 Miles Off," *New York Times*, August 9, 1945, 5; McCaskey, "Pikadon," 63, 75; "Leaflets and Radio Tell Japanese Bad News; Urge They Seek Peace," *New York Times*, August 10, 1945, 1.

67. "Russia Joins against Japan," *New York Times*, August 9, 1945, 20; "Truman Reveals Move of Moscow; Announces War Declaration Soon After Russian Action—Capital Is Startled," *New York Times*, August 9, 1945, 1; "Second Russo-Japanese War," *New York Times*, August 13, 1945, 18.

68. "Yielding Unqualified, Truman Says: President Announcing Surrender of Japan; the War Ends; President Addresses Crowd; Plan on the Emperor," *New York Times*, August 15, 1945, 1.

69. "Fall of Japan," *Time*, August 20, 1945, cover; "V-J Revelry Erupts Again with Times Sq. Its Focus; 4 Deaths Charged to Events; Banks to Be Open Today," *New York Times*, August 16, 1945, 1; "World War II; Its Six-Year Toll," *New York Times*, August 12, 1945, E2; Hanson W. Baldwin, "The Atomic Weapon; End of War Against Japan Hastened but Destruction Sows Seed of Hate; Result Is Unpredictable," *New York Times*, August 7, 1945, 10; Edwin L. James, "End of War Will Bring Gigantic World Issues: Problems of Political and Economic Reorganization Everywhere to Tax Statesmen of Allied Nations," *New York Times*, August 12, 1945, E3. Eisenhower envisioned a "useful postwar job" for a hundred journalists like Pyle to go "full out to tell the truth about the infantry combat

soldier" because "education along this one simple line might do a lot toward promoting future reluctance to engage in war." Eisenhower to Pyle, December 15, 1944, in Miller, *Pyle,* 399.

70. Censorship to End when Japan Quits; Price Ready to Cancel Curbs on All Communications to Outside Countries; Australia to Follow Suit; Britain May Take Longer; Cairo Censorship Criticized," *New York Times,* August 14, 1945, 19; Margaret A. Blanchard, *Exporting the First Amendment: The Press-Government Crusade of 1945–1952* (New York: Longman, 1986), 23; Teel, *McGill,* 187–206.

71. Teel, *McGill,* 187–206.

72. Jack Gould, "A Backward Glance; Programs Business," *New York Times,* December 30, 1930, 23.

73. Walter H. Waggoner, "Most Controls Go; Krug Says WPB Will Lift Them This Week to Let Industry Speed Up; Materials in Plenty; Swift Production Urged to Use up Supplies—Inflation Danger Told," *New York Times,* August 16, 1945, 1; "'From War to Peace—A Challenge' as Depicted in Report to President by John W. Snyder," *New York Times,* August 16, 1945, 12; "The News of the Year in Review: Outstanding Events and Trends," *New York Times,* December 30, 1945, 43; "State Department Backs Bloom Bill; Chiefs Declare Information Service Is Essential to Foreign Policy," *New York Times,* December 15, 1945, 23; "Plans Are Set up to 'Sell' U.S. Abroad; Benton Tells of State Department Program for Information and Culture Service; Cost Is Not Estimated; 2,654 Would Be Employed in Sending News, Films, Radio Broadcasts about America; Nine Points Are Outlined; Will Continue Radio Programs," *New York Times,* December 29, 1945, 9.

Afterword

Historians researching the wide range of American journalism during the first 45 years of the twentieth century have inestimable guidance from two major developments that provide a continuity of insight throughout the period. Early in the century there emerged from within journalism of a series of writers in a distinctly new genre—press criticism—distinguished from earlier critics by their skills in articulation of argument, documentation, and dissemination. Almost simultaneously, again from within journalism, there arose a robust initiative for the reform of journalistic practices, also distinguished from earlier efforts by emphatic public declarations and substantial financial commitments. As the period progressed, critics and reformers, joined by another new cadre—educators at the university level—continuously focused attention on what became known as professional practices. This extensive body of discourse elevated the concepts of ethics and responsibility that became the underpinnings for a vision of the press as a profession with obligations to the public.

Many of the questions raised in the press criticism focused on the subjects of politics and economics. Critics questioned the political role of the commercialized press, especially the extensive influence of publishers who were energetically engaged in building media empires. During the Progressive Era, Will Irwin's extensive *Collier's* magazine series on the press, done at the behest of Columbia University, alleged that newspaper publishers' commercial and political considerations had corrupted journalism by dictating news and editorial decisions. A generation later, as that trend toward media concentrations was expanding into radio, press critic George Seldes sounded more alarms about the insidious influence of the so-called lords of the press.

The national discourse of criticism was amplified at times by political leaders, including those in the White House. In the Progressive Era, Theodore Roosevelt maligned the zeal of investigative journalists, sticking them with the label "muckrakers." Warren Harding, himself a newspaper publisher, publicly urged the American Society of Newspaper Editors to adopt a national code of ethics, which they did in 1923.

As early as 1904 questions were raised about educational requirements for journalists. Editors who still championed Horace Greeley's model for training newspapermen on the job were challenged by substantial thinkers, notably by Joseph Pulitzer in his seminal essay in 1904 in the *North American Review*. Pulitzer backed his vision with enough money to establish a school of journalism at Columbia University. Such ideas, as they gained support, inspired the development of an extensive curriculum at numerous universities.

In the context of 1904, Pulitzer's doctrinaire declaration that daily journalism needed a new level of intelligence recognized the ground-breaking investigative journalism recently accomplished in the magazine field. In 1903, *McClure's* monthly magazine had published a series of investigative articles that caught the attention not only of publishers but of President Roosevelt and Congress. The publisher, Samuel S. McClure, had proven to be an excellent judge of talent and had given selected writers—Ida Tarbell, Lincoln Steffens, and Ray Stannard Baker—both more time and better pay to produce articles that required extensive investigation and corroboration. His investments paid off. In the landmark issue of January 1903, *McClure's* carried three articles documenting evasions and violations of law and ethics. Steffens, with the help of an accountant, exposed municipal corruption in "The Shame of Minneapolis," a city run, in McClure's words, "by crooks and incompetents." Tarbell published the third of her 19-part series alleging "force and fraud" that John D. Rockefeller used to build the Standard Oil Company. Baker's "The Right to Work" documented the torments of nonstrikers during the 1902 coal mine strike in Pennsylvania. The magazine aimed to set an agenda for government reforms but at the same time demonstrated some standards and practices for investigative and advocacy journalism. McClure, who like Pulitzer was an immigrant who appreciated the American way, stated that these articles sadly showed Americans' contempt for law: "We are doing our worst and making the public pay."

The work of these and other so-called muckrakers in the magazine field contributed significantly to the climate of journalistic reform that Pulitzer acknowledged, admired, and supported. Throughout the first decade of the twentieth century, the magazines' publication of series— notably those written by Upton Sinclair, Samuel Hopkins Adams, David Graham Phillips, and Will Irwin—led the movement toward modernity.

Journalists took inspiration from what they read in *McClure's*, in *Collier's*, and in Hearst's *Cosmopolitan*.

The economic underpinnings of the magazine press can explain some of its boldness in publishing such controversial series as Phillips's "Treason of the Senate," which aroused Roosevelt to condemn the "muckrakers." By 1900, the newer magazines had dropped their prices, gained in circulation, and begun attracting a broader base of national advertising that promoted national brands. Magazines in effect had become the country's main national medium. Unlike local advertisers in newspapers, national companies were less vulnerable to readers' complaints about content and thus were far less likely to drop ads because of a controversial article. In Hearst's case, he certainly had the fortune to bankroll *Cosmopolitan* even if all its advertisers had dropped out.

For the sake of the press and the public, the new surge in support of journalism education came none too soon, for it would take more than a decade to develop much education at the college level. Meanwhile, press critics Walter Lippmann and Charles Herz lamented the level of reporting by American journalists, notably their disastrous coverage of the Russian Revolution. Almost as defenseless were journalists' general failure in the 1920s to understand and report the weakness of economic structures that collapsed in the Great Crash of 1929. In both cases, in war and peace, overseas and at home, critics could contend, as did Lippmann and Herz in the case of Russia, that reporters were swayed by rumors rather than facts and based stories on "seeing not what was, but what men wished to see."

America's entrance into World War I in 1917 raised questions about the Constitution's guarantee of freedom of speech and of the press. Was the First Amendment absolute? Were there reasonable limits in wartime? The Wilson administration, Congress, and the Supreme Court all argued for such limits. The executive branch, citing the need to protect national security, issued a presidential order that called for a "voluntary" censorship, which seemed at times compulsory. Congress legislated stricter laws that curtailed First Amendment rights. The Supreme Court, for the first time, upheld Congress's authority to limit the First Amendment in the presence of a "clear and present danger." The primary sources from the war years of 1917–1918 and 1941–1945 document the fact that powerful publishers, notably William Randolph Hearst and Robert McCormick, could use their power to contest and resist such restrictive edicts by government. Between the wars, McCormick's insistent defense of one powerless publisher led the Supreme Court to affirm the Constitutional protection against prior restraint. In sum, the war years and those in between witnessed both losses and gains in the legal interpretation of the First Amendment.

America's emergence as a world power, largely a legacy of the Spanish-American War, was reflected in the contemporary press in two distinct ways. First, editors expanded their concepts of news values to include more international news, especially that which affected their readers. In 1900, stories about Filipino insurgents fighting the American military occupation could find a place on page one. Second, larger newspapers and news agencies began investing in expanded coverage of foreign wars.

Beginning with the U.S. military efforts in the Philippines, almost the entire period from 1900 to 1945 was marked by social and political unrest, often by bloody revolts, invasions, and outright war. This engendered the development of a new breed of war correspondents, some of whom enjoyed a sort of romantic glamour as adventurers. They covered the 1904–1905 war between Japan and Russia, the U.S. military conflict with Mexico, numerous European clashes before 1914, the German invasion of Belgium and France that triggered First World War, and the American soldiers who joined that same war in 1917. Others covered the Russian Revolution. After the Treaty of Versailles, correspondents reported from various peace and armament conferences in Europe, covered the Italian invasion of Ethiopia, the Japanese invasion of China, Nazi Germany's takeover of Austria and Czechoslovakia, the Spanish Civil War, and the outbreak of the Second World War in 1939. Throughout the era, they challenged numerous government and military restrictions on access to battlefields and censorship of information, often risking liberty and life. Nonetheless, many war correspondents acknowledged, as did novelist John Steinbeck, that their stories were "warped and one-sided," because of military orders, self-preservation, and the correspondents' own invented self-censorship springing from "a huge and gassy thing called the War Effort." Early in the century, Winston Churchill proclaimed that war kills liberalism, including of course the liberal dedication to freedom of the press. Philip Knightley confirmed in his monumental study of war reporting that the first casualty of war was truth.

While journalists generally came to terms with wartime propaganda, they were less skillful in dealing with its peacetime offspring, the growing business that in the 1920s became known as public relations. Practitioners who had trained in the Wilson administration's war propaganda operations became articulate leaders advocating psychological and other scientific techniques for manipulating public opinion. Chief among them was Edward Bernays, a nephew of Sigmund Freud, who became famous for staging events that attracted news coverage to clients. In 1929 Bernays, working for Lucky cigarettes, publicized cigarettes as suitable for young women to smoke in public by parading debutantes with smokes in the Easter Parade. Public relations specialists also developed methods of damage control when their clients were attacked—or about to be attacked—in the press. Many practitioners were former journalists, now making more money by getting stories and viewpoints planted in the media.

In peacetime as well, truth could be held hostage by both journalists and publishers. This was clearly the case with Washington correspondents, according to an PhD dissertation by a University of Chicago scholar, Leo Rosten. In 1937, he published this first sociological analysis of the capital press corps, which had grown both in importance and in numbers as Americans looked to Washington for solutions for the economic morass. Rosten systematically analyzed the correspondents' functions, techniques, and social backgrounds. He concluded that journalism's new professional standard of objectivity was impossible to achieve, given the inclinations of reporters and the wishes of their publishers.

The interaction during the 1930s between the press and the Roosevelt presidency can be viewed through an abundance of primary sources. Supplementing the reports and recollections of correspondents are the diaries and correspondence of Roosevelt Administration insiders, notably Harold Ickes, the former Chicago reporter and lawyer who became Roosevelt's Secretary of the Interior.

The economic pattern of mergers, closings, and consolidations was well set by the 1930s. In addition to newspaper holdings, some publishers owned stakes in news agencies and the film industry. Then, having failed to suppress competitive radio news, some publishers bought stations. Nationally, Hearst reigned supreme and independent, generally recognized as the voice dominating his many papers' editorial pages. Roy Howard had ascended to lead the Scripps-Howard chain. In the Midwest, Ira Clifton Copley in 1928 had purchased a record number of newspapers in one year, extending his chain from Illinois to the West Coast. In New York, Frank E. Gannett had been buying and merging newspapers since 1906 and had become a political force to be reckoned with when Roosevelt was governor of New York, and, entering politics officially, tried unsuccessfully to win the Republican nomination for president in 1940. John S. Knight, who inherited an Ohio newspaper, set about building his chain by purchasing the *Miami Herald* and other papers in Detroit and Chicago. James M. Cox added to his Ohio and Florida papers in 1939 with the purchase of the evening *Atlanta Journal,* which also gave him the newspaper's radio station, WSB; at the same time he bought Hearst's evening *Atlanta Georgian,* then promptly closed it to eliminate competition with his *Journal.*

The constant effort by publishers to expand their enterprises was the dominant economic reality of the period and set the pattern for later media mergers. Press critics, among them Oswald Garrison Villard, grandson of the famous abolitionist editor William Lloyd Garrison, lamented the steady loss of independent dailies as they were consumed by chains and often closed to eliminate competition. His 1944 book, *The Disappearing Daily,* serves as a fitting epitaph for a period that, at its beginning, had the greatest number of newspapers and greatest diversity of voices.

Selected Bibliography

UNPUBLISHED PAPERS AND DOCUMENTS

Ackerman, Carl W. Papers. Library of Congress. Record Group 216, File 012 D/4 Atom Smashing, January 1945, National Archives.

Baker, Ray Stannard. Papers, Library of Congress.

British Intelligence Records and Correspondence, War of 1914–1918, KV2 files, Public Record Office, London.

Capa, Robert. Capa Exhibit. National Museum of American History, Washington, D.C.

Creel, George. "A Historical Look at U.S. Immigration Policy: Number of Immigrants to the U.S. Per Decade, 1820–1990." Papers, Library of Congress. U.S. Bureau of the Census, 1993.

Davis, Elmer. Papers. Library of Congress.

Ickes, Harold. Papers. Library of Congress.

McGill, Ralph Emerson. Papers. Special Collections, Emory University, Atlanta, GA.

Pulitzer, Joseph. Papers, Library of Congress.

Roberts, Elmer Earle. Papers, Manuscript Department, Southern Historical Collection, University of North Carolina, Chapel Hill.

PUBLISHED PAPERS, LETTERS, AUTOBIOGRAPHIES, MEMOIRS, DIARIES, COLLECTIONS, AND DOCUMENTS

Agee, James. *Selected Journalism.* Ed. by Paul Ashdown. Knoxville: The University of Tennessee Press, 1985.

Bierce, Ambrose. *Collected Works.* 1912. Reprint, Staten Island, NY: Gordian Press, 1960.

Dorr, Rheta Childe. *A Woman of Fifty*. New York, 1924.

Broun, Heywood. *Collected Edition of Heywood Broun*, compiled by Heywood Hale Broun. New York: Harcourt, Brace and Company, 1941.

Gelhorn, Martha. *The Face of War*. New York: Simon and Schuster, 1959.

Hemingway, Ernest. *By-Line, Ernest Hemingway*. Ed. by William White. New York, 1967.

Hemingway, Ernest. *Selected Letters, 1917–1961*. Ed by Carlos Baker. New York: Charles Scribner's Sons, 1981.

Ickes, Harold L. *The First Thousand Days, 1933–1936*. In *The Secret Diary of Harold Ickes*. Vol. 1. New York: Simon and Schuster, 1953.

Kahn, Frank J., ed. *Documents of American Broadcasting*. 4th ed. Englewood Cliffs, NJ: Prentice-Hall, 1984.

Kaltenborn, H. V. *Fifty Fabulous Years 1900–1950: A Personal Review*. New York: Putnam's, 1950.

Lichty, Lawrence W., and Malachi C. Topping, eds. *American Broadcasting: A Source Book on the History of Radio and Television*. New York: Hastings House Publishers, 1975.

Liebling, A. J. *The Most of A.J. Liebling*. Selected by William Cole. New York: Simon and Schuster, 1963.

Liebling, A. J. *The Road Back to Paris*. Garden City NY: Doubleday, 1944.

Lippmann, Walter. *Public Philosopher: Selected Letters of Walter Lippmann*. Ed. by John Morton Blum. New York: Ticknor & Fields, 1985.

McClure, S. S. *My Autobiography*. New York: Frederick A. Stokes Co., 1914.

McGill, Ralph. *The South and the Southerner*. Boston: Atlantic Monthly Press, 1963.

Mencken, H. L. *Thirty-Five Years of Newspaper Work: A Memoir*. Ed. by Fred Hobson, Vincent Fitzpatrick, and Bradford Jacobs. Baltimore, MD: The Johns Hopkins University Press, 1994.

Moley, Raymond. *After Seven Years*. New York: Harper Brothers, 1939.

Monks, Noel. *Eyewitness*. London: Fredrick Muller, 1956.

Older, Cora Baggerly. *William Randolph Hearst, American*. New York: Appleton-Century, 1936.

Paley, William S. *As It Happened: A Memoir*. Garden City, NY: Doubleday & Co., 1979.

Pyle, Ernie. *Brave Men*. Lincoln: University of Nebraska Press, 2004.

Pyle, Ernie. *Ernie's America: The Best of Ernie Pyle's 1930s Travel Dispatches*. Ed. by David Nichols. New York: Random House, 1989.

Pyle, Ernie. *Ernie's War: The Best of Ernie Pyle's World War II Dispatches*. Ed. by David Nichols. New York: Random House, 1986.

Pyle, Ernie. *Last Chapter*. New York: Henry Holt and Company, 1946.

Roosevelt, Franklin D. *The Public Papers of Franklin D. Roosevelt*. Ed. by Samuel I. Rosenman. New York: Random House, 1938.

Roosevelt, Franklin D. *F.D.R.: His Personal Letters*. Ed. by Elliott Roosevelt. Vols. 3, 4. New York: Duell, Sloan and Pearce, 1947–1950.

Sevareid, Eric. *Not So Wild A Dream*. New York: Atheneum, 1976.

Shirer, William L. *The Start, 1904–1930*. In *20th Century Journey: A Memoir of A Life and The Times*. Vol I. New York: Simon and Schuster, 1976.

Shirer, William L. *The Nightmare Years, 1930–1940*. In *20th Century Journey: A Memoir of A Life and the Times*. Vol II. Boston: Little, Brown and Co., 1984.

Shirer, William L. *Berlin Diary: The Journal of a Foreign Correspondent, 1934–1941.* New York: Alfred A. Knopf, 1941.

Steinbeck, John. *Once There Was a War.* New York: The Viking Press, 1958.

White, William Allen. *The Autobiography of William Allen White.* New York: The Macmillan Co., 1946.

White, William Allen. *Selected Letters of William Allen White.* Ed. by Walter Johnson. New York: Henry Holt and Company, 1947.

Wilson, Woodrow. *The Papers of Woodrow Wilson.* Ed. by Arthur S. Link. Princeton: Princeton University Press, 1983.

INTERVIEWS AND ORAL HISTORIES

Bennett, Lerone. Telephone interview by author, April 1989.

Bluford, Lucile. Interview by Fern Ingersoll. August 26, 1989. Women in Journalism Oral History Project of the Washington Press Club Foundation. National Press Club, Washington.

Cooke, Marvel. Interview by Kathleen Currie. October 31, 1989. Women in Journalism Oral History Project of the Washington Press Club Foundation. National Press Club, Washington.

Davis, Frank Marshall. Interview by Carol Oukrop. Honolulu, March 29, 1984. Kansas State University, Manhattan, Kansas.

Nash, Ruth Cowan. Interview by Margot Knight. March 21, 1988. Women in Journalism Oral History Project of the National Press Club Foundation, Washington.

OTHER PRIMARY SOURCES: CONTEMPORANEOUS NEWSPAPER, MAGAZINE AND JOURNAL ARTICLES, BIOGRAPHIES, BOOKS, DIRECTORIES, AND OTHER PUBLICATIONS

Abbot, Willis J. "The A.S.N.E. and Its Ethical Code." *The New Republic,* May 22, 1929, 15–16.

Adams, Franklin P. *The Diary of Our Own Samuel Pepys.* New York, 1935.

Adams, Franklin P. *Something Else Again.* Garden City, NY, 1920.

Adams, Samuel Hopkins. "The Great American Fraud." *Colliers,* October 7, 1905, 14–15, 29.

"Added Ads Cheer Publishers; Assembling for Convention, They Are Pleased by Higher Lineage in Their Newspapers. Magazines Also Gain 13." *Business Week,* April 18, 1936, 14.

"Again." *Chicago Tribune,* March 27, 1911, 8.

Agee, James, and Walker Evans. *Let Us Now Praise Famous Men.* New York: Ballantine Books, 1960.

Ainsworth-White, Marian. "The Higher Education of Women: Women in Journalism." *Arena,* 33 (June 1900): 669–72.

"All Saved from Titanic After Collision." *Evening Sun* (New York), April 15, 1912 (final edition).

Allen, Frederick Lewis. *Since Yesterday: The Nineteen Thirties in America.* New York: Bantam Books, 1961.

Allen, Robert S., and Drew Pearson. *Washington Merry-Go-Round*. New York: Horace Liveright, 1931.

"America Last." *Saturday Evening Post,* 194 (March 4, 1922).

"American Industry Closed by Roosevelt's Attack on Business." *Chicago Tribune,* February 15, 1936.

"An American War Correspondent," *The Literary Digest,* April 24, 1915, 954–55.

"Amsterdam News Correspondents Were Protected." *Amsterdam News,* April 12, 1933, 2.

"Another Rhodes Scholar." *The Journalism Bulletin* 1 (1924), 9.

"Asphixiating Gases in Warfare." *The Times* (London), April 24, 1915, 8.

Bacon, C. F. "College Literature and Journalism." *Critic* 37 (July 1900): 21–30.

Baker, Ray Stannard. "Railroad Rebates." *McClure's,* December 1905.

Barton, Winfield. "What Broadcasting Does for a Newspaper." *Radio Broadcast* 4 (February 1924), 344–45.

"Begin Procedure to Deport Reds." *The New York Times,* January 6, 1920, 1.

Bell, Edward Price. "The Interview." *The Journalism Bulletin* 1 (1924): 13–18.

Bent, Silas. "The Hall-Mills Case in the Newspapers." *The New Republic,* December 8, 1926, 581.

Bickel, Karl L. *New Empires*. Philadelphia: J. B. Lippencott, 1930.

Bleyer, Willard Grosvenor. "Journalism in The United States, 1933." *Journalism Quarterly* 10 (1933): 300.

Bleyer, Willard G. *Main Currents in the History of American Journalism*. Boston: Houghton Mifflin, 1927.

Bok, Edward. "Is the Newspaper Office the Place for a Girl?" *The Ladies Home Journal* 18 (February 1901): 18.

"Bomb Conspirators." *New York Times,* June 4, 1919, 14.

"Borah Goes to Aid of the President on New Tax Plan; 'Absurd' to Call it a 'Soak-the-Rich' or 'Share-Wealth' Program, He Says." *New York Times,* June 24, 1935, 1.

Bourke-White, Margaret. *The Photographs of Margaret Bourke*. Ed. by Sean Callahan. New York: Bonanza Books, 1972.

"The British Advance; Hand-to-Hand Fighting; Heavy Losses." *The Times* (London), April 21, 1915, 8.

Britt, George. *Forty Years—Forty Millions: The Career of Frank A. Munsey*. New York: Farrar & Reinhart, Inc., 1935.

Broun, Heywood. *The Collected Edition of Heywood Broun*. New York Harcourt Brace, and Co., 1941.

Broun, Heywood. *It Seems to Me*. New York Harcourt Brace, and Co., 1935.

"Canons of Journalism, Adopted by the American Society of Newspaper Editors, April 1923." *World's Work* 49 (November 1924): 45.

Cantril, Hadley. "Technical Research: How Accurate Were The Polls?" *The Public Opinion Quarterly* 1 (January 1937): 97, 100, 102–103.

"The Case of Mr. Hearst and His Newspapers." *Current Opinion* 65 (July 1918): 5–8.

"Censorship and Suppression." *The Nation* 104 (April 12, 1917): 424–25.

"Chooses France." *Chicago Defender,* July 23, 1932, 20.

"The Church's New Voice." *Outlook* 137 (May 28, 1924): 131–32.

Clark, S. A, and E. Wyatt, "Shirtwaist Makers and Their Strike." *McClure's* 36 (November 10, 1910), 70–86.

Cobb, Irvin S. *Paths of Glory*. New York: G.H. Doran, 1915.

Coblentz, Edmond D. *William Randolph Hearst: A Portrait in His Own Words*. New York: Simon and Schuster, 1952.

Comstock, S. "Uprising of the Girls," *Collier's* 44 (December, 25 1909): 14–16.

Connolly, Charles B. "The Ethics of Modern Journalism." *Catholic World* 75 (July 1902): 453.

Corse, M.B. "The Best Plan to Save Magazine Literature." *World's Work* 2 (September 1901): 1222–24.

"Country Against City." *The New York Times*, January 19, 1920, 8.

Creel, George. "Melting Pot or Dumping Ground?" *Collier's* 68 (September, 3 1921).

Creel, George. "Close the Gates! The Way to Shut a Door Is to Shut It." *Collier's* 69 (6 May 1922).

Crossley, Archibald M. "Straw Polls in 1936." *The Public Opinion Quarterly* 1 (January 1937): 24.

Damrosch, Walter. "Radio and Music Education." *NEA Journal* 17 (November 1928): 11–12.

"Darkest Side of the Great War," *The Literary Digest*, September 12, 1914, 441–42.

Davis, Elmer. *War Information*. Washington: U.S. Government Printing Office, 1943.

Davis, Frank Marshall. "Kansas Joins." *Atlanta World*, April 20, 1932, 6.

Davis, Frank Marshall. "Touring the World." *Atlanta World*, February 17, 1932, 6.

Davis, Hartley. "The Journalism of New York." *Munsey's* 24 (November 1900): 217–18, 233.

Davis, Richard Harding. *With the Allies*. New York: Scribner's Sons, 1914.

Day, Donald. "Moscow Orders Reds in U.S. to Back Roosevelt," *Chicago Daily Tribune*, August 9, 1936.

Day, Dorothy. "The Use of Force." *The Catholic Worker*, November 1936, 4.

"Ebony with Pictures," *Newsweek*, September 24, 1945, 86.

"Epidemics in Germany." *New York Times*, July 26, 1918, 20.

Essary, J. Frederick. *Covering Washington: Government Reflected to the Public in the Press*. Boston: Houghton Mifflin, 1927.

"Ethel Waters at a Mere Trifle of $7,000 per Week." *Norfolk Journal and Guide*, February 24, 1934, 13.

"Ethel Waters Wins Laurels in New Show; Star of Palais Royal Floor Show in New York." *Norfolk Journal and Guide*, February 10, 1934, 14.

"Expert Medical Advice on Influenza." *Literary Digest* 59 (December 28, 1918): 23.

"The Falsehoods of Hearst; Remarkable Articles in his Pro-German Newspapers; Why He Is Barred." *Daily Express*, October 12, 1916.

"50 Reds Bagged in Night Raids Here...House Gets Sedition Bill With Teeth; Friend of Trotzky is Taken; Gregory Weinstein, Co-Editor of Soviet Leader, Now on Ellis Island; Communist Leader Held...Foreign Papers Seized." *The New York Times*, January 6, 1920, 1.

Finnegan, Richard. Editorial. September 2, 1936, *Daily Times* (Chicago).

Finnegan, Richard. "Prove *Tribune* Story—$5,000." *Daily Times* (Chicago), August 28, 1936, 1.

"*Fortune* Quarterly Survey: Hearst Papers' Influence on National Politics," *Fortune* 14 (July 1936): 148.

"*Fortune* Survey: Newspapers versus News Broadcasts." *Fortune* 17 (April 1938): 104–5.

"Fremont Older's Exposé of Newspaper Ethics: A Startling Recital of Secret and Unwritten History of San Francisco and California." *Current Opinion* 66 (January 1919): 39–40.

"French Mannequin." *Chicago Defender,* July 17, 1932, 1.

Gallup, George. "Putting Public Opinion to Work," *Scribner's* (November 1936): 38.

"Germans with Fever Drop in Their Tracks." *New York Times,* July 9, 1918, 10.

"Germany's Six Hundred." Editorial. *Pittsburgh Courier,* February 17, 1934, 10.

Godkin, E. L. "The Influence of the Press." *The Nation* 65 (November 25, 1897): 410.

Harmsworth, Alfred. "The Simultaneous Newspapers of the Twentieth Century." *The North American Review* 172 (January 1901): 72, 79, 80–83, 85, 89–90.

"Hearst Anti-Entente Propaganda." *The New York American,* September 4, 1917.

"The Hearst Issue." *Time,* September 7, 1936, 9.

Hemingway, Ernest. "Voyage to Victory." *Collier's,* July 22, 1944, 11–13, 56–57.

Hersey, John. "A Reporter at Large: Hiroshima." *The New Yorker,* August 31, 1945, 15–36.

"Hitler Plans to Destroy European Jews." *The Hebrew Christian Alliance Quarterly,* (Winter 1943): 25–26.

"Hoover on the Ether's 'Howls and Growls.'" *The Literary Digest,* December 19, 1925, 45.

"Hope for More Titanic Survivors Faint." *Evening Sun* (New York), April 16, 1912, 1.

Hopkins, M. A. "Newark Factory Fire." *McClure's* 36 (April 11, 1911), 663–72.

Horne, Charles F., and Walter F. Austin, eds. *Source Records of the Great War.* 11 vols. National Alumni, 1923.

"House Passes Bill to Curb Red Aliens." *New York Times,* December 21, 1919, 3.

"How the Flu Mask Traps the Germ." *Literary Digest* 59 (December 21, 1918), 21.

"Hughes Asks Rigid Immigration Ban. Calls Restriction of Aliens Imperative; Siegel, in Reply, Condemns Listing of Armenians, Jews and Persians as Unfit." *New York Times,* April 20, 1921, 1.

"Hughes Sent Files, Not Views on Races; Official Denial Is Made That Secretary Gave Opinion in Immigration Curb." *New York Times,* April 21, 1921, 1.

Hutchinson, Woods. "The Hygienic Aspects of the Shirtwaist Strike." *Survey* 23 (January 22, 1910): 545.

"Immigrants Arriving at Ellis Island." New York *Daily News,* January 1, 1922, 1.

"Influenza Epidemic." *Science* 48 (December 13, 1918), 594.

"Irish Freedom Born at Conference between Lloyd George and Glynn; So Declared Carl W. Ackerman at Banquet Last Night." *Albany Times-Union,* March 18, 1922.

Irwin, Will. "The American Newspaper: A Study of Journalism in Its Relation to the Public—The Power of the Press." Part 1. *Collier's* January 21, 1911, 15–18.

Irwin, Will. "The American Newspaper—The Fourth Current." Part 3. *Collier's,* February 18, 1911, 15

Irwin, Will. "The American Newspaper—The Spread and Decline of Yellow Journalism." Part 4. *Collier's* March 4, 1911, 19–20.

Irwin, Will. "The American Newspaper—What Is News?" Part 5. *Collier's* March 18, 1911), 16.

Irwin, Will. "The American Newspaper—The Editor and the News." Part 6. *Collier's* April 1, 1911, 18–19, 28.

Irwin, Will. "The American Newspaper—The Reporter and the News." Part 7. *Collier's* April 22, 1911, 19–20, 35–36.

Irwin, Will. "The American Newspaper—The Advertising Influence." Part 9 *Collier's* (May 27, 1911, 15–16, 23–25.

Irwin, Will. "The American Newspaper—The Unhealthy Alliance." Part 10. *Collier's* June 3, 1911, 17–19, 28.

Irwin, Will. "The American Newspaper—Our Kind of People." Part 11. *Collier's* June 17, 1911, 17–18.

Irwin, Will. "The American Newspaper—The Foe from Within." Part 12. *Collier's,* July 1, 1911, 17–18, 30.

Irwin, Will. "The American Newspaper—The Voice of a Generation." Part 15, *Collier's* July 29, 1911, 15.

"Is Sane and Honest Journalism Possible?" *Review of Reviews* 41 (January 1910): 93–94.

"Is the Influenza a Chinese Plague?" *Literary Digest* 59 (December 7, 1918): 26–27.

Jackson, Joseph H. "Should Radio Be Used for Advertising?" *Radio Broadcast* 2 (November 1922): 72–76.

"Jim Crow for Jews Now." *Afro-American* (Baltimore), October 14, 1933, 16.

Johnson, Robert Underwood. "The Responsibilities of the Magazine, an Address to the School of Journalism at Columbia University." *Independent* 73 (December 26, 1912): 1489.

Johnston, Stanley. "Navy Had Word of Jap Plan to Strike at Sea." *Chicago Tribune,* June 7, 1942, 1.

Jones, William N. "Day by Day." *Afro-American* (Baltimore), October 1, 1932, 6.

"The Kaiser and the Mailed Fist." *The World's Work* (September 1914): 68–71.

"Kansas Candidate." *Time,* May 18, 1936, 15.

Kent, Frank R. "Mr. Coolidge." *American Mercury* (August 1924): 385–90.

Krock, Arthur. "Why Our Newspapers Can't Tell the Truth." *Reader's Digest* (November 1942): 75.

"The Landon Build-Up," *The Nation,* June 27, 1936, 833.

"Landon: Little Known Man Who Captured the Front Page." *Newsweek,* June 13, 1936.

"Landon Prepares Crucial Speeches; Aides Expect 'Make or Break' Farm and Social Security Declarations This Week; Won't 'Outpromise' Rival; Will Say This in Des Moines and Milwaukee Talks—Trade Pack to be Hit in Minneapolis." *New York Times,* September 20, 1936, 1.

Landry, Robert J. "Edward R. Murrow; Scribner's Examines a Radio Foreign Correspondent ... His Technique, Rivals, and Influence on American Opinion ... His Tactics in Columbia's Battle Abroad with NBC." *Scribner's Magazine,* 4 (December 1938): 10.

"Lawlessness and the Press: Topics of the Time." *The Century Magazine* 82 (May 1911): 146, 148.

"The Lessons of the Equitable Building Fire." *Scientific American* 106 (January 20, 1912).

"*Life's* Bourke-White Goes Bombing." *Life,* March 1, 1943, 17.

Lippmann, Walter. *Interpretations, 1931–1932.* Ed. by Allan Nevins. New York: The Macmillan Co., 1932.

Lippmann, Walter. *Liberty and the News.* New York: Harcourt, Brace and Howe, 1920.

Lippmann, Walter. *Public Opinion.* 1922. Reprint, New York: The Macmillan Co., 1938.

Lippmann, Walter. "To-day and To-morrow: Magical Prosperity." *New York Herald Tribune,* September 8, 1931, 19.

Lippmann, Walter, and Charles Merz. "A Test of the News." *The New Republic* 23 (August 4, 1920): 1–42.

"Lynchings Go Up," *Afro-American* (Baltimore), October 21, 1933, 16.

Mailly, W. "Working Girls' Strike: The Shirtwaist Makers of New York." *Independent* 67 (December 23,1909): 1416–20.

"Man About the World [Ernie Pyle]." *Time,* May 1, 1943.

"The March of Radio: Real Information on the Size of Radio Audiences." *Radio Broadcast* 4 (April 1924): 468–69.

Martin, Olga J. *Hollywood's Movie Commandments: A Handbook for Motion Picture Writers and Reviewers.* New York: The H. W. Wilson Co., 1937.

Matthews, Ralph. "Looking at the Stars." Baltimore *Afro-American,* October 21, 1933, 18.

McFarlane, A. E. "Fire and the Skyscraper: Problem of Protecting the Workers in New York's Tower Factories." *McClure's* 37 (September 1911): 466–82.

McFarlane, A. E. "Triangle Fire: The Story of a Rotten Risk." *McClure's* 51 (May 17, 1913).

McGill, Ralph. "McGill Foils Nazi Terror to Aid Refugee; Writer Brings Memorized Message to Vienna Victims." *Atlanta Constitution,* May 2, 1938, 5.

McGill, Ralph. "McGill in Vienna; Hitler Invests Salute to Viennese with Pompous Drama." *Atlanta Constitution,* April 29, 1938, 1.

McGill, Ralph. "McGill in Vienna; Only a Fool Will Deny Hitler Hasn't Done Much for Germany and Will Do Much for Austria, Writer Declares." *Atlanta Constitution,* May 4, 1938, 7.

McGill, Ralph. "McGill in Vienna; Orgy of Adulation Accorded Hitler, the 'Build-Up' of Herr Goebbels Described in Dramatic Detail by Writer." *Atlanta Constitution,* April 18, 1938, 1.

McGill, Ralph. "McGill in Vienna: People of Austria Were Skillfully Coerced Into Voting 'Ja' in Humorless Plebiscite With Fine Goebbels Touch." *Atlanta Constitution,* May 1, 1938, 9K.

McGill, Ralph. "V-Bomb Attacks On This Nation?" *Atlanta Constitution,* January 13, 1945, 4.

McKee, Thomas H. "When Cowboys Heard Bedtime Stories: An Adventure in Receiving at a Grand Canyon Dead Spot." *Radio Broadcast* 4 (February 1924): 338–40.

McMeans, Orange Edward. "The Great Invisible Audience." *Scribner's Magazine* 73 (April 1923): 410–16.

McMillan, Allan. "Chicago Nite Life." *Baltimore Afro-American,* October 21, 1933, 19.

Mencken, H. L. "Editorial." *The American Mercury* 1 (January 1924): 27.

Mencken, H. L. "Editorial." *The American Mercury* 2 (June 1924): 155–60.

Mencken, H. L. "Editorial." *American Mercury* 3 (October 1924): 155.

Mencken, H. L. "Editorial." *American Mercury* 6 (September 1925): 16.

"Michael Collins Interviewed; No Compromises; Sinn Fein Victory Assured." *London Morning Post*, April 16, 1921.

Mix, Jennie Irene. "The Listeners' Point of View: How Shall We Get Great Artists to Broadcast?" *Radio Broadcast* 5 (May 1924): 11–17.

Moley, Raymond. *The Hays Office*. Indianapolis: Bobbs-Merrill, 1945.

"More Newspaper Cannibalism." *The Nation* 116 (February 28, 1923): 232.

Morrow, John. "Radio—A New Field for Investment: An Analysis of the Industry and Three Companies Whose Shares Are in the Public Eye." *Radio Broadcast* 5 (September 1924): 373–78.

"Moscow Backs Roosevelt." Editorial. *Chicago Herald and Examiner*, September 21, 1936.

Mossler, Sadie L. "They Call Me the Hen Editor: The Story of a Small-Town Newspaper Woman." *Woman's Home Companion* 45 (October 1918), 32.

Moulton, Robert H. "Linking the Farmer with His Market: How the Chicago Board of Trade Brings the Wheat Pit to the Farm." *Radio Broadcast* 5 (July 1924), 261–65.

"Mr. Hearst's Loyalty." *The Literary Digest*, May 25, 1918, 12–13.

Munsey, Frank. "The Journalists and Journalism of New York." *Munsey's* (January 1892).

"Munsey Destroys Another Daily." *The Nation* 118 (March 26, 1924), 334.

Nathan, George Jean, and H. L. Mencken. "Repetition Generale." *The Smart Set*, 44: 3 (March 1921): 40, 42.

"Nation has 3,000 'Perfect Cases' Behind Bars." *The New York Times*, January 6, 1920, 1.

"Negro Entertainers in Europe." *Amsterdam News*, September 2, 1928, 6.

"A New German Weapon; Poisonous Gas for Our Troops; The Control of Modern Battles." *The Times* (London), April 9, 1915.

"New Jersey and the Newark Fire." *Survey* 26 (July 15, 1911): 575–78.

"New Tax Program Pressed Despite a Revolt in House; Yield is Put at $340,000,000; Tentative New Tax Rates." *New York Times*, June 26, 1935, 1.

"New York and the Asch Fire." *Survey* 26 (July 15, 1911): 578–80.

"New York Plans to Lessen Fire Risks." *Survey* 26 (April 29, 1911): 180–82.

"Newspaper Criminals in Chicago." *The Nation* 131 (July 23, 1930): 88.

"Notes on the Schools: Missouri's Largest Class." *The Journalism Bulletin* 1 (1924): 9.

"141 Men and Girls Die in Waist Factory Fire; Trapped High Up in Washington Place Building; Street Strewn with Bodies; Piles of Dead Inside." *New York Times*, March 26, 1911, 1.

"The Ousting of Hearst." *Outlook* September 17, 1930.

"Pass Anti-Beer Bill in House 250 to 93."*New York Times*, June 28, 1921, 1.

"The 'Patent-Medicine' Curse." *Ladies Home Journal* (May 1904) and (July 1904).

Paxson, Fredric L. "The American War Government, 1917–1918." *The American Historical Review* 26:1 (October 1920): 55.

Pekor, Charles. "An Adventure in Georgia." *American Mercury*, 7 (August 1926): 410.

"Philadelphia Shirtwaist Strike Settled." *Survey* 23 (February 19, 1910): 757–58.

Phillips, David Graham. "The Treason of the Senate." *Cosmopolitan Magazine* (March 1906–November 1906).

"Plot in Manila." *Washington Post,* January 1, 1900, 1.

"President Beats Gun Denying Publisher's Red Blast." *Time* 8 (September 26, 1936).

Price, Byron. *Code of Wartime Practices.* Washington: U.S. Government Printing Office, 1942.

Price, Byron. "What Can and What Cannot Be Printed In War Time." *Congressional Digest,* February 1942.

"Profession Approves Schools." *The Journalism Bulletin* 2 (1926): 17.

"Program to Combat Influenza." *Survey* 41 (December 28, 1918): 408–9.

Pulitzer, Joseph. "The College of Journalism." *North American Review* 570 (May 1904): 641.

Pulitzer, Joseph. "The College of Journalism." *Review of Reviews* 29 (June 1904): 735–37.

"Radio Educational Program of Walter Damrosch." *School and Society* 28 (August 4, 1928): 138.

"Radio—the New Social Force." *Outlook* 136 (March 19, 1924): 465–67.

Ramsaye, Terry. *A Million and One Nights: A History of the Motion Picture Through 1925.* New York: Simon & Schuster, 1926.

Raymond, Allen. "The Follies of Radio." *New Outlook* 162, no 2: 38–41

"Religious Journalism." *Outlook* 71 (August 2, 1902), 821.

Rice, Grantland. *The Tumult and the Shouting: My Life in Sport.* New York, 1954.

"Roosevelt Asks Inheritance Taxes and Other Levies on Big Fortunes; Tax Move a Big Surprise; The President Proposes Money Be Segregated to Pay National Debt; Concentrated Riches Hit; Points in Tax Message." *New York Times,* June 10, 1935, 1.

Ross, Ishbel. *Ladies of the Press: The Story of Women in Journalism by an Insider.* New York: Harper & Brothers, 1936.

Rosten, Lee C. *The Washington Correspondents.* New York: Harcourt, Brace, 1937.

Runyon, Damon. "Horse and Buggy Governor." *Cosmopolitan Magazine* (November, 1935): 5–6.

St. John, Milton. "True Stories de Luxe." *The Nation,* 132 (March 4, 1931): 239–40.

Sandburg, Carl. *The Chicago Race Riots.* 1919. Reprint, New York: Harcourt, Brace and World, 1969.

"A School of Journalism." *The Independent* 55 (August 27, 1903): 2061–62.

"A School of Journalism." *The Outlook* 74 (August 22, 1903): 968–69.

"The School of Journalism of Columbia University." *Popular Science Monthly* 63 (October 1903): 570.

Scott, M. F. "What the Women Strikers Won." *Outlook* 95 (July 2, 1910), 480–81.

Scott, W. A. "Publisher's Note." *Atlanta World,* March 14, 1932, 1.

Seitz, Don Carlos. *Joseph Pulitzer: His Life & Letters.* New York: Simon & Schuster, 1924.

Seldes, George. *Even The Gods Can't Change History: The Facts Speak for Themselves.* Carol Publishing Group, 1976.

Seldes, George. *Freedom of the Press.* New York: Garden City Publishing, 1937.

Seldes, George. *The George Seldes Reader.* Ed. by Randolph T. Holhut. New York: Barricade Books, 1994.

Seldes, George. *Lords of the Press.* New York: Julian Messner, 1938.

Seldes, George. *You Can't Print That: The Truth Behind the News, 1918–1928.* Garden City, NY: Garden City Publishing, 1929.

"Seven Steamships Carrying 7,000 People." *Daily News* (New York), July 1, 1922, 1.

"Shall We Advertise By Radio? *Literary Digest* 77 (May 26, 1923): 27.

Shaver, John W. "Radio's N.B.C.: A Manufacturing Enterprise with 50,000,000 Final Inspectors." *Factory and Industrial Management* 79 (January 1930): 59–61.

Sheldon, Charles M. "The Experiment of a Christian Daily." *Atlantic* 134 (November 1924): 624–33.

Sinclair, Upton. "The Jungle: A Tale of the Beef Trust." Advertisement. *The Appeal to Reason,* December 9, 1905, 4.

Sinclair, Upton. *The Brass Check.* Rev. ed. New York: Albert and Charles Boni, 1936.

Sinclair, Upton. *The Jungle.* New York: Bantam Classic, 2004.

"Sinclair Consolidated in Big Oil Deal with U.S.; Contract Signed with Government and Sinclair Oil Interests for Development of Teapot Dome in Wyoming; Dome Estimated to Contain 150,000,000 to 200,000,000 Barrels of High-Grade Oil." *The Wall Street Journal,* April 14, 1922, 1.

"Sissle and Band will Remain at Ambassadeurs." *Amsterdam News,* August 29, 1928, 7.

"Statistics of the New York Times." *The New York Times,* May 12, 1926, 34.

"Suffragists Split by Party Politics; Mrs. Bass Attacks Republican Women Who Spread Propaganda at Convention." *The New York Times,* February 13, 1920.

Sumner, M. B. "Spirit of the Strikers." *Survey* 23 (January 22, 1910): 550–55.

Swope, Herbert Bayard. *Inside the German Empire: In the Third Year of the War.* New York : The Century, 1917.

"Tax Plan Assailed as 'Confiscation'; Executive Committee of Board of Trade Calls Proposal Class Legislation." *New York Times,* June 28, 1935, 2.

"Thaw Murders Stanford White." *New York Times,* June 26, 1906, 1.

"They Combine to Beat Us; But We Shall Make a Good Showing in Twenty Towns Tomorrow." *The Daily Socialist* (Boston), December 7, 1903, 1.

Thompson, Dorothy. *I Saw Hitler!* New York: Farrar and Rhinehart, 1932.

Thompson, Dorothy. "Good-by to Germany." *Harper's Magazine* 170 (December 1934): 43–51.

Thompson, Dorothy, and Benjamin Stolberg. "Hitler and the American Jew." *Scribner's Magazine* 94 (September 1933): 136.

"Through German Eyes. Poisonous Gases. A Quick and Painless Death." *The Times* (London), April 29, 1915, 6.

"Titanic's Passengers Are Transshipped." *Evening Sun* (New York), April 15, 1912 (Wall Street Night Edition), 1.

"Topics of the Day: What Women Like to Read in Newspapers." *Literary Digest* 117 (May 12, 1934): 9.

"Triangle Owners Acquitted by Jury; Harris and Blanck Leave Court with a Strong Police Guard to Protect Them; The Jurors Smuggled Out; Throng in the Street Hisses and Reviles the Defendants—To Be Tried on Another Indictment." *New York Times,* December 18, 1911, 1.

"True and False Sympathy in Strikes." *Century* 79 (March 1910): 791–92.

"U.S. Auto Plants Are Closed." *Life* 12, no 7 (February 16, 1942): 24, 27.

"Vaccination against Influenza." *Literary Digest* 59 (December 28, 1918): 25.

"Verdicts Rendered by Coroner's Jury on the Race Riot Cases." *The Race Riots: Biennial Report, 1918–1919.* In Ellen O'Brien and Lyle Benedict,. "Deaths, Disturbances, Disasters, and Disorders in Chicago." Chicago Public Library.

"Vienna Racked by Break Riots: German Hunger Spreads Disease." *New York Times,* June 21, 1918, 7.

Villard, Oswald Garrison. *The Disappearing Daily: Chapters in American Newspaper Evolution.* New York: Knopf, 1944.

Villard, Oswald Garrison. "Frank A. Munsey: Dealer in Dailies." *The Nation* 116 (June 20, 1923): 713.

Villard, Oswald Garrison. "The Press Today: The Associated Press." *The Nation,* April 16, 1930, 443–44.

Villard, Oswald Garrison. "Sex, Art, Truth and Magazines." *Atlantic Monthly,* 137 (March 1926): 388–96.

"Walter Lippmann," Advertisement. *New York Herald Tribune,* September 2, 1931, 10.

White, Horace. "The School of Journalism." *North American Review* 556 (January 1904): 25–26, 28, 31.

"White House Hits 'Malice' in Attack; Charges 'Notorious Newspaper Owner' Is Framing People by False Tales; Believed to Mean Hearst; His Aides Here Answer by Giving Out Proofs of Article Appearing Today." *New York Times,* September 20, 1936, 1.

Whittemore, Laurens E. "Development of Radio." *Annal of the American Academy* 142, supplement (March 7, 1929): 1, 7.

"Why Schools of Journalism?" *The New Republic,* October 29, 1930, 283–84.

"Will a Gandhi Arise?" *Chicago Defender,* November 5, 1932, 14.

"The Woman of Thirty." *New York Times,* August 29, 1920.

"The Worker and the Drone." *Chicago Tribune,* February 26, 1936.

SELECTED SECONDARY SOURCES

Adams, Larry L. *Walter Lippmann.* Boston: Twayne Publishers, 1977.

Adams, Samuel Hopkins. *Alexander Woollcott.* New York, 1945.

Allerfeldt, Kristofer. *Race, Radicalism, Religion, and Restriction: Immigration in the Pacific Northwest, 1890–1924.* Westport, CT: Praeger Publishers, 2003.

Altschull, J. Herbert. *From Milton to McLuhan: The Ideas Behind American Journalism.* New York: Longman, 1990.

Anderson, Douglas A. "The Muckraking Books of Pearson, Allen, and Anderson." *American Journalism* 2, no. 1 (1985): 16.

Anderson, Oscar Edward, Jr. *The Health of a Nation: Harvey W. Wiley and the Fight for Pure Food.* Chicago: University of Chicago Press, 1958.

Asher, Brad. "The Professional Vision: Conflicts over Journalism Education, 1900–1955." *American Journalism,* 11, no. 4 (Fall 1994): 306.

Baker, Carlos. *Ernest Hemingway: A Life Story.* New York: Bantam Books, 1970.

Banner, Lois W. *Women in Modern America: A Brief History.* New York: Harcourt, Brace, Javanovich, 1974.

Barnouw, Erik. *Tube of Plenty: The Evolution of American Television.* Rev. ed. New York: Oxford University Press, 1982.

Barone, Michael. *Our Country: The Shaping of America from Roosevelt to Reagan.* New York: Macmillan, the Free Press, 1990.

Barry, John M. *The Great Influenza: The Epic Story of the Deadliest Plague in History.* New York: Viking Press, 2004.

Barzun, Jacques. *From Dawn to Decadence: 1500 to the Present: 500 Years of Western Cultural Life.* New York: HarperCollins Publishers, 2000.

Bates, James Leonard. *The Origins of Teapot Dome: Progressive Parties and Petroleum, 1909–1921.* Reprint, Westport, CT: Greenwood Press, 1978.

Baughman, James L. Review of Edward E. Scharff, *Worldly Power: The Making of the Wall Street Journal.* New York: Beaufort Books, 1986. In *Journalism Quarterly* (Winter 1986): 863–64.

Becker, Stephen. *Comic Art in America: A Social History of the Funnies, the Political Cartoons, Magazine Humor, Sporting Cartoons and Animated Cartoons.* New York: Simon and Schuster, 1959.

Belford, Barbara. *Brilliant Bylines: A Biographical Anthology of Notable Newspaperwomen in America.* New York: Columbia University Press, 1986.

Benson, Jackson J. *The True Adventures of John Steinbeck, Writer.* New York: Penguin Books, 1984.

Berger, Meyer. *The Story of the New York Times, 1851–1951.* New York: Simon and Schuster, 1951.

Berland, Elaine Prostak. "'Up in the Air': Re-considering the Cultural Origins of Broadcasting and the Myth of Entertainment During the 1920s." *American Journalism,* 9, no. 3–4 (Summer-Fall 1992): 63–64.

Bessie, Simon M. *Jazz Journalism: The Story of the Tabloid Newspapers.* New York, 1938.

Biagi, Shirley. *Media/Impact: An Introduction to Mass Media.* 2d ed. Belmont, CA: Wadsworth Publishing, 1992.

Blakely, Debra E. "Social Construction of Three Influenza Pandemics in *The New York Times.*" *Journalism and Mass Communication Quarterly* 80, no. 4 (Winter 2003): 887–88.

Blanchard, Margaret A. *Exporting the First Amendment: The Press-Government Crusade of 1945–1952.* New York: Longman, 1986.

Boylan, James. *Pulitzer's School: Columbia University's School of Journalism, 1903–2003.* New York: Columbia University Press, 2003.

Brian, Denis. *Pulitzer: A Life.* New York: John Wiley & Sons, 2001.

Brown, Pamela A. "George Seldes and the Winter Soldier Brigade: The Press Criticism of *In Fact,* 1940–1950." *American Journalism,* 6, no 2 (1989): 101.

Brown, Theodore M. "A Legend That Was Largely True." In *The Photographs of Margaret Bourke-White.* Ed. by Sean Callahan. New York: Bonanza Books, 1972.

Bulliet, Richard W., ed. *The Columbia History of the 20th Century.* New York: Columbia University Press, 1998.

Bunyan, John. *The Pilgrim's Progress.* New York: The Pocket Library, 1957.

Burlingame, Roger. *Don't Let Them Scare You: The Life and Times of Elmer Davis.* Philadelphia: J. B. Lippincott, 1961.

"Carl Mydans, Photographer." Obituary. *Atlanta Constitution,* August 18, 2004.

Chatterton, Wayne. *Alexander Woollcott.* Boston: Twayne publisher, 1978.

Chilton, John. *Sidney Bechet: The Wizard of Jazz.* New York: Oxford University Press, 1987.

Clark, Tom. *The World of Damon Runyon.* New York, 1978.

Coogan, John W. *The End of Neutrality: The United States, Britain and Maritime Rights, 1899–1915.* Ithaca: Cornell University Press, 1981.

Cornwell, Elmer C., Jr. *Presidential Leadership of Public Opinion.* Bloomington: Indiana University Press, 1965.

Crichton, Judy. *America 1900: The Turning Point.* New York: Henry Holt, 1998.

Crozier, Emmet. *American Reporters on the Western Front, 1914–1918.* New York: Oxford University Press, 1959.

Culbert, David Holbrook. *News for Everyman: Radio and Foreign Affairs in Thirties America.* Westport, CT: Greenwood Press, 1976.

Davis, Elmer. *History of the New York Times, 1851–1921.* New York: The New York Times, 1921.

Davis, Kenneth S. *FDR: The New York Years, 1928–1933.* New York: Random House, 1979.

Desmond, Robert W. *Crisis and Conflict: World News Reporting Between Two Wars 1920–1940.* Iowa City: University of Iowa Press, 1982.

Desmond, Robert W. *Tides of War: World News Reporting 1940–1945.* Iowa City: University of Iowa Press, 1984.

D'Itri, Patricia Ward. *Damon Runyon.* Boston: Twayne Publishers, 1982.

Douglas, George H. *The Early Days of Radio.* Jefferson, NC: McFarland, 1987.

Eaton, John P., and Charles A. Haas. *Titanic: Triumph and Tragedy.* New York: W. W. Norton, 1986.

Evensen, Bruce J. "Jazz Age Journalism's Battle over Professionalism, Circulation and the Sports Page." *Journal of Sport History* 30 (Winter 1993).

Facey, Paul W. *The Legion of Decency: A Sociological Analysis of the Emergence and Development of a Social Pressure Group.* New York: Arno Press, 1974.

Fang, Irving E. *Those Radio Commentators!* Ames: University of Iowa Press, 1977.

Fielding, Raymond. *The American Newsreel, 1911–1967.* Norman: University of Oklahoma Press, 1972.

Fisher, Charles. *The Columnists.* New York: Howell, Soskin, 1944.

Flemion, Jess. and Colleen M. O'Connor, eds. *Eleanor Roosevelt: An American Journey.* San Diego: San Diego State University Press, 1987.

Friendly, Fred W. *Minnesota Rag: The Dramatic Story of the Landmark Supreme Court Case That Gave New Meaning to Freedom of the Press.* New York: Random House, 1981.

Gabriel, Jurg Martin Gabriel. *The American Conception of Neutrality After 1941.* Rev. ed. New York: Palgrave Macmillan, 2002.

Galbraith, John Kenneth. *The Great Crash: 1929.* Boston: Houghton Mifflin, 1961.

Gibbons, Edward. *Floyd Gibbons, Your Headline Hunter.* New York, 1935.

Gilbert, Douglas. *Floyd Gibbons: Knight of the Air.* New York, 1930.

Gill, Brenden. *Here at the "New Yorker."* New York: Random House, 1975.

Ginger, Ray. *Six Days or Forever? Tennessee vs. John Thomas Scopes.* Boston: Beacon Press, 1958.

Goldberg, Vicki. *Margaret Bourke-White.* New York: Harper & Row, 1986.

Goldstein, Tom, ed. *Killing the Messenger: 100 Years of Media Criticism.* New York: Columbia University Press, 1989.

Haag, Jan. "Carl Mydans Still Making Photographic History." *United Press International,* January 15, 1987.

Heald, Morrell. *Transatlantic Vistas: American Journalists in Europe, 1900–1940.* Kent, Ohio: Kent State University Press, 1988.

Herzstein, Robert E. *Roosevelt and Hitler: Prelude to War.* New York: Paragon House, 1989.

Hicks, Granville. *John Reed: The Making of a Revolutionary.* New York: Macmillan, 1937.

Higgins, Marguerite. *News Is a Singular Thing.* Garden City, NY: Doubleday, 1955.

Higham, John. "Another Look at Nativism." *Catholic Historical Review* 44 (1958): 147–58.

Hilliard, Robert L. and Michael C. Keith. *The Broadcast Century: A Biography of American Broadcasting.* Boston: Focal, 1992.

Hobson, Fred. *H. L. Mencken: A Life.* New York: Random House, 1994.

Hofstadter, Richard. *The Age of Reform: From Bryan to F.D.R.* New York: Alfred A. Knopf, 1955.

Howard, Michael and Wm. Roger Louis, eds. *The Oxford History of the Twentieth Century.* Oxford: Oxford University Press, 1998.

Howard-Pitney, David. *The Afro-American Jeremiad: Appeals for Justice in America.* Philadelphia: Temple University Press, 1990.

Hosley, David H., and Gayle K. Yamada. *Hard News: Women in Broadcast Journalism.* New York: Greenwood Press, 1987.

Hudson, Robert V. *The Writing Game: A Biography of Will Irwin.* Ames: The Iowa State University Press, 1982.

Jeurgens, George. *Joseph Pulitzer and the New York World.* Princeton, NJ: Princeton University Press, 1966.

Johnson, Gerald. *An Honorable Titan: A Biographical Study of Adolph S. Ochs.* New York: Harper & Brothers, 1946.

Kahn, Ely J. *The World of Swope.* New York: Simon and Schuster, 1965.

Kalko, Gabriel. *The Triumph of Conservatism: A Reinterpretation of American History, 1900–1916.* London: The Free Press of Glencoe/Collier-Macmillan, 1963.

Kemler, Edgar. *The Irreverent Mr. Mencken.* Boston: Atlantic Monthly Press, 1950.

Knightley, Phillip. *The First Casualty: The War Correspondent as Hero and Myth-Maker from the Crimea to Kosovo.* Rev. ed. Baltimore: The Johns Hopkins University Press, 2000.

Kobler, John. *Luce: His Time, Life, and Fortune.* New York: Doubleday, 1968.

Koop, Theodore F. *Weapon of Silence.* Chicago: University of Chicago Press,1946.

Kramer, Dale. *Heywood Broun: A Biographical Portrait.* New York: Current Books-A. A. Wynn, 1949.

Kramer, Dale. *Ross and the New Yorker.* New York, 1952.

Kraut, Alan M. *Silent Travelers: Germs, Genes, and the "Immigrant Menace."* New York: Basic Books, 1994.

Kurth, Peter. *American Cassandra: The Life of Dorothy Thompson.* Boston: Little, Brown and Co., 1990.

Kurzman, Dan. *Disaster! The Great San Francisco Earthquake and Fire of 1906.* New York: William Morrow, 2001.

Kyvig, David E. *Daily Life in the United States, 1920–1939: Decades of Promise and Pain.* Westport, CT: Greenwood Press, 2002.

Lamme, Meg. "Snatching Defeat from the Jaws of Victory: Communications of the Anti-Saloon League of America, 1920–1933." *Atlanta Review of Journalism History* (Fall 2003): 1–49.

Langford, Gerald. *The Richard Harding Davis Years: The Biography of a Mother and Son.* New York, 1961.

Lasswell, Harold D. *Propaganda Technique in World War I.* Cambridge, MA: The M.I.T. Press, 1971.

Lawson, Anita. *Irvin S. Cobb.* Bowling Green, Ohio: Bowling Green State University Popular Press, 1984.

Leuchtenberg, William E. *The Perils of Prosperity, 1914–1932.* Chicago: University of Chicago Press, 1972.

Levin, Harvey J. "Competition Among Mass Media and the Public Interest." *Public Opinion Quarterly* 18:1 (Spring 1954): 62.

Lewis, Jon E., ed. *The Mammoth Book of Journalism.* New York: Carroll & Graf Publishers, 2003.

Link, Arthur S., and William A. Link. *American Epoch: A History of the United States Since 1900.* Vol 1, 7th ed. New York: McGraw-Hill, 1993.

Loengard, John. *LIFE Photographers: What They Saw.* Boston: Little, Brown and Co., 1998.

Lofton, John. *The Press as Guardian of the First Amendment.* Columbia, SC: University of South Carolina Press, 1980.

Lowitt, Richard, and Maurine Beasley, eds. *One Third of a Nation: Lorena Hickok Reports on the Great Depression.* Urbana.: University of Illinois Press, 1981.

Lucas, Stephen E. "Theodore Roosevelt's 'The Man with the Muck-Rake': A Reinterpretation." *The Quarterly Journal of Speech* 59 (1973): 453–54.

Lundberg, Ferdinand. *Imperial Hearst: A Social Biography.* New York: Equinox Cooperative Press, 1936.

Lynn, Kenneth S. *Hemingway.* New York: Simon and Schuster, 1987.

MacDonald, J. Fred. *Don't Touch That Dial: Radio Programming in American Life, 1920–1960.* Chicago: Nelson-Hall, 1979.

Marzolf, Marion. *Up From the Footnote: A History of Women Journalists.* New York: Hastings House, 1977.

McChesney, Robert W. "Conflict, Not Consensus: The Debate over Broadcast Communication Policy, 1930–1935." In *Ruthless Criticism: New Perspectives in U.S. Communication History.* Ed. by William S. Solomon and Robert W. McChesney. Minneapolis: University of Minnesota Press, 1993.

McChesney, Robert W. "Franklin Roosevelt, His Administration, and the Communications Act of 1934." *American Journalism* 5 (1988): 207, 228–29.

McCoy, Donald R. *Landon of Kansas.* Lincoln: University of Nebraska Press, 1966.

Mencken, H. L. *Menckeniana: A Schimpflexikon.* Reprint, New York: Octagon Books, 1977.

Merriam, Charles E. *The Making of Citizens: A Comprehensive Study of Methods of Civic Training.* Chicago: University of Chicago Press, 1931.

Meyers, W. Cameron. "The Chicago Newspaper Hoax in the '36 Election Campaign." *Journalism Quarterly* 37 (1960): 356–64.

Miller, Lee G. *The Story of Ernie Pyle.* New York: The Viking Pres, 1950.

Mock, James R. and Cedric Larson. *Words that Won the War: The Story of the Committee on Public Information, 1917–1919.* Princeton, NJ: Princeton University Press, 1939.

Morris, Edmund. *Theodore Rex.* New York: Random House, 2001.

Nasaw, David. *The Chief: The Life of William Randolph Hearst.* Mariner edition. Boston: Houghton Mifflin, 2001.

Neuman, Fred Gus. *Irvin S. Cobb: His Life and Achievements.* New York: Beekman Publishers, 1974.

Noggle, B. *Teapot Dome Oil and Politics in the 1920s.* W.W. Norton, 1965.

O'Connor, Richard. *Heywood Broun: A Biography.* New York: Putnam Publishing Group, 1975.

Paper, Lewis J. *Empire: William S. Paley and the Making of CBS.* New York: St. Martin's Press, 1987.

Paxson, Frederic L. *American Democracy and the World War: Postwar Years: Normalcy, 1918–1923.* Berkeley: University of California Press, 1948.

Pilat, Oliver. *Drew Pearson: An Unauthorized Biography.* New York, 1973.

Pollard, James K. *The Presidents and the Press.* New York: Macmillan, 1947.

Ponder, Stephen. "That Delightful Relationship: Presidents and the White House Correspondents in the 1920s." *American Journalism* 14, no. 2 (Spring 1997).

Ponder, Stephen. *Managing the Press: Origins of the Media Presidency, 1897–1933.* New York: St. Martin's Press, 1998.

Ponder, Stephen. "Presidential Publicity and Executive Power: Woodrow Wilson and the Centralizing of Government Information." *American Journalism* 11, no 3 (Summer 1994): 258.

Prange, Gordon W., Donald M. Goldstein, and Katherine V. Dillon. *Miracle at Midway.* New York: McGraw-Hill Book, 1982.

Ritchie, Donald A. *American Journalists: Getting the Story.* New York: Oxford University Press, 1997.

Ritchie, Donald A. *Press Gallery: Congress and the Washington Correspondents.* Cambridge, MA: Harvard University Press, 1991.

Riley, Sam G. *The American Newspaper Columnist.* Westport, CT: Praeger Publishers, 1998.

Roberts, J. M. *Twentieth Century: The History of the World, 1901 to 2000.* New York: Viking, 1999.

Rosen, Philip T. *The Modern Stentors: Radio Broadcasters and the Federal Government, 1920–1934.* Westport, CT: Greenwood Press, 1980.

Ross, Robert W. *So It Was True: The American Protestant Press and the Nazi Persecution of the Jews.* Minneapolis: University of Minnesota Press, 1980.

Safire, William. "Media Quiet About Own Power." *Atlanta Constitution,* January 20, 2003, A9.

Sanders, Marion K. *Dorothy Thompson: A Legend in Her Time.* Boston: Houghton Mifflin, 1973.

Sann, Paul. *The Lawless Decade: A Pictorial History of a Great American Transition from WWI Armistice and Prohibition to Repeal and the New Deal.* Outlet Publishers, 1957.

Scharff, Edward E. *Worldly Power: The Making of the Wall Street Journal.* New York: Beaufort Books, 1986.

Schlesinger, Arthur M., Jr., and Roger A. Bruns, eds. *Congress Investigates: A Documented History, 1792–1974.* New York: Chelsea House Publishers, 1975.

Schlesinger, Arthur M., Jr. *The Coming of the New Deal.* Vol. 1 of *The Age of Roosevelt.* Boston: Houghton Mifflin, 1958.

Schlesinger, Arthur M., Jr. *The Crisis of the Old Order, 1919–1933.* Vol. 2 of *The Age of Roosevelt.* Boston: Houghton Mifflin, 1957.

Schlesinger, Arthur M., Jr. *The Politics of Upheaval.* Vol. 3 of *The Age of Roosevelt.* Boston: Houghton Mifflin, 1960.

Schudson, Michael. *Discovering the News: A Social History of American Newspaper.* New York: Basic Books, 1978.

Schudson, Michael. "Journalism." *Oxford Companion to United States History.* Ed. by Paul S. Boyer. New York: Oxford University Press, 2001.

Schudson, Michael. *The Power of News.* Cambridge, MA: Harvard University Press, 1995.

Serrin, Judith and William Serrin. *Muckraking! The Journalism that Changed America.* New York: The New York Press, 2002.

Shaw, Donald L. "The Rise and Fall of American Mass Media." Roy W. Howard Public Lecture. Bloomington: Indiana University, 1991.

Sloan, Wm. David. "Historians and the American Press, 1900–1945: Working Profession or Big Business?" *American Journalism,* 3, no. 3 (1986): 154.

Sloan, Wm. David. "The Media in Trying Times." In *Perspectives on Mass Communication History.* Hilsdale, NJ: Lawrence Erlbaum Associates, 1991, 283–99.

Sloan, Wm. David, Julie K. Hedgepeth, Patricia C. Place, and Kevin Stoker. *The Great Reporters: An Anthology of News Writing at Its Best.* Northport, AL: Vision Press, 1992.

Sperber, A. M. *Murrow: His Life and Times.* New York: Freundlich Books, 1986.

Startt, James D. "American Film Propaganda in Revolutionary Russia." *Prologue: Quarterly of the National Archives and Records Administration,* 30, no. 3 (Fall 1998): 167–79.

Startt, James D. "American Propaganda in Britain During World War I." *Prologue: Quarterly of the National Archives and Records Administration,* 28, no. 1 (Spring 1996): 17–33.

Startt, James D. *Journalism's Unofficial Ambassador: A Biography of Edward Price Bell, 1869–1943.* Athens: Ohio University Press, 1979.

Startt, James D. "The Media and Political Culture." *The Significance of the Media in American History.* Ed. by James D. Startt and Wm. David Sloan. Northport, AL: Vision Press, 1994.

Startt, James D., and Debra Reddin van Tuyll. "The Media and National Crises." *The Media in America: A History.* Ed. by Wm. David Sloan, 5th ed. Northport, AL: Vision Press, 2002.

Steele, Richard W. *Propaganda in an Open Society: The Roosevelt Administration and the Media, 1933–1945.* Westport, CT: Greenwood Press, 1985.

Stein, Leon. *The Triangle Fire.* New York: J. B. Lippencott, 1952.

Sterling, Christopher H., and John M. Kittross. *Stay Tuned: A Concise History of American Broadcasting.* 2nd ed. Belmont, CA: Wadsworth Publishing, 1990.

Swanberg, W. A. *Citizen Hearst: A Biography of William Randolph Hearst.* New York: Charles Scribner's Sons, 1961.

Swanberg, W. A. *Luce and His Empire.* New York: Charles Scribner's Sons, 1972.

Swanson, Walter S. J. *The Thin Gold Watch: A Personal History of the Newspaper Copleys*. New York: Macmillan, 1964.

Tax, Meredith. *The Rising of the Women*. New York: Monthly Review Press, 1980.

Teel, Leonard Ray. "The African-American Press and the Campaign for a Federal Antilynching Law, 1933–34: Putting Civil Rights on the National Agenda." *American Journalism* 8, no. 2–3 (Spring/Summer, 1991): 84–107.

Teel, Leonard Ray. "The Jazz Rage: Carter G. Woodson's Culture War in the African-American Press." *American Journalism* 11, no. 4 (Fall 1994): 349–50.

Teel, Leonard Ray. *Ralph Emerson McGill: Voice of the Southern Conscience*. Knoxville: University of Tennessee Press, 2001.

Teel, Leonard Ray. "The Shaping of a Southern Opinion Leader: Ralph McGill and Freedom of Information." *American Journalism* 5 (January 1988): 14–27.

Teel, Leonard Ray. "W. A. Scott and the Atlanta World." *American Journalism* 6, no. 3 (July 1989): 158–78.

Thurber, James. *The Years with Ross*. Boston: Little, Brown, 1959.

Tichenor, Daniel J. *Dividing Lines: The Politics of Immigration Control in America*. Princeton, NJ: Princeton University Press, 2002.

Tobin, James. *Ernie Pyle's War*. Lawrence: University Press of Kansas, 1997.

Tompkins, Jerry R., ed. *D-Days in Dayton*. Baton Rouge: Louisiana State University, 1965.

Vaughn, Stephen. *Holding Fast the Inner Lines: Democracy, Nationalism, and the Committee on Public Information*. Chapel Hill: University of North Carolina Press, 1980.

Wagner, Jean. *Runyonese: The Mind and Craft of Damon Runyon*. Paris: Stechert-Hafner, 1965.

Wagner, Lilya. *Women War Correspondents of World War II*. New York: Greenwood Press, 1989.

Washburn, Patrick S. "The Office of Press Censorship's Effort to Control Press Coverage of the Atomic Bomb During World War II." *Journalism Monographs* (1990).

Washburn, Patrick S. *A Question of Sedition: The Federal Government's Investigation of the Black Press During World War II*. New York: Oxford University Press, 1986.

Wendt, Lloyd. *Chicago Tribune: The Rise of a Great American Newspaper*. Chicago: Rand McNally, 1979.

White, Graham J. *FDR and the Press*. Chicago: University of Chicago Press, 1979.

Whited, Charles. *Knight: A Publisher in the Tumultuous Century*. New York: E. P. Dutton, 1988.

Williams, Lee E., and Lee E. Williams II. *Anatomy of Four Race Riots*. Hattiesburg: The University and College Press of Mississippi, 1973.

Winfield, Betty Houchin. *FDR and the News Media*. Urbana: University of Illinois Press, 1990.

Wright, Benjamin F. *Five Public Philosophies of Walter Lippmann*. Austin: University of Texas Press, 1973.

Young, J. Harvey. *The Toadstool Millionaires*. Princeton, NJ: Princeton University Press, 1961.

Zeman, Z.A.B. *Nazi Propaganda*. London: Oxford University Press, 1964.

UNPUBLISHED RESEARCH

Beasley, Maurine H. "Mary Marvin Breckinridge Patterson: Case Study of One of 'Murrow's Boys.'" Paper presented to the Association for Education in Journalism and Mass Communication (AEJMC), Boston, August 1991.

Brescoach, Sharon Wills. "The Press and Political Patronization: A Historical Study of the Coverage of Izetta Jewell Brown Miller, 1920s Woman Politician." Unpublished paper, presented at the Association for Education in Journalism and Mass Communication (AEJMC) Southeast Regional Colloquium, Lexington, KY, March 5, 1999.

Burt, Elizabeth V. "Women in the Workplace: Newspaper Coverage of The Triangle Shirt Waist Factory Fire, 25 March 1911." Paper presented to the American Journalism Historians Association (AJHA), Billings, MT, October 3, 2003.

Eberhard, Wallace B. "Restraining a Free Press in Wartime: Voluntary Censorship at the Grassroots Level." Paper presented to the American Journalism Historians Association (AJHA), University of Kansas, October 1, 1992.

Hardin, Marie. "Georgia Journalism and H. L. Mencken: The Rewards and Perils of 'Southbaiting.'" Paper presented at the Association for Education in Journalism and Mass Communication (AEJMC) Southeast Colloquium, Lexington, KY, March 5, 1999.

Hardin, Marie. "Mildred Seydell." PhD dissertation, Georgia State University.

McChesney, Robert W. "Strange Days Indeed! Louis G. Caldwell, the American Bar Association, the American Legal Community and the Changing Attitude Toward Federal Regulation of Broadcasting, 1928–1938." Paper presented at Association for Education in Journalism and Mass Communication (AEJMC), Minneapolis, August 1990.

Streitmatter, Rodger. "An African-American Woman Journalists Who Agitated for Racial Reform." Paper presented to the Association for Education in Journalism and Mass Communication (AEJMC), Boston, August 1991.

Streitmatter, Rodger. "Defying the Ku Klux Klan: Three 1920s Newspapers Challenge the Most Powerful Nativist Movement in American History." Paper presented to the Association for Education in Journalism and Mass Communication (AEJMC), August 10, 1996.

Taylor, Sue D. "Casting Radicals upon the Waters: Press Support of the Deportation Campaign of 1919–1920." Paper presented to the History Division of the Association for Education in Journalism and Mass Communication (AEJMC), National Conference, Chicago, 1999.

REFERENCE GUIDES AND RESEARCH WEBSITES

"1920 NAACP Conference in Atlanta: Civil Rights Action Through the Media." The Museum of Public Relations, 65 Broadway, New York, http://www.prmuseum.com/bernays/bernays_1920.html.

An American Time Capsule: Three Centuries of Broadsides and Other Printed Ephemera, in American Memory Historical Collections for the National Digital Library, Library of Congress, http://memory.loc.gov.

Black Holocaust Society, Inc., http://www.blackwallstreet.freeservers.com.

Blanchard, Margaret A. *History of the Mass Media in the United States*. Chicago: Fitzroy Dearborn Publishers, 1998.

Digital Archive of the AntiSaloon League Archive and Temperance Collection, Westerville Public Library, Westerville, OH.

House of Representatives Debate, April 20, 1921, Document Archive, American Civil Rights Review, http://www.americancivilrightsreview.com/docs-immigration1921.htm.

Klein, Leo Robert. "Red Scare (1918–1921): An Image Database." William and Anita Newman Library, Baruch College, City University of New York.

McKerns, Joseph. *Biographical Dictionary of American Journalism*. Westport, CT: Greenwood Press, 1989.

The Museum of Public Relations, 65 Broadway, New York.

NAACP Conference in Atlanta: Civil Rights Action through Media." The Museum of Public Relations, http://www.prmuseum.com/bernays/bernays_1920.html.

The New York *Daily News*, www.dailynewspix.com.

The *New York Times*. Historical Index, www.nytimes.com/1851archive.

O'Brien, Ellen, and Lyle Benedict. "Deaths, Disturbances, Disasters, and Disorders in Chicago: A Selective Bibliography of Materials." Municipal Reference Collection, Chicago Public Library.

Pickett, Calder M., ed. *Voices of the Past: Key Documents in The History of American Journalism*. New York: Macmillan Publishing, 1977.

A Political Atlas of the African Diaspora, The Institute for Diasporic Studies, Northwestern University, http://diaspora.northwestern.edu/cgi-bin/WebObjects/DiasporaX.woa/wa/displayArticle?atomid=604.

Stewart, Mary E. "Sherwood Anderson and William C. Stewart at *Today*." Memoir, Department of Journalism, University of Richmond, online at http://journalism.richmond.edu/studentvoice/mary_stewart1.htm.

Index